MONITORING FUNDAMENTAL RIGHTS IN THE EU

Coherent laws enforced by a central authority are part of the reason why human rights protection works at the national level in Europe. But when it comes to the EU these dimensions are lacking. The present system for protecting fundamental rights emerged on an ad hoc basis, with measures being improvised to respond to particular problems. In the next couple of years, however, this situation is likely to change very significantly. The proposed European Constitution incorporates the EU Charter of Fundamental Rights, and a specialized EU Fundamental Rights Agency is likely to be established. As a result, the situation of the EU will more closely resemble that of its Member States. Fundamental rights will occupy a central role, and coherent and systematic arrangements will be in place to protect rights, using both judicial and non-judicial means. The Fundamental Rights Agency, in particular, has immense potential to ensure effective monitoring of fundamental rights in the EU, and to ensure a unified strategy for their promotion in EU law and policy.

This volume is the first to critically examine the proposals put forward by the European Commission in October 2004 on the creation of the EU Fundamental Rights Agency. Leading scholars in the field of European and international human rights law analyse the potential significance of this innovative Agency, and seek to locate it in relation to various other human rights mechanisms, both in the EU's constitutional structure and within Member States. They review the tasks which the Agency could be called upon to perform, and make proposals as to how it can function most effectively. The relationship of EU law to the international law of human rights emerging from both the United Nations and the Council of Europe is examined. The authors also address the challenge of ensuring improved coherence between EU law and the other human rights obligations undertaken by the Member States. Taken together, these contributions address urgent questions facing the EU at a time when the central unifying function of fundamental rights has been recognized but the way forward remains largely uncharted.

Monitoring Fundamental Rights in the EU

The Contribution of the Fundamental Rights Agency

Edited by
Philip Alston and
Olivier De Schutter

·HART·
PUBLISHING

OXFORD AND PORTLAND, OREGON
2005

Hart Publishing
Oxford and Portland, Oregon

Published in North America (US and Canada) by
Hart Publishing c/o
International Specialized Book Services
5804 NE Hassalo Street
Portland, Oregon
97213-3644
USA

Hart Publishing is a specialist legal publisher based in Oxford, England.
To order further copies of this book or to request a list of other
publications please write to:

Hart Publishing, Salter's Boatyard, Folly Bridge,
Abingdon Road, Oxford OX1 4LB
Telephone: +44 (0)1865 245533 or Fax: +44 (0)1865 794882
e-mail: mail@hartpub.co.uk
WEBSITE: http//www.hartpub.co.uk

British Library Cataloguing in Publication Data
Data Available
ISBN 1–84113–534–8 (hardback)

Typeset by Hope Services (Abingdon) Ltd.
Printed and bound in Great Britain by
TJ International Ltd., Padstow, Cornwall

Contents

Part III. The EU Fundamental Rights Agency in a Wider Context

Introduction
Addressing the Challenges Confronting the EU Fundamental Rights Agency

OLIVIER DE SCHUTTER* AND PHILIP ALSTON**

H UMAN RIGHTS DEPEND for their protection on adequate legislative and regulatory frameworks, as well as on the possibility of effective judicial enforcement. They depend on the allocation of adequate resources. What this collection of essays illustrates is how the realisation of human rights depends also on appropriate governance mechanisms designed to ensure that human rights are taken fully into account, especially in the preliminary stages of policy setting and law-making, and on the participation of the relevant stakeholders in the design and implementation of these policies.

This third dimension is of particular importance in the context of the European Union. The present study of the potential contribution to be made by a new EU Fundamental Rights Agency not only considers how best it might perform its work; taking this debate as its departure point, it also identifies, more broadly, the challenges that face all such agencies in the human rights field.

1. THE BACKGROUND

Towards a Fundamental Rights Agency

In a report prepared for the *Comité des Sages* responsible for drafting *Leading by Example: A Human Rights Agenda for the European Union for the Year 2000*, Philip Alston and JHH Weiler insisted on the need for the establishment of a monitoring centre for human rights within the European Union.[1] The main

---

* Professor at the University of Louvain and Co-ordinator of the EU Network of independent experts on fundamental rights, Member of the Global Law School Faculty at New York University.
** Professor at New York University, previous Chair of the UN Committee on Economic, Social and Cultural Rights.

[1] P Alston and JHH Weiler, "An 'Ever Closer Union' in Need of a Human Rights Policy: The European Union and Human Rights", in P Alston, with M Bustelo and J Heenan (eds), *The European Union and Human Rights* (Oxford, Oxford University Press, 1999), p 3.

argument in favor of the creation of such a body was that it could encourage the Union to adopt a more preventive approach to human rights. The argument ran as follows: instead of human rights simply being monitored *post hoc* by the possibility of judicial review in the event of violation, what was required was a tool alerting the institutions to the need to address certain issues, where they had been given the power to do so and where an initiative on their part would be justified because these issues could not be satisfactorily addressed by the Member States acting individually, and because the objectives to be achieved could be better achieved by an initiative adopted at the level of the Union. "Systematic, reliable, and focused information", it was then argued, "is the starting point for a clear understanding of the nature, extent, and location of the problems that exist and for the identification of possible solutions".

The Union has moved towards implementing this proposal, albeit using a remarkably indirect route. In a communcation of 2001 on the Union's external human rights policy, the Commission had stated, in answer to a call to follow upon this proposal, that such an additional supervisory body was not required, as the Commission "does not lack sources of advice and information. It can draw on reports from the United Nations, the Council of Europe and a variety of international NGOs".[2] Although this communication only concerned the human rights policy of the Union vis-à-vis third countries, many saw in this pronouncement a definitive rejection of the idea. When the Heads of States and Governments of the Member States of the European Union announced at their Brussels European Council of 13 December 2003 their intention to extend the mandate of the EU Monitoring Centre on Racism and Xenophobia[3] in order to create a "Human Rights Agency" entrusted with the mission to collect and analyse data in order to define the policy of the Union in this field, the decision therefore took most observers by surprise. Indeed, not only was the very proposal for such an Agency unexpected; but the proposal to build on the existing EUMC, was equally not an obvious one. On the basis of an external evaluation of the activities of the EUMC between its creation in 1998 and end 2001,[4] the Commission had considered that "the Centre should continue to concentrate on racism" and that "an extension to other fields would be an unwelcome distraction within the limits of the resources likely to be available to the Centre and that it would lead to a weakening of the emphasis on racism".[5] In a commun-

[2] Communication from the Commission to the Council and the European Parliament, The European Union's Role in Promoting Human Rights and Democratisation in Third Countries, COM(2001) 252 final, p 7.

[3] The EU Monitoring Centre was created by Council Regulation (EC) 1035/97 of 2 June 1997 establishing a European Monitoring Centre on Racism and Xenophobia, OJ L 151 of 10.6.1997, p 1. Based in Vienna, it has a staff of approximately 30 persons. In 2003, its budget was 6.5 million euros.

[4] http://europa.eu.int/comm/employment_social/fundamental_rights/pdf/origin/eumc_eval2002_en.pdf

[5] Communication from the Commission to the Council, the European Parliament, the European Economic and Social Committee and the Committee of the Regions on the Activities of the European Monitoring Centre on Racism and Xenophobia, together with proposals to recast Council Regulation (EC) 1035/97, COM(2003)483 final of 5.8.2003.

ication of 5 August 2003, the Commission therefore had proposed a number of amendments to the Regulation establishing the EU Monitoring Centre in order to improve its effectiveness and the coherence of its tasks.

By announcing the decision to move towards the establishment of a Fundamental Rights Agency (as the Commission was soon to call it) by extending the mandate of the EUMC, the Brussels European Council of December 2003 answered the question of what should be done with the EUMC: the answer was that it should be transformed into something else. That decision however opened another question, namely what contribution a Fundamental Rights Agency could make to improving the monitoring of fundamental rights in the Union, and how that new body should relate to the mechanisms already existing in the field of the promotion and protection of fundamental rights in the Union.

It is this question which the essays of this volume seek to address. The authors examine the present situation of monitoring human rights in the Union and the possible contribution the Fundamental Rights Agency could make to the human rights policy of the Union. They address these questions at a particularly important time. Indeed, five recent and interrelated developments illustrate the central position fundamental rights have come to occupy in the constitutional discourse of the Union and in the practice of its institutions. The Charter of Fundamental Rights has been adopted and shall be incorporated in the Constitution now proposed for ratification by the 25 Member States. An EU Network of independent experts in fundamental rights has been established. The Council may adopt sanctions against, or address recommendations to, a Member State threatening to breach the values—including respect for human rights—on which the Union is founded. If and when the Constitution enters into force, the Union shall have the competence to accede to the European Convention on Human Rights. Finally, the division of powers between the Union and its Member States has evolved to the extent that the development of a fundamental rights policy of the Union has become a genuine possibility, although the identification of the circumstances in which the Union can and will use its powers to that effect remains a matter of controversy. Together, these developments form the background of the debate on the tasks of the future Agency, and on how it will fit into the institutional landscape. Each of these developments is significant in its own right, but they are also related to one another in complex ways.

The Adoption of the Charter of Fundamental Rights

The Charter of Fundamental Rights was adopted at the Nice European Summit of December 2000, as a solemn declaration from the European Council, the European Commission and the European Parliament. Though formally a non-binding document, the Charter was immediately perceived by the commentators as the single most authoritative restatement of the acquis of the Union in the field of human and fundamental rights, and its impact was immediate on the practice of the institutions. In a Communication of 11 October 2000, the European Commission had insisted that the binding character of the Charter as a codification of that acquis should not depend on the formal integration of the Charter into the European Treaties.[6] In March 2001, a requirement was imposed on the services of the European Commission to accompany all legislative proposals which could have an impact on fundamental rights with an indication that these proposals were considered to be compatible with the requirements of the Charter.[7] When Working Group II of the European Convention presided over by Commissioner A. Vitorino had to examine the issue of the incorporation of the Charter into the Constitution for Europe which was prepared in the framework of the Convention between February 2002 and July 2003, its members unanimously agreed on the principle of full incorporation.[8] While preserving the substantive provisions of the Charter, the members of the Working Group nevertheless agreed on certain adaptations being made to its general provisions, which although presented as mere clarifications of the initial understanding of the drafters of the Charter, raised certain fears as to the invocability of the Charter before courts applying Union law or acts adopted by the Member States in the scope of application of Union law. The Charter now forms part II of the Treaty establishing a Constitution for Europe. If and when the Constitution enters into force, it will be relied upon by the European Court of Justice in reviewing the validity of secondary Union law, although the Court of Justice should also continue to develop, alongside its reliance on the Charter, those fundamental rights which are protected as general principles of Union law.

Although by no means a revolutionary development changing the nature of the Union—and, indeed, this was not the intention of the European Council when, in June 1999, it initially agreed on the codification of the acquis of the Union in the field of fundamental rights—, the constitutionalisation of fundamental rights in the Union nevertheless gives them a heightened visibility within the legal order of the Union.[9] Even before the entry into force of the

---

[6] Communication from the Commission on the legal nature of the Charter of fundamental rights of the European Union, COM(2000) 644 final, of 11.10.2000 (stating, at para 9, that "it is reasonable to assume that the Charter will produce all its effects, legal and others, whatever its nature. [. . .] it is clear that it would be difficult for the Council and the Commission, who are to proclaim it solemnly, to ignore in the future, in their legislative function, an instrument prepared at the request of the European Council by the full range of sources of national and European legitimacy acting in concert").

[7] Memorandum of M Vitorino and the Presidency: Application of the Charter of Fundamental Rights, SEC(2001) 380/3.

[8] See the Final Report presented by the Chairman of Working Group II "Incorporation of the Charter/Accession to the ECHR", CONV 354/02, 22 October 2002.

[9] See, for further examples of the impact the Charter has had since its proclamation, the Report on the impact of the Charter of Fundamental Rights of the European Union and its future status (2002/2139(INI)) adopted by the Committee on Constitutional Affairs (rapporteur: Andrew N Duff) (doc EP A5-0332/2002, 8 October 2002).

Constitution, the adoption of the Charter makes it easier for national courts, before which litigants contest the validity of acts adopted by the Union, to decide whether a referral to the European Court of Justice is required. It encourages individuals affected by Union law or by state measures adopted in the scope of application of Union law to claim that their fundamental rights are being violated, either in order to file a complaint with the European Commission, or to challenge these acts before the national courts or the Court of First Instance. Moreover, the adoption of the Charter of Fundamental Rights encourages the development of political forms of monitoring, on which the Charter confers a greater degree of objectivity and thus also of legitimacy. In particular, since 2000, the European Parliament's annual report on the situation of fundamental rights in the Union uses the Charter of Fundamental Rights as its main source of reference, and as the authoritative template on which to base its examination of the evolution of fundamental rights in the Member States.

The Creation of the EU Network of Independent Experts on Fundamental Rights

It is this monitoring by the European Parliament which led to the creation, in September 2002, of the EU Network of independent experts on fundamental rights.[10] Indeed, the Network was set up by the European Commission (DG Justice and Home Affairs), in response to the resolution of the European Parliament based on the Report on the state of fundamental rights in the European Union in the year 2000.[11] The EU Network of Independent Experts on Fundamental Rights is currently[12] composed of 25 experts—one per Member State—, and monitors the situation of fundamental rights in the Member States and in the Union, on the basis of the EU Charter of Fundamental Rights. It currently holds three meeting sessions each year. Its tools are the publication of annual reports which examine the situation of fundamental rights in each

---

[10] One of the co-editors of this volume (Olivier De Schutter) chairs the Network. Three of the other authors are members of the Network (Manfred Nowak, Rick Lawson and Martin Scheinin). The positions adopted here of course are formulated by these authors in their personal capacity, and should not necessarily be seen as reflecting the position of the Network.

[11] In its resolution of 5 July 2001 on the situation of fundamental rights in the European Union (2000) (2000/2231(INI)) (rapporteur Mr Thierry Cornillet, MEP), the European Parliament recommended "that a network be set up consisting of legal experts who are authorities on human rights and jurists from each of the Member States in order to ensure a high degree of expertise and enable the Parliament to receive an assessment of the implementation of each of the rights laid down in the European Union Charter of Fundamental Rights, taking into account developments in national laws, the case-law of the Luxembourg and Strasbourg Courts and any notable case-law of he Member States' national and constitutional courts".

[12] Initially, only 15 experts, one from each Member State, composed the Network. Independent experts covering the new Member States joined the Network in 2003, simultaneously with the signature of the Accession Treaty. They submitted their first full reports in January 2004, prior to the formal date of accession of the new Member States.

Member State and the activities of the institutions of the Union, as well as the publication of a consolidated report synthesizing on an annual basis its main conclusions and recommendations, which are addressed both to the Member States and the Union institutions. The Network also prepares Thematic Comments, examining cross-cutting issues which, typically, concern both the Member States and the Union and may therefore pose the problem of coordination between both levels in the promotion and protection of fundamental rights in the Union.[13] Further, it submits opinions on issues relating to the protection of fundamental rights in the Union, usually based on a comparison, as complete as possible, of the situations which exist in the different Member States on a given question, and systematically seeking to take into account the state of international and European human rights law.[14]

The Role of the Council in the Prevention of Human Rights Violations

How, it may be asked, could such monitoring be justified, when not only the institutions of the Union but also the Member States are monitored in relation to all of their fields of activity, whether or not they are acting in the scope of application of Union law? After all, Article 51 of the Charter of Fundamental Rights limits the scope of application of the Charter to the institutions of the Union and to the Member States only in their implementation of Union law. However—and this illustrates the impact the adoption of the Charter has had, beyond and prior to any strictly legally binding effect it may have in the future— the Network of independent experts on fundamental rights took the view that the Charter also constitutes a catalogue of common values of the Member States of the Union. In that respect, the Charter may be taken into account in the interpretation of Article 6(1) EU. This provision identifies human rights as part of the values on which the Union is based,[15] and the Charter, while not exclusive of other fundamental rights, constitutes an authoritative catalogue of the rights recognized as fundamental in the legal order of the Union. Moreover, Article 6(1) EU is referred to by Article 7 EU. This provision was initially inserted in the

---

[13] The Thematic Observation appended to the 2003 Synthesis Report (covering the year 2002) relates to "The Balance between Freedom and Security in the Response by the European Union and its Member States to the Terrorist Threats". The Thematic Comment contained in the 2004 Synthesis Report (covering the year 2003) examines "Fundamental Rights in the External Activities of the European Union in the Fields of Justice and Asylum and Immigration". The Thematic Observation appended to the 2005 Synthesis Report (covering the year 2004) will focus on the protection of minorities in the Union.

[14] The opinions of the Network, as well as the report on the activities of the institutions of the Union and the synthesis report, are available online at http://europa.eu.int/comm/justice_home/ cfr_cdf/index_en.htm. The country reports are currently accessible online at www.cpdr.ucl.ac.be/ cridho ("documentation online").

[15] These values include democracy, respect for human rights and fundamental freedoms, and the rule of law. Article 49 EU provides that respect for these values is a condition for membership of the Union.

Treaty of the European Union by the Treaty of Amsterdam which entered into force on 1 May 1999. It was limited, then, to providing the possibility for the Council of the Union to adopt certain sanctions against a Member State persistently committing serious violations of the values on which the Union is based: clearly, the provision was conceived in order to meet certain fears raised by the perspective of the enlargement of the Union to certain newly democratized States, especially at a time where the Union was being attributed further powers in the fields of justice and home affairs. Since the entry into force of the Nice Treaty on 1 February 2003,[16] Article 7 EU gives the Council the possibility to determine that there exists a clear risk of a serious breach by a Member State of the common values on which the Union is based. This preventive mechanism, provided for in Article 7(1) EU, now complements the possibility of adopting sanctions against a State which, according to the determination made by the Council, has seriously and persistently breached the principles mentioned in Article 6(1) EU.[17]

As recounted by Manfred Nowak in his contribution to this volume, this improvement of Article 7 EU was proposed by the *Comité des Sages* which reported in September 2000 to the European Council on the human rights situation in Austria and the means by which the EU could respond to possible human rights problems in an EU Member State.[18] However, in order to ensure that such a mechanism is used in a non-selective manner, it should proceed on the basis of a systematic monitoring by independent experts, providing comparable data and objective assessments on the situation of fundamental rights in all the Member States of the Union. It is with this objective in mind that the communication which the Commission presented to the Council and the European Parliament on Article 7 EU entitled "Respect for and promotion of the values on which the Union is based"[19], notes that, by its reports, the Network of independent experts in fundamental rights may help to "detect fundamental rights anomalies or situations where there might be breaches or the risk of breaches of these rights falling within Article 7 of the Union Treaty"; and that it may "help in finding solutions to remedy confirmed anomalies or to prevent potential breaches". Therefore, while the adoption by the Network of the Charter of Fundamental Rights as the catalogue of rights on which its monitoring should be based was motivated both by the practice inaugurated in 2000 by the annual reports of the European Parliament and by the understanding of the Charter as a codification of the fundamental rights which were considered to be part of the common values on which the Union is based, it is Article 7 EU which explains

---

[16] OJ C 180, of 10.3.2001.

[17] Art 7(2) to (4) EU (Art I–59 of the Treaty establishing a Constitution for Europe) ("Suspension of certain rights resulting from Union membership") and, for the implementation of these sanctions in the framework of the EC Treaty, Art 309 EC.

[18] The report was submitted by Martti Ahtisaari, Jochen Frowein and Marcelino Oreja, adopted in Paris on 8 September 2000: See http://www.virtual-institute.de/en/Bericht-EU/report.pdf.

[19] COM (2003) 606 final, of 15.10.2003.

the reliance on the Charter even with regard to situations which, under Article 51 of the Charter, would in principle not fall under its scope of application. The need for an objective and impartial assessment of the situation of fundamental rights in the Member States of the Union, in order to facilitate the exercise by the institutions of their constitutional functions under this article, has been clearly recognized, and one of the most important functions fulfilled by the Network of independent experts is to offer such an assessment.

The Accession of the European Union to the European Convention on Human Rights

After having failed to seize the opportunities created by the intergovernmental conferences for the revision of the treaties of 1996–1997 and of 1999–2000, which led respectively to the treaties of Amsterdam and of Nice, the Heads of State and Government agreed, in adopting the Treaty establishing a Constitution for Europe, to provide a legal basis for the accession of the Union to the European Convention on Human Rights.[20] Of course, although the political will now appears to be present, both within the Member States of the Union and within the overwhelming majority of the Member States of the Council of Europe, a number of technical difficulties remain, which will have to be solved before the Protocol providing for the accession of the Union to the European Convention on Human Rights can be opened for signature and ratification. But even the simple prospect of such accession constitutes a strong encouragement to the Union to ensure that fundamental rights are adequately protected within its own legal order, in order to limit the risk that, in the future, it may be found by the European Court of Human Rights to have violated them. Such pressure has been rising since the European Court of Human Rights first concluded in 1999, in the case of *Matthews v the United Kingdom*, that a Member State of the Union, which is a Party to the European Convention on Human Rights, could be in violation of its obligations under the Convention even where the source of the violation is located in an act of the Union. Although the Court still has to clarify the precise implications of this judgment—and, especially, whether it extends to acts of secondary Union law which the European Court of Justice

---

[20] This was required by the Opinion delivered by the European Court of Justice on 28 March 1996, concluding that the European Community could not rely on its implicit powers in order to accede to the European Convention on Human Rights, because of what the Court called the "constitutional significance" of such a change in the regime of protection of human rights in the legal order of the Community: see Opinion 2/94 [1996] ECR I–1759. The Court stated in that opinion that the Community institutions do not have at their disposal a "general power to enact rules on human rights or to conclude international conventions in this field", although it did not question that respect for human rights constituted a "condition of lawfulness of Community acts": see paras 27 and 34 of the opinion. On this opinion, see, inter alia, O De Schutter and Y Lejeune, 'L'adhésion de la Communauté européenne à la Convention européenne des droits de l'homme. A propos de l'avis 2/94 de la Cour de justice des Communautés européennes', (1996) *Cahiers de droit européen*, 555; G Gaja, 'Opinion 2/94', (1996) 33 *Common Market Law Review* 973.

may review for compatibility with the fundamental rights protected in the legal order of the Union—, it can hardly be argued today that the Union may ignore the requirements of the ECHR where it legislates, if it wishes to avoid engaging the Member States' international responsibility in the implementation of Union law.

There is no reason in principle to consider that the European Convention on Human Rights should be given a specific legal status, distinguishing it from any other international human rights treaty in force with respect to one or more of the EU Member States. Even those who may believe it premature to envisage the accession of the Union to instruments other than the European Convention on Human Rights or the Council of Europe Convention for the Protection of Individuals with regard to Automatic Processing of Personal Data[21] could hardly deny that, as its powers are being extended, and as it exercises more of the powers conferred upon it by the Member States, the Union is not in a position to ignore, in its law- and policy-making, the requirements of international and European human rights instruments. Indeed, the EU Network of independent experts in fundamental rights has been consistent in its preoccupation with this dimension of the protection of fundamental rights in the legal order of the Union. In the explanatory introduction to its conclusions and recommendations on the situation of fundamental rights in the Union in 2003, it emphasized that the privileged status recognized to the European Convention on Human Rights by the text of the EU Charter of Fundamental Rights should not lead to an underestimation of the need to take into account other international or European human rights treaties in the interpretation of the Charter. It noted:

> . . . in accordance with Article 52(3) of the EU Charter of Fundamental Rights, the Network reads the provisions of the Charter which correspond to rights guaranteed by the Convention for the Protection of Human Rights and Fundamental Freedoms as having the same meaning and the same scope than those rights, as interpreted by the European Court of Human Rights; in certain cases, the provisions of the Charter however are recognized a broader scope, as confirmed by the second sentence of Article 52(3) of the Charter. The Network also takes into account the fact that other provisions of the Charter have to be read in accordance with the rights guaranteed in instruments adopted in the field of human rights in the framework of the United Nations, the International Labour Organisation or the Council of Europe. Where this is the case, these provisions of the Charter are interpreted by taking into account those instruments and the interpretation given to them in the international legal order.[22]

One of the most underestimated, yet crucial, stakes of the future system of monitoring fundamental rights in the Union concerns the role of instruments

---

[21] See the Amendements to the Convention for the Protection of Individuals with regard to Automatic Processing of Personal Data authorizing the accession of the European Communities adopted by the Committee of Ministers of the Council of Europe at its 675th meeting, on 15 June 1999.

[22] EU Network of Independent Experts on Fundamental Rights, *Synthesis report on the situation of fundamental rights in the Union in 2003: Conclusions and Recommendations*, March 2004, p 10.

adopted within the United Nations or within the Council of Europe in the fundamental rights policy of the Union. When the Charter of Fundamental Rights was adopted, certain fears were expressed that it could result in diverging interpretations of the requirements of fundamental rights by the institutions of the Union—including the European Court of Justice—on the one hand, and the European Court of Human Rights, on the other hand. Article 52(3) of the Charter was adopted in order to alleviate that fear. It would be a paradoxical consequence of that effort if it resulted in encouraging, *a contrario* of the clauses of the Charter which are considered to correspond to provisions of the European Convention on Human Rights, an interpretation of the other clauses of the Charter which would not take into account what may be referred to as the emerging common law of international human rights.

The Rise of the Category of Shared Competences

Finally, one last aspect of the current situation should be highlighted. Although fundamental rights have emerged in the jurisprudence of the European Court of Justice as limits imposed on EC law from outside, respect for which should be controlled by the Court as one aspect of its constitutional mission to ensure that the law is respected,[23] they have now assumed, in many respects, a different status. Although they are not actually ranked among the objectives of the Union—thus ruling out the possibility that the Union may legislate on the basis of its implied powers[24]—, they may nevertheless inspire the adoption of legislation where there exists an adequate legal basis therefor in the Treaties. There are many such legal bases in the existing treaties.[25] Together, they form a canvass through which an authentic fundamental rights policy of the Union can be envisaged—a policy, that is, which would go beyond judicial protection, in a purely reactive mode, of victims of human rights violations, but which would be proactive, anticipating the risk of violations occurring in the legal order of the Union by the adoption of the necessary legislative instruments.[26] The Treaty

---

[23] Art 220 EC (ex art 164 of the EC Treaty).

[24] Art 308 EC (ex art 235 of the EC Treaty).

[25] For an overview of the competences of the EU in the field of fundamental rights, see, e.g. P Alston and JHH Weiler, 'An "Ever Closer Union" in Need of a Human Rights Policy: The European Union and Human Rights', in P Alston, with M Bustelo and J Heenan (eds), *The European Union and Human Rights*, cited above n 1, at pp 24–25 (see also in the same volume JHH Weiler and S Fries, 'A Human Rights Policy for the European Community and Union: the Question of Competences'); section II of the Introduction to the *Report on the Situation of Fundamental Rights in the European Union and Its Member States in 2002*, presented by the EU Network of Independent Experts in March 2003, at pp 12–19; and O De Schutter, "The Implementation of the Charter of Fundamental Rights through the Open Method of Coordination", in O De Schutter and S Deakin (eds), *Social Rights and Market Forces. Is the open coordination of employment and social policies the future of Social Europe?* (Bruxelles, Bruylant, 2004) (also available as a *Jean Monnet Working Paper*, www.JeanMonnetProgram.org).

[26] See JHH Weiler, 'Editorial Comments: Does the European Union Truly Need a Charter of Rights?', (2000) 6 *European Law Journal*, 95, at 96.

establishing a Constitution for Europe confirms in this respect the many developments which previous treaties have prepared.

First, certain fundamental rights are ranked among the objectives of the Union as defined in Article I–3 of the Treaty establishing a Constitution for Europe, which has been proposed for ratification by the Member States.[27] The realization of those objectives could justify using the flexibility clause now located in Article I–18 of the Constitutional Treaty. These objectives include in particular: 'combat[ing] social exclusion and discrimination'; promoting 'social justice and protection'; pursuing 'equality between women and men' and 'solidarity between generations'; and protecting children's rights. For the fulfilment of these values, the flexibility clause may apply, according to which 'If action by the Union should prove necessary within the framework of the policies [of the Union] to attain one of the objectives set by the Constitution, and the Constitution has not provided the necessary powers, the Council of Ministers, acting unanimously on a proposal from the Commission and after obtaining the consent of the European Parliament, shall take the appropriate measures.' This provision, which retains and somewhat enlarges Article 308 EC (ex Article 235 of the EC Treaty), therefore makes it possible for the Union to adopt certain measures for the realization of the abovementioned objectives, provided of course there exists the political will to do so.

Second, like the existing European Treaties, the Treaty establishing a Constitution for Europe has conferred upon the Union a number of powers which, although not necessarily framed as powers to realize fundamental rights, nevertheless could easily fulfil that objective—and, indeed, have already been used for that purpose. For instance, Article III–124 of the Treaty establishing a Constitution for Europe provides that the Council acting unanimously may adopt a European law or framework law in order to establish the measures needed to combat discrimination based on sex, racial or ethnic origin, religion or belief, disability, age or sexual orientation. It may also, acting by qualified majority, establish basic principles for Union incentive measures and define such incentive measures, and support action taken by Member States in order to contribute to combating discrimination. This provision corresponds to Article 13 EC, as revised by the Treaty of Nice. It is on the basis of this article that the Council has adopted Directive 2000/43/EC of 29 June 2000 implementing the principle of equal treatment between persons irrespective of racial or ethnic origin[28] and Directive 2000/78/EC of 27 November 2000 establishing a general framework for equal treatment in employment and occupation.[29] Under Article III–125 of the Treaty establishing a Constitution for Europe, European laws or framework laws may be adopted in order to facilitate the exercise of the right of every citizen of the Union to move and reside freely and the Constitution. It is

---

[27] In the renumbered version signed in Rome on 29 October 2004 (CIG 87/2/4 REV 2).
[28] OJ L 180 of 19.7.2000, p 22.
[29] OJ L 303 of 2.12.2000, p 16.

on the basis of Article 18 EC, which has inspired Article III–125 of the Constitutional Treaty, that the European Parliament and the Council adopted Directive 2004/38/EC of 29 April 2004 on the right of citizens of the Union and their family members to move and reside freely within the territory of the Member States.[30] Articles III–266 and III–267 concern, respectively, the development by the Union of a common policy on asylum, subsidiary protection and temporary protection, and the development of a common immigration policy. The first of these provisions restates Articles 63, al. 1 and 2, EC, and 64(2) EC; the second provision is a reformulation of Article 63, al. 3 and 4, EC. It is on these bases that the Council adopted Directive 2003/86/EC of 22 September 2003 on the right to family reunification[31] and Directive 2003/9/EC of 27 January 2003 laying down minimum standards for the reception of asylum-seekers[32]— all instruments may be presented either as fulfilling, albeit imperfectly, certain rights of the Charter of Fundamental Rights, and thereby as contributing to the fundamental rights policy of the Union. Article III–270(2) of the Treaty establishing a Constitution for Europe provides that, to the extent necessary to facilitate mutual recognition of judgments and judicial decisions and police and judicial cooperation in criminal matters having a cross-border dimension, European framework laws may establish minimum rules which may concern, inter alia, the mutual admissibility of evidence between Member States, the rights of individuals in criminal procedure, or the rights of victims of crime. It is on the basis of Article 31 EU, from which Article III–270 is inspired, that the European Commission recently proposed the adoption of a Council Framework Decision on certain procedural rights in criminal proceedings throughout the European Union.[33] Such examples could be multiplied.

The importance of this development for the future of monitoring fundamental rights in the Union—and for the definition of the tasks of the Fundamental Rights Agency, the object of this book—could hardly be overstated. Indeed, the implication is that monitoring by the Union of the situation of fundamental rights in the EU Member States will not only serve to ensure that fundamental rights are respected by the national authorities, either because they are to comply with the Charter of Fundamental Rights and other fundamental rights recognized among the general principles of Union law when they act in the scope of application of Union law, or because the institutions of the Union have been granted the power to adopt sanctions against a Member State found to be in serious and persistent violation of these rights, and may address recommenda-

---

[30] Dir 2004/38/EC of the European Parliament and of the Council of 29 April 2004 on the right of citizens of the Union and their family members to move and reside freely within the territory of the Member States amending Reg (EEC) No 1612/68 and repealing Dirs 64/221/EEC, 68/360/EEC, 72/194/EEC, 73/148/EEC, 75/34/EEC, 75/35/EEC, 90/364/EEC, 90/365/EEC and 93/96/EEC, OJ L 158, 30.4.2004, p 77.

[31] OJ L 251 of 3.10.2003, p 12.

[32] OJ L 31 of 6.2.2003, p 18.

[33] COM(2004) 328 final, 28.4.2004.

tions to a Member State at clear risk of committing a serious breach of those rights. Monitoring, indeed, must also fulfill another, non-contentious function: it will serve to identify issues on which it would be justified for the Union to exercise its powers to contribute to the promotion and the protection of fundamental rights, because the decentralized action of the Member States, acting individually, appears incapable of attaining that objective, and because that objective could be better fulfilled by an initiative of the Union.[34] We see, then, that the current evolution of the relationship between the Union and its Member States, which leads (to express this in fashionable jargon) to a system of "multi-level governance", invests the monitoring of fundamental rights in the EU Member States with another function, as yet insufficiently explained in the debates on the status of fundamental rights in the Union. It is this dimension of its monitoring which the Network of independent experts on fundamental rights sought to explain when it stated that it would address certain recommendations to the EU institutions

> either where the EU Network of Independent Experts on Fundamental Rights arrives at the conclusion that certain violations of fundamental rights or risks of such violation by Member States are serious enough to justify that the attention of the European Parliament be drawn upon them, as they could imperil the mutual trust on which Union policies are founded, *where it is found that certain initiatives taken by the EU in the limits of its attributed powers could truly add value to the protection of fundamental rights in the Union,* or where the violations which are found to have occured [...] have their source in the law of the European Union, requiring that this situation be remedied.[35]

The italicized passage shows how monitoring may serve, in effect, to inaugurate what may be called an open method of coordination in the field of fundamental rights,[36] at least if we agree to detach that notion from the specific institutional forms it has now taken under the EC Treaty in the Titles concerning

---

[34] Most of the powers conferred upon the Union by the Member States, and which it could use in order to develop a fundamental rights policy, fall into the category of competences which it shares with the Member States, and which the Treaty establishing a Constitution for Europe defines as the residual category, comprising all competences which are neither exclusive to the Union, nor limited to the carrying out of supporting, coordinating or complementary action: see Art I–14 of the Constitutional Treaty. In these areas of shared competence, among which the Treaty explicitly mentions social policy for the aspects defined in Part III of the Constitution and the establishment of an area of freedom, security, and justice, the Union is bound to respect the principles of subsidiarity and proportionality. It may therefore only act "if and insofar as the objectives of the proposed action cannot be sufficiently achieved by the Member States, either at central level or at regional and local level, but can rather, by reason of the scale or effects of the proposed action, be better achieved at Union level" (Art I–11(3) of the Constitutional Treaty).

[35] EU Network of Independent Experts on Fundamental Rights, *Synthesis report on the situation of fundamental rights in the Union in 2003: Conclusions and Recommendations*, March 2004 (see the "Explanatory note" preceding the Conclusions).

[36] See also section V of the Introduction to the *Report on the situation of Fundamental Rights in the European Union and Its Member States in 2002*, cited above, at pp 25–27.

Employment[37] and Social Policy,[38] and return to the original meaning of such a form of coordination as a process by which the Member States may insure themselves against the risk of destructive competition by mutually observing themselves, by seeking to identify good practices and by encouraging the dissemination thereof rather than falling into opportunistic and non-cooperative behavior in the absence of harmonization. The assertion that a decentralized implementation of fundamental rights, where these are defined at the level of the Member States without any attempt to harmonize at the level of the Union, may produce suboptimal effects, is equivalent to saying that the power which the Member States may attribute to the Union is not necessarily power which is subtracted from the Member States. The relationship is not a zero-sum game. On the contrary, it has been written, 'power is increased to mutual benefit by the very fact of action in common', so that arguments about the allocation of power cannot be framed as arguments about 'who wins and who loses'.[39] The mutual observation of the Member States which would be made possible by an open form of coordination should enable the identification—with respect to particular rights—of situations where implementing measures should ideally be adopted.

The Charter of Fundamental Rights, then, would begin a new life. Beyond its political significance as a solemn statement of fundamental values, but also beyond its legal significance as a catalogue of rights contained in the Constitution once in force, the Charter could serve to guide a search mechanism in a dynamic understanding of the division of competences between the Member States and the Union.[40]

[37] See Art 129 EC, al. 1: "The Council, acting in accordance with the procedure referred to in Art 251 and after consulting the Economic and Social Committee and the Committee of the Regions, may adopt incentive measures designed to encourage cooperation between Member States and to support their action in the field of employment through initiatives aimed at developing exchanges of information and best practices, providing comparative analysis and advice as well as promoting innovative approaches and evaluating experiences, in particular by recourse to pilot projects".

[38] Under Art 137(2)(a), the Council 'may adopt measures designed to encourage cooperation between Member States through initiatives aimed at improving knowledge, developing exchanges of information and best practices, promoting innovative approaches and evaluating experiences, excluding any harmonization of the laws and regulations of the Member States' with a view to achieving the objectives of 'the promotion of employment, improved living and working conditions, so as to make possible their harmonization while the improvement is being maintained, proper social protection, dialogue between management and labour, the development of human resources with a view to lasting high employment and the combating of exclusion', 'having in mind fundamental social rights such as those set out in the European Social Charter signed at Turin on 18 October 1961 and in the 1989 Community Charter of the Fundamental Social Rights of Workers' (Art 136 EC).

[39] S Weatherill, 'Competence', in B de Witte (ed), *Ten Reflections on the Constitutional Treaty for Europe* (European University Institute, Robert Schuman Centre for Advanced Studies and Academy of European Law, 2003) p 45, at p 46.

[40] There are signs that this significance is progressively being recognized. For instance, the European Social Agenda—as presented by a Communication of the Commission of 30 June 2000 (COM(2000) 379 final) and as approved by the Nice European Council in December 2000 (OJ C 157 of 30.5.2001, p 4)—mentions the importance of the Charter of Fundamental Rights for the future development of social policy in the Union and, indeed, borrows much of its terminology from the Charter of rights. See also N Bernard, "A 'New Governance' Approach to Economic, Social and Cultural Rights in the EU", in T Hervey and J Kenner (eds), *Economic and Social Rights under the EU Charter of Fundamental Rights. A Legal Perspective* (Oxford, Hart Publishing, 2003) p 245, esp at pp 263–67.

2. THE ORGANIZATION OF THE ESSAYS

The essays collected in this volume take the background set out above as their departure point. Their immediate preoccupation is with the establishment of the European Fundamental Rights Agency; their real contribution is to a larger debate on the future of monitoring fundamental rights within the Union and how the Agency shall fit into this larger panorama of tools and bodies. The essays have been completed after the publication, on 25 October 2004, of the communication in which the European Commission presented a public consultation document in order to launch the debate on which its proposals, expected in mid-2005, are to be based.[41] They should be seen, however, as going beyond that debate, since most of the chapters contain proposals not only as to how the tasks of the Fundamental Rights Agency should be defined, but also as to how the different strands of fundamental rights protection in the Union should be woven together, in order to overcome the sense of patchiness which still emerges from any systematic overview of past achievements in the field.

The essays are structured around three questions. First, how should the creation of the Fundamental Rights Agency be interpreted, when placed in the larger scheme of the constitutionalisation of EU law, and how can we ensure that it will truly add value to the existing mechanisms which promote and protect fundamental rights within the Union? Second, how should the tasks of the Agency be defined, in its different domains of action, if—as suggested by the consultation document of the Commission[42]—the Charter of Fundamental Rights is to constitute its reference point? Third and finally, should the Agency relate to the global environment in which the Union operates? Should it take into account, alongside the Charter, the acquis of international and European human rights law, in order to ensure a greater consistency between the standards which apply to the Member States and those which apply in the legal order of the Union? Should it extend its mandate to the external action of the institutions of the Union, whether they act directly beyond the territories of the Member States or whether they seek to promote respect for human rights in third countries?

---

[41] Commission of the European Communities, Fundamental Rights Agency. Public consultation document, COM(2004) 693 final, 25.10.2004.

[42] See Commission of the European Communities, Fundamental Rights Agency. Public consultation document, cited above, at p 7 (the Charter "already constitutes an authentic expression of the fundamental rights protected by Community law as a set of general principles. As such, it constitutes an essential reference document in the discussion on the definition of the Agency's areas of intervention").

The Fundamental Rights Agency and its Constitutional Background

The four essays constituting the first part of the book situate the Fundamental Rights Agency in its constitutional background. They are concerned less with the content of the tasks to be entrusted to the Agency than with the way these tasks are to be fulfilled, and the relationships the Agency might develop with other institutional actors. Gráinne de Búrca situates the topic of the Fundamental Rights Agency in the broader context of the use of so-called 'new modes of governance', in the EU, and more specifically in the context of the increasing 'agencification' of the EU. Her chapter examines why such modes of governance might be used in the field of human rights protection, questioning whether their use is indeed appropriate in this field, and more particularly whether there is a tension between these governance values and human rights values. Finally, her chapter questions the possible political motivation for the recent decision to establish an EU fundamental rights agency by extending the mandate of the Vienna Monitoring Centre on Racism and Xenophobia (EUMC), looking both at the decision of the European Council to this effect and at the tenor of the Commission's recent communication on the subject, and at the apparent use of the EUMC as a model for the new agency. The chapter concludes by questioning whether the proposed Agency is likely to contribute to strengthening the EU's emerging human rights policy.

In chapter 2, Olivier De Schutter proposes that the time has come for the mainstreaming of fundamental rights in all law- and policy-making by the institutions of the Union. Mainstreaming goes beyond the banal obligation imposed on the institutions to comply with fundamental rights, and to verify systematically that the acts they adopt are compatible with those requirements. The concept of mainstreaming requires, rather, that institutions be incentivized to use their powers in order to contribute to the realisation of fundamental rights, even when they act in sectors which present no apparent risk of violating these rights and, indeed, even when they take initiatives which seem to present no relationship with fundamental rights as traditionally conceived. Seen in this light, the objective of mainstreaming presents, at two levels, a paradoxical relationship to the setting up of a Fundamental Rights Agency. First, there is a risk that being entrusted to an Agency, fundamental rights become sectoralized where they should be made transversal, sidelined to the policy margins where they should instead be brought to the centre. Second, there is a risk that if expertise in fundamental rights is located within the Agency, institutional learning would be discouraged: in relying on the Agency for advice, the services of the Commission might lose the incentive to build fundamental rights within their institutional culture. O. De Schutter seeks to identify how the two components of the mainstreaming strategy he proposes—impact assessments and the preparation of action plans—could be devised in order to limit these risks.

As a member of both the UN Human Rights Committee and the EU Network of independent experts on fundamental rights, Martin Scheinin was ideally placed to reflect upon the relationship between this network and the Fundamental Rights Agency. His analysis in chapter 3 is based on a distinction between what may be called, in the vocabulary which best describes the current functions of the European Union Monitoring Centre on Racism and Xenophobia, data collection and analysis, on the one hand, and monitoring in the normative sense of the term, on the other hand. Data collection and analysis consists in providing policy-makers with the information they require in order to exercise their competences; whereas monitoring requires the "legal assessment of complex information against the normative grid of of human rights/fundamental rights norms, [in which] the ability of an independent expert body to formulate a position as to the compatibility or lack of compatibility of a law, practice or situation with applicable human rights/fundamental rights norms, is an end in itself". Whilst the Agency could, building on the experience of the EUMC, develop its mission of data collection and analysis, Scheinin identifies the need for the EU Network of independent experts on fundamental rights to continue to exercise its monitoring function, which is unique and irreducible to what an Agency within the Union could perform. Scheinin concludes by envisaging different modes of coexistence of these two bodies, described respectively as "loose cooperation", "close cooperation", and "institutional merger".

In chapter 4, Manfred Nowak focuses on the possible relationships which the Agency could establish with the national institutions for the promotion and protection of human rights. Ten such institutions, established according to the so-called "Paris Principles" on the status of national institutions, have been established in the EU Member States and recognized by the International Co-ordinating Committee of National Institutions for the Promotion and Protection of Human Rights. Three or four more would seem to qualify under these same Principles, although the assessments differ. Nowak examines both the extent to which it would be desirable, or even feasible, to conceive of the Fundamental Rights Agency on the model of such national institutions for the promotion and protection of human rights, and whether, if the choice is rather made to remain broadly within the framework which is currently that of the EUMC, the Agency should cooperate with the network of national institutions for the promotion and protection of human rights established within the Union, perhaps contributing thereby to accelerate the establishment of such institutions in States where they currently are lacking and reinforcing the independency and capacities of the existing institutions. This chapter asks to what extent the Fundamental Rights Agency might in time become a facilitator of the mechanisms existing at the level of the Member States, perhaps helping to coordinate their efforts where issues with a European dimension are concerned, rather than a simple replication, at the level of the Union, of what is or should be achieved at the national level.

The Tasks of the Fundamental Rights Agency

The essays grouped in the second part of the volume, instead of examining the positioning of the Agency in the existing institutional landscape, focus on the tasks which it might be attributed. In his examination of the contribution the Fundamental Rights Agency could make to the promotion and protection of civil and political rights, Steve Peers confronts in chapter 5 the difficulties inherent in the creation of an institution operating across the different pillars of the European Union, each of which still at present retains its own specificity, and in a system where the actions of the Member States and those of the Union complement one another, forming what has already been referred to as the "multi-level" system of governance characteristic of the Union. What is required, he concludes, rather than an Agency replicating the model of national institutions for the promotion and protection of human rights, is that "a *sui generis* entity" be set up, "which should be carefully adapted to its unique legal and political environment". Peers sees its role as consisting in "examining existing, proposed or potential legal measures, issuing reports, ensuring compatibility of EU and relevant national measures with national and international human rights standards, and in contributing to education, research and publicity related to the EU's role in human rights".

Although the debate on the future tasks of the Agency is only beginning at the time of the writing of this Introduction, calls have been made already to ensure that the current focus of the EUMC on racism and xenophobia will not be abandoned, and that non-discrimination issues, in general, still constitute one of the priorities of the extended Agency. Christopher McCrudden, the author of chapter 6, has been one of the main actors in the debate which led to the adoption of the Northern Ireland Act 1998. This Act established a new Equality Commission for Northern Ireland and a separate Northern Ireland Human Rights Commission, and it contained a provision (section 75) imposing on each public authority carrying out functions relating to Northern Ireland that it have "due regard" to the need to promote equality of opportunity between certain different individuals and groups, thus mainstreaming the requirement of equality in all the activities of public authorities in Northern Ireland. In his chapter, McCrudden reflects on the debates which have concerned the setting up of equality and human rights bodies in Northern Ireland and in the rest of the United Kingdom, and examines which lessons can be drawn from these debates for the transformation, at European level, of the EUMC into an Agency with an extended mandate.

Philip Alston's contribution, in chapter 7, begins by insisting on the need to ensure that economic and social rights will make up an important part of the work of the FRA. He draws attention to the fact that this category of rights is not as easily defined as most observer would assume and notes that the distinction between 'principles' and 'subjective rights' which was introduced at the last moment into the EU Charter complicates matters considerably. In his view the distinction is confusing and unhelpful. He then briefly traces the evolution of social rights policy within the EU and the role accorded to those rights in the Charter. He argues that the way in which the role of the FRA is conceptualized will be of major importance in determining the type of activities which it carries out in the field of economic and social rights. Examining the assumptions which underpinned the various proposals for creating such an Agency can help to give a better appreciation of the sort of roles that it needs to play. Against that background he then looks briefly at the lessons which might be learned by the FRA from the experience of other international endeavours to monitor social rights and concludes with a number of specific policy recommendations addressed to the new Agency.

In chapter 8 of the book, Brian Bercusson offers a wide panorama of the different legal strategies which were deployed in the Union in order to promote the fundamental rights of workers—strategies alternatively judicial, administrative, and based on industrial relations. He relates those strategies to the evolving context in which these rights were pursued, now characterized by the Lisbon Strategy and the emphasis put on the open coordination of social and employment policies as well as on social dialogue. The Fundamental Rights Agency will succeed in contributing effectively to the promotion of workers' rights if it acknowledges the central role of labour and industrial relations in the European social model, and engages with the open method of coordination and social dialogue. It should, in sum, act as a facilitator of these processes, by specifying minimum procedural safeguards, by obliging and providing incentives to social partners to engage into social dialogue in a spirit of cooperation, and by guaranteeing, in particular, that the rights to information and consultation are fully respected. This, indeed, would be in conformity with Article I–48 of the Treaty establishing a Constitution for Europe ("The social partners and autonomous social dialogue"), in which the Union "recognises and promotes the role of the social partners at its level, taking into account the diversity of national systems", and in which the Union undertakes to "facilitate dialogue between the social partners, respecting their autonomy".

The Fundamental Rights Agency in the Global Context

The final two chapters seek to place the Agency and its mandate in the global environment in which it operates. In chapter 9, Rick Lawson examines the relationship between the Charter of Fundamental Rights and international and European human rights treaties, as well as its interactions with other sources of fundamental rights, in particular the common constitutional traditions of the Member States which Article I–9(3) of the Treaty establishing a Constitution for Europe identifies, alongside the European Convention on Human Rights, as the source of fundamental rights as general principles of EU law. The chapter examines how these sources form different combinations with one another in three situations, around which the chapter is structured: where the fundamental rights recognized in the Union limit the exercise by the institutions of the competences which have been conferred upon them; where they serve to avoid a conflict with international standards obligatory for the Member States, and therefore, indirectly, for the Union; and finally, where the Union advocates compliance with human rights in its relations with third countries. The essay shows that even if, as may be anticipated, the Charter of Fundamental Rights constitutes the main reference instrument for the activities of the Agency, it should also take into account developments in international and European human rights law, although the respective weight of each source of fundamental rights will vary according to the type of activity concerned.

The final chapter of the book, authored by Mielle Bulterman, closely relates to the essay of Rick Lawson. This chapter examines whether the Agency should have a role in the external policies of the Union. It distinguishes between the situations where the institutions of the Union directly exercise their external powers—in which case the Charter of Fundamental Rights is binding upon them, although they also have to seek to promote human rights with the partners with whom they interact[43]—, and the situations in which they seek to promote respect for human rights in third countries. The Commission repeats in the document submitted for public consultation on 25 October 2004 its previous position, already expressed in the communication of May 2001 and confirmed by the Council, that it is unnecessary to extend the mandate of the Agency to third countries. Bulterman identifies however the circumstances in which an objective and systematic collection of information regarding the situation of such countries could contribute to the efficacy and consistency of the human rights policy of the Union vis-à-vis those countries.

A final note of caution may be in order. The chapters have been written independently from one another, and although the authors have shared their drafts in the course of preparing their contributions, they have not in any way sought to achieve a unified perspective or to present a single coherent set of proposals. Indeed, on certain important issues, such as in particular whether or not the Agency should be assigned certain tasks with respect to third countries, whether it should be endowed with the institutional characterstics of "independence" within the meaning of the Principles Relating to the Status of National Institutions, whether it should be built according to the model of the current EUMC on Racism and Xenophobia, or whether it should have a role in the mechanism of Article 7 EU (Article I–59 of the Treaty establishing a

---

[43] Art III–292 of the Treaty establishing a Constitution for Europe states that "The Union's action on the international scene shall be guided by the principles which have inspired its own creation, development and enlargement, and which it seeks to advance in the wider world: democracy, the rule of law, the universality and indivisibility of human rights and fundamental freedoms, respect for human dignity, the principles of equality and solidarity, and respect for the principles of the United Nations Charter and international law".

Constitution for Europe), significant differences of opinion emerge from the various contributions. The purpose of this collection of essays is not to offer a blueprint for the future. It is instead to enrich the debate by bringing into it arguments which the authors feel may contribute to what should remain the overall objective: that of improving compliance in the EU with the full set of fundamental human rights recognized in the Charter of Fundamental Rights and in general international and European human rights law.

Part I

The Constitutional Background

1

New Modes of Governance and the Protection of Human Rights

GRÁINNE DE BÚRCA*

I. INTRODUCTION

THIS CHAPTER EXAMINES the operation of agencies as an element of the emerging "new modes of governance" in the EU, and considers whether such modes of governance are in tension with the requirements of human rights protection. Most of the other chapters in this collection begin from the perspective of human rights protection, and proceed to consider how an agency dealing with fundamental rights[1] might operate within the EU system. This chapter, by way of contrast, begins by looking at the particular character of EU governance, and more specifically at the recent rise in the establishment and use of agencies at European level, situating this development in the more general context of changing approaches to regulation in the EU. Thus the chapter begins with a brief discussion of the notion of 'new modes of governance' and specifically with the trend towards greater use of such modes in the European Union context. It moves on to consider how the rise of agencies can be understood as one aspect of this broader trend. Focusing then on the subject of human rights protection, the possible reasons for embracing certain new governance modes in this area in the EU as well as the possible reasons for caution or concern in so doing will be set out. Finally, the chapter will focus on the proposal to establish an EU fundamental rights agency by extending the mandate of the Vienna Monitoring Centre on Racism and Xenophobia (EUMC), looking both at the Commission's communication and at the decision of the European Council to this effect. It concludes by considering how the new institution might operate, and whether this 'new governance tool' is likely to be a positive move in the area of EU human rights protection and whether it is likely to contribute to the EU's emerging human rights policy.

---

* Professor of European Law at the European University Institute, Florence; Member of the Global Law School Faculty at New York University.
[1] For a reflection on the Commission's decision to change the title of the proposed agency from one dealing with "Human Rights" to "Fundamental Rights", see the chapter by M Nowak, 'The Agency and National Institutions for the Promotion and Protection of Human Rights' in this volume, at footnote 1.

II. WHAT IS MEANT BY NEW MODES OF GOVERNANCE?

There has been an outpouring of writing in recent years about the emergence of new modes of governance in the EU and beyond. The label 'new' might be a questionable one, but what is implied by the notion of new governance is the perception that a shift has occurred in the traditional paradigm of regulation and lawmaking. That shift can broadly be characterised in the following way. In the first place, the language of 'governance' rather than 'government' signifies: (i) a decline in the centrality of national and territorial boundaries and the growing relevance of the multilevel and transnational context; (ii) the decentralization and dispersal of authority; and (iii) a blurring of the public-private distinction (the involvement of private/social as well as public/official actors). Secondly, the language of *new* governance carries with it a number of further implications: (i) a shift away from hierarchical to more heterarchical forms of law- and policy-making; (ii) a move towards more flexible, softer (less binding or non-binding) and less detailed forms of law; (iii) a move towards reflexive (self-amending or readily adaptable) forms of law. In the EU context in particular, new modes of governance have expressly been contrasted with the 'classic Community method', which implies decision-making which originates in a proposal by the Commission, results in a binding law which is adopted by the Council or Parliament and Council together, and is reviewable by the Court of Justice.[2] In terms of their function, new governance modes are said to promote change by persuasion, monitoring and mutual learning, rather than by hierarchy, fiat or sanction. While there has been scepticism in particular about the effectiveness and accountability of new governance modes, their potential virtues are said to include greater responsiveness, suitability to a multi-level and diverse transnational system, the involvement of a more diverse range of voices, and the emergence of better informed policies.

III. THE RISE OF AGENCIES AS AN ASPECT OF NEW GOVERNANCE IN THE EU

The rise of agencies—and more particularly their rapid proliferation in recent years—has been identified as one of the manifestations of a transformation in European governance.[3] Agencies in the EU context, by comparison with the US where they tend to be autonomous and powerful decision-making bodies ('the fourth branch of government') have until recently tended to be institutions

---

[2] J Scott and D Trubek "Mind the Gap: Law and New Approaches to Governance in the EU" (2001) *European Law Journal* 1.

[3] R Dehousse, 'Misfits: EU Law and the Transformation of European Governance', Jean Monnet Working Paper 2/2002, http://www.jeanmonnetprogram.org/papers/02/020201.html

whose powers were primarily information-based.[4] More recently, however, the Commission has proposed the establishment of 'regulatory agencies' in the sense of agencies which would have power either to take binding decisions or to carry out or implement policies which have been adopted by others.[5] A number of EU agencies with particular powers of this kind already exist, for example the Office for Harmonisation in the Internal Market, the Community Plant Variety Office, and the European Agency for the Evaluation of Medicinal Products. Apart from these, many of the previously established agencies at EU level are charged with gathering, analysing and disseminating information on the policy area with which they are concerned, such as the European Environment Agency, the European Monitoring Centre for Drug and Drug Addiction, and indeed the Vienna EUMC. In many such cases, they have also been mandated to liaise with or to coordinate networks of actors in the relevant policy field, and they have sometimes been required to conduct research and to make proposals. Without necessarily having binding decision-making powers, EU agencies can feed into policy making in more or less influential ways by the data they gather, the expertise they marshal, the actors they mobilize and the advice they provide. There is therefore a collection of rather different kinds of bodies currently in existence in the EU, all of which are referred to as agencies, but many of which have different tasks and powers from others, and some of which are more powerful or more influential than others. A great many scholarly categorizations and taxonomies of EU agencies have been proposed,[6] analysing 'three waves of agencification' which are said to have occurred so far. Yet whichever taxonomy is preferred, it is undeniable that the establishment of agencies is a rapidly proliferating phenomenon in the EU context. These agencies, for all their variety and range, can be seen as one manifestation or dimension of the new governance trend in so far as they are transnational, information-based, largely non-hierarchical, network-coordinating organs, operating in a multi-level context and feeding into the policy-making process in different ways.

Below, the likely shape of the new fundamental rights agency will be considered, but for now suffice it to say that it seems to be the case that there is no political will to establish the proposed human rights agency as a regulatory or

---

[4] G Majone, 'The new European agencies: Regulation by Information' (1997) 4 *Journal of European Public Policy* 262–75.

[5] See COM(2002)718, 'The Operating Framework for European Regulatory Agencies', and the subsequent report of the European Parliament (doc A5 0471/2003) of December 2003, and the Conclusions of the Council of 29 June 2004.

[6] Some examples are E Vos, 'Reforming the European Commission: What role to play for EU agencies?' (2000) 37 *Common Market Law Review* 1113, M Everson 'Independent Agencies: Hierarchy Beaters?' (1995) 1 *European Law Journal* 180, A Kreher, 'Agencies in the European Community—a step towards administrative integration in Europe' (1997) 4 *Journal of European Public Policy* 225, M Shapiro, 'The problems of independent agencies in the United States and the European Union' (1997) 4 *Journal of European Public Policy* 276, M Flinders, 'Distributed public governance in the European Union' (2004) 11 *Journal of European Public Policy* 520, D Geradin and N Petit, 'The Development of Agencies at EU and National Levels: Conceptual Analysis and Proposals for Reform', Jean Monnet Working Paper 1/2004.

executive agency with any kind of decision-making powers of the kind described by the Commission in its 2002 communication on agencies, and possibly not even as an agency with a monitoring function like the recent European Aviation Safety Authority—but rather it seems so far to have been officially conceived largely as an informational tool and resource for the EU.

Finally, it should be said that the spread of European agencies is a development which has not necessarily been greeted as a positive or even neutral development by all. On the one hand, it seems that the creation or designation of a new actor or organ is a quasi-automatic response of the EU these days to any perceived policy deficit, whether in the form of an anti-terrorism 'Tsar', a defence and armaments agency, or even the mooted proposal for a Lisbon-Agenda 'super commissioner'. On the other hand, the problem of the accountability of agencies, and the suspicion that the creation of new agencies and the delegation of tasks to them could be a way for the main political institutions to evade political responsibility has also been raised.[7]

IV. HUMAN RIGHTS PROTECTION AND NEW MODES OF GOVERNANCE: AN UNLIKELY COUPLING?

Apart from the fact that the mushrooming of EU agencies has been explained as part of a transformation in the modes of European governance, however, why should the subject matter of this book, which is the proposed EU Fundamental Rights Agency, be considered from the perspective of the spread of new modes of governance? A first answer to this question is that a number of proposals have recently been made about the desirability and practicability of promoting human rights in the EU context by means of new modes of governance such as the open method of coordination,[8] and indeed some traces of this approach can already be seen.[9] Both as a means of avoiding some of the cul-de-sacs of the competence debate and because the task of shaping a Europe-wide policy in a broad and

---

[7] C Harlow, *Accountability in the European Union* (Oxford, OUP, 2002), pp 75–78.

[8] See the two annual reports of the EU network of independent experts on fundamental rights in 2002 and 2003, http://europa.eu.int/comm/justice_home/cfr_cdf/index_en.htm#. Also G de Búrca, 'Beyond the Charter: How Enlargement has Enlarged the Human Rights Policy of the EU' in O De Schutter and S Deakin (eds), *Social Rights and Market Forces. Is the open coordination of employment and social policies the future of Social Europe?* (Bruxelles, Bruylant, 2004); and O De Schutter, 'The Implementation of EU Fundamental Rights Through the Open Method of Coordination', Jean Monnet Paper 7/2004, http://www.jeanmonnetprogram.org/papers/04/040701.html

[9] Apart from the work of network of independent experts, ibid., other traces can be seen in the trend towards establishing monitoring and evaluation procedures—whether by groups of experts or by Member States together with the Commission, or even by an agency—both under specific pieces of legislation (such as under Directive 2000/43/EC of 29 June 2000 implementing the principle of equal treatment between persons irrespective of racial or ethnic origin, OJ L 180 of 19.7.2000, p 22, or under Directive 2000/78/EC of 27 November 2000 establishing a general framework for equal treatment in employment and occupation, OJ L 303 of 2.12.2000, p 16) and in particular policy areas governed by primary law, such as in Art III–260 of the new constitutional text concerning mutual 'objective and impartial evaluation' by member states, together with the Commission, of the implementation of policies under chapter IV on the Area of Freedom, Security and Justice.

diverse field such as that of human rights protection is a complex one, the soft, flexible, iterative and comparative dimension of some of the new modes of governance is potentially attractive to those seeking to shape a way forward for an EU human rights policy. It offers the prospect of a better way of reconciling the requirements of EU single market freedoms with the protection of fundamental human rights, including social rights, at the national and the European level,[10] particularly in view of the political unwillingness to render economic and social rights justiciable under the Charter of fundamental rights.[11] In other words, quite apart from the possibility that they may constitute more effective alternatives to traditional regulation, the lack of legal competence to adopt traditional regulatory measures is precisely one of the reasons which has been suggested to explain the recourse to new or experimental modes of governance in the EU in areas such as social protection. This argument would clearly also be applicable to the domain of human rights protection and promotion.

This is because the field of human rights protection and promotion is a very different one, in the European Union context, from that of the state, and it is one in which the 'competences problem' looms large. States, generally speaking, have open-ended legislative and policy powers, and questions of their legal competence to act to protect human rights (other than in federally divided systems) rarely arise. The opposite is the case in the EU, where the question of competence has dominated the debate on human rights for years now, in particular since the opinion of the European Court of Justice on accession to the ECHR.[12] Despite a number of significant changes over the last decade, the position remains that the EU does not have general competence in the field of human rights, and neither the Charter nor the new constitutional treaty, would significantly change this formal position. In the area of human rights protection and promotion, which is not itself a specific policy field but rather a set of compelling interests cutting across all areas of policy, the EC and EU's legal competence to enact rules (regulatory powers) have been few. Until the addition of Article 13 EC empowering the Community to act to combat discrimination, the fields of sex discrimination, together with certain dimensions of social policy, development policy and some other aspects of external policy, were really the only areas of EU activity in which the promotion of human rights was a clearly acknowledged component. Although the discourse of the EU on human rights and the attention given in official documents and debates to human rights issues

---

[10] O De Schutter, n. 8 above.

[11] See Art II–112(5) of the new constitution "The provisions of this Charter which contain principles may be implemented by legislative and executive acts taken by institutions, bodies, offices and agencies of the Union, and by acts of Member States when they are implementing Union law, in the exercise of their respective powers. They shall be judicially cognizable only in the interpretation of such acts and in the ruling on their legality".

[12] Opinion 2/94 on accession to the European Convention on Human Rights [1996] ECR I–1759. See also JHH Weiler and S Fries "A Human Rights Policy for the European Community and Union: the Question of Competences" in P Alston, M Bustelo and J Heenan (eds), *The European Union and Human Rights* (Oxford, OUP, 1999).

has expanded greatly over the past five or six years, not much has changed as far as legal competences are concerned. The anti-discrimination powers added by the Amsterdam Treaty to Article 13 EC remain the only prominent new arena of human rights activity, and otherwise the concern with limiting the legal powers of the EU to act in the field of human rights protection is as evident as ever. It is reflected in various of the provisions of the new constitutional text dealing with human rights, including Article I-9 (2) concerning accession to the ECHR,[13] and II–111 dealing with the scope and impact of the Charter.[14] Probably the most significant treaty provision to date dealing with the role of the EU in relation to human rights protection is Article 7 TEU, building on Article 6. Although this is not a legal competence but rather a provision allowing for the suspension of the rights of a Member State which is found to be in serious and persistent violation of the values of human rights, democracy and the rule of law mentioned in Article 6 TEU, it has proved in particular in its amended form following the Nice Treaty, to be a significant trigger for human rights activity at EU level—not least in the form of the establishment of the network of independent experts in 2002. Another consequence of the lack of legal powers and thus the lack of focus on human rights issues in much of the EU's legislative program is a corresponding lack of experience and expertise on the subject. Apart from the relevant parts of the EU institutions which deal fairly regularly with human rights issues in the context of social policy or justice and home affairs, for example, there is unlikely to be much specialised knowledge or awareness of the human rights implications of much of the EU's legislative and other activities.[15] And in fact this perceived importance of expertise and specialised knowledge has played a central part of the debate on the need for the establishment of agencies in the EU. Relatedly, the cross-cutting and non-sectoral nature of human rights concerns resonates with several of the characteristics of new governance approaches, specifically the emphasis on policy integration, linkage and co-ordination

Finally, the attraction of newer modes of governance is not only the existing lack of explicit legal powers, but also the lack of political will either to transfer such competence to the EU or the lack of political will to use any harder legal powers which already exist. Given that fact, and given the consequent lack of institutional experience and expertise, recourse to other tools and instruments

---

[13] "The Union shall accede to the European Convention for the Protection of Human Rights and Fundamental Freedoms. Such accession shall not affect the union's competences as defined in the Constitution".

[14] "1. The provisions of this Charter are addressed to the institutions and bodies of the Union with due regard for the principle of subsidiarity and to the Member States only when they are implementing Union law. They shall therefore respect the rights, observe the principles and promote the application thereof in accordance with their respective powers and respecting the limits of the powers of the Union as conferred on it in the other Parts of the Constitution. 2. This Charter does not extend the field of application of Union law beyond the powers of the Union or establish any new power or task for the Union, or modify powers and tasks defined in the other parts of the Constitution".

[15] This problem is discussed in Olivier De Schutter's chapter on mainstreaming in this volume.

of governance such as the monitoring, coordinating, promotional and informational work of agencies appears to make sense.

A note of caution should, however, be sounded here. Even if the competence problems and the related expertise and linkage problems of human rights in the EU policy context render attractive a move towards the use of new governance methods, there may also be risks in such a move. One should question whether the so-called new modes of governance, with their emphasis on non-binding, non-justiciable instruments and on coordinating and informational mechanisms, are appropriate for the area of human rights protection, given that what is generally said to differentiate 'rights' in law from other claims or interests is the availability of a legal remedy, usually a remedy which can be individually enforced, and usually in judicial proceedings. Is there a risk that the shift towards new modes of governance for the protection and implementation of human rights could denude them of their character as rights, undermining the idea of a core content, and rendering the standards of protection ultimately fluid and flexible? There seems to be a tension between a 'rights' model and a 'governance' model which suggests the need for caution before a monitoring, informational and coordinating approach to human rights protection is wholeheartedly embraced. Various aspects of this tension can be identified: a human rights model is suspicious of voluntarism and of self-regulation and is premised on an element of hierarchy in terms of answerability for the pursuit of overarching norms, while a new governance approach is premised on a more heterarchical set of arrangements with an emphasis on peer or reputational accountability. Secondly, a human rights model places importance on a degree of definition and clarity in the content of the commitment in question, while a new governance approach prioritizes revisability and open-endedness in the specification of goals, with an emphasis on the role of ongoing processes to give content to those goals in changing circumstances. Thirdly, the human rights model posits a significant role for courts in enforcing the content of the legal commitment, while in the new governance model the role of courts is at best a residual one to monitor the adequacy of the processes established and to allow for their disruption where they are malfunctioning.

V. A SUPPLEMENTARY ROLE FOR NEW GOVERNANCE FORMS

Having identified some of the potential risks of a new governance approach to human rights protection, however, two further observations should be made. In the first place, the proposed new EU human rights agency is not envisaged as a substitute or a replacement for other existing elements of EU fundamental rights protection, but rather is intended to supplement whatever role the ECJ develops in enforcing the Charter, the role of the political institutions in adopting legislation in areas such as anti-discrimination, and the role of bodies like the European Parliament and possibly the network of independent experts in monitoring respect for fundamental rights by the EU and the member states. In the second place, both in the international human rights field and in domestic law, a supplementary role for informational, advisory and monitoring bodies which do not have traditional lawmaking powers or judicial functions is a common feature. In particular, the Paris principles (discussed in several other chapters in this volume) which were endorsed in 1992 by the UN Human Rights Commission and in 1993 by the General Assembly, envisage the role of an agency or other non-judicial body to be complementary to a traditional, legal-judicial rights-based approach.

In a 1998 document on national human rights institutions the Council of Europe referred to "an awareness that the classic means of protecting human rights, through independent and impartial courts, while indispensable in a democratic society based on the rule of law, may not always be sufficient for ensuring, at the national level, that human rights are fully respected by national authorities . . . Independent national bodies such as human rights commissions can play a key role in advising the public authorities (at national, regional and local level) on relevant human rights standards and their significance for the legislation and practice of a member state. In relation to the general public, they can take an active part in promoting the provision of information and education in the human rights field."[16] It is evident that the model of a national human rights institution may not be directly transposable to the EU context, given the different and specific nature, powers and political structure of the European Union. Indeed national human rights institutions were originally conceived at the UN level as a kind of mediator between the international and national levels to educate, inform and advise local and national bodies and actors about international human rights obligations in an effort to further their implementation. Nonetheless the general point remains valid, i.e. that a non-judicial non-lawmaking agency could also operate in the EU to supplement more 'classic' means (in so far as they exist) of protecting and implementing human rights, through an informational, advisory, networking and monitoring role, and possibly even a role in addressing or receiving complaints. Regardless of the particular powers and functions given to such a body, however, what seems crucial to the international understanding of a 'national human rights institution' is the independence of the body from the government and executive of the day, and to a lesser extent its representativity and pluralist composition.

VI. ASSESSING THE DECISION TO ESTABLISH AN EU FUNDAMENTAL RIGHTS AGENCY

The chapter so far has discussed the phenomenon of agencification of the EU, the controversy over competence which has dogged the field of human rights

---

[16] "Non-Judicial Means for the Protection of Human Rights at the National Level", Council of Europe's Directorate General on Human Rights (May 1998).

protection in the EU, and the arguments which could be marshalled in favour of extending a 'new governance' approach in this field. Given each of these points, the proposal to establish a European fundamental rights agency may seem an obvious one. Despite the growth in rhetoric and debate about an EU human rights policy over the last five or six years years, it remains an uncertain and patchy field of EU policy-making, and the establishment of an institution exclusively devoted to human rights issues which could bring together and render more coherent the fragmented elements of this field would appear to be desirable. Nevertheless, at least two features of the current debate on the creation of a fundamental rights agency give cause for a somewhat more critical or at least reflective appraisal of the move. In the first place, the political decision to establish the Agency—announced by the European Council late in 2003—was extremely unexpected,[17] and the reasons for the change in strategy (in particular since the Commission some years previously had rejected the proposals of at least two groups of 'wise persons' to establish an EU human rights agency[18]) have not been obvious. Secondly, the reaction of the Commission to the European Council's decision in its communication on a fundamental rights agency does not suggest a particularly ambitious or open response. Let us consider these two facts a little further.

The European Council decision to create a human rights agency for the EU, and in so doing to transform the existing Vienna Monitoring Centre, EMUC, came as a surprise to many. It was commented upon in parts of the media mainly as part of an unsavoury distribution of spoils amongst the Member States when the location of various EU agencies was being decided during the fractious December 2003 meeting, following the failure to agree on the EU constitution. Austria was said to have been aggrieved by having only a small agency located in Vienna, and the decision to expand the remit of the EUMC was interpreted in the context of this.[19] However anecdotal, temporally contingent or trivial these comments may seem, the suspicion to which they refer that the sudden decision to create this agency might not have been underpinned by a real political commitment to promoting human rights in the EU is a serious one, and is relevant to a critical appraisal of the current proposals on the nature, shape and tasks of the new agency.

---

[17] See for instance the surprise expressed by Joke Swiebel in the European Parliament LIBE committee's working document of 25 March 2004, discussing the Commission's proposal (later withdrawn, due to the European Council's decision to establish a human rights agency) to recast the Council Regulation on the European Monitoring Centre on Racism and Xenophobia, EU Doc PE 339.635.

[18] These are the Comité des Sages *Leading by Example* report of 1998, annexed in P Alston et al (eds) *The European Union and Human Rights,* n 12 above, and the M Ahtisaari, J Frowein and M Oreja Report on the situation of fundamental rights in Austria of September 2000.

[19] Martin Walker, United Press International editor-in-chief, reported to this effect on the debate which took place at the European Council meeting in 2003, in the Globalist magazine, www.TheGlobalist.com

Secondly, as noted in different ways by Manfred Nowak and Mielle Bulterman in their contributions to this book,[20] the communication published by the Commission in October is rather cautious in several respects.[21] For example, sections 2.1 and 2.2 of the communication suggest that the agency's remit should be primarily to monitor the EU, rather than the Member States under Article 7 EU, section 4 argues against a role for the agency in external policy, section 1 rules out a complaints or petitions role, and section 8 suggests that the agency will be a 'lightweight' structure in terms of resources (staff and budget). The preferences thus expressed by the Commission in its communication are very likely to reflect at least in part the ongoing discussion taking place with Member States, and the Commission's sense of what will be politically acceptable. However, not all of the cautious dimensions of the communication can be attributed to this sensibility, and it seems likely that the communication also broadly reflects the vision which the Commission itself has of the future agency, i.e. not as a body entrusted with significant powers but rather as "a crossroads facilitating contact between the different players in the field of fundamental rights".[22]

A third matter to consider in reflecting on the political decision to establish an EU human rights agency concerns the implications of it being presented as a decision to extend the mandate of the EUMC. This raises the question whether there was an implicit intention to confine the tasks of the new human rights agency to those currently carried out by the EUMC, i.e. primarily to data-gathering and dissemination, and to the coordination of a network of national focal points. However, it also raises the question whether the model which the European Council may have had in mind for the new agency was based on the general experience and practice of the EUMC to date. Without engaging here in a proper analysis of the operation and work of the EUMC, it is clear that it has thus far a mixed record. It has encountered a range of difficulties, including practical, political (in relation to the initial non-publication of a controversial report on anti-semitism in Europe) and management problems.

Although established in 1997[23] the Centre did not actually have fixed premises from which to operate until 1999 and was not fully staffed until 2000, and its profile in the field of European anti-racism activities has not as yet been very high. The smaller Council of Europe body—the European Commission on Racism and Intolerance (ECRI)—appears to have been more successful in building relationships with NGOs in carrying out very similar tasks to the EUMC in the 'wider Europe', despite having fewer resources. According to the external evaluation report of the EUMC which was carried out in 2002, despite the fact that almost six years had passed since the adoption of the Regulation establishing the Monitoring Centre, it remained impossible to measure the effect or

---

[20] M Nowak, n 1 above, and M Bultermann "The Fundamental Rights Agency and the External Relations of the European Union".

[21] COM(2004)693, Public Consultation Document on the EU Fundamental Rights Agency, 25 October 2004.

[22] *Ibid*, section 1.

[23] Reg (EC) No 1035/97 of 2 June 1997 (OJ L 151, 10.6.1997).

impact of its output, so that 'value for money' for the budget which it had committed could not be demonstrated. The Commission subsequently accepted most of the criticisms made by the external evaluators, and—before withdrawing the proposal when the European Council announced the decision to establish a human rights agency—proposed some changes to the regulation establishing the EUMC to address these.[24] In the first place the Commission accepted that with regard to the agency's data-collection function, the objective of comparability had not yet been achieved to any substantial degree, nor had any assessment of the effectiveness of the anti-racist policies of individual member states been possible on the basis of its work. Part of the reason for this was said to be delay and another was the variability of member state responses to the Agency's attempt to hold regular round tables, to bring together national civil society actors, researchers, governments etc. The lack of a communications strategy for disseminating information and data was also criticised. The evaluation report had also criticised the structure and membership of the management board, on the basis that it was insufficiently skilled for the tasks faced by the board, and recommended that the board should consist of member state representatives. Given the obvious problems of independence which this proposal would pose, the Commission in its response had suggested a compromise solution whereby the membership of the management board could draw on the expertise of the existing heads of the national specialised bodies (whether equality agencies, ombudspersons etc) which were required to be set up under the Race Directive. This question of independence from 'government' (which in the EU context should be read as freedom both from Member State government as well as from the influence of the EU Council and Commission), as noted above in the discussion of the Paris Principles, is an absolutely crucial one for the functioning of a serious human rights institution or agency.

The choice to create an EU human rights agency by extending the remit of the existing EUMC clearly calls for reflection on the problems in the functioning of the EUMC to date. While it seems evident that the political will detected by the Commission, and perhaps shared also by it, is to create a body which would be primarily a data-gathering, information-providing and advisory body—and thereby possibly reserving to the committee of independent experts the member-state monitoring function which it currently exercises[25]—one can only hope that there is not also a political wish to maintain for the new agency the relatively low profile, low impact and under-resourced character of the EUMC.

The variety of different agency models in the EU is broad and diverse, and indeed the variety of human rights institutions at national level is broad and

---

[24] Commission Communication on the European Monitoring Centre on Racism and Xenophobia, COM(2003)483.

[25] The Commission appears open-minded on this point in section 7.3 of its Communication, but more positive about seeking a firm future role for the network of independent experts in question 6 of its list of questions prepared for consultation in advance of the public hearing scheduled for January 2005: "Following the creation of the Agency, how can the added value of the network of independent experts be assured?"

diverse, leaving quite a range from which to choose in designing a human rights agency for the EU. And even if—as the debate so far seems to indicate—a broadly informational model is chosen over one of the more powerful varieties with either decision-making, executive, monitoring or dispute-resolution functions, this certainly would not of itself consign the agency to a marginal role. As much of the experimentalist governance literature suggests, a well-designed body with a clear data-gathering, information-providing, mainstreaming,[26] advisory and network-coordinating role can, if sufficiently well-resourced and politically supported, play a powerful role in governing by information, advice, persuasion and learning. Whether the future agency will be an example of the latter rather than a marginalised player remains to be seen. In the meantime, however, the crucial factors determining the success of the agency will be the responsiveness of the Commission to the submissions of relevant civil society actors during the public consultation process, and more importantly the genuineness of the political commitment to create and support a meaningful body to help in strengthening the emergent but still fragmented and uncertain human rights policy of the EU.

[26] See O De Schutter's chapter in this volume "Mainstreaming Human Rights in the European Union".

2

Mainstreaming Human Rights in the European Union

OLIVIER DE SCHUTTER*

WHAT MAY THE creation of a new Fundamental Rights Agency contribute to the protection of human rights in the Union? This chapter seeks to develop one answer to this question, based on the idea of mainstreaming human rights and the facilitating role the Agency may play in this regard. A number of presuppositions have oriented the proposals put forward. In explaining these, Part I sets the general framework within which the proposal develops. Part II then describes briefly the concept of mainstreaming human rights and its original contribution to the protection of fundamental rights more generally. The two following parts then review the tools which could facilitate mainstreaming human rights in the Union, building on a critical examination of one mainstreaming tool which already exists in European governance—Impact Assessments—(III), and seeking inspiration, for the other tool of mainstreaming which consists in the adoption of human rights action plans, from the recommendations of human rights treaty bodies (IV). The paper concludes by identifying the specific role the EU Fundamental Rights Agency could fulfil in the implementation of those tools (V).

I. THE GENERAL FRAMEWORK

The proposals made in this paper in favour of mainstreaming human rights in the Union are based on an understanding of the role of the Fundamental Rights Agency which is compatible with the constitutional limitations imposed by the principle of subsidiarity governing the exercise of competences shared between the Member States and the Union (a), as well as by the restrictions imposed by

---

* Professor at the University of Louvain (Belgium) and Co-ordinator of the EU Network of Independent Experts in Fundamental Rights. The opinions expressed in this contribution are strictly personal and they commit neither the Network nor the institutions which have mandated the Network.

the European Court of Justice to the delegation of powers by the institutions of the Union (b). These proposals are also based on the conviction of the author that further developments of Union law should develop in conformity with the international and European law of human rights (c), and that the chances of the Fundamental Rights Agency succeeding in fulfilling its future tasks will be improved if it builds on the governance mechanisms already existing in the Union (d).

a) Subsidiarity

Any proposal relating to the future tasks of the Fundamental Rights Agency must take into account the constitutional framework within which the Agency will have to operate. In particular, the creation of the Agency and the definition of its tasks should comply with the principle of subsidiarity, under which:

> in areas which do not fall within its exclusive competence, the Union shall act only if and insofar as the objectives of the proposed action cannot be sufficiently achieved by the Member States, either at central level or at regional and local level, but can rather, by reason of the scale or effects of the proposed action, be better achieved at Union level.[1]

It must therefore be demonstrated (i) that the issues which the Agency will deal with cannot be satisfactorily addressed by the Member States acting individually, and (ii) that the objectives can be better achieved by an initiative adopted at the level of the Union. The realisation of the fundamental rights of the EU Charter of Fundamental Rights is not an exclusive competence of the European Union, with the exception of a limited number of provisions which concern only the activities of the institutions, such as the right to vote and stand in elections for the European Parliament,[2] the right to complain to the EU Ombudsman,[3] or the right to petition the European Parliament.[4] With respect to the rights, freedoms and principles of the Charter which are relevant both to the activities of the Union and the activities of the Member States, the principle of subsidiarity requires that the Agency should only act if, and to the extent that, the mechanisms which exist at the national level to ensure that these rights are complied with are insufficient, for instance because problems of externalities require a better coordination at the level of the Union.

This restriction, as well as the limited scope of application of the Charter itself,[5] counsel against extending the mandate of the Agency beyond the activi-

---

[1] Under the formulation of the principle now in Art I–11(3), al 1, of the Treaty establishing a Constitution for Europe (CIG 87/04), now proposed for ratification to the 25 Member States (hereafter referred to as the 'Constitution').

[2] Art 39 of the Charter (Art II–99 of the Constitution).

[3] Art 43 of the Charter (Art II–103 of the Constitution).

[4] Art 44 of the Charter (Art II–104 of the Constitution).

[5] Art 51 of the Charter (Art II–111 of the Constitution).

ties of the institutions, organs and agencies of the Union.[6] Where the Member States act in the field of application of Union law—whether they implement Union law or restrict a fundamental freedom under Union law in accordance with the Treaty or the case-law of the European Court of Justice[7]—they are of course bound by the Charter and by the general principles of Union law which the Court of Justice identifies in ensuring the application of Union law.[8] But the Member States are parties to a large array of international treaties which, in many respects, not only cover those fundamental rights, but go beyond them. They generally have detailed catalogues of rights in their national constitutions, with constitutional and administrative courts effectively controlling the acts of the national legislature and of the Executive according to such constitutionally protected rights. A majority of the Member States have set up a national institution for the promotion and protection of human rights in conformity with the 'Principles of Paris,' as endorsed by the United Nations General Assembly of 20 December 1993.[9] Moreover, both national jurisdictions—if necessary in

---

[6] Indeed, the creation of the European Union Monitoring Centre for Racism and Xenophobia under Reg no 1035/97 of 2 June 1997, OJ L 151 of 10.6.1997, p. 1, has been criticised for not complying with the principle of subsidiarity: see D Geradin and N Petit, 'The Development of Agencies at EU and National Levels: Conceptual Analysis and Proposals for Reform' Jean Monnet Working Paper 01/04, New York University School of Law, at p 39 (the authors refer in particular to the 'elliptic justification for the choice of the EC level,' in recital 16 of the Preamble to Reg n° 1035/97 ('Whereas racism and xenophobia are phenomena which manifest themselves at all levels within the Community: local, regional, national and Community, and therefore the information which is collected and analysed at the Community level can also be useful to the Member States authorities in formulating and applying measures at local, regional and national level in their own spheres of competence.'))

[7] See Case 353/89 *Commission v Netherlands* [1991] ECR 4089 (Recital 30); Case 288/89 *Stichting Collectieve Antennevoorziening Gouda et al v Commissariaat voor de Media* [1991] ECR 4007 (Recital 23); Case 148/91 *Vereniging Veronica Omroep Organisatie v Commissariaat voor de Media* [1993] ECR 513 (Recitals 9 and 10); Case C–368/95 *Familiapress* [1997] ECR I–3689 (Recital 24); Case C–112/00 *Schmidberger* [2003] ECR I–5659 (Recital 81). On the precise delineation of the situations in which the Member States are bound by fundamental rights as general principles of EC or EU law, see especially J Weiler, 'The European Court at a Crossroads: Community Human Rights and Member State Action' in *Du droit international au droit de l'intégration. Liber amicorum Pierre Pescatore* (Baden-Baden, Nomos Verlagsgesellschaft, 1987) p 821; J Temple Lang, 'The Sphere in Which Member States are Obliged to Comply with the General Principles of Law and Community Fundamental Rights Principles' *Legal Issues of European Integration* 1991/2, p 23; J Weiler, 'Fundamental Rights and Fundamental Boundaries: On Standards and Values in the Protection of Human Rights' in N Neuwahl and A Rosas (eds), *The European Union and Human Rights* (The Hague, Martinus Nijhoff Publishing, 1995) p 56; and K Lenaerts, 'Le respect des droits fondamentaux en tant que principe constitutionnel de l'Union européenne' in M Dony and A De Walsch (eds), *Mélanges en hommage à Michel Waelbroeck* (Bruxelles, Bruylant, 1999) p 423.

[8] See Art I–9 of the Constitution.

[9] See UN doc A/RES/48/134, adopted by the 85th plenary meeting of the UN General Assembly, 'National institutions for the promotion and protection of human rights.' A comparative study completed early in 2004 concludes however that 11 of the current 25 Member States of the Union do not have a national institution set up following the 'Paris principles': see EU Network of Independent Experts on Fundamental Rights, Opinion no 1–2004 regarding the role of national institutions for the protection of human rights in the Member States of the European Union, March 2004, available from www.europa.eu.int/comm/justice_home/cfr_cdf/index_en.htm. The Member States who appear not to have acted according to those principles are Austria, Belgium, Finland, Hungary, Malta, the Netherlands, Poland, Portugal, Slovenia, Spain and the United Kingdom. Such a listing must be considered with caution, however, as in the countries which have set up such institutions, the body

cooperation with the European Court of Justice through the referral procedure—and the European Court of Justice ensure a *post hoc* judicial protection
where the Member States would be acting in violation of the Charter of
Fundamental Rights or other fundamental rights recognised under the general
principles of Union law in the scope of application of Union law. And finally, in
order to improve the capacity of the European Commission to monitor that the
Charter of fundamental rights will be complied with in the implementation of
Union law, it may build on the EU Network of independent experts in fundamental rights or any equivalent committee which could take over the tasks this
group currently performs.[10]

Of course, what by definition may not be done at the level of each Member
State is the drawing of comparisons between the situation of fundamental rights
in each State, in order to alert the institutions of the Union either where certain
divergences emerge which could threaten the unity of the internal market or the
mutual trust on which the area of freedom, security and justice is based, or
where there appears a clear risk of a serious violation of the values on which the
Union is founded, which could justify the adoption of an initiative under Article
7 EU.[11] An EU-based monitoring of the Member States justified by the need for
such comparisons and the requirement to ensure that the Member States do not
breach those values identified as fundamental, however, is currently performed
by the EU Network of Experts on Fundamental Rights[12]—a light structure, but
sufficiently well equipped to cover all the Member States in order to provide the
institutions of the Union with the information they require to adequately perform their constitutional functions. Entrusting a new Agency with the task of

may not comply with all the requirements set forth in the 'Paris principles'; conversely, in a number
of the States which have no institution created in accordance with those principles, other institutions,
especially ombudspersons with a general competence to protect human rights or with a competence
limited to certain rights, may fulfil at least certain of the functions which institutions created under
the 'Paris principles' would otherwise be entrusted with.

[10] The expected Framework decision on certain procedural rights in criminal proceedings
throughout the European Union may signal the beginning of a systematization of this form of monitoring. In the extended Impact Assessment of the proposal of the Commission on this instrument,
the Commission calls for 'a regular monitoring exercise on compliance. This should be on the basis
of Member States themselves submitting data or statistics compiled by their national authorities and
submitted to be collated and analysed by the Commission. The Commission could use the services
of independent experts to analyse the data and assist with the drawing up of reports. One possible
team of independent experts is the EU Network of Independent Experts on Fundamental Rights.'
(SEC(2004) 491, of 28.4.2004, p 22). Indeed, the proposal of the Commission for a Council
Framework decision in this area contains a specific clause on evaluating and monitoring the effectiveness of the Framework Decision (Article 15), with one possibility being to be assisted in this by
an independent monitoring by the EU Network of Independent Experts in Fundamental Rights (see
paras 83 and 84 of the Explanatory Memorandum, *Proposal for a Council Framework Decision on
certain procedural rights in criminal proceedings throughout the European Union*, COM(2004) 328
final of 28.4.2004).

[11] See Art I–59 of the Draft Constitution.

[12] See the communication which the Commission presented to the Council and the European
comment on Art 7 EU, *Respect for and promotion of the values on which the Union is based* COM
(2003) 606 final, of 15 October 2003.

such a monitoring may constitute a source of unnecessary confusion, although as a matter of course this does not mean that the Agency could not offer a logistical support to the Network of Independent Experts or any similar body to be created in the future on a firmer legal basis.

b) Delegation of Powers

Another important component of the constitutional framework constraining which tasks may be entrusted to the Fundamental Rights Agency derives from the doctrine according to which the institutions of the Union may not:

> confer upon the authority [to which certain powers are attributed], powers different from those which the delegating authority itself received under the Treaty;

and that such a delegation may involve only:

> clearly defined executive powers the exercise of which can, therefore, be subject to strict review in the light of criteria determined by the delegating authority.[13]

According to the European Commission,[14] this would imply that although agencies may be granted the power to take individual decisions 'in areas where a single public interest predominates and the tasks to be carried out require particular technical expertise,' they may not be given the power to adopt general regulatory measures, nor be given decision-making power in areas in which they would have to 'arbitrate between conflicting public interests, exercise political discretion or carry out complex economic assessments.' Moreover, agencies 'cannot be given responsibilities for which the Treaty has conferred a direct power of decision on the Commission'—for example, to launch infringment proceedings against the Member States not complying with their obligations under the Treaty, or to propose to the Council to adopt a decision determining that there is a clear risk of a serious breach by a Member States of the values on which the Union is founded. On the other hand, the strict limits imposed under *Meroni* to the delegation of powers would not appear to create an obstacle to the exercise in an independent fashion of the responsibilities envisaged for national institutions for the promotion and protection of human rights by the 'Paris Principles,' especially the responsibility to submit non-binding opinions, recommendations, proposals and reports on 'any matters concerning the promotion and protection of human rights.'

---

[13] Case 9/56 *Meroni v High Authority* [1957–8] ECR 133, at paras 40 and 44. On the basis of another provision (Art 211 EC Treaty, which defines the tasks of the Commission), the European Court of Justice had considered that 'a body such as the administrative commission [of the European Communities on social security for migrant workers] may not be empowered by the Council to adopt acts having the force of law.' (Case 98/80 *Giuseppe Romano v Institut national d'assurance maladie-invalidité* [1981] ECR 1241).

[14] See Commission of the European Communities, *European Governance: A White Paper*, COM(2001) 428 final, of 25 July 2001, p 24.

c) The International Law of Human Rights and the Union

A third presupposition which may be worth making explicit is that, in the view of the author, the European Union should now act in the field of human rights as if it were bound by the main international instruments for the protection of human rights, adopted either within the framework of the Council of Europe or within the United Nations, to which a significant number of the Member States are parties.[15] Aligning Union law with international and European human rights law would present advantages even in the absence of a legal obligation for the Union to do so.[16] First, it would limit the risk of situations occurring where the Member States would be facing conflicting obligations under Union law, on the one hand, under international agreements concluded in the field of human rights to which they are parties, on the other hand—conflicts which, under the current constitutional scheme, are not satisfactorily dealt with. Second, it would contribute to legal certainty, as a number of vague provisions from the Charter of Fundamental Rights could be read in accordance with the requirements of the international and European human rights law. Third, developing a human rights policy within the Union in accordance with the international and European human rights instruments obligatory upon the Member States would prepare the accession of the European Union to those instruments—an accession which, in the medium term, seems inevitable. At a minimum, what is proposed here is simply that in thinking about how to conceive the contribution of the Fundamental Rights Agency to the development of a fundamental rights policy in the Union, we seek inspiration from the requirements set forth by the human rights bodies set up within the United Nations or the Council of Europe, insofar as, drawing upon the experience accumulated through a number of years, these bodies have made suggestions concerning the mechanisms which States should set up in order to prevent human rights from being violated and to improve their further realization (see IV, below). By taking these requirements into account, we will not only draw upon that accumulated knowledge; we also will be preparing within the Union the institutional frame which, later in time, may greatly facilitate the accession of the Union to those international instruments, economizing the cost of reforms which would otherwise have to be made to made in order to comply.

---

[15] The arguments mentioned in this paragraph are developed in O De Schutter, 'The Implementation of the Charter of Fundamental Rights through the Open Method of Coordination' in O De Schutter and S Deakin (eds), *Social Rights and Market Forces. Tthe open coordination of employment and social policies the future of Social Europe?* (Bruxelles, Bruylant, forthcoming, 2004) (also available as a *Jean Monnet Working Paper*, at: www.JeanMonnetProgram.org).

[16] Some have argued that, as a 'successor' to its Member States in the areas where it has been been attributed certain powers, the Union should recognise that it is bound by the same international obligations. This view has been decisively rejected by the European Court of Justice: see Case 812/79 *Attorney General v Juan C Burgoa* [1980] ECR 2787 (Recital 9); or Joined Cases 50 to 58/82 *Dorca Marina* [1982] ECR 3949 (Recitals 6 and 7).

d) Economizing Change

A fourth presupposition guiding the proposals which follow is that in imagining the tasks of the Fundamental Rights Agency, we should build, as much as possible, on the mechanisms and working methods which already exist within the Union. Of course the procedures may be changed, new working methods imposed, and this may in certain cases be necessary. But where certain procedures already exist in European governance which could serve as a channel for the mainstreaming of human rights, it is these procedures which should be used. In fact, the very idea of mainstreaming is that instead of creating specific devices, or apart from those, we seek to implement the requirements of fundamental rights in the course of all the activities of the institutions concerned, in order to ensure that the respect for, and the promotion of, fundamental rights become part of their normal way of functioning.

II. THE CONCEPT OF MAINSTREAMING FUNDAMENTAL RIGHTS

a) A Proposal for Mainstreaming

Adapting to fundamental rights generally the definition used by the European Commission to define more specifically gender mainstreaming,[17] we may see the mainstreaming of fundamental rights as involving:

> the systematic integration of [fundamental rights] in all policies [. . .] with a view to promoting [fundamental rights] and mobilising all general policies and measures

---

[17] Of course, the concept of mainstreaming owes immensely to the efforts of scholars who have sought to develop the implications of gender mainstreaming, especially after it was given prominence at the United Nations World Conference on Women held at Beijing in 1995 (see *Report of the Fourth World Conference on Women*, UN doc A/Conf.177/20 (1995) (objective H2)). My personal debts are especially to F Beveridge, S Nott and K Stephen, 'Mainstreaming and the engendering of policy making: a means to an end ?' (2000) 7.3 *Journal of European Public Policy* 385–405; S Nott, 'Accentuating the Positive: Alternative Strategies for Promoting Gender Equality' in F Beveridge, S Nott and S Stephen (eds), *Making Women Count. Integrating Gender into Law and Policy-making* (Ashgate, Dartmouth, 2000) pp 247–276; T Rees, *Mainstreaming Equality in the European Union* (London, Routledge, 1998); M Pollack and E Hafner-Burton, 'Mainstreaming gender in the European Union' (2000) 7.3 *Journal of European Public Policy* 432–457; A Woodward, 'Gender Mainstreaming in European Policy: Innovation or Deception ?' Discussion paper FS I 01–103, Wissenschaftszentrum Berlin für Sozialforschung, 2001; M Verloo, 'Another Velvet Revolution ? Gender Mainstreaming and the Politics of Implementation' IWM Working Paper No 5/2001, Institut für die Wissenschaften vom Menschen, Vienna, 2001. Another major influence on the approach explored in this chapter is the experience in mainstreaming equality in Northern Ireland after the multi-party 'Good Friday' Agreement of April 1998. On this, see especially Ch McCrudden, 'Mainstreaming Equality in the Governance of Northern Ireland' (1999) 22 *Fordham International Law Journal* 1696–1775; and C McCrudden, ' Equality' in CJ Harvey (ed), *Human Rights, Equality and Democratic Renewal in Northern Ireland* (Oxford, Hart Publishing, 2001) p 75.

specifically for the purpose of [realising them] by actively and openly taking into account, at the planning stage, their [impact on fundamental rights].[18]

Although this 'definition' may seem laborious,[19] which it certainly is stylistically, it does serve to highlight what is novel about mainstreaming, and how it complements the monitoring of fundamental rights. Mainstreaming implies, at its core, that fundamental rights should not be pursued only via ear-marked, distinct policies, but must be incorporated in all the fields of law- and policy-making: fundamental rights thus, should be seen as 'an integral part of all public policy making and implementation, not something that is separated off in a policy or institutional ghetto.'[20] Mainstreaming is transversal, or horizontal. But it should also be seen as operating *ex ante* rather than *post hoc*: it influences the way legislations and public policies are conceived and different alternative paths compared to one another; it does not simply require that such legislations and policies do not violate fundamental rights. It is pro-active, rather than reactive.

The proposal may be briefly stated as follows. Since 2000 especially, the European Commission has taken a series of initiatives in order to improve European governance.[21] It has adopted a White Paper on European Governance in July 2001, which proposes a number of ways to improve the involvement of stakeholders in the shaping of the policy and legislation of the Union, as well as the openness and accountability of the institutions.[22] In two later communications, the Commission examined how legislation making could be improved and be made more responsive to the diversity of contexts in which it is to apply,[23] and defined the general principles of impact assessment, which is seeks to impose, since 2003, to all major initiatives.[24] Following one of the proposals made in the White Paper on European Governance, the Commission also

---

[18] Comp Commission of the European Communities, *Incorporating Equal Opportunities for Women and Men into All Community Policies and Activities*, COM(96) 67 final of 21 February 1996, p 2.

[19] For an extensive discussion of the different definitions of mainstreaming which have been proposed, see A Woodward, 'Gender Mainstreaming in European Policy: Innovation or Deception ?' n 17 above, pp 5–10.

[20] Ch McCrudden, 'Mainstreaming Equality in the Governance of Northern Ireland' n 17 above, p 1699.

[21] It would seem that, in the eyes of the public and some commentators, this development was in immediate response to the fraud and mismanagement scandals which led in March 1999 to the fall of the Santer Commission. In fact, the reflection on the reform of European governance has been launched since 1996–1997 within the European Commission, especially under the Forward Studies Unit created by J Delors. See a set of consultation papers collected after a seminar held in 1996–1997, O De Schutter, N Lebessis and J Paterson (eds), *Governance in the European Union*, OOPEC, Luxembourg, 2000.

[22] COM(2001) 428 final, of 25 July 2001.

[23] Communication from the Commission, *European Governance: Better Lawmaking* COM(2002) 275 final of 5 June 2002.

[24] Communication from the Commission, *Impact Assessment* COM(2002) 276 final of 5 June 2002. This communication has been completed a few months later by a set of practical guidelines relating to impact assessment.

adopted a communication defining the general principles and minimum standards for the consultation of interested parties by the Commission.[25]

It is submitted that, on the basis of this *acquis* in European governance, it is possible to transplant methods developed elsewhere, by which human rights may be mainstreamed into European policy- and law-making. The European Fundamental Rights Agency could be entrusted with ensuring that these methods will indeed be effective, and the requirement of mainstreaming human rights adequately implemented by the civil servants concerned. Specifically, two obligations could be imposed on the different services of the European Commission which the Agency could follow upon.

First, the *impact assessments* which the services of the Commission must prepare could be improved in order both to clarify their relationship to a compatibility assessment, and to encourage a more systematic consultation of selected stakeholders, whose comments may lead the Commission to revise its proposals. The facilitating role of the Agency in this process could consist in assisting in both the preparation of these fundamental rights impact assessments by providing the Commission, upon its request, with any expert advice the Commission might require, and in identifying the relevant stakeholders and ensuring that the consultation takes place in a fully satisfactory manner. One major argument favoring such a facilitating role of the Agency is that it is simply unrealistic to postulate that all the services within the Commission producing impact assessments possess both the expert knowledge about fundamental rights and an understanding of the sociological field of relevant actors to drive this process satisfactorily.

Second, the services of the Commission could be required to submit *action plans*, for instance on a biennial basis, describing how they intend to mainstream human rights in the definition of the policies for which they are responsible. These plans could be submitted to the Agency, which might be given the possibility to either approve of them, or transmit them to the European Parliament with its observations, thus giving the Parliament the possibility to request from the Commission that it justifies its choices and, if so required, that it gives its answers in response to the observations of the Agency.

b) The Advantages of Mainstreaming

Before developing this proposal, however, we may briefly summarise certain of the advantages it has to offer. Christopher McCrudden writes:

> Mainstreaming approaches are intended to be anticipatory, rather than essentially retrospective, to be extensively participatory, rather than limited to small groups of

---

[25] Communication from the Commission, *Towards a reinforced culture of consultation and dialogue—General principles and minimum standards for consultation of interested parties by the Commission* COM(2002) 704 final, of 11 December 2002.

the knowledgeable and to be integrated into the activities of those primarily involved in policy-making.[26]

The usefulness of mainstreaming, where implemented as proposed here, may be attributed to the following characteristics:

1) It is an incentive to develop new policy instruments.

Mainstreaming displaces questions which were sectorialised from the vertical to the horizontal, from the policy margins to their centre. It therefore requires from policy-makers that they ask new questions about old themes. It is a lever for political imagination. For instance, the mainstreaming of disability issues within the European Commission[27] has led it to pay attention to these issues in all its socio-economic policies, programmes and projects,[28] leading it to include provisions in favour of the professional integration of persons with disabilities in the regime of State aids,[29] in the adoption of the guidelines under the European Employment Strategy,[30] or in the revision of the rules relating to public procurement.[31] Mainstreaming disability issues has thus obliged the policy-makers to identify how, in their particular sector, they could contribute to the social and professional integration of persons with disabilities: rather than remedying the exclusion from employment of persons with disabilities, mainstreaming seeks to combat such exclusion by tackling the phenomenon at its root, in the market mechanisms which produce it. Similarly, mainstreaming corporate social responsibility—the idea that corporations not only owe to their shareholders an obligation to make profits, but also must integrate social and environmental concerns in their business operations—will lead the policy-

[26] C McCrudden, 'Mainstreaming Equality in the Governance of Northern Ireland,' n 17 above, p 1769.

[27] See recently the Communication of the Commission, *Equal Opportunities for People with Disabilities. A European Action Plan*, COM(2003)650 final of 30 October 2003.

[28] See also: Resolution of the Council of 15 July 2003 on promoting the employment and social integration of people with disabilities, OJ C 175 of 24.7.2003, p 1 (calling upon the Member States to reinforce 'the mainstreaming of the disability perspective into all relevant policies at the stages of policy formulation, implementation, monitoring and evaluation,' and insisting on the need for statistical information for such monitoring and evaluation as well as for the need of cooperation with bodies and civil society organisations concerned with people with disabilities).

[29] Commission Reg (EC) No 2204/2002 of 12 December 2002 on the application of Arts 87 and 88 of the EC Treaty to State aid for employment, OJ L 337 of 13.12.2002, p 3 (determining that certain categories of State aid schemes which seek to favour employment, and especially employment of target groups, including workers with disabilities, may be considered compatible with the common market within the meaning of Art 87(3) EC and be exempted from the notification requirement of Art 88(3) EC).

[30] Council Decision of 22 July 2003 on guidelines for the employment policies of the Member States, OJ L 197 of 5 August 2003, p 13.

[31] See Dir 2004/18/EC of the European Parliament and of the Council of 31 March 2004 on the coordination of procedures for the award of public works contracts, public supply contracts and public service contracts (OJ L 134, 30 March 2004, p 114) (which provides that contract performance conditions may seek to favour the employment of people experiencing particular difficulty in achieving integration).

makers to identify in different sectors such as employment and social affairs policy, enterprise policy, environmental policy, consumer policy or procurement policy, which consequences this new understanding of the role of business in its societal context may have.[32] An obligation imposed on all policy-makers to identify how they could facilitate the realization of the objective which is mainstreamed, in this sense, is a first step towards identifying means by which the mechanisms producing undesirable outcomes may be modified: it rewards imagination above the reproduction of routine solutions.[33]

2) *Mainstreaming is a source of institutional learning.*

A group of experts commissioned by the Council of Europe defines gender mainstreaming as:

> the reorganisation, improvement, development and evaluation of policy processes, so that a gender equality perspective is incorporated in all policies at all levels and at all stages, by the actors normally involved in policy-making.[34]

This definition presents the advantage of laying the accent on one of the important virtues of mainstreaming, which is to oblige policy-makers to identify issues which are present in the policies they pursue or the sectors these policies impact upon, but which would otherwise be obliterated and marginalised. As they get acquainted with the new tools mainstreaming requires, these actors will learn about these implications which previously may have gone unnoticed. They will progressively gain an expertise in the issues mainstreaming requires them to consider. The objective is that, in time, the institutional culture within the organisation will evolve, and that both awareness to fundamental rights issues and the capacity to address them will augment.

---

[32] See Communication from the Commission, *Corporate Social Responsibility: A business contribution to Sustainable Development* COM(2002) 347 final, of 2 July 2002, especially point 7.

[33] See also, inter alia: the comments of the Committee on the Rights of the Child, stating that it 'has [. . .] found it necessary to encourage further coordination of government to ensure effective implementation [of the Convention on the Rights of the Child]: coordination among central government departments, among different provinces and regions, between central and other levels of government and between Government and civil society. The purpose of coordination is to ensure respect for all of the Convention's principles and standards for all children within the State jurisdiction; to ensure that the obligations inherent in ratification of or accession to the Convention are not only recognised by those large departments which have a substantial impact on children—education, health or welfare and so on—but right across Government, including for example departments concerned with finance, planning, employment and defence, and at all levels.' (General comment No 5, *General measures of implementation of the Convention on the Rights of the Child* (arts 4, 42 and 44, para 6), adopted at the thirty-fourth session of the Committee (2003), in *Compilation of the general comments or general recommendations adopted by human rights treaty bodies*, UN doc HRI/GEN/1/Rev7, 12 May 2004, p 332, at par 18).

[34] Council of Europe, Gender mainstreaming: Conceptual Framework, Methodology and Presentation of Good Practices. Final Report of the Activities of the Group of Specialists on Mainstreaming (EG-S-MS (98)2), Strasbourg 1998, p 6.

3) It improves the implication of civil society organisations in policy-making.

In most cases, the requirement to identify the policies which best take into account the objective to be mainstreamed, imposed on policy-makers who have no specialised knowledge in the issue, will require them to consult externally. They may of course limit that consultation to experts. But they may also be incentivised to consult more widely, within the community of stakeholders, in order not only to better evaluate the impact the proposed policies may have— as such an impact may be difficult to anticipate and often will be impossible to measure—but also to stimulate the formulation of alternative proposals, better suited to the conciliation of the different objectives pursued and, therefore, more satisfactory in a mainstreaming perspective.

4) It improves transparency and accountability.

The obligation to formulate policies or legislative proposals by referring to the impact they may have on the realization of fundamental rights not only will incentivise the policy-makers to develop alternatives they may have had no good reason previously to consider, but the adverse impact of which on fundamental rights may be less important, and to consult more widely with a view both to identifying such alternatives and to measuring such impacts. It also will lead the proposals to be more richly justified, as the policy-maker will have to explain why a particular route was chosen and preferred above alternative possibilities, after having examined those possibilities and evaluated their potential impact. It is in that sense that impact assessment, one of the two tools of the strategy for mainstreaming human rights which is proposed here—the other tool being the formulation of action plans by the different services concerned—reinforces participation, to which it gives meaning and which it serves to better inform, thus equipping the stakeholders participating with the informational resources they require for their participation to be effective.

5) It improves coordination between different services.

The sectoralization of policies, although inevitable in any large organisation, may lead to the development of policies effectively contradicting one another. The example classicly proposed of such policy inconsistencies is where certain polluting industries are subsidised on the one hand, and financial incentives and taxation schemes are developed, on the other hand, to discourage their polluting activities. But examples abound in the domain of fundamental rights. For instance, under European legislation, the Member States of the Union may be under an obligation to adopt regulations ensuring health and safety at work, while at the same time having to guarantee the principle of equal treatment with respect to person with disabilities in employment—although it is well documented that the two objectives may conflict with one another, and that some form of coordination between the two sets of rules may be therefore desirable.[35] The Member States are encouraged to promote diversity in business, yet at the same time the rules relating to the protection of personal data may constitute an obstacle for employers seeking to develop such diversity policies by monitoring the representation of ethnic groups in the workforce.[36] Because it is transversal and creates horizontal bridges between vertical sectors, mainstreaming may serve to identify such tensions, in order to remedy them. It is a way to restore communication between different services or departments, as one of its tools may consist in the organisation of common meetings with representatives from different services to compare the schemes they are proposing and identify potential conflicts or redundancies, or other failures in coherence.

6) It aims at the causes of the problems identified rather than at their surface manifestations.

Mainstreaming addresses the definition of policies at their initial stages and throughout their implementation. Therefore its transformative character is much more powerful than that of *post hoc* monitoring, where the impact of policies is measured. But mainstreaming is also much more powerful even than 'impact-analysis,' as usually conceived and as currently practiced. Indeed, although impact assessment may be a tool of mainstreaming and does operate *ex ante*, ie, in the initial stages of policy-selection, mainstreaming goes one step further in that it imposes on authorities a positive duty to identify how they may contribute to achieving the objective pursued. It therefore obliges them not only to examine whether the policy they have been pursuing or which they intend to pursue adversely impacts upon that objective, as if this objective, although an objective of the community as a whole, would not be for them to pursue: instead, once it is identified, the objective is one they are requested to consider as their own, and they are to take that objective as part of the set of objectives they are pursuing and which, in combination with other objectives, will dictate the shape of policies. Again, the mainstreaming of disability may serve to illustrate this: it is one thing to measure the impact of certain policies on persons with disabilities, and choose the policy which appears to have the least adverse impact on them—for instance, where policies are devised which seek to create

---

[35] For a study of this tension, see O De Schutter, *Pre-Employment Inquiries and Medical Examinations as Barriers to the Employment of Persons with Disabilities: Reconciling the Principle of Equal Treatment and Health and Safety Regulations under European Union Law*, European Commission, DG Employment and Social Affairs, July 2004; and J Davies and W Davies, 'Reconciling Risk and the Employment of Disabled Persons in a Reformed Welfare State' (2000) 29 *Industrial Law Journal* 347–377.

[36] See EU Network of Independent Experts on Fundamental Rights, Report on the situation of fundamental rights in the European Union in 2003, January 2004, pp 97–100, and the reference to a study completed in October 2003, 'The Costs and Benefits of Diversity: A Study on Methods and Indicators to Measure the Cost-Effectiveness of Diversity Policies in Enterprises' report drawn up by the Centre for Strategy and Evaluation Service (CSES) on behalf of the European Commission. Available at: http://europa.eu.int/comm/employment_social/fundamental_rights/prog/studies_en.htm.

incentives to work and therefore to raise the level of activity of the active segment of the population; it is quite another to consider that employment policies should contribute actively to the professional integration of persons with disabilities, and that the absence of adverse impact on persons with disabilities—or the adoption of measures mitigating any adverse impact there may be—is therefore necessary, but not sufficient.

c) The Institutional Make-up of Mainstreaming

Of course, the extent to which these different virtues are realised depends on the institutional devices in which mainstreaming gets translated. In particular, the implication of civil society organisations and the greater accountability of the policy-makers—the third and fourth virtues listed above—will only result from the adoption of a 'participative-democratic' model of mainstreaming, in the vocabulary proposed by S Nott.[37] By way of contrast, a purely 'expert-bureaucratic' model of mainstreaming would consist in an expertise being provided to the policy-maker about how to include the particular objective to be mainstreamed in his or her approach, without any 'external' consultation otherwise taking place with the affected stakeholders. It is important however to emphasize that these models are not necessarily mutually exclusive.[38] On the contrary, they are complementary. Indeed, it may be useful not only to ensure that the policy-maker will consult with the interested stakeholders, and on the basis of those consultations perhaps modify his or her proposal if it appears that certain dimensions of the problem have been ignored or their importance underestimated—but also to provide both the policy-maker and the stakeholders concerned with the expert knowledge they require to ensure that their dialogue is fully informed. We should not see the kind of deliberation which a mainstreaming approach should encourage as a zero-sum game, as if the power to influence decision-making existed in a fixed quantity, so that all the particles of power which are given to the 'experts' or the 'stakeholders' which are consulted are substracted from the 'policy-maker,' and so that the 'stakeholders' and the 'experts' are competing for influence. This view from public choice theory[39] is simply misleading. Rather, in a truly deliberative process, the position of each actor is reinforced by the presence of all the others. That co-existence represents a net gain in both legitimacy and in understanding: if, under the influence of

---

[37] S Nott, 'Accentuating the Positive: Alternative Strategies for Promoting Gender Equality,' n 17 above, pp 269–270. See also: TB Donaghy, 'Mainstreaming: Northern Ireland's participative-democratic approach' (2004) 32 *Policy and Politics* 49–62, especially pp 51–52.

[38] See especailly S Nott, 'Accentuating the Positive: Alternative Strategies for Promoting Gender Equality,' n 17 above, p 270.

[39] See, eg: DA Farber and PhP Frickey, 'Jurisprudence of Public Choice' (1987) 65 *Texas Law Review* 873; DA Farber and PhP Frickey, 'Legislative Intent and Public Choice' (1988) 74 *Virginia Law Review* 423; W Macey, 'Promoting Public-Regarding Legislation Through Statutory Interpretation: An Interest Group Model' (1986) 86 *Columbia Law Review* 223.

either the experts or the stakeholders, the policy-maker is led to modify the position he or she initially adopted, the position finally taken will be stronger—better informed, better reasoned, more legitimate—than it otherwise might have been. Governance may gain in reflexivity.[40] It is this gain which the requirement of mainstreaming may offer. As noted in the Communication from the Commission on consultation, 'both the Commission and outside interested parties will benefit from understanding the perspective of the other.'[41]

III. MAINSTREAMING FUNDAMENTAL RIGHTS: IMPACT ASSESSMENTS

Mainstreaming is not a new phenomenon in European governance. It is constitutionally mandatory under the EC Treaty with respect to equality between men and women[42] as well as with respect to the protection of the environment[43] and the protection of consumers.[44] The Treaty establishing a Constitution for Europe, now proposed for ratification by the Member States, not only confirms this,[45] but extends the requirement of mainstreaming to the combating of discrimination based on sex, racial or ethnic origin, religion or belief, disability, age or sexual orientation.[46] Of course, there is no constitutional mandate to 'mainstream' all the provisions of the EU Charter of Fundamental Rights. But neither is there any prohibition to do so: as the examples of anti-racism[47] and disability[48] mainstreaming already exhibit, the institutions may choose to take into account certain legitimate objectives in all the policy areas, as long as this does not lead them to exercise powers which have not been attributed to them.[49]

---

[40] For developments concerning this view of the contribution civil society organisations can make to governance, see O De Schutter, 'Europe in Search of its Civil Society' (2002) 8 *European Law Journal* 198–217.

[41] Communication from the Commission, *Towards a reinforced culture of consultation and dialogue—General principles and minimum standards for consultation of interested parties by the Commission* COM(2002) 704 final, of 11 December 2002, at p 18.

[42] See Art 3(2) EC ('In all the activities referred to in this Article, the Community shall aim to eliminate inequalities, and to promote equality, between men and women.')

[43] See Art. 6 EC ('Environmental protection requirements must be integrated into the definition and implementation of the Community policies and activities referred to in Article 3, in particular with a view to promoting sustainable development.')

[44] See Art 153(2) EC ('Consumer protection requirements shall be taken into account in defining and implementing other Community policies and activities.')

[45] See Art III–116 (equality between men and women), Art III–117 (environmental protection), and Art III–120 (protection of the consumers) of the Constitution.

[46] See Art III–118.

[47] See COM(1998) 183 final, of 25 March 1998; for a study of the potential of mainstreaming anti-racism in the future, the report commissioned by the European Network against Racism (ENAR) to J Shaw, *Mainstreaming Equality in European Union law and policy-making*, July 2004, p 80.

[48] See nn 26–30 above.

[49] The integration of fundamental rights into all the policies and activities of the Union, according to the devices proposed here, would not lead the Union to become a 'human rights organisation' whose objective would be to fulfil human rights. Compare: A von Bogdandy, 'The European Union as a Human Rights Organization? Human Rights and the core of the European Union' (2000) 31 *CML Rev* 1307.

Since March 2001, the services of the European Commission are required to accompany all their legislative proposals which could have an impact on fundamental rights with an indication that these proposals are compatible with the requirements of the Charter.[50] The proposal made in this chapter is to add a more preventive dimension to this compatibility control, and to translate this into specific institutional mechanisms fitting into the current mechanisms by which European governance has sought to redefine itself.[51]

a) The Current Practice of Impact Assessments

How, precisely, would human rights mainstreaming fit into the *acquis* of European governance? At present, an evaluation of the impact on fundamental rights is part of the general impact assessment imposed for all major initiatives adopted by the Commission, ie, those which are presented either in the Annual Policy Strategy of the Commission or those which are included in the Work Programme of the Commission. For the civil servants of the Commission responsible for the formulation of proposal—the political responsibility of which remains in the hands of the Commissioners,[52] the impact assessment (IA) serves to ensure that the decision-maker receives all the required information, presented in adequate format, in order to make the final choice as to which policy to pursue, and under which form.[53] IA develops in two stages, corresponding to two different formats of IA. All major initiatives are subjected to a *preliminary assessment*, which should offer a brief overview of the issue, the objectives, the main policy options available, and preliminary indications on the expected impact. This preliminary assessment serves to determine whether or not an *extended impact assessment* is required. This brings us into a second stage of IA, which is only reached where the Commission concludes from the preliminary assessment that the proposal will result in substantial economic, environmental and/or social impacts on a specific sector or several sectors,

[50] Memorandum of M Vitorino and the Presidency, *Application of the Charter of Fundamental Rights* SEC(2001) 380/3.

[51] This proposal was also made in the first report of the EU Network of Independent Experts in Fundamental Rights, *Report on the situation of fundamental rights in the European Union and its Member States in 2002*, March 2003, p 17.

[52] The Communication from the Commission on Impact Assessment states in this regard that 'Impact assessment is an aid to decision-making, not a substitute for political judgment. Indeed, political judgment involves complex considerations that are go far [sic] beyond the anticipated impacts of a proposal. An impact assessment will not necessarily generate clear-cut conclusions or recommendations. It does, however, provide an important input by informing decision-makers of the consequences of policy choices.' p 3.

[53] For further details, the reader is referred to the Communication from the Commission, *Impact Assessment* see n 24 above, as well as to the *Handbook for Impact Assessment in the Commission: How to do an Impact Assessment*, no date (but presumably from late 2002), 34 pages, and the accompanying 13 Technical Annexes, 41 pages.

might have a significant impact on major interested parties, or represents a major policy reform in one or several sectors.[54]

The extended IA consists, first, in identifying with precision the problem which has to be addressed and its causes, and whether or not an intervention at the level of the Union is desirable and, indeed, justifiable in terms of subsidiarity and proportionality where the subject matter belongs to an area shared with the Member States. Second, a clear identification of the objective pursued is required, in order in particular to ensure that the policy objective will not conflict with other EU policies and that it will be possible to monitor progress and report on the achievements, ideally on the basis of indicators. Third, the different options have to be identified, including the 'no-policy change' option. Fourth, the impacts of each of these policies are to be measured. The policy-maker should examine the economic, environmental and social impacts. He or she should identify the distributive effects of the different options—who will 'win' and 'lose' in each proposal. He or she should compare the different impacts expected according to analytical tools such as cost-benefit analysis where this is possible, or alternatively cost-effectiveness analysis or a multi-criteria analysis, while taking into account the risks and uncertainties inherent in each policy choice, as well as discounting the evaluation of the costs and benefits where they are expected to occur later in time, rather than immediately. Fifth, the result of this impact analysis should be presented to the Commissioners in the most transparent and understandable way possible, in order to facilitate the exercise of the final choice by the College of Commissioners.

The Guidelines prepared within the Commission on Impact assessment provide that in the course of such an extended IA, both the stakeholders concerned ('interested parties') and outside experts may be consulted. The need for such external consultations and the choice of the persons or organisations consulted are defined on a case-to-case basis. The objective is to gather information about both the problem and the possible impacts of different policy routes, and to identify policy options which may have been overlooked by the policy-maker at the initial stage. The consultation of the interested parties should take place in accordance with the general principles and minimum standards defined by the Commission in one of the communications following upon the White Paper on European Governance.[55] However, this communication clearly provides that there is no obligation to consult imposed on the Commission. Such a 'legally-binding approach' is rejected, first, in order to avoid any confusion between the informal consultation process and the formal decision-making procedures stipulated in the Treaties; secondly, such an approach might result in:

---

[54] See, on the two stages of the general impact assessment, the Communication from the Commission, *Impact Assessment,* see n 24 above, para 3, pp 6–9.

[55] Communication from the Commission, *Towards a reinforced culture of consultation and dialogue—General principles and minimum standards for consultation of interested parties by the Commission* COM(2002) 704 final of 11 December 2002.

a situation in which a Commission proposal could be challenged in the Court on the grounds of alleged lack of consultation of interested parties;

which:

would be incompatible with the need for timely delivery of policy, and with the expectations of the citizens that the European Institutions should deliver on substance rather than concentrating on procedures.[56]

Again in order to preserve the effectiveness of the decision-making process, the Commission rejects the idea of 'feedback statements,' ie, of having to provide feedback on an individual basis to all the interested parties having taken part in the consultation.[57] As to the consultation of experts, it should conform with the good practices identified in the communication on the collection and use of expertise by the Commission, called *Improving the knowledge base for better policies.*[58]

b) The Difficulties Entailed by the Inclusion of Fundamental Rights in Impact Assessments

Among the 'social impacts' to be considered in such an IA, the Commission lists 'impact on fundamental/human rights, compatibility with the Charter of Fundamental Rights of the European Union.'[59] A Unit within General Directorate Justice and Home Affairs of the European Commission[60] has prepared directives for the purpose of effectuating such a 'human rights impact analysis' within the different services of the Commission, as the extended IA is normally conducted within the DG responsible for the policy sector concerned by the proposal.[61] The inclusion of fundamental rights into such an approach, however, appears unsatisfactory for a number of reasons.

---

[56] *Ibid.*

[57] *Ibid* p 12.

[58] Communication from the Commission on the collection and use of expertise by the Commission: Principles and Guidelines, *Improving the knowledge base for better policies* COM002) 713 final of 11 December 2002.

[59] Communication from the Commission, *Impact Assessment*, see n 24 above, p 15; and *Handbook for Impact Assessment in the Commission: How to do an Impact Assessment*, see n 53 above, at p 20.

[60] Now renamed DG Justice, Freedom and Security, since the Barroso Commission took over from the Prodi Commission.

[61] These directives are currently under revision. A study has been commissioned by DG Justice and Home Affairs the aim of which is to 'assist in the design of a conceptual framework for more intensified integration of fundamental rights in the impact assessment of legislative proposals.' It should focus on how to assess the redistributive impacts of a given legislative proposal, on how to include in such an assessment the principle of proportionality as well as the need to balance certain rights against one another, and on the identification of 'undesirable consequences and negative spillovers' on fundamental rights by initiatives which concern other sectors.

1) The lack of adequate expertise within each responsible General Directorate.

A first major difficulty is that the choice to include fundamental rights within general impact assessment mechanisms and to have each responsible DG effectuate that assessment without necessarily receiving outside expert advice will lead, all too often, the fundamental rights dimension of the different proposals to be obscured or treated superficially. Indeed, it requires expertise to decide whether or not any proposal raises issues under the Charter of Fundamental Rights which may justify calling for an outside expertise, and it is precisely at this preliminary stage that the risk of non-specialists underestimating that dimension are highest. The absence of an expert body operating transversally to offer that expertise raises doubts about the credibility of this aspect of the impact assessment.[62] But three other difficulties are potentially more important still.

2) The confusion between mainstreaming fundamental rights and ensuring compliance with fundamental rights.

A second difficulty consists in the confusion between the mainstreaming of fundamental rights and the verification of the compatibility with the requirements of fundamental rights, which the current mechanisms for the inclusion of a fundamental rights dimension in impact assessments seem to operate.[63] The risk is that such a confusion may result both in a failure to effectively mainstream fundamental rights, and at the same time, in a devaluation of fundamental rights raising the risk of these rights being violated: by seemingly wishing to embrace both objectives through one single tool, we may end up attaining neither. *Mainstreaming* fundamental rights requires that we take into account, in the policy choices we make, the impact the different policy options we have

---

[62] The competent Unit in DG Justice and Home Affairs may be asked by other services from the Commission to offer expert advice where issues relating to fundamental rights are raised. This Unit is genuinely committed to ensuring that any initiative of the Commission which might interfere with the requirements of the Charter of Fundamental Rights will be carefully scrutinised and, if necessary, modified. However, the Unit is under-resourced and the time it may dedicate to such assessments is limited. Moreover, the civil servants composing the Unit are not necessarily specialists in all areas covered by the Charter, and the usual rules on mobility within the Commission apply to them, which implies that the expertise they acquire will have to be re-created as they depart. Finally, although expertise external to the Commission may be requested, this solution presents its own problems: by its very nature, it cannot result in building an expertise in fundamental rights in the long term, capable of developing a learning relationship with the different services of the Commission.

[63] Such a confusion may be seen in the very language by which the 'social impacts' to be screened are identified by the Commission: 'impact on fundamental/human rights, compatibility with [EU] Charter of Fundamental Rights' are mentioned alongside, as if these were two species of the same genre or even interchangeable. See Communication from the Commission, *Impact Assessment*, n 24 above, p 15; and *Handbook for Impact Assessment in the Commission: How to do an Impact Assessment*, n 53 above, at p 20.

at our disposal will produce on our capacity to further realise those rights. The realisation of rights is however an objective which, it is submitted, is better understood as a *process* than as an *outcome*, as a general *direction* in which to move, than as a *target* we either hit or miss. By way of contrast, where we verify the *compatibility* of certain policy or legislative proposals with the requirements of fundamental rights, our answer will present itself in the binary mode which characterises the adjudicatory approach in general: either the proposal will be found to comply, or it will not. These are different modes of evaluation, and for any single legislative or policy proposal, they may lead to different conclusions. For instance, we may say that a proposal made in the field of competition fails to contribute to the realisation of pluralism in the media as it does not offer safeguards against certain forms of concentration in that sector,[64] yet the same proposal may still be compatible with the requirements of freedom of expression, and even with the obligation imposed by the Charter that the pluralism of the media be 'respected.'[65] Or we may note that a new information technology has not been designed in such a way as to minimise the impact on privacy and to facilitate the exercise by the individual concerned of the rights which safeguard from abuse in the processing of personal data (right of information, access and rectification, objection and appeal),[66] and yet, find at the same time that such technology does not violate the requirements of Article 8 of the Charter of Fundamental Rights or the applicable legislation which develops its requirements.

In making this distinction between the objective of mainstreaming fundamental rights into all policies and the objective of ensuring that these policies comply with the requirements of fundamental rights, this paper is not asserting that one mode of evaluation should be recognised a priority above the other. Nor is it questioning that the efforts an entity makes in order to achieve progress in the realization of fundamental rights may be subjected to an objective evaluation and be considered either sufficient or wanting—and indeed, human rights bodies routinely do evaluate whether the States they monitor are investing enough efforts in the progressive realization of fundamental rights. The point

---

[64] In which sense it fails to contribute to the realization of freedom of expression, which pluralism of information facilitates: see Recommendation 1506(2001) 'Freedom of expression and information in the media in Europe,' adopted on 4 April 2001 by the Parliamentary Assembly of the Council of Europe: 'A pluralist and independent media system is also essential for democratic development and a fair electoral process. It is thus essential to eliminate oligopolism in the media, and to ensure that the media are not used to gain political power, especially in countries where a mixed public-private system would enable political movements, supported by the private sector, to control all information after elections, especially through radio and television.' (para 12). For references to the case law, see EU Network of Independent Experts on Fundamental Rights, *Report on the situation of Fundamental Rights in the European Union in 2003*, n 51 above, at pp 70–73.

[65] Art 11(2) of the Charter of Fundamental Rights.

[66] On the need to develop Privacy Enhancing Technologies (PET) and to conduct privacy-impact-analyses where new technologies are introduced, see EU Network of Independent Experts on Fundamental Rights, *Report on the situation of Fundamental Rights in the European Union in 2003*, n 51 above, at pp 65–66.

made is simply methodological: mainstreaming fundamental rights in order to encourage that all policies seek to contribute to their further realisation, on the one hand, and ensuring the compatibility of these policies with the requirements of fundamental rights, on the other hand, are requirements of a different nature, which each deserve to be treated according to a specific method.

3) *The valuation problems raised by Impact Assessments.*

Neither is this distinction between impact assessments and compatibility assessments a purely academic one. The risk of the current state of confusion between the two modes of evaluation is not only that we may fail to seize upon the opportunities which offer themselves to better mainstream the requirements of the Charter of Fundamental Rights into the EU policies and legislative proposals subjected to IA—as we may content ourselves with the reassuring finding that the Charter is not violated by those policies or proposals. It is also that we may degrade the requirement to comply with the Charter into a balancing exercise, in which considerations linked to fundamental rights will be weighed on the same scale as, for instance, the need not to impose excessive administrative burdens on small and middle-size enterprises or to keep consumer prices at an affordable level. In fact, the insistence in IA on an objective evaluation of the impacts, if possible quantitative or at least measurable, although it fits within a larger movement which in many respects has contributed to improve the rationality of regulations and the accountability of the legislator and of policy-makers,[67] may in many cases lead to underestimate the 'value' of fundamental rights, because such violations are hardly ever expressed in monetary terms.

The Commission recognises this difficulty, of course:

> Expressing all impacts in money terms makes it easier to compare different impacts, because everything is then expressed in the same units. However, not all impacts can be expressed in money terms.[68]

But the methods which are proposed for valuing the impacts for which no market exists only serve to reinforce our scepticism. The two methods which Annex 7 to the *Handbook for Impact Assessment in the Commission* proposes for the valuing of non-market impacts consist in mimicking the market, in the pure tradition of post-Coasian economic analysis of law. 'Stated preference methods' consist of 'constructing hypothetical markets and asking people via questionnaires and interviews the value of a given outcome.'[69] 'Revealed preference methods' are 'based on evidence from market transactions, for example the

---

[67] On the debates provoked by the expansion of cost-benefit analysis, see especially RH Frank, 'Why is Cost-Benefit Analysis so Controversial ?' (2000) 29 *Journal of Legal Studies* 913; CR Sunstein, 'Cognition and Cost-Benefit Analysis' (2000) 29 *Journal of Legal Studies* 1059; MD Adler and EA Posner, 'Rethinking Cost-Benefit Analysis' (2000) 109 *Yale Law Journal* 165.

[68] *Handbook for Impact Assessment in the Commission: How to do an Impact Assessment*, see n 53 above, at p 23.

[69] *Ibid.*

correlation of noise disturbance with house prices.'[70] Apart from the disturbing consequence—but not necessarily fatal—which follows from such an approach, that a price tag risks being attached to encroachments upon rights,[71] these methods which serve to offer a monetary evaluation of the 'values' to be considered in impact assessments fail to take into account that such evaluations will be highly context-dependent. In particular, such valuations will reflect the need in which the persons concerned find themselves as much as the value they would otherwise attach to what they are asked to sacrifice.[72] Which sum of money will compensate you, in your estimation, for the pollution of your neighbourhood, will depend on how much you need money, and not only on how much you are affected by pollution: indeed, in the hypothetical proposed by the *Handbook* of the Commission, it would become much easier to justify polluting a neighbourhood inhabited by poor communities, who would be satisfied to receive 100 euros per child risking to develop respiratory problems, than to justify polluting an affluent neighbourhood, whose inhabitants would not accept to live nearby a polluting source even if compensated with 10 000 euros per child affected. Moreover, such valuations, whether they are 'contingent valuations' based on surveys of the 'willingness to pay' in the absence of markets or whether they are based on the preferences exhibited by economic agents through the choices they

[70] *Handbook for Impact Assessment in the Commission: How to do an Impact Assessment*, see n 53 above, at p 26.

[71] To the question 'Why do we want a monetary value of risk?', Annex 7 answers: 'If we seek to balance the costs of a policy against its benefits, then we must compare the benefit of reductions in risk against costs. Any decision in this context means placing an implicit monetary value on health benefits. Decision-making will be easier and become more consistent if we have a monetary estimate of the value of health benefits. The monetary value represents the strengths of society's preferences' (at p 26). Although the Annex states that 'We cannot—and do not seek to—place a monetary value on our own lives or on other individuals' lives' (p 26), it adds that 'changes in risks are a different matter,' as indeed the prevention of certain risks, even if potentially fatal, may be considered excessively costly as resources preventing risks to health could be put to a more efficient use. Unsurprisingly, the Handbook for Impact Assessment offers an example in which the value of one human life is evaluated at 1 million euros, so that it will be justified, insofar as it will save 1000 persons from premature death (1 billion euros), to impose the installation of air pollution equipment despite the cost for companies, estimated at 400 million euros in the area concerned. See the *Handbook for Impact Assessment in the Commission: How to do an Impact Assessment*, n 53 above, at p 28. On the difficulties raised by such valuation, see, eg: J Broome, 'Trying to Value a Life' (1978) 9 *Journal of Public Economics* 91 (arguing specifically that contingent valuation approaches—in which, in the absence of a market for human lives, the valuation of human life (or the 'price' we attach to it) depends on non-contextual estimations, per definition relating to unknown persons—will lead to grossly underestimate the importance of human life: projects in which only unknown persons will die will go forward even where the loss of life is compensated for by ridiculously low economic compensations, because neither the persons surveyed, nor the authorities, know who in particular will be dying as a result of that project); F Ackerman and L Heinzerling, 'Pricing the Priceless: Cost-Benefit Analysis of Environmental Protection' (1998) 150 *University of Pennsylvania Law Review* 1553; and CR Sunstein, 'Incommensurability and Valuation in Law' (1994) 92 *Michigan Law Review* 779.

[72] On the difference between actual consent and hypothetical consent, see HM Hurd, 'Justifiably Punishing the Justified' (1992) 90 *Michigan Law Review* 2203, 2305; and M Adler, 'Incommensurability and Cost-Benefit Analysis' (1998) 146 *University of Pennsylvania Law Review* 1371.

make in the market, have been demonstrated to be strongly baseline-dependent[73]: the position already occupied by any individual will shape his or her estimation of the value of any regulatory benefits or sacrifices.

It is true that, when confronted with a similar question, in a case where the applicants were complaining that the adoption by the United Kingdom government of new regulations on the night flights above Heathrow airport resulted in a violation of their right to private and family life because of the disturbances caused to their sleep—which had obliged some of them to move to another location—the European Court of Human Rights reiterated that:

> in matters of general policy, on which opinions within a democratic society may reasonably differ widely, the role of the domestic policy maker should be given special weight.[74]

Moreover, perhaps regrettably, the Court noted in its judgment that:

> house prices in the areas in which [the applicants] live have not been adversely affected by the night noise. The Court considers it reasonable, in determining the impact of a general policy on individuals in a particular area, to take into account the individuals' ability to leave the area. Where a limited number of people in an area (2 to 3% of the affected population, according to the 1992 sleep study [commissioned by the UK authorities before the adoption of the new legislation]) are particularly affected by a general measure, the fact that they can, if they choose, move elsewhere without financial loss must be significant to the overall reasonableness of the general measure.[75]

However, the relatively wide margin of appreciation left to the public authorities where planning schemes or general economic and social policies are concerned may not be considered the general rule: in other areas, where the fundamental rights of the individual are more directly interfered with, the European Convention on Human Rights requires that a stricter scrutiny be applied, and that, in particular, any interference be justified by referring to the necessity to achieve a pressing social goal.[76] Indeed, *Hatton* may not be considered typical,

---

[73] E Hoffman and ML Spitzer, 'Willingness to Pay vs. Willingness to Accept: Legal and Economic Implications' (1993) 71 *Washington University Law Quarterly* 59; M Adler, 'Incommensurability and Cost-Benefit Analysis,' see 72 above, at pp 1396–1398. Another, related, difficulty is that we value not only our position in absolute terms, but also relative to the position of others; see RH Frank and CR Sunstein, 'Cost-Benefit Analysis and Relative Position' (2001) 68 *University of Chicago Law Review* 323.

[74] EurCtHR (GC), *Hatton and others v the United Kingdom* (Application No 36022/97) judgment of 8 July 2003, s 97. See also, eg: *James and others v the United Kingdom* Series A no. 98 (1986) p 32, s 46, where the Court found that the margin of appreciation 'available to the legislature in implementing social and economic policies should be a wide one'; EurCtHR, *Buckley v the United Kingdom* judgment of 25 September 1996, *Reports of Judgments and Decisions* 1996–IV, ss 75 ('It is not for the Court to substitute its own view of what would be the best policy in the planning sphere or the most appropriate individual measure in planning cases [. . .] By reason of their direct and continuous contact with the vital forces of their countries, the national authorities are in principle better placed than an international court to evaluate local needs and conditions. In so far as the exercise of discretion involving a multitude of local factors is inherent in the choice and implementation of planning policies, the national authorities in principle enjoy a wide margin of appreciation.')

[75] *Hatton and others v the United Kingdom*, n 74 above, at s 127.

[76] *Ibid* at s 123.

but rather the normal test of compatibility with the requirements of the European Convention on Human Rights is whether the measure interfering with the enjoyment of a fundamental right or freedom pursues a legitimate aim and is strictly tailored to fulfil that aim, and whether there exists a reasonable relationship of proportionality between the aim pursued—which must correspond to a 'pressing social need'—and the seriousness of the interference.[77] Although it would far exceed the scope of this paper to describe the variations around that test which the European Court of Human Rights has used in different settings, the point is that the balancing of interests as performed in *Hatton* is not representative of the proportionality requirement as it is usually applied. In principle, fundamental rights are not simply one factor among others to be included in the general weighing exercise: when they are interfered with, this requires a special justification from the author of the measure, who must demonstrate that no alternatives would have achieved the same legitimate aim with the same efficiency, and that moreover the seriousness of the interference with the fundamental right in question is justified by the importance of the objective pursued.

Moreover, even in situations where it is alleged that the enjoyment of fundamental rights is affected by general economic or social policies or by land planning schemes, and where, accordingly, the margin of appreciation left to the public authorities is widest, the European Court of Human Rights appears to require that the impact of such policies or schemes on the most vulnerable segments of the population be examined with care.[78] Where negative impacts

---

[77] It is impossible to offer even a sample of the voluminous case-law on this issue. With regard to the right of access to a court for instance, as read into Article 6 s 1 of the European Convention on Human Rights, the Court verifies whether 'the limitations applied do not restrict or reduce the access [to a court] left to the individual in such a way or to such an extent that the very essence of the right is impaired. Furthermore, a limitation will not be compatible with Article 6 s 1 if it does not pursue a legitimate aim and if there is no reasonable relationship of proportionality between the means employed and the aim sought to be achieved' (EurCtHR (GC), *Al-Adsani v the United Kingdom* (Application No 35763/97) judgment of 21 November 2001, s 53; EurCtHR (GC), *Waite and Kennedy v Germany* (Application No 26083/94) judgment of 18 February 1999, s 59, ECHR 1999–I). With regard to interferences with the right to respect of private life, the Court notes that 'an interference will be considered "necessary in a democratic society" for a legitimate aim if it answers a pressing social need and, in particular, is proportionate to the legitimate aim pursued; (EurCtHR (3rd s), *Smith and Grady v the United Kingdom* (Applications No 33985/96 and 33986/96) judgment of 27 September 1999, s 87). In the context of interferences with freedom of expression as protected under Art 10 ECHR, the Court traditionally emphasises that 'the adjective "necessary," within the meaning of Art 10 § 2, implies the existence of a "pressing social need,"' and that the supervisory task of the Court is not 'limited to ascertaining whether the respondent State exercised its discretion reasonably, carefully and in good faith,' but 'what the Court has to do is to look at the interference complained of in the light of the case as a whole and determine whether it was "proportionate to the legitimate aim pursued" and whether the reasons adduced by the national authorities to justify it are "relevant and sufficient."' (*Handyside v the United Kingdom* Series A no 24 (1976), p 23, s 49; *Lingens v Austria* Series A no 103 (1986), p 26, s 41; *The Sunday Times v the United Kingdom* (no 2) Series A no 217 (1991), p 29, s 50; EurCtHR, *Hertel v Switzerland*, judgment of 25 August 1998, s 46).

[78] See *Hatton and others v the United Kingdom*, n 74 above, at s 118: 'It is true that the applicants have not submitted any evidence in support of the degree of discomfort suffered, in particular they have not disproved the Government's indications as to the "objective" daytime noise contour measured at each applicant's home [. . .] However, as the Government themselves admit, and as is

occur for the most vulnerable, mitigating measures should be adopted to minimise those impacts.[79] In certain cases, exceptions may have to be provided in generally applicable regulations in order to accommodate the specific situation of certain groups, the application to whom of the general rule might result in discrimination.[80] This applies not only to the adoption of regulatory measures or policies which risk impacting negatively on the enjoyment of fundamental rights, but also to the adoption of measures contributing to the further realization of fundamental rights: in the context of the right to education, the European Committee of Social Rights thus noted that:

> When the achievement of one of the rights [recognised in the (revised) European Social Charter] is exceptionally complex and particularly expensive to resolve, [measures must be adopted] to achieve the objectives of the Charter within a reasonable time, with measurable progress and to an extent consistent with the maximum use of available resources. States parties [to the (revised) European Social Charter] must be particularly mindful of the impact that their choices will have for groups with heightened vulnerabilities as well as for other persons affected including, especially, their families on whom falls the heaviest burden in the event of institutional shortcomings.[81]

Finally, whether they risk impacting negatively upon the enjoyment of fundamental rights or whether they contribute to the fulfilment of fundamental rights but risk not targeting sufficiently the most vulnerable segments of the population, the measures adopted must be held under constant review, in order to ensure that changing conditions will not result in the impacts becoming more severe than initially anticipated.[82]

---

evident from the 1992 sleep study on which they rely, sensitivity to noise includes a subjective element, a small minority of people being more likely than others to be awoken or otherwise disturbed in their sleep by aircraft noise at night. The discomfort caused to the individuals concerned will therefore depend not only on the geographical location of their respective homes in relation to the various flight paths, but also on their individual disposition to be disturbed by noise. In the present case the degree of disturbance may vary somewhat from one applicant to the other, but the Court cannot follow the Government when they seem to suggest that the applicants were not, or not considerably, affected by the scheme at issue.'

[79] See *Hatton and others v the United Kingdom*, n 74 above, at ss 74 and 125. In the judgment delivered by a Chamber of the Court before the case was referred to the Grand Chamber, the Court had considered that 'States are required to minimise, as far as possible, the interference with these rights, by trying to find alternative solutions and by generally seeking to achieve their aims in the least onerous way as regards human rights. In order to do that, a proper and complete investigation and study with the aim of finding the best possible solution which will, in reality, strike the right balance should precede the relevant project.' (*Hatton and others v the United Kingdom* s 97). Although it arrives at a different conclusion on the basis of another understanding of the facts presented by the parties, the Grand Chamber does not contradict this statement in its judgment of 8 July 2003.

[80] See EurCtHR (GC), *Thlimmenos v Greece* (Application No 34369/97) judgment of 6 April 2000, s 44 ('The right not to be discriminated against in the enjoyment of the rights guaranteed under the Convention is also violated when States without an objective and reasonable justification fail to treat differently persons whose situations are significantly different.')

[81] European Committee of Social Rights, *Autisme-Europe v France*, complaint no 13/2002, decision on the merits adopted on 4 November 2003, para 53.

[82] See *Hatton and others v the United Kingdom*, n 74 above, at s 125.

In sum, although there may exist in certain cases a superficial analogy between the inclusion of fundamental rights concerns in impact assessments and the scrutiny required to ensure that fundamental rights are not violated by the adoption of any particular measure—and this may explain, indeed, the tendency to conflate both methods in the IA tool—these remain approaches analytically distinct from one another, which, if correctly applied, may lead to different conclusions. Both tests are useful, but their purposes are different: impact assessments (IA) serve to mainstream fundamental rights into the policies and legislative proposals of the EU, when compatibility assessments (CA) should constitute a preventive mechanism, required in order to avoid the adoption of measures which may be found later, in the course of judicial proceedings, to be in violation of the requirements of fundamental rights. We will only realise the full potentialities of mainstreaming fundamental rights through IA if we clearly separate this exercise from an assessment of the legality of the measures proposed, ie, of their compatibility with fundamental rights.

4) The lack of adequate procedural safeguards ensuring participation in Impact Assessments.

A fourth set of difficulties with IA as it is currently conceived and implemented in European governance concerns its procedural aspects. As it fears to commit itself formally to certain forms of consultation with interested parties, the Commission has considered that it would be unwise to choose to select the most representative organisations in the field of human rights in order to provide those organisations a right to consultation on a more systematic and structured basis.[83] Indeed, the variety of the organisations listed in the CONECCS directory[84] and the absence of any accreditation mechanism would make it wholly unrealistic to require from the different Commission services to consult these organisations: for consultation to be effective, it must be structured in some formal manner, and it must be codified by binding rules.[85] The current situation

---

[83] The Commission did set up a directory of civil society organisations (CONECCS: Consultation, the European Commission and Civil Society) which it may consult, however it clearly stipulates that 'The directory is established on a voluntary basis and it is intended only for information. Inclusion in the directory does not constitute any recognition on the part of the Commission.' In September 2004, 47 civil society organisations were listed in the CONECCS database under the heading 'human rights.' Although as a condition for their registration on the database these organisations must present a certain number of qualities—in particular, they must be non-profit representative organisations at the European level, be active and have expertise in one or more of the policy areas of the Commission—their representativity, level of expertise, and—indeed—their relationship to the promotion of human rights all appear to be extremely variable. Moreover, major actors in the field such as the unions, the European Roma Rights Centre, the European Forum for Persons with Disabilities or the International Commission of Jurists are absent from the list.

[84] *Ibid.*

[85] On the need to give an adequate legal status to mainstreaming instead of relying on 'soft law' mechanisms, see C McCrudden, 'Mainstreaming Equality in the Governance of Northern Ireland,' n 17 above, at p 1772. On the need for civil society organisations to be better structured in order for a right to be consulted to emerge, see O De Schutter, 'Europe in Search of Its Civil Society,' n 40 above, *passim.*

where the consultation processes remain informal—although they are broadly circumscribed by the general principles and minimum standards defined in the Communication from the Commission of 11 December 2002[86]—and where the 'interested parties' are identified on a purely *ad hoc* basis not only results in the absence of a recognition of a 'right to be consulted' for stakeholders, but in fact also in the lack of effectiveness of consultation altogether, as the responsible DG, which in principle should decide which interested parties it should consult, may have difficulties identifying them adequately. Moreover, even where a consultation of interested parties does take place in the performance of an extended impact assessment exercise, the general principles and minimum standards on the consultation of interested parties by the Commission which apply since 2003 are silent about the need to provide those parties with the information, the resources and, more generally, the capabilities they require in order for their participation to be effective.

5) *The inadequacy of Impact Assessments for the identification of an obligation to adopt measures.*

A last difficulty is that IA, as it is currently conceived of and practiced in order to ensure the implementation of fundamental rights in the activities of the Commission, is insufficient to identify situations which call for an initiative of the Union, because a 'no-policy' course of action would create a risk of human rights violations. It cannot be excluded *a priori* that the Charter may impose on the Union institutions a positive obligation to adopt certain measures, where this appears necessary for the effective protection of fundamental rights within

---

[86] On this question, the Minimum Standards proposed in the Communication stipulate that 'For consultation to be equitable, the Commission should ensure adequate coverage of the following parties in a consultation process: those affected by the policy; those who will be involved in implementation of the policy; bodies that have stated objectives giving them direct interest in the policy.' However, other elements as well should guide the choice of the Commission as to whom to consult: the Commission mentions the need to take into account 'the wider impact of the policy on other policy areas, eg environmental interests or consumer policy'; 'the need for specific experience, expertise or technical knowledge, where applicable'; 'the need to involve non-organised interests, where appropriate'; 'the track record of participants in previous consultations'; and the need for a proper balance between different categories of organisations. See Communication from the Commission, *Towards a reinforced culture of consultation and dialogue—General principles and minimum standards for consultation of interested parties by the Commission,* n 25 above, at pp 19–20. Interestingly, the reference to environmental interests as interests which might be affected by policy initiatives adopted in other sectors that the environmental sector strictly defined (for instance, a number of initiatives taken by DG internal market (' MARKT') could impact on the environment, and not only those originating in DG Environment) is justified in the Communication by a reference to the 'environment mainstreaming' clause of Art 6 EC, n 43 above (now replicated in Art III–117 of the Treaty establishing a Constitution for Europe). The proposal made in this chapter with respect to the mainstreaming of human rights would imply, in the same vein, a more systematic consultation of representative human rights organisations existing permanently at the European level, not limited to the proposals of policies or instruments which concern directly the implementation of fundamental rights.

the legal order of the Union.[87] Article 51(1) of the Charter mentions that the institutions and organs of the Union and the Member States, to which the Charter is addressed, are obliged to 'promote the application' of the rights, freedoms and principles contained in the Charter. The formulation suggests at least that the drafters of the Charter recognised that it may impose obligations beyond the purely negative duty to abstain from interfering without justification with these rights, freedoms and principles. But IA of course only applies to policy or legislative proposals which are initiated on other grounds, and which may impact, directly or less directly, on fundamental rights or on the capacity of the Member States to fulfil them in the fields in which they remain competent. As such, IA therefore is not sufficient to ensure the mainstreaming of fundamental rights into EU legislations and policies, as mainstreaming implies not only that we ensure that these legislations and policies do not impact negatively upon fundamental rights, but also that the tools the EU institutions have at their disposal are used in order to affirmatively promote them. Where a legislative or policy proposal is made, the IA of course includes an examination of the 'no-policy option,' ie, of the *status quo*. But no IA will be made where no such proposal is presented: the impact on fundamental rights of inaction, of the institutions of the Union not exercising the competences conferred upon them by the Member States, is not examined. This deficiency should not be attributed to the way impact assessments are performed, but to the procedure leading those assessments to be made in the first place. It reveals a lack of awareness that, in the field of fundamental rights in general—and not only in the field of social rights or the environment, areas in which the argument has become a familiar one[88]—

---

[87] Indeed, even before the adoption of the Charter of Fundamental Rights, it has been argued that the jurisprudence of the European Court of Justice may be read as affirming 'that there is a positive duty of the institutions [of the Union] "to ensure the observance of fundamental rights." In other words, they are obligated not simply to refrain from violating them, but to ensure that they are observed within the respective constitutional roles played by each institution' P Alston and JHH Weiler, 'An "Even Closer Union" in Need of a Human Rights Policy: The European Union and Human Rights' in P Alston, M Bustelo and J Heenan (eds), *The EU and Human Rights* (Oxford, Oxford University Press, 1999) p 3, at p 25. In the context of the discussion of the Charter, however, a more sceptical view has been expressed on the same point: see J Kenner, 'Economic and Social Rights in the EU Legal Order: The Mirage of Indivisibility' in T Hervey and J Kenner (eds), *Economic and Social Rights under the EU Charter of Fundamental Rights: A Legal Perspective* (Oxford, Hart Publishing, 2003) p 1, at p 19. For further developments on the positive obligations which may be derived from the Charter of Fundamental Rights, see O De Schutter, 'The Implementation of the EU Charter of Fundamental Rights through the Open Method of Coordination,' n 15 above.

[88] See, eg: R Stewart, 'Pyramids of Sacrifice? Problems of Federalism in Mandating State Implementation of National Environmental Policy' (1977) 86 *Yale Law Journal*. 1196; R Stewart, 'The Development of Administrative and Quasi-Constitutional Law in Judicial Review of Environmental Decisionmaking: Lessons from the Clean Air Act' (1977) 62 *Iowa Law Review* 713; and the counter-argument from R Revesz, 'Rehabilitating Interstate Competition: Rethinking the "Race-to-the-Bottom" Rationale for Federal Environmental Regulation' (1992) 67 *New York University Law Review* 1210. In the field of social rights, see, eg: C Sunstein, 'Constitutional After the New Deal' (1987) 101 *Harvard Law Review* 421, 505 (recalling that, when the New Deal was being envisioned, there was good reason to believe that 'Competition among the States would generate a "race to the bottom" that would both harm the disadvantaged and prevent coordinated action. New Deal reformers willingly abandoned the belief in self-determination through local

regulatory competition between the Member States of the Union may have damaging consequences.[89] What may be required instead is a screening mechanism ensuring that the institutions of the Union are alerted to the need to take action where a 'race to the bottom' occurs as a consequence of the lack of harmonisation or coordination between the Member States: due to what may be called their reactive character—they are made where proposals are presented or envisaged, and not in anticipation of such proposals—impact assessments as currently conceived may not be capable to meet that challenge.

IV. MAINSTREAMING FUNDAMENTAL RIGHTS: ACTION PLANS

The last difficulty identified with the practice of Impact Assessments may be met, in part, by the attribution to the EU Network of independent experts on fundamental rights of the task to alert the Union institutions where there appears to be a need for intervention at the level of the Union, in the face of trends observed within the Member States. The Commission has noted in this regard that the Network:

> has an essential preventive role in that it can provide ideas for achieving the area of freedom, security and justice or alerting the institutions to divergent trends in standards of protection between Member States which could imperil the mutual trust on which Union policies are founded.[90]

government and looked instead to national institutions, and in particular to regulatory agencies and to the presidency, to fulfil democratic aspirations.') For a larger perspective on the relationship between the values of federalism and decentralisation and rights, see R Stewart, 'Federalism and Rights' (1985) 19 *Georgia Law Review* 917. As is well known, the European Court of Justice has recognised the validity of this argument. The second *Defrenne* case, for instance, clearly recalled the economic foundation of Art 119 EEC, stating that the aim of this provision was 'to avoid a situation in which undertakings established in states which have actually implemented the principle of equal pay suffer a competitive disadvantage in intra-Community competition as compared with undertakings established in states which have not yet eliminated discrimination against women workers as regards pay' (Case 43/75, *Defrenne* (no 2), [1976] ECR 455).

[89] For further developments, see O De Schutter, 'The Implementation of the EU Charter of Fundamental Rights through the Open Method of Coordination,' n 15 above.

[90] Communication from the Commission presented to the Council and the European Parliament on Art 7 EU, *Respect for and promotion of the values on which the Union is based* COM (2003) 606 final, of 15 October 2003. This function resembles one which is defined, for the Working Party on Data Protection instituted by Art 29 of Dir 95/46/EC of the European Parliament and of the Council of 24 October 1995 on the protection of individuals with regard to the processing of personal data and on the free movement of such data (OJ L 281 of 23 November 1995, p 31), by Art 30(2) of this Dir, which states that 'If the Working Party finds that divergences likely to affect the equivalence of protection for persons with regard to the processing of personal data in the Community are arising between the laws or practices of Member States, it shall inform the Commission accordingly.' Indeed, the language of the Communication from the Commission of 15 October 2003 replicates that used in the Report on the situation of fundamental rights in the European Union and its Member States in 2002, in which the EU Network of Independent Experts on Fundamental Rights already proposed this analogy (at pp 14–15).

The externalisation of this function—which is to identify the situations which appear to call for the intervention of the Union in order to ensure that fundamental rights are adequately protected within the Union—presents certain advantages, of course. It provides for an independent appreciation of the need to act for the Union institutions, which moreover is based on a direct and systematic examination of the evolution of the situation of fundamental rights in the Member States, a form of mutual observation which would be difficult to ensure for any service within the Commission. However, apart from the fact that this group of experts has not for the moment made permanent, this externalisation also presents the disadvantage that it contributes only weakly to collective learning within the Commission, as the services concerned are not asked to identify by themselves, proactively, in which way they may contribute to the promotion of fundamental rights within the limits of their attributed powers, taking into account the principles of subsidiarity and proportionality which govern the exercise by the institutions of the Union of the competences they share with the Member States. This may constitute a serious lacuna, at least if we conceive of mainstreaming, as we should, not only as consisting in the injection of an expert knowledge of the issues mainstreamed in law- and policy-making, but also as a mechanism for the progressive transformation of the culture within the organisation within which the mainstreaming takes place.[91]

One tool by which both to impose the positive duty on the Commission to affirmatively promote fundamental rights, and to encourage this institutional learning—which may greatly improve the sensitivity of the members of the institution to fundamental rights issues and ensure that, progressively, their inclusion will become 'automatic'—would consist in imposing on the services concerned an obligation to present, at regular intervals (every two years for instance), an action plan defining how they intend to contribute to the promotion of fundamental rights in the policy area of which they are in charge.[92] This should not be seen as a substitute for the formulation of recommendations by an independent body, which has its own virtues—as has been mentioned, the very fact that such a group remains external and acts independently, while closely following the situation of fundamental rights within the Member States, makes it an important tool in the overall strategy for the improvement of the promotion and protection of human rights in the Union. However, the adoption

---

[91] Alison Woodward writes for instance in the context of gender mainstreaming that 'if the goal of mainstreaming is transformation of the perception of the average bureaucrat and institutional transformation, then external experts need to be couples to a training process and evaluation to create learning carry over. Otherwise the departure of the expert will mean the departure of awareness.' (AE Woodward, 'Gender Mainstreaming in European Policy: Innovation or Deception?', see n 17 above, pp 18–19).

[92] In the field of equality, a good example of this mainstreaming tool is offered by the obligation imposed on public bodies in Northern Ireland under section 75 of the Northern Ireland Act 1998 and, in Britain, under the Race Relations (Amendment) Act 2000, to present 'equality schemes' detailing the measures they intend to adopt in order to fulfil their obligation to promote equality (limited to racial equality under the latter legislation), with an accompanying timeframe for their adoption and implementation. The reader is referred to ch 6 in this volume by C McCrudden.

of action plans by the services of the Commission, or even of a consolidated action plan by the Commission as a whole, would complement this and lead a more anticipatory, or proactive, mainstreaming of fundamental rights in the legislations and policies of the Union. This would be fully in line with the idea that the European Union should begin acting as if it were bound by the international human rights instruments which are binding on the Member States, in order to pave the way to accession to those instruments.[93] The World Conference on Human Rights held in Vienna in June 1993 recommended that each State:

> consider the desirability of drawing up a national action plan identifying steps whereby that State would improve the promotion and protection of human rights.[94]

Indeed, the expert bodies created under the United Nations human rights treaties insist—both in their general comments and in the concluding observations made upon their examination of the reports submitted by States parties—on the usefulness of preparing such action plans in order to facilitate the implementation of the different rights which the States parties have undertaken to observe.[95] The preparation of such action plans should not be considered simply as a means for States to comply with their obligation to 'take steps' in order to realise the fundamental rights they have undertaken to fulfil, especially those aspects of which still have to be progressively realised.[96] Nor should they be seen as a purely bureaucratic process, imposing on States yet further administrative burdens adding to those already imposed on them in the system of international and regional human rights treaties. Rather, the preparation of such plans should be envisaged as an opportunity for the administrations preparing them to present imaginative solutions to the problems they face in the implementation of fundamental rights, by learning from the experiences of other jurisdictions and from the outside contributions they may receive in the course of the preparation of such plans. Not only does the preparation of action plans oblige their authors to identify these problems of implementation—ideally, by developing adequate indicators in order to follow the developments in time a particular issue undergoes—; it also offers the opportunity to consult widely with civil society organisations in order to identify which solutions can

---

[93] See I–c above.

[94] Vienna Declaration and Programme of Action, adopted by the World Conference on Human Rights on 25 June 1993 (UN doc. A/CONF.157/23, 12 July 1993), at para 71.

[95] The UN Committee on Economic, Social and Cultural rights considers that 'At a minimum, the State party is required to adopt and implement a national educational strategy which includes the provision of secondary, higher and fundamental education in accordance with the Covenant. This strategy should include mechanisms, such as indicators and benchmarks on the right to education, by which progress can be closely monitored.' (General comment No 13: The right to education (art 13), adopted at the twenty-first session of the Committee (1999), para 52, in *Compilation of the general comments or general recommendations adopted by human rights treaty bodies*, UN doc HRI/GEN/1/Rev.7, 12 May 2004, p 71.

[96] See Art 2(1) of the International Covenant on Economic, Social and Cultural Rights, GA Res 2200, UN GAOR, 21st session, Supp No 16, at p 49, UN Doc A/6316 (1966).

be successful; and it may serve to highlight inconsistencies between different approaches to a same problem, thus fulfilling what has been identified above as one of the main virtues of a mainstreaming approach to the fulfilment of human rights.[97] Most importantly, action plans complement impact assessments, which constitute the other tool of mainstreaming in the conception presented here: indeed, the authorities responsible for the preparation, the discussion, the adoption and the implementation of such plans are incentivised to act pro-actively in order to improve the protection and to promote fundamental rights, rather than to react on an *ad hoc* basis to any identified violation of fundamental rights, by remedying the situation which has led to that violation. The preparation of action plans as a component of a strategy for the implementation of fundamental rights, in sum, does not constitute an end in itself, but should be seen as an instrument furthering a number of important aims. Such plans may, in particular:

1) serve to improve the coordination between different administrative bodies or departments, either because the schemes will be consolidated schemes presented jointly by these entities, or because, where each entity presents its own scheme, the preparation of the scheme and the publicity given to it will facilitate the identification of coordination problems;

2) constitute a tool in order to promote participatory processes, as the contribution the relevant stakeholders can make to the discussion of the scheme will incentivise these stakeholders to invest into the process[98];

[97] In recommending the adoption of a national strategy to ensure food and nutrition security, the UN Committee on Economic, Social and Cultural Rights notes that such a strategy 'will facilitate coordination between ministries and regional and local authorities and ensure that related policies and administrative decisions are in compliance with the obligations under article 11 of the Covenant. The formulation and implementation of national strategies for the right to food requires full compliance with the principles of accountability, transparency, people's participation, decentralization, legislative capacity and the independence of the judiciary. Good governance is essential to the realization of all human rights, including the elimination of poverty and ensuring a satisfactory livelihood for all. Appropriate institutional mechanisms should be devised to secure a representative process towards the formulation of a strategy, drawing on all available domestic expertise relevant to food and nutrition. The strategy should set out the responsibilities and time frame for the implementation of the necessary measures.' (General comment No 12: *The right to adequate food* (art 11), adopted at the twentieth session of the Committee (1999), paras 21–24 (UN doc E/C.12/1999/5), in *Compilation of the general comments or general recommendations adopted by human rights treaty bodies*, UN doc HRI/GEN/1/Rev.7, 12 May 2004, p 63). See also, with respect to national strategies—including the adoption of action plans—in order to promote the right to the highest attainable standard of health: General comment No 14: *The right to the highest attainable standard of health* (art 12), adopted at the twenty-second session of the Committee (2000), paras 53–54 and 56, in *Compilation of the general comments or general recommendations adopted by human rights treaty bodies*, UN doc HRI/GEN/1/Rev.7, 12 May 2004, p 86. In the context of the Convention on the Rights of the Child, see General comment No 5: *General measures of implementation of the Convention on the Rights of the Child* (arts 4, 42 and 44, para 6), adopted at the thirty-fourth session of the Committee (2003), in *Compilation of the general comments or general recommendations adopted by human rights treaty bodies*, UN doc HRI/GEN/1/Rev.7, 12 May 2004, p 332, at paras 28–34.

[98] Conversely, the action plans will be dependent for their quality on such participation, as the implementation of any plan will be greatly facilitated if both the policy-makers and the stakeholders understand what the objectives are and which steps are required to attain these objectives.

3) constitute a source of reflexivity within the public bodies presenting such schemes: they will be obliged to think about the definition of attainable targets, benchmarking and indicators to measure progress, and the resources required for the achievement of the stated goals.

At the same time, just like fundamental rights impact assessments discussed above, the success of action plans as a component of a broader strategy for the mainstreaming of fundamental rights in the Union requires that an entity monitors the process and ensures and adequate coordination between the different services of the Commission. The contribution of the EU Fundamental Rights Agency to this process, therefore, could be of decisive importance. It is to this question that the next section turns.

V. THE ROLE OF THE AGENCY IN MAINSTREAMING FUNDAMENTAL RIGHTS IN THE UNION

We may conclude from what precedes that, although certain of the developments resulting from the recent reforms of European governance offer fertile soil for the implementation of a mainstreaming strategy of fundamental rights, these developments remain in many respects unsatisfactory. Impact assessments exist. They are systematic for all major proposals since 2003. They include an examination of the impact of these proposals on fundamental rights. However, as they are currently performed, these impact assessments fall into a confusion between impact assessments as a tool for mainstreaming fundamental rights, and a verification of the compatibility with the requirements of the Charter of Fundamental Rights, neither for which the responsible General Directorates really may claim to possess the required expert knowledge. These impact assessments are not truly participatory, despite the potential they present in this regard: although interested parties may be consulted, when this happens and whom is consulted remains left to the appreciation of the responsible DG, notwithstanding what we may suspect will be, more often than not, its lack of experience with fundamental rights issues and with the relevant stakeholders in the field.

Moreover, impact assessments may not constitute the only tool of mainstreaming. For this strategy of promoting and protecting fundamental rights to be truly innovative, it requires to be proactive and anticipatory: not only in the obvious sense that violations should be prevented from occurring, but also in the sense that public authorities should be led to ask themselves what they might contribute to improving the promotion and protection of fundamental rights, by *taking action* and not simply by *avoiding to adversely impact on fundamental rights in the actions they take*. Therefore, the preparation of action plans for the realization of fundamental rights should be required either from each service of the Commission, or from the Commission as a whole. In fact, such plans are occasionally produced, on questions such as, for instance, the integration of persons with disabilities or the fight against racism. But there is no unified strategy behind these plans. More importantly, there lacks an external monitoring of these plans, which are neither validated in their content, nor verified in their implementation once they are adopted.

It has been remarked that:

> much of the success of mainstreaming will depend on the institutional and organizational setting and the methods used to carry out the project.[99]

Indeed. With respect both to improving the fundamental rights component of impact assessments and to the preparation and implementation of action plans for the promotion of fundamental rights, the Fundamental Rights Agency may have a decisive role to play. In order to facilitate *fundamental rights impact assessments*, the Agency could provide the Commission, upon its request, with any expert advice the Commission might require. And, in order to encourage a more systematic consultation of selected stakeholders, whose comments may lead the Commission to revise its proposals, the Agency may help identify the relevant stakeholders and ensure that the consultation takes place in a fully satisfactory manner. The networks which the Agency may be expected to build in the human rights community, especially the partnerships it may have with non-governmental organisations, will greatly contribute to it fulfilling this role.

As a second component of a fundamental rights mainstreaming strategy in the Union this paper has proposed, the services of the Commission could be required to submit *action plans*, describing at regular intervals how they intend to promote human rights in the definition of the policies for which they are responsible. This, it has been suggested, will result in a more pro-active or anticipatory strategy, according to which the services of the Commission will be asking themselves not only—as with impact assessments—how to minimise the negative impact on fundamental rights of the policies or legislations they propose, but also what they may do—which policies or legislations they may propose—in order to implement fundamental rights, where they possess the required competences to do so and where the decentralised actions of the Member States cannot be trusted to adequately ensure such implementation, so that such implementation can be better achieved at Union level. In this mechanism also, the creation of a Fundamental Rights Agency may constitute a unique opportunity to improve the Union's fundamental rights policy. The Agency could facilitate the identification of the relevant stakeholders to be consulted in the preparation of such action plans, in order to make them more participatory, and therefore both better informed and more legitimate. Once adopted, these plans could be submitted to the Agency. The role of the Agency at this stage would be to verify whether the authors of the plan have demonstrated that they

---

[99] AE Woodward, 'Gender Mainstreaming in European Policy: Innovation or Deception?' see n 17 above, p 17.

have made sufficient efforts to identify what could be done in order to protect and promote fundamental rights in the definition of the policies for which they are responsible; whether the plan submitted does not reveal certain inconsistencies with other policies developed by the Commission which impact fundamental rights; and whether the plan, as it has been adopted, does not betray a misunderstanding of the requirements of the Charter of Fundamental Rights or other fundamental rights included in the general principles of Union law. Exercising such examination, the Agency might be given the possibility to either approve of the plan which is submitted, or transmit the plan to the European Parliament accompanied with its observations, thus giving the Parliament the possibility to request from the Commission that it justifies its choices and, if so required, that it gives its answers in response to the comments of the Agency.

Two final comments are in order. First, the processes which have been described should be clearly defined as having as their objective to improve the quality of the impact assessments and action plans adopted by the different services of the Commission. It would be politically and legally unjustifiable to present the Fundamental Rights Agency as 'monitoring' the Commission's action with respect to the requirements of fundamental rights: the Agency should act, rather, as the 'facilitator' of a process of 'self-monitoring,' the tools of which are fundamental rights impact assessments and action plans, and the objective of which is collective learning. Indeed, the implementation of such tools should lead, progressively, to the kind of organisational learning which is at the basis of any mainstreaming strategy.

Second, for all it has to offer, it would be a mistake to consider that the Fundamental Rights Agency could centralise all which needs to be done for an effective fundamental rights policy to be developed at the level of the Union. Even if facilitated by the Agency, 'self-monitoring' may not be sufficient therefore. Although the potential of mainstreaming in the transformation of administrative culture constitutes one of its advantages—it may contribute to raising the awareness of public bodies and to their progressive acquisition of the expert knowledge they will require to become effective participants in the process—it remains crucial that an external perspective be preserved. This paper has highlighted at least two functions which a structure similar to the Network of Independent Experts on Fundamental Rights should continue to perform, alongside the Fundamental Rights Agency. First, such a group of experts may be called upon to perform, where requested to do so, an examination of the compatibility of certain policy or legislative proposals with the requirements of the Charter of Fundamental Rights.[100] Such an examination, it has been submitted, should not be confused with a 'fundamental rights impact assessment.' Rather, it constitutes an exercise of a different kind, requiring a form of normative appreciation which can only be performed by independent experts in

---

[100] This is a function the Network already performs, by delivering opinions on specific questions relating to fundamental rights upon the request of the Commission.

fundamental rights.[101] Second, such a structure could be required in order to monitor the situation of fundamental rights within the different Member States, so as to alert the institutions to the need to adopt certain initiatives where this appears necessary to avoid a 'race to the bottom' in the field of fundamental rights or, more generally, to alert them where, in the absence of adequate coordination, the Member States arrive at sub-optimal solutions as they act individually in order to implement the Charter of Fundamental Rights.[102]

---

[101] The reader is referred to the contribution by M Scheinin in ch 3 of this volume for further developments on the function of 'monitoring.' It should be emphasised that, although such monitoring can be performed *ex ante*, when a legislative or policy proposal is envisaged, it may also be done *ex post*, after a particular policy has been implemented or a legislative or regulatory instrument adopted. The paper by M Scheinin focuses on this second form of monitoring by the Network of Independent Experts.

[102] The need for such information to be collected and analysed can hardly be contested, even if, as argued in this paper, the mandate of the Fundamental Rights Agency is limited to the scope of application of Union law. Indeed, although the Communication of the Commission on the Fundamental Rights Agency (COM(2004)693 final, of 25 October 2004) asks 'whether retaining the two structures [the Fundamental Rights Agency and the EU Network of Independent Experts on Fundamental Rights] will give real added value to the promotion and protection of fundamental rights' (in para 7.3), it notes that 'The network of independent experts for fundamental rights could also be an important source of information for the Agency.' (para 5.1).

3

The Relationship between the Agency and the Network of Independent Experts

MARTIN SCHEININ*

T HIS CHAPTER DISCUSSES the respective functions and mandates of the future EU Fundamental Rights Agency (the Agency) and the existing EU Network of Independent Experts on Fundamental Rights (the Network). It is asserted that there will be a meaningful role for the Network or a corresponding independent monitoring institution also after the establishment of the Agency. With reference to experiences from the monitoring mechanisms under human rights treaties, the author also discusses available options for institutional links between the Agency and the Network.

The approach taken in this chapter is based on a conceptualization of the notion of monitoring in respect of fundamental rights. Although the notion of monitoring is occasionally also used in respect of the mandate of the future Agency, the author emphasises the legal-normative nature of true monitoring as something quite distinct from the planned profile of the Agency which relates to the collection and analysis of data for the purpose of providing input for policy-making. To the extent such a profile can at all be described as monitoring, it resembles more an 'observatory' than an international expert body making a normative assessment. Monitoring in the more demanding, normative sense of the term is typically a function of independent expert bodies entrusted with one or more mechanisms of judicial or quasi-judicial nature, allowing for a normative assessment of the compliance by states or other entities under a given set of substantive norms on human or fundamental rights.

The chapter also addresses the question of which division of tasks could exist between the EU Network of Independent Experts and the Agency.

---

* Armfelt Professor of Constitutional and International Law, Director of the Institute for Human Rights, Åbo Akademi University (Finland), member of the of the EU Network of Independent Experts on Fundamental Rights, and, until December 2004, member of the United Nations Human Rights Committee.

I. THE COMMUNICATION FROM THE COMMISSION

The December 2003 decision by the Brussels European Council[1] to create an EU Human Rights Agency by extending the mandate of the European Monitoring Centre on Racism and Xenophobia was, in October 2004, developed further in the form of a communication from the Commission.[2] This Communication includes a specific section related to the relationships of synergy to be developed between the Agency and other bodies operating, broadly speaking, in the same field. After speaking in favour of the Agency's cooperation with Council of Europe institutions such as the European Commission against Racism and Intolerance and the Commissioner for Human Rights, and of setting up a network between the Agency and national human rights institutions or equivalent bodies in the Member States, the Communication moves to address the relationship between the Agency and the Network as follows:

> It is necessary to identify the synergies which the Agency could develop with the network of independent experts on fundamental rights, set up by the Commission at the request of the European Parliament, and to determine whether retaining the two structures will give real added value to the promotion and protection of fundamental rights.[3]

Below it is asserted that such real added value exists, provided that the need for and importance of independent fundamental rights monitoring is accepted and respected by the Member States and the EU institutions.

II. EXPERIENCES FROM HUMAN RIGHTS TREATY MONITORING

a) What is International Human Rights Monitoring?

In order to understand the role fundamental rights monitoring may and should have in the EU context, lessons should be drawn from the experiences of international monitoring mechanisms under human rights treaties. In this respect, the most important issue to understand is that such human rights monitoring is *normative* in nature. Although various mechanisms under human rights treaties do have a dimension of fact-finding in order to enable a normative assessment, for the most part they rely on fact-finding made by others, and consist of a normative assessment of the established set of facts against the normative grid of the legal obligations of a State Party to an international treaty. Such activity is quasi-judicial, or in some cases judicial, in nature, and it strives towards the non-selective, foreseeable and coherent application of human rights law in

---

[1] See http://ue.eu.int/ueDocs/cms_Data/docs/pressData/en/ec/78364.pdf.

[2] Communication from the Commission. *The Fundamental Rights Agency*, Public consultation document 25 October 2004, COM(2004) 693 final (Commission Communication).

[3] *Ibid* p 10.

respect of all States Parties to a treaty. The application of the normative grid in question is complex and cannot be reduced to the use of a given set of indicators that would allow an assessment directly on the basis of empirical data. Typically, it will require knowledge not only of the empirical data to be addressed and of the applicable treaty provisions but also of the institutionalised practices of interpretation (case law in the broad sense of the term) that exist under the treaty in question and under comparable substantive provisions of other human rights treaties, and of practices within, and implications for, a wide range of national legal systems.

The generally applicable institutional solution for pursuing human rights monitoring is the establishment of a multi-member expert body where the members have different backgrounds as to nationality and legal system and serve in a judicial or otherwise independent capacity. Arrangements for the modalities of monitoring mechanisms at the disposal of the body, for professional secretariat services and for the legal effect of the findings made by the body differ, but the normative nature of human rights monitoring is the same across the board.

The notion of 'monitoring' is here used as a general characterisation of the common task of normative assessment performed by treaty-based human rights courts or expert bodies. The treaties in question, or the bodies established by those treaties, may use other concepts when referring to the activity in question. For instance, Article 19 of the European Convention on Human Rights (ECHR) entrusts the European Court of Human Rights with the task 'to ensure the observance of the engagements undertaken by the High Contracting Parties in the Convention and the Protocols thereto.' The Court itself often uses the more far-reaching notion of 'supervision' as a characterization of its function in respect of states and their authorities.[4] Generally speaking, the United Nations human rights treaties are more ambiguous in the sense that they avoid any general characterisation of the function of the independent expert bodies established under them.[5] However, the term 'monitoring' has become the most widely used one in academic scholarship.[6]

Roughly speaking, the monitoring functions of independent expert bodies established under human rights treaties can be divided into two forms of applying a normative grid over a set of facts: assessing laws, practices or situations *in abstracto* for the purpose of addressing their *compatibility* with human rights, and dealing *in concreto* with the case of an alleged victim of a human rights *violation*.

---

[4] See, eg: EurCtHR (GC Judgment of 13 February 2003) in the case of *Refah Partisi (Welfare Party) and Others v Turkey*, para 100.

[5] For instance, in the CCPR and its two Optional Protocols expressions such as 'consider' and 'examine' are used when referring to the functions of the Human Rights Committee.

[6] Reference can be made to book titles such as: P Alston and J Crawford (eds), *The Future of UN Human Rights Treaty Monitoring* (New York, Cambridge University Press, 2000); G Alfredsson et al (eds), *International Human Rights Monitoring Mechanisms* (The Hague, Martinus Nijhoff Publishers, 2001); and J Symonides (ed), *Human Rights: International Protection, Monitoring, Enforcement* (UNESCO Publishing 2003).

b) Human Rights Monitoring in Abstracto

The first-mentioned version of monitoring is applied under all six major United Nations human rights treaties that have been ratified by all 25 EU Member States.[7] This means also that EU Member States are subject to monitoring by the six expert bodies established under the treaties, through their respective reporting procedures. The end result of a reporting cycle is a set of country-specific Concluding Observations where the treaty body in question applies the normative grid of the treaty in respect of the factual information covered by the State Party report and its oral consideration before the treaty body.[8] Typically, the normative conclusions are categorised as 'positive aspects,' situations of 'concern' or instances of 'incompatibility.'

Similar monitoring occurs under the 185 conventions so far adopted within the International Labour Organization. Many of the ILO conventions overlap with the provisions of the EU Charter of Fundamental Rights. There is no need to give a detailed account of the ratification practice of EU Member States under ILO conventions.[9] Here it suffices to state that these conventions are subject to a regular reporting procedure that includes a normative assessment by a Committee of Experts, in the form of country-specific Individual Observations.

Comparable reporting procedures exist under certain Council of Europe treaties, notably the European Social Charter (ESC) and the Framework Convention on National Minorities. All EU Member States are parties either to the 1961 European Social Charter or the Revised European Social Charter of 1996 and hence subject to the reporting procedure under the ESC. A specific feature of the ESC framework is that the available complaint procedure is one of collective and not individual complaints, leading to an assessment of whether there is 'unsatisfactory application' of the ESC in a state party.[10] For this reason, the complaints procedure also comes close to an *in abstracto* assessment. Only 40 per cent of EU Member States have accepted the procedure for collective

---

[7] See http://www.ohchr.org/english/bodies/docs/RatificationStatus.pdf (1 October 2004). The six treaties in question are the International Convention on the Elimination of All Forms of Racial Discrimination (CERD), the International Covenant on Economic, Social and Cultural Rights (CESCR), the International Covenant on Civil and Political Rights (CCPR), the Convention on the Elimination of All Forms of Discrimination against Women (CEDAW), the Convention against Torture and Other Cruel, Inhuman or Degrading Treatment or Punishment (CAT) and the Convention on the Rights of the Child (CRC). None of the EU Member States have ratified the seventh UN human rights treaty, the 1990 International Convention on the Protection of the Rights of All Migrant Workers and Members of Their Families.

[8] In its consideration of a report, a treaty body makes use of a wide range of independent sources of information, such as reports and submissions by national and international non-governmental organisations.

[9] The 2003 Synthesis Report by the Network includes, as Annex 2, a ratification chart for 25 EU Member States and 12 ILO Conventions identified as having particular relevance related to the Charter.

[10] Art 1 of the Additional Protocol to the European Social Charter Providing for a System of Collective Complaints (1995, CETS No 158).

complaints which strengthens the modalities of international monitoring.[11] The end result of the monitoring by the European Committee of Social Rights on state reports is called Conclusions and, respectively, Decisions on the Merits as for collective complaints.

Also, the Advisory Committee, under the Framework Convention for the Protection of National Minorities, produces country-specific Opinions as the outcome of the reporting procedure. The FCNM has been ratified by three quarters of the EU Member States, this meaning that six Member States[12] are not bound by the substantive obligations of the FCNM and not subject to the monitoring mechanism of periodic reporting.

Article 52 of the European Convention on Human Rights provides for an inquiry procedure under which a Contracting Party shall:

> furnish an explanation of the manner in which its internal law ensures the effective implementation of any of the provisions of the Convention.

Potentially, but with little application so far, this provision would enable a normative *in abstracto* assessment of the laws and practices of states.[13] To some extent this is true also for the inter-state complaints mechanism under Article 33 of the ECHR, which speaks of an alleged 'breach' of the Convention, instead of using the notion of a 'violation' as Article 34 which relates to individual applications by persons with victim status.[14]

c) Human Rights Monitoring *in Concreto*

Procedures for individual complaints form the second main method of human rights monitoring by judicial or otherwise independent expert bodies. Through them, the bodies in question make a determination whether there has been a human rights violation *in concreto,* in respect of an identified individual or group of individuals as victims of that violation. The European Convention on Human Rights is, of course, the prime example of this method of monitoring. All EU Member States have ratified the ECHR, although not every one of them has ratified all of its Protocols.

---

[11] Belgium, Cyprus, Finland, France, Greece, Ireland, Italy, Portugal, Slovenia and Sweden; see ratifications and declarations available at http://conventions.coe.int/Treaty/EN/v3MenuTraites.asp.

[12] Belgium, France, Greece, Latvia, Luxembourg and the Netherlands.

[13] Efforts have been made to use ECHR Art 52 in order to monitor the human rights situation in Chechnya/the Russian Federation, but, at least so far, without much success. See *Consolidated report containing an analysis of the correspondence between the Secretary General of the Council of Europe and the Russian Federation under Art 52 of the European Convention on Human Rights,* prepared by Mr T Bán, Mr F Sudre and Mr P Van Dijk, SG/Inf (2000)24. Some of the conclusions made by the three experts were that the Secretary General had made legitimate and appropriate use of his power under Art 52 of the ECHR and that the Russian Federation had failed in its legal obligations as a Contracting State under Art 52.

[14] Note also that the admissibility criteria are different for the two categories of complaints. Inter-state complaints are subject only to the requirements of Art 35, para 1, whereas individual applications must meet the more demanding admissibility requirements of paras 2 and 3.

Brief reference was already made to the collective complaints procedure under the ESC. Similar mechanisms exist also under ILO conventions.

Of the six major UN human rights treaties mentioned above, four are monitored through procedures for individual complaints, that is, CCPR, CERD, CAT and CEDAW. Most EU Member States have accepted even these procedures for individual complaints.[15] The exceptions are as follows: Estonia, Latvia and the United Kingdom have accepted only one of the four available complaint procedures, these being the CCPR for Estonia and Latvia and the CAT for the UK. Lithuania allows for complaints under the CCPR and the CEDAW but not under CERD or CAT. Greece has not accepted the complaints procedure under the CERD, Malta not under the CEDAW and Slovenia not under the CAT.

In addition to providing access to justice on the international level the complaint procedures under human rights treaties are extremely relevant as a form of normative assessment of the conduct of States Parties under the treaty. Human rights law is defined and developed through the sedimentation of jurisprudence, which greatly assists the application of the normative grid of the same provisions in the procedures for assessment *in abstracto*.

d) Subsidiary Functions of Human Rights Monitoring Bodies

Some of the human rights treaties referred to above also provide for independent fact-finding mechanisms through procedures of inquiry or country visits. For the purpose of human rights treaty monitoring, these functions should be seen as subsidiary ones. They provide for independent, direct fact-finding in order to assist the expert body in question in its normative assessment under the provisions of the treaty. An inquiry procedure exists under the CAT[16] and CEDAW,[17] and the Advisory Committee under the FCNM has developed a practice of country visits.[18] Also the European Court of Human Rights makes

---

[15] As reflected in the chart maintained by the Office of the High Commissioner for Human Rights as of 1 October 2004, including ratifications that will enter into force during 2004. See http://www.ohchr.org/english/bodies/docs/RatificationStatus.pdf.

[16] CAT Art 20.

[17] Art 8 of the Optional Protocol to the CEDAW (1999).

[18] On the FCNM website, the practice of country visits is described as follows: 'With respect to various working methods designed over the first years of its operation, perhaps the most important step was the introduction of country-visits by the relevant working groups of the Advisory Committee as a customary element of the monitoring procedure. The Advisory Committee visited Albania, Armenia, Austria, Azerbaijan, Bosnia and Herzegovina, Bulgaria, Cyprus, Croatia, Czech Republic, Denmark, Estonia, Finland, Germany, Hungary, Ireland, Italy, Lithuania, Moldova, Norway, Poland, Romania, the Russian Federation, Serbia and Montenegro, Slovakia, Slovenia, Sweden, Switzerland, 'the former Yugoslav Republic of Macedonia', Ukraine, and the United Kingdom.' Available at: http://www.coe.int/T/E/human_rights/minorities/1._GENERAL_PRESENTATION/Overview%20E.asp (31 October 2004).

fact-finding visits in the course of its consideration of a case, including by hearing witnesses within the country concerned.[19]

The European Convention for the Prevention of Torture and Inhuman or Degrading Treatment or Punishment (CPT) is a special case among human rights treaties, as it does not include substantive normative provisions but, instead, is built on the idea of country visits as a preventive mechanism. As a consequence, direct fact-finding has more than a subsidiary role in the operation of the CPT. Nevertheless, the operation of the respective CPT-Committee should be understood as applying a normative grid over the facts that are established, albeit the applicable normative standards in question are not spelled out in the text of the treaty.[20] Instead, the CPT-Committee itself codifies, through periodic updating, its understanding of applicable standards.[21]

e) Law and Policy in Human Rights Treaty Monitoring

Although the essence of the monitoring function of independent expert bodies established under human rights treaties is in normative (legal) assessment of the law and practice of a state party, there are differences in degree as to how much restraint a body exercises in confining itself to the judicial or quasi-judicial application of the law, or whether it proceeds from a normative assessment to the issuing of a policy recommendation on what measures should be taken to remedy the human rights violation or otherwise alleviate the concern expressed on normative grounds. As a general assessment of such differences it is asserted that the closer a body is to a genuine court, the more careful it tends to be in practice to restrict itself to the judicial resolution of the legal issue. The European Court of Human Rights establishes through interpretation the applicable law under the ECHR, proceeds to the determination whether there has been a violation of the Convention in respect of the applicant and finally pronounces on the grounds and amounts for just satisfaction to be paid by the state in question. In this strictly judicial variant of monitoring, or 'supervision,' the Court leaves it for the Committee of Ministers of the Council of Europe to oversee that the state in question not only complies with its obligation to pay the just satisfaction ordered by the Court, but that it also makes the necessary changes in its law and practice in order to prevent similar violations in the future.[22]

---

[19] See, eg: Press release (No 528) issued by the Registrar on 24 October 2003, *Fact-finding missions in the case of Shamayev and Others v Georgia and Russia*, available at: http://www.echr.coe.int/eng/press/2003/oct/fact%2Dfindingmissionshamayev.htm.

[20] In CPT Art 10, para 1, the mandate of the CPT-Committee is spelled out as follows: 'After each visit, the Committee shall draw up a report on the facts found during the visit, taking account of any observations which may have been submitted by the Party concerned. It shall transmit to the latter its report containing any recommendations it considers necessary.'

[21] See *The CPT standards*, CPT/Inf/E (2002) 1—Rev 2004, available at: http://www.cpt.coe.int/en/documents/eng-standards-scr.pdf.

[22] According to Art 46 of the ECHR ratifying states 'undertake to abide by the final judgment of the Court' and the Committee of Ministers 'shall supervise its execution.'

The United Nations human rights treaty bodies, in turn, consider periodic reports by states, and some of them consider individual complaints as well. There is no political body of the United Nations that would under the treaties be entrusted with the implementation or enforcement of the findings made by the treaty bodies.[23] In practice, for instance, the Human Rights Committee operating under the CCPR tends, in its Final Views on individual cases, to move from the establishment of violations of the Covenant, to a declaration that the state party in question has pursuant to Article 2, paragraph 3, of the Covenant a legally binding obligation to afford an effective remedy, and then to the Committee's view on what the remedy should be in the concrete case.[24] The concluding observations issued by UN human rights treaty bodies in the consideration of periodic reports by states go even further in combining a normative operation of legal interpretation with a policy recommendation. For instance, the concluding observations by the Human Rights Committee are systematically structured so as first to include a paragraph that expresses a concern or establishes a finding of incompatibility as a matter of interpretation and then to make a recommendation on the steps the state party should take to improve its implementation of the CCPR.[25]

III. THE EU NETWORK OF INDEPENDENT EXPERTS AS A MONITORING BODY

In the light of the above account of monitoring mechanisms existing under human rights treaties one may ask what purpose is being served by a separate EU Network of Independent Experts on Fundamental Rights. The normative grid to be applied by the Network is the EU Charter on Fundamental Rights, reflecting the norms enshrined in European and international human rights treaties. To a large extent the Network can build its findings upon the pronouncements by human rights treaty bodies on the laws, practices and individual grievances in EU Member States. Therefore, one may ask whether the

---

[23] The CESCR forms a special case, since originally the Arts 16–22 of the Covenant entrusted a political body, the Economic and Social Council, with the task of considering state party reports. The independent expert body, the Committee on Economic, Social and Cultural Rights, was established only later on, through a resolution by the ECOSOC (1985/17). Potentially this resolution would allow that ECOSOC would play, under Arts 21 and 22 of the Covenant, a role of political enforcement in relation to the findings made by the CESCR Committee.

[24] See M Scheinin, 'The Human Rights Committee's Pronouncements on the Right to an Effective Remedy—an Illustration of the Legal Nature of the Committee's Work under the Optional Protocol' in N Ando (ed), *Towards Implementing Universal Human Rights: Festschrift for the Twenty-fifth Anniversary of the Human Rights Committee* (Leiden, Martinus Nijhoff, 2004) pp 101–115.

[25] See, eg: *Concluding observations on the Dominican Republic*, CCPR/CO/71/DOM: '13. The Committee is seriously concerned at the statement in paragraph 78 of the report that applications for habeas corpus are heard weeks or months after receipt. This is incompatible with Article 9 of the Covenant. The State party should take prompt action to enable the courts to rule on the legality of detentions as quickly as possible.'

work of the Network is merely repetitive in respect of treaty-based human rights monitoring mechanisms.

It is submitted that the Network has added value, as compared to the monitoring performed under human rights treaties, due to a number of factors:

(1) The scope of the Charter is broader than that of human rights treaties, even taken together. Articles 18, 36–38, 41–44 and 46 do not have direct counterparts in the treaties adopted within the United Nations, Council of Europe or ILO. This means that one of the benefits of the operation of the Network is that it applies a richer normative grid than what is available through international human rights treaties.

(2) The nature of the Charter as a comprehensive catalogue of the fundamental rights of all members of society, within a single document, is unique. There are wide human rights treaties applicable in respect of a category of persons, such as children. And there are human rights treaties that apply to the benefit of all persons subject to the jurisdiction of a state. But no treaty applicable in respect of EU Member States combines these two features. Consequently, the principle of interdependence and indivisibility of all human/fundamental rights can, under the Charter, be taken further, as a principle of law, than under any human rights treaty. In its work the Network has sought systematically to read the requirements of the EU Charter in accordance with international and European human rights law, even where this is not explicitly required by the Charter itself. Nevertheless, the mere fact that the EU Charter is broader in scope than any one of existing human rights treaties takes it beyond the approach of duplicating the monitoring that is taking place through the separate mechanisms established under human rights treaties.[26]

(3) The nature of the Charter as an agreed common normative grid in respect of all 25 EU Member States remedies certain problems that arise under human rights treaties due to differences in the ratification patterns of states or due to reservations by some of them. For instance:

a) Articles 21 and 22 of the Charter are applicable in respect of all 25 Member States, although Belgium, France, Greece, Latvia, Luxembourg and the Netherlands have not ratified the Framework Convention for the Protection of National Minorities and France has a (questionable) reservation to article 27 of the CCPR.

b) Articles 15, 25–35 of the Charter are fully applicable in respect to all 25 Member States although most of them have accepted only a part of the provisions of the European Social Charter.

---

[26] Already in its first annual report the Network described its method of 'indexing' the EU Charter by interpreting it against the background of all relevant human rights treaties; see EU Network of Independent Experts in Fundamental Rights, *Report of the Situation of Fundamental Rights in the European Union and its Member States in 2002*, pp 21–24, available at: http://europa.eu.int/comm/justice_home/cfr_cdf/doc/rapport_2002_en.pdf.

(4) Furthermore, the nature of the Charter as a regional set of standards gives added value to monitoring by a body of independent experts from the same region and with in-depth knowledge of all the legal systems within the region. This situation results in a well-informed comparative approach in making assessments.[27]

(5) The Charter is fully applicable not only in respect to Member States but also for the EU institutions, whereas, at least for the time being, the monitoring mechanisms under human rights treaties procedurally apply only in respect to states and is then substantively subject to considerable restraint what comes to holding states accountable for their conduct within or through an international organisation.

IV. OUTLINE OF RESPECTIVE SPHERES OF COMPETENCE OF THE AGENCY AND THE NETWORK

Already the Brussels European Council stressed the importance of 'human rights data collection and analysis' for the purpose of 'defining Union policy in this field' as the rationale for creating a Human Rights Agency. The formulation used did not make a choice between, as one alternative, focusing on Member States and Union institutions, and the second alternative of primarily addressing the human rights situation in other countries. However, the genesis of the idea of a Human Rights Agency and also the later decision to create the Human Rights Agency by extending the mandate of the European Monitoring Centre on Racism and Xenophobia suggested that an internal focus would be the starting-point. Against this background it is logical that the Commission Communication uses the notion of a Fundamental Rights Agency and proposes a mandate that excludes functions related to third countries.[28]

Judging on the basis of the Commission Communication, the Agency will be an entity that collects and analyses data for the purpose of contributing towards the formulation of policy in the field of fundamental rights. According to the communication, it will carry out:

---

[27] In the Network's *Report on the Situation of Fundamental Rights in the European Union in 2003*, p 13, this advantage was reflected upon as follows: 'The comparison of national situations which the EU Network of Independent Experts in Fundamental Rights presents at least on an annual basis for all the rights listed in the Charter of Fundamental Rights, does not have as unique objective to identify the initiatives which [. . .] the Union could take to preserve the unity of the area of freedom, security and justice and of the internal market. Such a comparison also has another function to perform, where the Union does not have the required competences to react to emerging divergences between the Member States in the field of fundamental rights and where the comparison does not indicate a clear risk of a serious breach of fundamental rights which could justify the use of Article 7(1) EU. Indeed, the comparison could be an occasion for mutual learning, by the sharing of experiences which it makes possible and more systematic.'

[28] Commission Communication, see n 2 above, p 8.

Highly technical, scientific or administrative tasks defined in the instrument setting it up and it will have no decision-making powers.[29]

In the same connection, the task of the Agency is described as one of 'providing support' for EU institutions, Member States and civil society.

In a separate section of the communication, the Commission presents the tasks of the Agency as follows:

a) Data Collection and Analysis.

The Agency's 'principal task' is defined as the collection and analysis of objective, reliable and comparable data at European level. According to the Commission, data should be collected 'in cooperation with,' inter alia, Member States, NGOs, national human rights institutions and Council of Europe. In this connection, the Network is referred to as 'an important source of information.'[30] This reference represents a fundamental misunderstanding of what human rights/fundamental rights monitoring is, by forgetting its main dimension of normative assessment and reducing it to collection of information. Thereafter the communication moves to describing an 'active'[31] and a 'passive'[32] approach to data collection by the Agency, without expressing a preference.

b) Opinions and Views Intended for the EU Institutions and Member States.

This task of the Agency is described by the Commission in three lines of text, merely indicating that the Agency would set outs its analyses in such opinions, presented in the form of published reports or otherwise.[33]

c) A Communications and Dialogue Strategy.

This third task of the Agency would be one of dissemination through the publication of reviews, information bulletins, studies, a website and a database.[34]

This suggested mandate of the Agency, based on the primacy of data collection and leaning towards the Agency being also in its 'opinions' an 'observatory' rather than a genuine monitoring entity making a normative assessment of law and practice, leaves plenty of room for the continued operation of the Network.

---

[29] Commission Communication, see n 2 above, p 4.
[30] *Ibid* p 8.
[31] Through data collection mechanisms set up by the Agency itself. Commission Communication, n 2 above, p 8.
[32] Through reports compiled by the EU institutions and Member States. *Ibid.*
[33] *Ibid* p 9.
[34] *Ibid.*

The rationale for the Network is quite different from the one planned for the Agency. The mandate of the Network is typical for a human rights *monitoring* body, adjusted to the role of the EU Charter of Fundamental Rights as the applicable set of standards. On the basis of information from various sources, independent experts acting in their individual capacity make a *normative* assessment on the compatibility of the law and practice of Member States and Union institutions with the EU Charter on Fundamental Rights which in turn reflects the legally binding treaty norms accepted by Member States through their ratification of a number of international human rights treaties, notably those adopted within the auspices of either the Council of Europe or the United Nations. Such a monitoring function is primarily one of legal assessment of complex information against the normative grid of human rights/fundamental rights norms. In such assessment, the ability of an independent expert body to formulate a position as to the compatibility or lack of compatibility of a law, practice or situation with applicable human rights/fundamental rights norms is an end in itself. The monitoring may not necessarily strive towards a policy recommendation as to what should be changed in order to reach compatibility. The Network does engage itself in issuing such recommendations, for instance in the form of identifying 'best practices' that are in place in some Member States and by recommending that other states follow those examples. Nevertheless, the value of monitoring by independent experts cannot be reduced to the formulation of policy recommendations.

The composition of the Network reflects its function of independent monitoring. Among the members of the Network there are persons who serve or have served on a human rights treaty body of the United Nations,[35] as an ombudsperson or judge in an international setting,[36] as a national ombudsperson, constitutional court judge or legal adviser to such entities,[37] as a member of the Venice Commission[38] or as ad hoc judge of the European Court of Human Rights.[39] Such a combination of relevant background experience gives the Network a capacity to address, in an objective and non-selective manner, the laws and practices in 25 Member States as well at the EU level, at the same time remaining conscious of the practice of a number of international or national bodies with similar functions.

---

[35] Morten Kjærum (CERD), Martin Scheinin (CCPR), Linos-Alexandre Sicilianos (CERD).

[36] Manfred Nowak (Human Rights Chamber of Bosnia-Herzegovina), Marek Antoni Nowicki (Kosovo ombudsperson), Pavel Sturma (Permanent Court of Arbitration). MA Nowicki is also a former member of the European Commission of Human Rights.

[37] Elvira Baltutyte, Lauri Mälksoo, Arne-Marjan Mavcic, Vital Moreira.

[38] Vital Moreira.

[39] Ineta Ziemele. Dean Spielmann, a previous member of the Network, is now a full-time judge of the European Court of Human Rights. Some other Network members have been on the national list of three candidates for the position of judge of the European Court of Human Rights and have been recognised by the Committee on Legal Affairs and Human Rights at the Parliamentary Assembly of Council of Europe, as meeting the required qualifications.

The current tasks of the Network have been described as follows:

- To draft an annual report of the state of fundamental rights in the European Union and its Member States, assessing the application of each of the rights set out in the EU Charter of Fundamental Rights.
- To provide the Commission with specific information and opinions on fundamental rights issues, when requested.
- To assist the Commission and the Parliament in developing European Union policy on fundamental rights.[40]

As indicated above, the rationale of the Network does not depend on whether its normative assessment leads to policy recommendations. Therefore the third task mentioned above is to be seen as subordinate to the primary task of monitoring Member States and EU institutions as to the human rights compatibility of their action.

The reporting by the Network should not be seen primarily as collection of data. Of course, data needs to be collected before the Network and its individual members can compile annual reports on law and practice. But the main task of the Network is one of normative assessment of that data on the basis of the Charter. This is not only true for the first task of the Network to prepare annual reports on the state of fundamental rights in the EU and its Member States, but also what comes to the second task of providing, upon request, 'specific information and opinions.' This task is performed by producing, outside the cycle of annual reports, opinions on topical issues.[41] While there might be some overlap between this function of the Network and the envisaged but so far unspecified role of the Agency in delivering 'opinions,' the differences in the overall design of the two institutions will most likely result in that the opinions by the Network will continue to emanate from a normative expert assessment under the EU Charter, whereas the opinions issued by the Agency will pertain to the field of policy. As demonstrated above with reference to the work of the UN human rights treaties the fact that an independent expert body primarily performs a task of normative assessment is not an obstacle for it also expressing recommendations on policy, as long as any such recommendations flow directly from a normative finding made through interpreting the applicable standards.

In addition to this fundamental difference between the tasks of the Network and the planned mandate of the Agency, there appear to be a number of further differences. According to the Commission Communication, the Agency will be required to 'monitor' fundamental rights 'by area' and not to prepare reports by country.[42] If this position will be adopted in the final design of the Agency, the need for country-specific reports alone will justify the separate continued existence of the Network. Further, in the light of the Commission Communication, it is by no means clear that the mandate of the Agency would

---

[40] Taken from http://europa.eu.int/comm/justice_home/cfr_cdf/index_en.htm#.

[41] For issued opinions, see http://europa.eu.int/comm/justice_home/cfr_cdf/list_opinions_en.htm.

[42] Commission Communication, n 2 above, p 5.

cover the full spectrum of fundamental rights, as reflected in the Charter. Although such a broad catalogue of fundamental rights is presented as one available option in defining the mandate of the Agency, the Commission Communication also puts forward another option, according to which the Agency's work would be focused on 'such thematic areas that have special connections with Community policies or the Union.'[43]

According to the Commission Communication, the Agency will not have the quasi-judicial power of some national human rights institutions to receive and consider complaints or petitions.[44] This is logical in the light of the mandate and functions of the Agency. It would, however, be fully compatible with its nature as a monitoring organ if the Network were to develop a complaints mechanism, either as a device for seeking information on laws or practices that should be assessed in the annual reports, or as a separate quasi-judicial decision-making procedure to address individual cases. To be clear, no such proposal of the Network starting to deal with complaints has been made so far.[45]

A further demarcation line in the respective competencies of the Agency and the Network will need to be drawn in relation to Article 7 EU which requires that Member States, also when they are not acting under EU law, do not breach the principles of liberty, democracy, respect for human rights and fundamental freedoms, and the rule of law. It is clear that one of the ultimate justifications for the existence of the Network lies in its systematic, non-selective and long-term monitoring of human/fundamental rights compliance by Member States. The series of annual reports on a particular Member State would be an indispensable tool if a situation were to arise where it is suggested that, and it will need to be verified whether, there is a clear risk of a serious breach of the principle of respect for human rights by a Member State.

As to the competencies of the Agency in respect of Article 7 EU, the Commission Communication gives two options. The first option would be to define the mandate of the Agency on the basis of EU law, so that Member States would be subject to its monitoring only when they are acting within the scope of EU law.[46] As stated in the Communication, such delimitation would have the advantage of avoiding duplication with the work by other bodies acting at international and national levels. The disadvantage, however, would be that even Article 7 EU would come into play only as far as the possible breach is related to the conduct of a Member State in the field of EU law.

---

[43] Commission Communication, n 2 above, p 7, where the following list of spheres is given: 'immigration, asylum, non-discrimination, ethical questions, guarantee of criminal proceedings, violence etc.'

[44] *Ibid* p 4.

[45] But see: the Network's *Report on the Situation of Fundamental Rights in the European Union in 2003*, n 27 above, p 142, where the possibility is mentioned that the deliberations and proposals by the Agency could be inspired by the content of the complaints or petitions that are lodged before other bodies where they are concerned with structural problems going beyond the case of the individual petitioner.

[46] Commission Communication, n 2 above, pp 5–6.

The second option presented in the Commission Communication is that the Agency would generally, and not only in respect of EU law, serve as 'an early warning instrument' in respect of situations covered by Article 7 EU. While not rejecting this option, the Communication nevertheless refers to considerable overlap with other mechanisms, including those of the Council of Europe, as a resulting disadvantage. In the light of the other proposed delimitations, such as that the Agency would 'monitor' developments in an area and not in individual countries and that in respect of Article 7 it would:

> in any event be required only to provide institutions with the expertise that allows them to base their decisions on reliable and objective data[47]

it cannot be expected to have a meaningful role in the assessment to be made under Article 7 EU, if modelled along the lines of the Commission Communication. On the basis of its independent status, its current tasks and its institutional memory being accumulated before the Agency is fully operative, the Network will be much better placed as an early warning mechanism under Article 7.

In its 2003 EU Report, the Network cites a Commission Communication on Article 7 EU and reflects upon its own role in relation to Article 7 as follows:

> The communication which the Commission presented to the Council and the European Parliament on Article 7 EU, 'Respect for and promotion of the values on which the Union is based,'[48] identifies the two missions which the EU Network of Independent Experts in Fundamental Rights can fulfil, in the specific context of that Article. First, the Network may contribute to 'detect fundamental rights anomalies or situations where there might be breaches or the risk of breaches of these rights falling within Article 7 of the Union Treaty': this is the monitoring function of the Network. Second, the Network can 'help in finding solutions to remedy confirmed anomalies or to prevent potential breaches': this is its recommendation function.[49]

Last but definitely not least, the Agency and the Network are clearly different entities as to their degree of independence. The Network currently operates on a contractual basis and is constituted of independent fundamental rights experts serving in their individual capacity. The Agency, in turn, would be a separate juridical person but nevertheless an entity of the EU. The Commission Communication is internally contradictory as to the degree of independence proposed for the Agency. On the one hand, it is stated that the Agency 'must be independent of all those with whom it will come into contact'[50] which is then specified as the Commission, European Parliament, Council, Member States and 'civil society' [*sic*]. But on the other hand it is suggested almost immediately thereafter that 'representatives appointed by' the Commission, the European Parliament, the Member States and Council of Europe would 'participate' in the management bodies of the Agency.

[47] *Ibid* p 6.
[48] COM (2003) 606 final, of 15 October 2003.
[49] The Network's *Report on the Situation of Fundamental Rights in the European Union in 2003*, n 27 above, p 10.
[50] Commission Communication on the Fundamental Rights Agency, n 2 above, p 10.

These formulations support the contention that also after the establishment of the Agency there will be room and need for independent fundamental rights monitoring by a group of independent experts. In fact, there appears to be a need to *strengthen* the independence of the Network as distinct from the political institutions of the EU, rather than transforming its monitoring function to the Agency. In this respect, it is of more than anecdotal interest that although the Commission maintains the internet pages of the Network and although it is announced on the Commission website that the national reports produced by the Network will be, as of January 2004, available there,[51] by 31 October 2004 the national reports have not yet been put on the Commission website. Instead, they so far appear, with an appropriate disclaimer,[52] on the website of the Interdisciplinary Research Cell in Human Rights (CRIDHO) at the Catholic University of Louvain (UCL).[53] The LIBE-Committee section of the website of the European Parliament, however, does include a link to the CRIDHO website.[54]

If seen as a monitoring mechanism similar to judicial and quasi-judicial bodies operating under human rights treaties, the continued existence of the Network is clearly justified also after the establishment of the Agency. If the distribution of tasks between the Agency and the Network is made clear at the outset, there arises a need to develop the methods of work and activities of the Network so that they enhance its role as a monitoring body. This may entail, for example, a transparent procedure for appointing the members of the network on the basis of their qualifications to serve as independent fundamental rights experts, as well as the greater involvement than until now of the Network as a collective body in the normative assessment made in the annual reports on individual Member States.

V. OPTIONS AS REGARDS INSTITUTIONAL LINKS BETWEEN THE AGENCY AND THE NETWORK

Finally, there is plenty of room for coordination and cooperation between the Agency and the Network. This issue should be discussed on the basis of three alternative models.

---

[51] 'From 2004, the national reports drafted by each network expert will be available on this website. The reports will be available in each expert's language and will be published on the website in January each year.' Available at: http://europa.eu.int/comm/justice_home/cfr_cdf/index_en.htm.

[52] This disclaimer states: 'The EU Network of Independent Experts on Fundamental Rights has been set up by the European Commission upon request of the European Parliament. It monitors the situation of fundamental rights in the Member States and in the Union, on the basis of the Charter of Fundamental Rights. It issues reports on the situation of fundamental rights in the Member States and in the Union, as well as opinions on specific issues related to the protection of fundamental rights in the Union. The content of this opinion does not bind the European Commission. The Commission accepts no liability whatsoever with regard to the information contained in this document.'

[53] Available at: http://www.cpdr.ucl.ac.be/cridho/index.php (under 'Online Documentation').

[54] Available at: http://www.europarl.eu.int/comparl/libe/elsj/charter/default_en.htm.

a) Loose Cooperation.

The Agency and the Network can both be developed on the basis of respecting their independent existence and autonomous spheres of competence. Even in this model there is a need for developing regular and institutionalised forms for the exchange of information, as well as specific forms of cooperation, such as joint conferences, on an ad hoc basis. An annual event for the publication of the reports by the Network would be an obvious form of regular cooperation.

b) Close Cooperation.

Another option is to strive towards clearly defined but mutually dependent spheres of competence. The key to such a solution is in the recognition of data collection and analysis as the core function of the Agency, whereas the rationale of the Network is in systematic normative assessment through annual reports and also upon request on a thematic basis. Much of the data to be used by the Network for performing the normative assessment could be collected and analysed by the Agency. Here, it would be for the Agency to represent scientific expertise in the areas of sociology, economics and statistics in the collection and compilation of data, whereas the legal expertise related to normative assessment would be centred in the Network. The identification, development and use of indicators for addressing compliance with the Charter could be a joint exercise for the two entities, bringing together scientific expertise in all relevant disciplines. The Agency could also have a role in disseminating the annual reports and thematic comments by the Network and in utilising them in training activities. Institutional links could be established through the Network being represented by an observer or adviser on the management board of the Agency and the Agency in turn through an observer within the Network.

c) Institutional Merger.

A third option is to transform the Network of Independent Experts on Fundamental Rights into a panel of independent experts operating as a part of the institutional structure of the Agency. In order to preserve its role as an independent monitoring body, the Network should not have management functions. In order to recognise its specific function of normative assessment, the Network should not be transformed into a Scientific Committee[55] of the Agency, such a scientific body necessarily representing also empirical social sciences. It remains to be seen whether the EU institutions and Member States are prepared to accept that the Agency would host an expert body with sufficient independence and

---

[55] See Commission Communication, n 2 above, p 11.

qualifications needed to make it an entity of genuine fundamental rights monitoring in the normative sense of the term.

Whatever is the chosen option, it should be understood that the EU Network of Independent Experts in Fundamental Rights would have a useful and distinct role also after the establishment of the Fundamental Rights Agency. Therefore, the establishment of the Agency should be seen as a historical opportunity for providing the Network with an adequate legal basis. Furthermore, the Agency should be encouraged to make use of the annual reports and other documents issued by the Network not only as one source of information but as normative assessments provided by a group of independent experts.

4

The Agency and National Institutions for the Promotion and Protection of Human Rights

MANFRED NOWAK*

I. INTRODUCTION

THERE ARE, IN principle, two ways that the establishment of an EU Human Rights/Fundamental Rights Agency[1] can be related to national institutions for the promotion and protection of human rights, as spelled out in the *Paris Principles* of the United Nations[2] and later

---

* Co-director of the Ludwig Boltzmann Institute for Human Rights in Vienna, Chairperson of the European Master's Degree in Human Rights and Democratization, and member of the EU Network of Independent Experts in Fundamental Rights.

[1] The European Council on 13 December 2003 decided to 'build upon the existing European Monitoring Centre on Racism and Xenophobia and to extend its mandate to become a Human Rights Agency to that effect.' When the Commission on 25 October 2004 presented its *Communication on the Agency* (COM(2004) 693 final), it simply changed the term 'Human Rights Agency' into 'Fundamental Rights Agency' and explained in fn 2 that for the purposes of this text, the expressions 'fundamental rights' and 'human rights' carry the same meaning. In legal terms, the expression 'human rights' usually refers to international law and the term 'fundamental rights' to domestic constitutional law; See M Nowak, *Introduction to the International Human Rights Regime* (Leiden/Boston, Martinus Nijhoff, 2003) p 4. Art 6 of the EU Treaty, by providing that the Union is founded on the principles of, inter alia, respect for human rights and fundamental freedoms, refers to international and European human rights law, above all to the European Convention for the Protection of Human Rights and Fundamental Freedoms (ECHR). On the other hand, the adoption of the EU Charter of Fundamental Rights in December 2000 illustrates the significance of this document as a domestic 'bill of rights' of the EU to be incorporated into a future EU Constitution. In principle, it is a question of terminology whether one refers to the Agency as Human Rights or Fundamental Rights Agency. Since the Communication of the Commission has been prepared by the DG Justice and Home Affairs, which in strong but unconvincing terms rules out any role of the Agency with respect to the external relations of the Union (ch 4.1), the suspicion arises that this change of name was intentional and carries a symbolic meaning. On this question, see also the contribution of M Bulterman, 'The Fundamental Rights Agency and the External Relations of the European Union' in ch 10 of this volume. In the following, the term Agency shall be used.

[2] Principles relating to the Status of National Institutions: See Commission on Human Rights resolution 1992/54 of 3 March 1992 and General Assembly resolution 48/134 of 20 December 1993. On the Paris Principles see, eg: United Nations, *National human rights institutions: a handbook on the*

documents.[3] Taking into account that the Union, with the recent adoption of a common Constitution for Europe,[4] which incorporates the EU Charter of Fundamental Rights of 2000, took a decisive step in its nation building endeavours, there might be a need to establish a non-judicial mechanism for the promotion and protection of human rights following the model of national human rights institutions. As Joke Swiebel, Rapporteur of the EU Parliament's Committee on Citizen's Freedoms and Rights, in a recent Working Document on the Agency suggested, 'it might be useful also to look at these types of institutions for inspiration' when it comes to designing an outline for an EU Human Rights Agency.[5] Most of the present contribution will follow this advice and analyse to what extent the Paris Principles might be a useful framework for designing the future mandate of the Agency.

The second approach builds on the experience of the *EU Monitoring Centre on Racism and Xenophobia* (EUMC). This Vienna based institution established in 1997[6] can only perform its task of monitoring the phenomena of racism and xenophobia in all 25 EU Member States by closely co-operating with so-called *national focal points* in all Member States. Since the future Agency, in the words of the European Council,[7] shall 'build upon the existing European Monitoring Centre on Racism and Xenophobia' by extending its mandate, the question arises whether the Agency will be in need of co-operation with general national human rights institutions in all EU Member States, similar to the co-operation between the EUMC and its specialised focal points. In a recent Opinion regarding the role of national institutions for the protection of human rights in the Member States of the European Union, submitted at the request of the Commission, the EU Network of Independent Experts in Fundamental Rights carried out a comparative analysis on national human rights institutions in the

---

establishment and strengthening of national institutions for the promotion and protection of human rights (New York/Geneva, 1995); Council of Europe, *Non-judicial means for the protection of human rights at the national level* (Strasbourg, 1998); Commonwealth Secretariat, *National Human Rights Institutions—Best Practice* (London, 2001); V Aichele, *Nationale Menschenrechts-institutionen in Europa* (Berlin, Deutsches Institut für Menschenrechte, 2004).

[3] See, eg: Recommendation No R(97)14 of the Committee of Ministers of the Council of Europe on the establishment of independent national institutions for the promotion and protection of human rights, adopted on 30 September 1997; General Comment 10 of the Committee on Economic, Social and Cultural Rights of 14 December 1998: *The role of national human rights institutions in the protection of economic, social and cultural rights*, UN Doc E/C.12/1998/25; Copenhagen Declaration, adopted on 13 April 2002 by the Sixth International Conference for National Institutions for the Promotion and Protection of Human Rights, held in Copenhagen and Lund, available at: http://www.nhri.net/SixthConference.htm.

[4] The Treaty establishing a Constitution for Europe (CIG 87/04) was signed on 29 October 2004 in Rome by the Heads of State or Government and Ministers of Foreign Affairs of the 25 EU Member States as well as Romania, Bulgaria and Turkey. It will be submitted to the 25 EU Member States for ratification.

[5] J Swiebel, *Working Document of 25 March 2004 on the proposal for a Council Regulation on the European Monitoring Centre on Racism and Xenophobia* (Recast version), EU Doc PE 339.635.

[6] The EUMC has been established by Council Regulation 1035/97. See its annual reports, available at: http://eumc.eu.int.

[7] See n 1 above.

Union.[8] According to this survey, 13 of the 25 EU Member States have established a national human rights institution, although it is sometimes difficult to assess whether these institutions actually comply with the Paris Principles.[9] In any case, the creation of the Agency will provide a *new impetus for EU Member States to establish a proper counter-part at the national level.*

II. FUNCTIONS OF NATIONAL INSTITUTIONS

a) In General

The idea of promoting national human rights institutions is based on the conviction that courts are only one of several mechanisms for the promotion and protection of human rights. In order to prevent future human rights violations and to establish a genuine culture of human rights, awareness-raising through human rights education and advocacy, preventive visits to places of detention, advisory services and similar *non-judicial mechanisms* seem to be as important as judicial review of alleged violations in the past. The *Vienna World Conference on Human Rights* reaffirmed the important and constructive role played by national institutions for the promotion and protection of human rights, in particular their advisory capacity to the competent authorities, their role in remedying human rights violations, their dissemination of human rights information, and education in human rights. It encouraged the establishment and strengthening of national institutions in line with the Paris Principles, and at the same time recognised that:

> it is the right of each State to choose the framework which is best suited to its particular needs at the national level.[10]

In practice, States have established a variety of different types of national human rights institutions, such as advisory committees (eg France, Greece and

---

[8] See EU Doc CFR-CDF.Opinion1.2004. The Network has been set up by the Commission upon request of the European Parliament in 2002. It monitors the situation of fundamental rights in the EU and its Member States on the basis of the EU Charter of Fundamental Rights. It issues annual reports as well as specific reports and opinions related to the protection of fundamental rights in the Union. On the relationship between the Network and the Agency see the contribution of M Scheinin in ch 3 of this volume.

[9] These States are Cyprus, the Czech Republic, Denmark, France, Germany, Greece, Ireland, Latvia, Luxembourg, Poland, Portugal, Sweden and Spain. All of these institutions with the exceptions of three (Cyprus, the Czech Republic and Latvia) have already been (semi-officially) recognised by the International Co-ordinating Committee of National Institutions for the Promotion and Protection of Human Rights, which was established in 1993 and consists of representatives of national institutions. See Aichele, n 2 above, pp 10–12; see also: http://www.nhri.net/ICCMembers.htm. But see: the contribution of O De Schutter in ch 2 of this volume, 'Mainstreaming human rights in the European Union,' who arrives at the conclusion that 14 EU Member States (including Italy, Estonia, Lithuania and the Slovak Republic) have in fact established a national institution.

[10] Para 36 of the Vienna Declaration and Programme of Action of 25 June 1993, UN Doc A/CONF.157/23. See M Nowak, *World Conference on Human Rights* (Vienna, Manz, 1994), p 168 at p 176.

Luxembourg), human rights institutes (eg Denmark, Norway and Germany), ombuds-type institutions (eg Sweden, Spain, Portugal and Poland) and national human rights commissions (eg Ireland, Bosnia and Herzegovina, Canada, Mexico, India, the Philippines, New Zealand, Uganda and South Africa).

In fact, not every national human rights institution recognised by the United Nations is entrusted with all the competences and responsibilities as provided in the Paris Principles of 1993.[11] But some of the key functions of promoting and protecting human rights as well as guarantees of independence and pluralism are essential conditions. The composition and sphere of competence shall be clearly set forth in a constitutional or legal text. The members shall be appointed in accordance with a procedure which affords all necessary guarantees to ensure the pluralist representation of civil society. In order to ensure independence from the Government, members shall be appointed by an official act which shall establish the specific duration of the mandate,[12] and the institution shall be guaranteed sufficient infrastructure (own staff and premises) and financial resources without being subject to financial control which might affect its independence. The competences and responsibilities can be summarised as follows:

1) Advisory Services

Any national institution shall have the responsibility to submit to the Government, Parliament and any other competent body, either at the request of the authorities concerned or on its own initiative, opinions, recommendations, proposals and reports on any matters concerning the promotion and protection of human rights. The national institution may decide to publish such opinions and reports. They may relate, for example, to any legislative, administrative or judicial act, to legislative bills and proposals, as well as to the factual situation of human rights in the country, including specific violations and human rights problems. The advisory function may also include the preparation of reports on the national human rights situation.

2) Co-operation with International Monitoring Bodies

Any national institution shall co-operate with the United Nations and regional organisations and institutions competent in the field of human rights. In particular, it shall encourage ratification of international and regional human rights treaties and ensure their implementation at the domestic level through all means, above all by promoting and ensuring the harmonisation of national legislation, regulations and practices with international human rights law. In

---

[11] See n 2 above.

[12] In interpreting this provision, the Commonwealth Secretariat, n 2 above, p 16, concludes that members shall be appointed for a fixed term of at least five years.

addition, national institutions shall have the responsibility of contributing to States reports to be submitted to international monitoring bodies and, where necessary, to express an opinion on the subject, with due respect for their independence.

3) *Human Rights Education and Awareness Raising*

National institutions shall assist in the formulation of programmes for the teaching of, and research into, human rights, and take part in their execution in schools, universities and professional circles. A particular focus shall be put on awareness raising and sensitivity training in the field of racial and other forms of discrimination, as well as the protection of vulnerable groups, such as children, migrant workers, refugees and persons with disabilities.

4) *Data Collection and Analysis*

In order to carry out the above-mentioned tasks, it is essential that national institutions can hear any person and obtain any information and/or any documents necessary for assessing the legal and factual situation of human rights in the country. The collection and analysis of all relevant data is a necessary precondition not only for any monitoring function, but also for advisory, co-operation and awareness raising responsibilities.

5) *Individual Complaints Procedure*

Most controversial is the competence to consider complaints and petitions concerning individual situations. Consequently, this function was laid down in 'Additional Principles concerning the Status of Commissions with Quasi-Jurisdictional Competence.' If a national institution has such a competence,[13] cases may be brought before it by individuals, their representatives, third parties, non-governmental organisations, associations of trade unions or any other representative organisations. Some national institutions are empowered to deliver binding decisions; others aim primarily at an amicable settlement through conciliation and mediation. If no amicable solution can be achieved, they may transmit the case to a court of law or other competent decision-making body. In any case the national institution shall be entitled to make recommendations to the competent authorities, including legislative proposals, on the basis of the facts established by means of individual complaints procedures.

---

[13] This is usually the case with national human rights commissions, such as Ireland, Bosnia and Herzegovina and many Commonwealth States, and with ombuds-type national institutions, such as in Sweden, Spain, Portugal and Poland. See Aichele, n 2 above, pp 20–43.

III. THE AGENCY AS A NATIONAL INSTITUTION OF THE EU?

a) The Monitoring Function

Can one apply the functions and responsibilities of national human rights institutions *per analogiam* to the future EU Agency? When the Heads of State and
Government decided in December 2003 to establish the Agency, they said very
little about its mandate. They only stressed 'the importance of human rights
data collection and analysis with a view to defining Union policy in this field,'
and agreed to extend the mandate of the EUMC to become a Human Rights
Agency to that effect. *To build upon the existing EUMC is an indicator for the
monitoring function of the Agency.* On the other hand, the European Council
deliberately deleted the word 'Monitoring' from the title of the Human Rights
Agency. When the idea of an Agency was proposed for the first time by a *Comité
des Sages*, which in 1998 prepared a Human Rights Agenda for the European
Union for the Year 2000, these four wise men and women, supported by a
research project at the European University Institute in Florence, had in mind a
Human Rights Monitoring Agency with the task of information-gathering, data
analysis and monitoring the human rights situation within the EU.[14] This idea
was taken up by the Austrian Presidency during the second half of 1998,[15] by the
Cologne European Council of June 1999,[16] and by another *Comité des Sages*,
reporting in September 2000 to the European Council on the *human rights situation in Austria* and proper ways for the EU to respond to possible human rights
problems in an EU Member State.[17]

The European Council of Nice, besides adopting the *EU Charter of
Fundamental Rights* on 7 December 2000, responded to the Austrian situation
and the proposals of the three wise men by amending Article 7 of the EU Treaty
to the effect that certain membership rights of an EU Member State may be suspended even for preventive purposes, ie, if the Council determines by a four-
fifths majority that there is a clear risk of a serious breach of fundamental rights.
Although the *new Article 7 procedure* requires effective monitoring and early
warning by an independent body,[18] neither the Commission nor the Council

[14] See Comité des Sages, consisting of Antonio Cassese, Catherine Lalumière, Peter Leuprecht
and Mary Robinson, *Leading by Example: A Human Rights Agenda for the European Union for the
Year 2000* (Florence, European University Institute, 1998), pp 7 and 10. See also: the Final Project
Report by Ph Alston and JHH Weiler, *ibid*, pp 89–96. See further Ph Alston (ed), *The EU and
Human Rights* (Oxford, Oxford University Press, 1999) pp 55–59.

[15] Despite the Austrian initiative, the idea of the Agency did not find its way into the Vienna
Declaration of 10 December 1998, adopted by the European Council on the occasion of the 50th
anniversary of the Universal Declaration of Human Rights.

[16] European Council of Cologne on 3 and 4 June 1999, Conclusions of the Presidency, para 46.

[17] Report by M Ahtisaari, J Frowein and M Oreja, adopted in Paris on 8 September 2000, available at: http://www.virtual-institute.de/en/Bericht-EU/report.pdf.

[18] See in this respect Communication of the Commission of the European Communities to the
Council and the European Parliament on Article 7 of the Treaty on the European Union, *Respect for
and promotion of the values on which the Union is based*, COM (2003) 606 final, of 15 October 2003.

were eager to further pursue the idea of an independent EU Human Rights Monitoring Agency. Of the EU institutions, only the European Parliament has supported the Agency idea from the very beginning.[19]

When the Parliament realised that the Monitoring Agency was not popular among the Commission[20] and the Council, it took the initiative of requesting the Commission to set up a less formal monitoring body. In 2002, the Commission (DG Justice and Home Affairs) responded to this request by establishing the *EU Network of Independent Experts on Fundamental Rights*, which has the function of monitoring and reporting on the situation of fundamental rights in the Union and its Member States, based on the *EU Charter of Fundamental Rights*.[21] Since this network has been operating in a truly independent manner since 2002, the question of the relationship between the Network and the Agency arises. In a contribution to the present volume, Martin Scheinin argues that true monitoring in the sense of a normative assessment of an established set of facts against the normative grid of legal obligations can better be achieved by the Network of Independent Experts than by an Agency which, as an institution of the EU, can never be fully independent.[22] This assumption seems to be supported by the experience of the EUMC, which in fact lacks the full independence necessary for a genuine monitoring body.[23] But by collecting and analysing data, the Agency could function in close co-operation with the Network.

Another issue would be the *monitoring of human rights in third countries*, such as candidate States, ACP countries and other States which have accepted a human rights clause as an essential element of their bilateral treaties with the Union. Although the Commission strongly rejects such a possibility,[24] there are good arguments in favour of such a monitoring mandate. First of all, the development and consolidation of the respect for human rights and fundamental freedoms is one of the main objectives of the Union's Common Foreign and Security Policy as well as its policy of development cooperation.[25] Secondly, the monitoring role of the EU Network of Independent Experts on Fundamental

---

[19] See Swiebel, n 5 above, p 3.

[20] See, eg: the Commission Communication of 8 May 2001, COM(2001)252 final, para 5.

[21] For the annual and special reports, as well as opinions of the Network, see http://www.europa.eu.int/comm/justice_home/cfr_cdf/index_en.htm. See also: n 8 above.

[22] See the contribution of M Scheinin, 'The Relationship between the Agency and the Network of Independent Experts,' in ch 3 of this volume.

[23] This statement is based on the experience of the author with the Austrian focal point for the EUMC.

[24] See the Commission's Communication on the EU's role in promoting human rights and democratisation in third countries of 8 May 2001, COM(2001)252 final, para 5. In its recent Communication on the Agency (see n 1 above, ch 4), the Commission argued as follows: 'Confining the Agency's scope to the Union would certainly underline the will to emphasise the importance of fundamental rights in the Union and would be an effective means of placing responsibility on its institutions in the field of fundamental rights [. . .] This message might be diluted if the Agency's remit were to be extended to third countries.' No reasoning was given to support this surprising assumption. But see: the criticism of M Bulterman, n 1 above.

[25] Arts 6, 11 and 49 EU, Art 177(2) EC, Arts 9(2) and 96 of the Cotonou Agreement of 23 June 2000 with 77 ACP States, human rights clauses in bilateral treaties etc.

Rights extends only to the situation in the EU and its Member States, but not to third countries. Thirdly, the future Agency might be more independent in monitoring the human rights situation in third countries than within the EU. Whether the Agency should publish an annual EU report on the human rights situation world-wide, as proposed by Mielle Bulterman,[26] or provide confidential information to the relevant EU institutions, seems to be a highly controversial matter, and there are indeed good reasons for keeping at least some reports and recommendations of the Agency (eg, on Article 7 matters) confidential.[27] But it seems difficult to deny the need for an independent EU monitoring of the human rights situation in the candidate and partner countries of the EU.

b) The Advisory Function

The advisory function is the main responsibility of national human rights institutes and has also been identified by the European Council for the Agency when it stressed the importance of human rights data collection and analysis 'with a view to defining Union policy in this field.'[28] As national institutions advise Governments, Parliaments and other competent bodies, the Agency should advise the Council, the Commission and the European Parliament, ie, the main political decision-making bodies of the Union. What does the European Council mean by the expression 'Union policy in this field'? The Commission suggested a fairly restricted scope of:

> thematic areas having a special connection with Community policies or the Union (immigration, asylum, non-discrimination, ethical questions, guarantee of criminal proceedings, violence etc).[29]

The Paris Principles, on the other hand, provide that a 'national institution shall be given as broad a mandate as possible.' Since the Agency will be the main EU institution in the field of human rights, and since the EU develops human rights policies in respect of a large variety of areas in its internal and external relations, it would seem to be prudent to define the Agency's advisory function in as broad terms as possible. As any well-functioning national human rights institution, the Agency should become a *think tank* which might be consulted by the main EU institutions on any relevant human rights issue, both in the internal and external relations of the Union. The range of issues on which the Agency might provide advice includes, eg, *early warnings* in relation to the preventive procedure envisaged in Article 7 EU, opinions on the fulfil-

---

[26] See Bulterman, n 1 above, p 14.

[27] There are, of course, limits to what may remain confidential. See Article 42 of the Charter of Fundamental Rights and Regulation (EC) No 1049/2001 of the European Parliament and of the Council of 30 May 2001 regarding public access to European Parliament, Council and Commission documents (OJ L 145 of 31 May 2001, p 43).

[28] See European Council, n 1 above.

[29] Commission, n 1 above, ch 3.

ment of the *Copenhagen admission criteria* in the field of human rights and minority protection vis-à-vis candidate countries, and recommendations on common positions, joint actions and bilateral human rights dialogues with third countries. Similar to any national institution, the Agency should be entrusted to provide advice on the request of the respective EU institutions as well as on its own initiative. It should also comment on draft regulations and directives in the field of human rights. The main point of reference for the Agency is certainly the *EU Charter of Fundamental Rights*, but in relation to external policies, the Agency would also have to take relevant international and regional human rights instruments into account.

c) Co-operation with International Monitoring Bodies

As long as the Union is not a party to the ECHR or any other European and international human rights treaty, there is no particular need for the Agency to co-operate with any European or international human rights monitoring body. In performing its data collection function, the Agency should, of course, also collect relevant data from human rights monitoring bodies, and in relation to its own monitoring, the Agency might build up a special working relation with such bodies, similar to the working relation between the EUMC and the Council of Europe's Commission against Racism and Intolerance (ECRI). But there is no need to contribute to the preparation of State reports or similar functions carried out by national human rights institutions.[30]

d) Human Rights Education and Awareness-raising

With the growing importance of human rights as essential element of the Union's internal and external policies, there is an increasing demand for a pre-service and in-service training of EU officials and diplomats in the field of human rights. In this respect, the Agency, similar to any national human rights institution, should play a leading and co-ordinating role. It could co-operate closely with the *European Inter-University Centre for Human Rights and Democratisation* (EIUC) in Venice, which was set up in 2002 with the active support of the European Union. In addition to organising, in co-operation with almost 40 European universities in all EU Member States, the *European Master's Degree in Human Rights and Democratisation* (EMA),[31] EIUC is in

---

[30] But see the proposals made in favour of a contribution of the Union to the compliance by the Member States with their obligations under international human rights treaties, *Report on the situation of fundamental rights in the Union in 2003*, submitted to the EU Network of Independent Experts on Fundamental Rights in January 2004, paras II.1 and II.2 of the Introduction (at pp 17–21 of the report).

[31] See http://www.ema-humanrights.org.

the process of developing a number of further teaching, training and research activities in the field of human rights.[32]

e) Data Collection and Analysis

The collection and analysis of human rights data is the only function of the Agency that was clearly spelled out in the Council decision of December 2003.[33] As with national human rights institutions, the geographic and thematic scope of the data collection is determined by the scope of its other responsibilities, above all its monitoring and advisory functions. Even if its monitoring mandate might be limited, its advisory function should be as broad as possible. This requires a comprehensive task of data collection, analysis and research. As the major human rights think tank for the EU institutions, the Agency has to develop considerable *research and documentation capacities*, similar to the national human rights institutions in Europe, such as the Danish or German Institutes of Human Rights. In this respect, the Agency might closely co-operate with relevant national human rights institutions in the EU Member States, as well as with relevant EU institutions, such as the European University Institute in Florence, the European Inter-University Centre for Human Rights and Democratisation (EIUC) in Venice, and the EU Network of Independent Experts on Fundamental Rights.

f) Individual Complaints Procedure

As stated above, the consideration of individual complaints and petitions is not an essential task of a national human rights institution. Only some of them have in fact been entrusted with such a quasi-judicial function. This is not surprising as the main reason for setting up national human rights institutions is the need to complement judicial bodies with non-judicial mechanisms. Individual complaints might not, however, necessarily lead to adjudication. Rather than deciding in a final and legally binding manner on a human rights complaint, national institutions might aim at a friendly settlement through conciliation and mediation procedures. Typical examples of these types of conflict resolution mechanisms are Ombuds-type institutions which, provided they show a strong human rights focus, are regarded as national institutions.

Should the Agency be entrusted to deal with individual complaints? Again, the Commission is very decisive in its recent Communication:

> Several national institutions also have quasi-judicial powers (dealing with complaints and petitions). The Agency will not have similar powers as the Treaty has already

---

[32] See http://www.eiuc.org.
[33] See n 1 above.

conferred them on the institutions: the Commission's role of supervising the proper application of Community law must be respected.[34]

Again, this argument does not seem to be particularly convincing. Nobody doubts the eminent role of the Commission as the guardian of the proper implementation of Community law by EU Member States. With the entry into force of the Treaty establishing a Constitution for Europe,[35] the EU Charter of Fundamental Rights will become part of primary EU law, and thereby become binding on the EU bodies and institutions as well as on the EU Member States when implementing Community law. In other words, the Commission will assume an important function of monitoring the compliance of other EU institutions and the EU Member States with their obligations deriving from the EU Charter of Fundamental Rights. Any violation of fundamental rights will be qualified as a breach of primary EU treaty law, and the Commission has the power to initiate infringement proceedings before the European Court of Justice.

But in the field of human rights, monitoring and protection by governmental bodies is not sufficient. The very notion of human rights includes the *right of victims* of a violation of their human rights to an *effective remedy and reparation*.[36] In other words, the rights-holders should have the legal possibility to initiate themselves individual complaints against the respective duty-bearers. Neither the EU Charter of Fundamental Rights nor other provisions in the Treaty establishing a Constitution for Europe provide for a proper individual complaints procedure against alleged violations of fundamental rights, and the standing of individuals before the European Court of Justice and the Court of First Instance for alleged human rights violations is fairly limited.[37] Although the situation shall be improved if and when the Constitution enters into force, the progress which has been made with respect to the *locus standi* of individuals seeking to annul Union acts of a general nature has not alleviated all the concerns which have been expressed in the past, both in academic circles and by certain members of the European Court of Justice.[38]

Can the complaints procedure before the *European Ombudsman* be regarded as an effective remedy? According to Article 195 of the EC Treaty, the European Ombudsman receives complaints from any citizen of the Union or any natural or legal person residing or having its registered office in a Member State, concerning instances of *maladministration* in the activities of Community institutions and bodies with the exception of the Court of Justice and the Court of

[34] Commission, n 1 above, ch 1.

[35] See n 4 above.

[36] See M Nowak, n 1 above, p 63.

[37] See the various contributions to a respective Symposium held in December 2003 at the European Inter-University Centre for Human Rights and Democratisation in Venice, to be published shortly in the Human Rights Law Journal.

[38] See for developments O De Schutter, 'Group Litigation before the European Court of Justice,' manuscript (November 2004).

First Instance acting in their judicial role. In 1997, the Ombudsman adopted the following definition of maladministration, which was later agreed upon by the European Parliament and the Commission:

> Maladministration occurs when a public body fails to act in accordance with a rule or principle which is binding upon it.[39]

In practice, human rights do not seem to play any significant role in the Ombudsman's activities. Of the rights guaranteed in the (presently still non-binding) EU Charter of Fundamental Rights, only the right to good administration in Article 41 has been applied in more recent cases.[40] A considerable number of cases concern discrimination.[41] Most cases are settled by means of mediation and friendly solutions. Only relatively few cases lead to critical remarks, draft recommendations (to which the institution or body concerned must respond with a detailed opinion within three months) or a special report of the Ombudsman. The Ombudsman has no power to refer a case to the European Court of Justice or any other judicial proceedings leading to a binding decision. In his Annual Report 2003, the present Ombudsman, P Nikiforos Diamondouros, stressed, however, that he will:

> need to complement attention to the rule of law and good administration, traditionally identified as core preoccupations of an ombudsman, with increased sensitivity to the protection of human rights.[42]

Nevertheless, in view of the limited competences vis-à-vis the EU institutions and the lack of any competences vis-à-vis the EU Member States when implementing Community law, the *European Ombudsman, at least in its present form, cannot be considered an effective remedy* for victims alleging a violation of any of the fundamental rights covered in the Charter. Since the future Agency, with or without a specific mandate, will be seized with many individual complaints, which need to be taken into account in one way or another as part of its data collection activities, its establishment might provide a good opportunity to think more carefully about a proper individual human rights complaints mechanism with respect to all rights enlisted in the EU Charter of Fundamental Rights. The Agency, as a non-judicial body, might be entrusted to receive and consider complaints based on alleged violations of the Charter with a view to establishing the facts and facilitating an amicable solution. Such a procedure can, however, only be considered as an effective remedy if the Agency has the possibility to refer complaints, if the friendly settlement procedure failed, to a

---

[39] See The European Ombudsman, *Annual Report 2003* (Brussels, European Communities, 2004) p 27. On the activities, see also: hppt://www.euro-ombudsman.eu.int.

[40] See, eg: the decision of the Ombudsman on complaint 1200/2003/OV against the Council on the Council's responsibility for ensuring that the European Union Police mission in Sarajevo respects fundamental rights, including the right of an employee to be heard before being dismissed for alleged serious misconduct. See Annual Report, *ibid*, pp 141–144.

[41] *Ibid*, p 268.

[42] *Ibid*, p 20.

court for adjudication. The direct power to launch infringement proceedings before the European Court of Justice would, of course, require an amendment of the EC Treaty or the Treaty establishing a Constitution for Europe. Such a procedure would resemble the one before the European Commission and Court of Human Rights before the entry into force of the 11th AP to the ECHR in 1998, the procedure before the Inter-American Commission and Court of Human Rights or the procedure before the Human Rights Commission for Bosnia and Herzegovina established by the Dayton Peace Agreement of 1995, which consisted of an Ombudsperson and a special human rights court, the Human Rights Chamber for Bosnia and Herzegovina.[43]

Since an amendment of primary EU law seems to be fairly unrealistic, one might think of a *more indirect involvement of the Agency in launching further proceedings* leading to binding decisions. It might be entrusted, eg, to bring specific individual human rights cases, which could not be solved by means of a friendly settlement, to the attention of the Commission with the request to launch infringement proceedings before the European Court of Justice. Similarly, on the basis of a variety of individual complaints, the Agency might bring a specific situation to the attention of the Commission, the Council or the European Parliament with the recommendation to take action in accordance with the procedure envisaged in Article 7 of the EU Treaty. This advisory and early warning function, based on the consideration of individual complaints, would be in line with the role of the Agency as a think tank and could be achieved within the framework of a Council Regulation.[44]

g) Legal Basis, Type, Composition and Independence of the Agency

The Paris Principles require a *legal basis* in a constitutional or legal text. Ideally, the Agency should have been incorporated into the Treaty establishing a Constitution of Europe. In the absence of a constitutional entrenchment, the proper legal basis would be a *Council Regulation*. In fact, the European Council decided in December 2003 to base the Agency on an amendment of Regulation 1035/97, by which the Council had established the EUMC in 1997.[45]

Of the four *types* of national human rights institutions outlined above, the mandate of the Agency, as presently discussed, would probably more resemble that of an *advisory committee* or a human rights institute (as exists, eg, in France, Greece, Luxembourg, Denmark and Germany) than that of an Ombuds-type institution or national human right commission (such as those existing in Ireland, Sweden, Spain, Poland and Portugal).

---

[43] On the latter procedure see *Human Rights Chamber for Bosnia and Herzegovina, Digest—Decisions on Admissibility and Merits 1996–2002*, with an 'Introduction' by M Nowak (Kehl/Strasbourg/Arlington, Engel Publishers, 2003).

[44] On the legal basis of the future Agency see, eg:, the contribution of O De Schutter in ch 2 of this volume, n 9 above.

[45] See nn 1 and 6 above.

As to the *composition*, the Paris Principles provide as follows:

> The composition of the national institution and the appointment of its members, whether by means of an election or otherwise, shall be established in accordance with a procedure which affords all necessary guarantees to ensure the pluralist representation of the social forces (of civilian society) involved in the promotion and protection of human rights.

Although the Paris Principles seem to presuppose a multi-member institution,[46] the variety of national institutions illustrates that pluralism can be achieved by different means. Even in a one-member institution, such as an Ombudsman, and a human rights institute or monitoring centre led by one Director,[47] the board of governors and advisory committees may ensure broad representation of civil society.

While the Paris Principles are fairly open with regard to the legal basis, the type and composition of a national institution, its *independence* constitutes an absolutely necessary feature.[48] Even though the guarantees of independence may be less strong than those of courts, the requirements developed in international law for the independence of the judiciary might provide useful guidance.[49] Members of national institutions must, therefore, be elected or appointed for a longer period of time,[50] shall not be subject to directives from the executive or other powers and should enjoy financial autonomy on the basis of a specific budgetary allocation from Parliament. For the Agency it seems most important that its members and staff are fully independent from political or financial pressure by the Commission, the Council and the Governments of EU Member States.

IV. CO-OPERATION BETWEEN THE AGENCY AND NATIONAL HUMAN RIGHTS INSTITUTIONS

One important function of the Agency will certainly be the collection and analysis of relevant legal and factual human rights data in the 25 EU Member States. In order to perform this task in a professional and cost-efficient manner, the Agency will have to develop co-operation with relevant institutions in the Member States. The RAXEN network of the EUMC consisting of *national focal*

---

[46] See, eg: Commonwealth Secretariat, n 2 above, p 14.

[47] The EUMC, as the legal model for the Agency, falls into this category: see n 6 above.

[48] See, eg: Commonwealth Secretariat, n 2 above, p 14; Aichele, n 2 above, pp 17–18 with further references.

[49] See, eg: the jurisprudence of the European Court of Human Rights in relation to Art 6 ECHR, and the 'Basic Principles for the Independence of the Judiciary,' adopted in 1985 by the 7th UN Congress on Crime Prevention in Milan and reinforced by UNGA resolutions 40/146 and 41/149.

[50] The Commonwealth Secretariat, n 2 above, p 16, refers to a fixed term of at least five years. During this term of office, members shall not be removed except for reasons specified in the enabling law. These reasons, and the method of removal, should parallel those applicable to members of the judiciary.

points in the Member States might form the nucleus of such a co-operation structure, but the resources allocated to these focal points would need to be considerably enlarged if they were requested to provide data on the human rights situation of their countries in general. While some focal points are based in a general human rights environment, others deal exclusively with racism and xenophobia.

The recent opinion of the EU Network of Independent Experts on Fundamental Rights regarding the role of national human rights institutions in the EU Member States shows that in the majority of EU Member States an official institution with a general human rights mandate has already been established and internationally recognised.[51] In the remaining States, similar institutions exist and plans for the creation of national human rights institutions in accordance with the Paris Principles and relevant UN resolutions as well as Council of Europe recommendations are ongoing. The question, therefore, arises whether the Council Regulation establishing the Agency should not be accompanied by an obligation of all EU Member States to designate an appropriate independent national human rights institution as the Agency's domestic counter-part. In other words, the *creation of the EU Human Rights Agency might facilitate the establishment of an EU network of national human rights institutions*, similar to the Asia Pacific Forum of National Human Rights Institutions.[52] In addition to providing relevant governmental and non-governmental human rights data in a systematic manner to the Agency, the respective national institutions might co-operate with the Agency in various fields, including human rights education, advocacy, and awareness raising activities.

V. CONCLUSION

The analysis of both the principles underlying the foundation of national human rights institutions and the practical experience with such institutions in Europe provides *useful guidance for the current discussion on the establishment of an EU Human Rights Agency*. On the one hand, the need of the Agency to co-operate closely with relevant domestic counter-parts might accelerate the establishment of national institutions in those EU Member States that still lack such an official non-judicial human rights body and, thereby, facilitate the creation of an EU network of national human rights institutions. On the other hand, the aims and objectives, structures, functions and responsibilities of national human rights institutions in Europe show a considerable variety and might serve as a source of inspiration for the structure, composition and the mandate of the future EU Agency.

[51] See nn 8 and 9 above.

[52] On the increasingly important function of the Asia Pacific Forum for the promotion and protection of human rights in the Asia Pacific region, see U Amarsaikhan, *Human Rights in Asia* (Vienna, Phd thesis, 2004).

Most importantly, the Agency should enjoy full *independence* from the EU institutions, above all the Commission and the Council, as well as from the Governments of EU Member States. It is equally important to stress that the Agency should not be a policy-making or policy-implementing body with enforcement powers,[53] but rather a *think tank* with the task of providing the EU institutions and its Member States with reliable and comparative data on the legal and factual human rights situation in the Union and its Member States, in candidate countries and in other countries that are of particular interest to the Union, be it in the framework of development co-operation, of bilateral trade relations or of the common foreign and security policy. These data should be collected, with the assistance of respective national institutions, analysed in a comparative manner by the research and documentation staff of the Agency, and made available, on its own initiative or on request, to the respective EU institutions in order to assist and advise them when taking measures or formulating policies within their respective spheres of competence.

Whether or not the collection of data includes a more formal *consideration of individual complaints* in a non-judicial mediation procedure is a question which needs to be further discussed. Without an amendment of primary EU law, the Agency cannot be entrusted with any judicial or quasi-judicial decision-making functions or with the power of initiating infringement procedures before the European Court of Justice. But the Agency might be entrusted to advise the Commission in its function of ensuring the proper implementation of Community law by the EU Member States, which includes its power to initiate infringement proceedings.

As an *advisory body*, the Agency should have the competence to act on the request of the relevant EU institutions and on its *own initiative*. It might, for instance, draw the attention of the Commission, the European Parliament or the Council to a deterioration of the human rights situation in a particular EU Member State, which would merit a closer scrutiny with a view of initiating a procedure in accordance with Article 7 of the EU Treaty. Similarly, it might report on certain events in a candidate country which are of relevance for the application of the *Copenhagen criteria* for admission to the Union. The same applies to the human rights situation in partner countries, since the Cotonou Agreement with 77 ACP States and most bilateral treaties contain a *human rights clause as essential element of the respective agreement*. A coherent and consistent human rights policy of the Union in its internal and external relations requires the thorough analysis of all relevant data by an independent and professional Agency, which has the right and obligation to draw the attention of the EU institutions to relevant developments and to elaborate policy options for strategic action.

---

[53] See the *Final Project Report on a Human Rights Agenda for the European Union for the Year 2000* by Ph Alston and JHH Weiler, n 13 above, pp 95–96.

Whether this function is called *monitoring* or merely *advisory* is in the final result a terminological question. Even if one applies the strict definition of Martin Scheinin, according to whom human rights monitoring is normative in nature and, therefore, a judicial or quasi-judicial activity,[54] one cannot deny that advising EU institutions on policy options in respect of a specific Member State, candidate or partner country, requires some normative assessment of the respective situation. More important than the designation of this activity as monitoring is the question whether the respective report and recommendation of the Agency may be made public or not. Usually, independent human rights monitoring is associated with *public reporting*. In the case of the EU Agency, there might, however, be good reasons to keep the reports confidential until the respective EU institution, to which the report is addressed, decides to publish it. Many objections of Governments towards a monitoring function of the Agency are in fact based on *fears of public reporting* rather than on concerns about the monitoring function as such.

In addition to data collection and analysis, comparative research and documentation, monitoring and advice, the Agency should have a strong role in *human rights advocacy, education and awareness raising* in relation to the EU institutions and its Member States. In this respect, the Agency should closely co-operate with relevant EU training centres as well as national human rights institutions.

[54] See M Scheinin, n 22 above.

Part II

The Tasks Ahead

5

The Contribution of the EU Fundamental Rights Agency to Civil and Political Rights

STEVE PEERS*

I. INTRODUCTION

GIVEN THE EXTENSIVE (some might say too extensive) scope of judicial protection for civil and political rights within the European Union and its Member States, what further role could the creation of an EU Agency play in protecting those rights? As we shall see, on the assumption that non-judicial bodies can have an important role to play supplementing and enhancing judicial remedies for enforcement of human rights—even justiciable civil and political rights—an Agency at EU level could also be useful, if it is able to address a sufficient range of rights, if it is given constructive and meaningful task to perform, and if there is an appropriate (but not excessive) scope for it to carry out its activities.

II. DEFINING THE RIGHTS TO BE PROTECTED

The sources of the human rights protected in EU law are (for the general principles of EU law) international human rights treaties, especially the European Convention on Human rights (ECHR) and national constitutions. Subsequently, the EU's Charter of Fundamental Rights (the 'Charter') has become a yardstick, at least for the EU political institutions, the Court of First Instance, and Advocates-General of the Court of Justice, if not (yet?) the latter Court itself.[1] It might be tempting to focus solely on the Charter and/or on the ECHR as the sole source(s) of civil and political rights, given their clarity and prominence as compared with the general principles. However, this approach

---

* Professor of Law at the University of Essex, affiliated to the University's Human Rights Centre and Centre for European Union Law.

[1] See App 1 in S Peers and A Ward (eds), *The EU Charter of Fundamental Rights: Politics, Law and Policy* (Oxford, Hart Publishing, 2004).

should be rejected, as the general principles, pending the entry into force of the proposed EU Constitution, remain the key source for the human rights protected within the EU legal order. Even under the Constitution, if it enters into force, the general principles will apparently remain as a separate source of legal rules distinct from the Charter and the EU's accession to the ECHR (which will take several years to arrange in any event). So civil and political rights which derive from other international human rights treaties (in particular the International Covenant on Civil and Political Rights), assuming that the EU cannot or at least will not become parties to them, or from any ECHR Protocols which the EU decides not to ratify, or from national constitutional principles not referred to in the Charter, will continue to exist as part of the general principles of EU law. For that matter, it could be argued that even where rights are recognised in both the general principles and in the Charter/ECHR, there could be cases where the general principles accord them a higher level of protection, a wider scope, or both.

Given the doctrine of the indivisibility of human rights, encapsulated in the Charter and in the Universal Declaration of Rights, there is no convincing reason that an EU Human Rights Agency should be limited to concern with some rights, but not others. For that reason, the Agency should be able to concern itself with the civil and political rights set out in the Charter, the ECHR, other international treaties, or national constitutions. These rights are at least the following rights, listing them in the order they appear in the Charter, then in the ECHR and other treaties (if they do not appear in the Charter):

a) the right to human dignity, although this right could also have application in the spheres of economic, social and cultural rights[2];
b) the right to life and abolition of death penalty[3];
c) the right to integrity of the person[4];
d) the right to be free from torture/inhuman or degrading treatment;[5]
e) the prohibition on slavery and forced labour, entailing also a prohibition on trafficking in persons[6];
f) the right to liberty and security of the person[7];
g) the right to respect for private and family life[8];

---

[2] Art 1 of the Charter (Art II–51 Constitution), recognised as forming part of the general principles in Case C–377/98 *Netherlands v EP and Council* [2001] ECR I–7079; see also: Case C–13/94 *P v S* [1996] ECR I–2143.

[3] Art 2 of the Charter (Art II–52 Constitution), also Art. 2 ECHR (referred to in Case C–112/00 *Schmidberger* [2003] ECR I–5659) and Protocols 6 and 13 ECHR.

[4] Art 3 of the Charter (Art II–53 Constitution).

[5] Art 4 of the Charter (Art II–54 Constitution); also Art 3 ECHR, referred to in *Schmidberger*, n 3 above).

[6] Art 5 of the Charter (Art II–55 Constitution); also Art 4 ECHR.

[7] Art 6 of the Charter (Art II–56 Constitution); also Art 5 ECHR.

[8] Art 7 of the Charter (Art II–57 Constitution); also Art 8 ECHR. On the right as part of the general principles of EU law, see cases on family reunion (Case 249/86 *Commission v Germany* [1989] ECR 1263; Case C–60/00 *Carpenter* [2002] ECR I–6279; Case C–459/99 *MRAX* [2002] ECR I–6591; Case C–413/99 *Baumbast and R* [2002] ECR I–7091; Case C–257/00 *Givane* [2003] ECR I–345; and

h) the right to protection of personal data[9];

i) the right to marry and found a family[10];

j) the freedom of thought, conscience and religion, including the right to conscientious objection[11];

k) the freedom of expression and information[12];

l) the freedom of assembly and association[13];

m) the freedom of the arts and sciences[14];

n) the right to asylum[15];

o) the prohibition on collective expulsions, along with the non-refoulement rule[16];

p) the right to vote and stand in elections for the European Parliament[17];

q) the right to vote and stand in municipal elections[18];

r) the right to good administration[19];

s) the right of access to documents[20];

t) the right to complain to the EU Ombudsman[21];

u) the right to petition the European Parliament[22];

Case C–109/01 *Akrich* [2003] ECR I–9607) and medical confidentiality (Case C–62/90 *Commission v Germany* [1992] ECR I–2575; Case T–10/93 *A v Commission* [1994] ECR II–179; Joined Cases T–121/89 and T–13/90 *X v Commission* [1992] ECR I–2195; Case C–404/92 *X v Commission* [1994] ECR I–4737). Children's' rights may also be relevant in family reunion cases (see Art 24 Charter, Art II–84 of the Constitution and the Convention on the Rights of the Child).

[9] Art 8 of the Charter (Art II–58 Constitution); also Art 8 ECHR. On the right as part of the general principles of EU law, see Case C–369/98 *Fisher* [2000] ECR I–6751; Joined Cases C–465/00, C–138/01, and C–139/01 *Osterreichischer Rundfunk* [2003] ECR I–4989; and Case C–101/01 *Lindqvist*, judgment of 6 November 2003, not yet reported.

[10] Art 9 of the Charter (Art II–59 Constitution); also Art 12 ECHR. See also: *P v S*, n 2 above, Case C–249/96 *Grant* [1998] ECR I–649 and Case C–117/01 *KB*, judgment of 7 January 2004, not yet reported.

[11] Art 10 of the Charter (Art II–60 Constitution); also Art 9 ECHR. On the right as part of the general principles of EU law, see Case 130/75 *Prais* [1976] ECR 1589.

[12] Art 11 of the Charter (Art II–61 Constitution); also Art 10 ECHR. On the right as part of the general principles of EU law, see, most recently: *Schmidberger*, n 3 above; Case C–245/01, *RTL Television*, judgment of 23 October 2003, not yet reported; and Case C–71/02 *Karner*, judgment of 25 March 2004, not yet reported.

[13] Art 12 of the Charter (Art II–62 Constitution); also Art 11 ECHR. On the right as part of the general principles of EU law, see most recently *Schmidberger*, n 3 above.

[14] Art 13 of the Charter (Art II–63 Constitution).

[15] Art 18 of the Charter (Art II–78 Constitution), which arguably forms part of the general principles of EC law pursuant to national constitutions and the Geneva Convention on the status of refugees, referred to in Art 63 EC.

[16] Art 19 of the Charter (Art II–79 Constitution); also Art 4 of Protocol 4 ECHR and case law on Art 3 ECHR respectively.

[17] Art 39 of the Charter (Art II–99 Constitution); also Art 3 of Protocol 1 ECHR as interpreted by the European Court of Human Rights in *Matthews v UK* (Reports of Judgments and Decisions 1999–I).

[18] Art 40 of the Charter (Art II–100 Constitution).

[19] Art 41 of the Charter (Art II–101 Constitution).

[20] Art 42 of the Charter (Art II–102 Constitution).

[21] Art 43 of the Charter (Art II–103 Constitution).

[22] Art 44 of the Charter (Art II–104 Constitution).

v)   the right of free movement and residence[23];

w) the right to diplomatic and consular protection[24];

x)   the right to an effective remedy and to a fair trial[25];

y)   the presumption of innocence and right of defence[26];

z)   the principles of legality, non-retroactivity and proportionality of criminal offences[27];

aa) the right not to be tried or punished twice for the same offence[28];

bb) prohibition of imprisonment for debt[29];

cc) the right to leave any country[30];

dd) the right of citizens to enter and reside in their own country[31];

ee) procedural safeguards relating to expulsion[32];

ff) the right of appeal in criminal matters[33];

gg) compensation for wrongful conviction[34];

hh) general rights to non-discrimination on various grounds, which include civil and political rights[35]; and

ii) the rights of children and minority rights, which include civil and political rights.[36]

This list is necessarily non-exhaustive, because of the open process of inclusion of human rights as part of the general principles of law forming part of the EU legal order. It might be objected that some of the above rights are not relevant to the activities of the EU, because, for instance, the EU does not operate prisons or police forces. But, even setting aside the relevance of all human rights to EU foreign policy, the rights set out above could all be relevant to the EU if we

---

[23] Art 45 of the Charter (Art II–105 Constitution); on the economic aspects of free movement, see Art 15 of the Charter (Art II–75 Constitution). See also: Art 2(1) of Protocol 4 ECHR.

[24] Art 46 of the Charter (Art II–106 Constitution).

[25] Art 47 of the Charter (Art II–107 Constitution); and Arts 6 and 13 ECHR. This clause could arguably apply to economic, social and cultural rights as well. On these rights as general principles of EC law, see particularly A Ward, 'Access to Justice' in S Peers and A Ward, n 1 above, 123–40.

[26] Art 48 of the Charter (Art II–108 Constitution); see Art 6 ECHR.

[27] Art 49 of the Charter (Art II–109 Constitution); see Art 7 ECHR.

[28] Art 50 of the Charter (Art II–110 Constitution); see Art 4 of Protocol 7 ECHR.

[29] Art 1 of Protocol 4 ECHR.

[30] Art 2(2) of Protocol 4 ECHR; this right forms an aspect of the right to free movement.

[31] Art 3 of Protocol 4 ECHR; the ECJ has recognised this right in relation to citizens of each Member State, but not as regards the entire EU. See Cases 41/74 *Van Duyn* [1974] ECR 1337, para 22; 115/81 and 116/81 *Adoui and Cornuaille* [1982] ECR 1665, para 7; C–370/90 *Singh* [1992] ECR I–[4375], para 22; C–65/65 and 111/95 *Shingara and Radiom* [1997] ECR I–3343, para 28; C–171/96 *Roque* [1998] ECR I–4607, para 37; C–348/96 *Calfa* [1999] ECR I–11, para 20; C–235/99 *Kondova* [2001] ECR I–6557, para 83; C–257/99 *Barkoci and Malik* [2001] ECR I–6427, para 80; C–63/99 *Gloszczuk* [2001] ECR I–6369, para 78; and C–100/01 *Olazabal* [2002] ECR I–10981, para 40.

[32] Art 1 of Protocol 7 ECHR.

[33] Art 2 of Protocol 7 ECHR.

[34] Art 3 of Protocol 7 ECHR.

[35] Art 26 ICCPR and the UN Conventions on Discrimination against Women and on Elimination of Racial Discrimination.

[36] Arts 24 and 27 ICCPR, the UN Convention on Rights of the Child and the Council of Europe Framework Convention on National Minorities.

recall that the general principles of EC law and the Charter apply to Member States when they are implementing EU law. So, any right linked to the criminal law process is relevant to EU law, because the EU has adopted measures requiring Member States to establish criminal law offences and to establish systems of mutual assistance as regards criminal procedure (assuming that the general principles as restated in Article 6(2) EU apply to all three EU pillars).[37] Any right relating to entry, residence or expulsion of any person is relevant to EU immigration or asylum law.

It might also be objected that a number of the rights referred to above, including some of those in the Charter, do not apply to all Member States, because some Member States have not ratified the Fourth, Seventh or Thirteenth Protocols to the ECHR.[38] Therefore, these rights should not be protected by EU law. However, even if we accept the assumption that the human rights standards binding the EU should be defined by reference to the Member States, all of the relevant rights, except for the ban on executions in wartime, are in fact set out in the ICCPR, which all Member States have ratified.[39] As for the Thirteenth Protocol, although it had only been ratified by 15 Member States as of 15 November 2004, it had been signed by all Member States, and so could be considered a treaty which Member States have 'collaborated' upon within the meaning of the Court of Justice case law identifying the sources of the general principles of EC law.[40]

III. SCOPE OF THE RIGHTS PROTECTED BY THE AGENCY

In the area of civil and political rights (as with other rights), it will be necessary to decide several issues concerning the scope of rights which will be addressed in the Agency's conduct of its activities. As we shall see, the determination of the scope of the rights protected plays a decisive role in determining whether the Agency could play a useful role in ensuring the protection of civil and political rights.

The first of these issues is the scope of the Agency as regards the *activities of Member States*. On this issue, the first option would be to give the Agency

---

[37] See the analysis in the Advocate-General's Opinion of 11 November 2004 in Case C–105/03 *Pupino*, pending.

[38] Greece, Spain and the UK have not ratified the Fourth Protocol; six Member States have not ratified the Seventh Protocol (Belgium, Germany, the Netherlands, Portugal, Spain and the UK); and ten Member States have not ratified the Thirteenth Protocol (Finland, France, Greece, Italy, Latvia, Luxembourg, the Netherlands, Poland, Slovakia and Spain).

[39] Freedom from imprisonment for debt appears in Art 11 ICCPR; various free movement rights are in Art 12 ICCPR; procedural rights regarding expulsion are in Art 13 ICCPR; and rights regarding criminal appeal, double jeopardy and compensation for wrongful conviction are in Art 14 ICCPR.

[40] For instance, the Court of First Instance has confirmed that a right referred to in Art 4 of Protocol 7 ECHR forms part of the general principles of EC law (Case T–224/00, *Archer Daniels Midland*, judgment of July 9 2003, not yet reported).

powers in relation to protection of all civil and political rights within the EU and the Member States. One argument for such a wide scope of powers would be the necessity to ascertain, in addition to monitoring the EU and actions of the Member States within the scope of EU law, whether a Member State had arguably committed or risked committing a serious and persistent breach of human rights, in violation of Article 7 ECHR, which could therefore result respectively in suspension from the EU or a warning from the Council.

The second option would be to give the Agency the same scope as the Charter,[41] which applies to the EU institutions and to the Member States when they are implementing EU law. A variation on this option would be to give the Agency the same scope as the general principles of EU law, which apply not just where the Member States are implementing EU law, but also where they derogate from it.[42] It is assumed that the general principles apply not only where Member States derogate from free movement law, but also from other EU rules; this is a crucial point for the application of many civil and political rights. These two variations on the scope may in fact merge in practice, as the Court of Justice could ultimately rule that despite its wording, the Charter also applies when Member States derogate from EU rules. After all, the Court has maintained its jurisdiction over human rights in the context of national application of and derogation from EC law,[43] in spite of the restrictive wording of Article 46 EU as amended by the Treaty of Amsterdam, which appears to restrict the Court to ruling on breaches of the general principles by the EU *institutions*.

In light of this wording set out in the Treaty, a potential third option would be to limit the Agency only to the activities of those institutions. It is assumed that an Agency competent to deal with any of these options could be created in accordance pursuant to Articles 285 and 308 EC, as far as EC law is concerned.[44] The Commission's consultation paper on the creation of the Agency assumes that the choice is between the first two options, although it refers expressly to only the first variation on the second option (Member States *implementing* EC/EU law, not *derogating* from it).[45]

As to the first option, there is a convincing argument in principle for survey-ing the human rights records of Member States at EU level in order to ascertain whether there is evidence for Article 7 EU to be invoked, particularly to address the concern that a potential 'double standard' would otherwise exist by com-parison with the fairly intensive scrutiny by the EU of the human rights records of *applicant* countries (although, given the politicised nature of the scrutiny

---

[41] See Art 51 Charter (Art II–111 of the Constitution).

[42] Cases C–260/89 *ERT* [1991] ECR I–2925, C–368/95 *Familiapress* [1997] ECR I–3689 and C–60/00 *Carpenter* [2002] ECR I–6279.

[43] See, eg: the judgments in Joined Cases C–20/00 and C–64/00 *Booker Aquaculture* [2003] ECR I–7411 and *Carpenter*, n 42 above.

[44] See the legal arguments in JHH Weiler and S Fries, 'A Human Rights Policy for the European Community and Union: The Question of Competences' in Ph Alston (ed), *The EU and Human Rights* (Oxford, Oxford University Press, 1999) p 147.

[45] COM (2004) 693, 25 October 2004.

which takes place during the accession process, the 'double standard' could only be reduced, not eliminated entirely). However, while this activity could be carried out by the Agency, it could also be carried out, as at present, by a Committee of Independent Experts. In light of the thorough reports by the experts to date, there seems no reason to conclude that the Agency would do a demonstrably better job of this sort of survey. However, if the Experts were unable to continue their current task for legal or other reasons, then the task of conducting this survey should be given to the Agency, to ensure that it the survey continues to take place.

On the other hand, it could be argued that such a survey is insufficient, and that the EU should have the task not merely of surveying national human rights protection in the context of Article 7 EU, but also of taking a far greater role in ensuring that civil and political rights are protected within Member States' jurisdiction. Such an approach to the role of the EU as regards human rights should be rejected.[46] First of all, it would clearly exceed any plausible interpretation of the competences conferred by the Member States upon the EC or EU under the current Treaty framework or the proposed EU Constitution. But this objection is not ultimately decisive, for in the longer term it would always be possible, if the political will could be mustered, to amend the current Treaties or the Constitution to this effect. The second, and decisive, objection is that there is simply no need for such an EU role, regardless of the legal powers of the EC and EU. There are already extensive judicial and non-judicial mechanisms at national and international level to ensure that civil and political rights are protected within the Member States; to the extent that such mechanisms do not exist or are insufficient, they could be created, improved or further developed. Such developments are not impossible to achieve in practice, as evidenced by the UK's *Human Rights Act* 1998 and the recent agreement on substantive and procedural Protocols to the ECHR. Surely a development of an existing mechanism, or the development of a new mechanism within an existing legal framework, is more likely to have a decisive impact in the protection of human rights within the Member States than the creation of a new EU Agency which would have difficulty establishing the (political) legitimacy or securing sufficient resources to undertake such a huge task.

As for the third option, it should be rejected. Given the extensive delegation to Member States to finance and administer the application of EC and EU law, and even (in many cases) legislate to give effect to EU and EC law, along with the role of Member States' national courts to deal with most arguments over EC or EU law in the first instance, limiting a Human Rights Agency to considering actions of the EU institutions would mean that its contribution to the protection of civil or political rights would be virtually non-existent. The only four civil

---

[46] See A Von Bogdandy, 'The European Union as a Human Rights Organisation? Human Rights and the Core of the European Union' (2000) 37 *CML Rev* 1307, who rejects any extensive increase in EU powers regarding human rights, although for different reasons than those set out here.

and political rights which essentially concern the EU institutions only are the right to good administration, the right of access to documents, the right to complain to the EU Ombudsman and the right to petition the European Parliament. The first two rights could be extended to Member States, but as worded in the Charter, they are not; and to the extent that maladministration in Member States could hinder the protection of human rights within the scope of EC law, it is addressed by the right to a fair hearing and effective remedy set out in the Charter and the general principles. Moreover, the first two rights are adequately protected by the EU Ombudsman (and the EU Courts, subject to concerns about standing which the creation of an Agency would not resolve), and the second two rights are effectively self-executing.[47]

The remaining rights wholly or largely fall within the scope of EC or EU law only when Member States implement EC or EU law or derogate from it. In such cases, there is a genuine gap in non-judicial remedies in the absence of any body at EU level which is capable of offering one, or which has the task of monitoring developments (other than the existing EU Monitoring Centre concerned with racism, xenophobia and anti-Semitism).

This leaves us with the second option: an agency concerned with civil and political rights within the scope of EU and EC law. Which variation of the second option should be chosen? Given that the Court of Justice could (and should) insist, as suggested above, that Member States' derogations from the Charter fall within the scope of its human rights jurisdiction (as in the case of the general principles); that the general principles are at present the primary source, and the sole binding source, of human rights rules in EU law; and that even if the Constitution enters into force, the general principles will apparently continue to exist distinctly from the Charter, it is essential to choose the second variation, and to insist that the Agency has a role whenever Member States derogate from EU law, not just where they implement it. Furthermore, this interpretation not only best fits in with the structure of human rights protection, but is likely to contribute more to the protection of civil and political rights in practice, due to its broader scope and the intrinsic difficulty of ensuring human rights protection in such situations linked to EU or EC law through national mechanisms.

The second key issue is the scope of the agency's powers as regards the EU's pillar system. Within the first pillar, there are no convincing grounds for excluding any area of Community law from the Agency's scope; in particular, there are no grounds for excluding immigration, asylum and civil law in Title IV or Part Three of the EC Treaty from its scope, since those areas raise many issues concerning civil and political rights and have fallen within the scope of Community law since 1999. The transitional period relating to the adoption of Title IV measures expired on 1 May 2004 and in any event, there is no plausible

---

[47] In the last resort, failures by the Ombudsman to carry out his or her duties can be sanctioned by damages actions before the EU courts; see Case C–234/02 P *Lamberts*, judgment of 24 March 2004, not yet reported.

reason why the existence of this transitional period (or the inclusion of these issues within the third pillar of the EU prior to 1 May 1999) should impact upon the scope of the Agency's activities. There are also broader concerns to take into account. A Human Rights Agency which was excluded from examining such high-profile topics raising critical human rights issues (and yet falling squarely within the scope of EC law) would be bereft of much legitimacy from the outset. In particular, given the historical background of the Agency as a Monitoring Centre concerned with racism, coupled with the importance of asylum and immigration issues to many racial minority communities and the links between far-right groups and racist attacks on foreigners and asylum-seekers, exclusion of asylum and immigration from the Agency's activities would widely be seen as a defensive, cynical and even (symbolically) dangerous decision by the Union.

In the alternative, if the Agency is to focus only on certain human rights issues as priorities, as suggested in the Commission communication on the Agency, immigration and asylum issues should be among those priority issues.[48] This would be justified by the importance of these issues from a human rights perspective, the extensive EC harmonization programme following the Treaty of Amsterdam, the Tampere conclusions of 1999, the Hague Programme of November 2004 and the draft Constitutional Treaty, along with the close link between these issues and the continuing anti-racist mandate of the Agency. In fact, the Hague Programme makes express reference to the Agency in the context of stressing the existence of the EU's human rights principles as part of the next multi-annual programme on Justice and Home Affairs, so again it would appear rather cynical if the Agency did not in fact deal with particular JHA issues. Indeed, the Commission communication on the Agency nominates the issues of asylum and immigration as likely priority issues for the Agency.[49]

We shall leave aside the second pillar to the discussion of the external aspects of EU human rights policy below. This brings us to the third pillar, concerning policing and criminal law, another high-profile area where the human rights concerns are acute, touching on many of the key civil and political rights, in particular the right to human dignity, the right to life, the right to be free from torture/inhuman or degrading treatment, the prohibition on trafficking in persons, the right to liberty and security of the person, the right to respect for private and family life, the right to protection of personal data, the right to an effective remedy and to a fair trial, the presumption of innocence and right of defence, the principles of legality, non-retroactivity and proportionality of criminal offences, the right not to be tried or punished twice for the same offence, the prohibition of imprisonment for debt, the right of appeal in criminal matters and the right to compensation for wrongful conviction. In light of this long list, there is clearly an overwhelming argument from a human rights perspective in

---

[48] See n 45 above.
[49] *Ibid.*

including such matters within the scope of the Agency. The Commission's discussion paper on the Agency does not discuss this issue fully, but at one point apparently considers the possible application of the Agency to the third pillar by implication (referring to possibly limiting the Agency to 'Community (or Union) law.')[50]

Yet there could remain a question from the perspective of EU law whether there might be an argument on grounds of policy or law for excluding third pillar matters from the scope of the Agency. The policy argument for excluding such matters from the Agency's remit would be that the subject-matter is regulated in an intergovernmental manner, and so should not be subject to the same arrangements as apply to human rights issues within the Community's remit. This argument would in any event only be valid up into the entry into force of the proposed EU Constitution, and has obviously lost much of its force in the meantime in light of the agreement on the Constitution. But it could still be argued that despite the planned application of almost all of the 'Community method' to policing and criminal law issues, nonetheless there is and would remain something intrinsically different about these subjects, given their link to the exercise of coercive authority and the core aspects of state sovereignty, that should preclude bringing them within the scope of an EU agency.

The answer to this objection is that whatever the case may be for regulating police and criminal law matters in an intergovernmental manner and whatever the intrinsic differences between these and other subjects, it does not follow that *human rights monitoring* related to those issues should be treated in a distinct manner.[51] After all, international human rights treaties and national constitutions do not treat the subject-matter of policing and criminal law as a separate category. Nor do the Paris principles for the creation of national human rights institutions, which instead specify that such institutions should have 'as broad a mandate as possible.'[52] The only convincing case for limiting the role of the Agency as regards civil and political rights is where the EU already has a body dealing with certain aspects of rights (the EU Data Protection Supervisor and data protection working party and the EU Ombudsman). Again, as noted above, it would be odd to exclude any JHA matters from the scope of the Agency's competence, given that the Hague programme setting an agenda for future JHA co-operation expressly refers to the creation of the Agency.

This leaves us with the legal objections to extending the scope of the Agency's activities to the third pillar. At first sight, these are strong objections: Articles 30 and 31 EU confer competences relating to specific policing and criminal law issues, and there is no equivalent of Article 285 or 308 EC in the third pillar. Article 41 EU requires or permits the application of certain EC Treaty rules to

---

[50] See n 45 above.

[51] In any event, the Opinion in the pending case of *Pupino*, n.37 above, argues that the third pillar is not as intergovernmental as might be thought.

[52] Point 2 of the annex to the General Assembly Resolution setting out the Principles; available at: http://www.ohchr.org/english/law/parisprinciples.htm.

the third pillar, but these rules do not include any that might be relevant to the creation of an EU Human Rights Agency. However, while Article 41 *a contrario* rules out the application of EC legislation creating an Agency as such to the third pillar, it does not rule out the adoption of parallel and interlinked first and third pillar acts. There are a number of precedents for such measures in the areas of the facilitation of illegal entry and residence, the Schengen Information System and the Customs Information System.[53] In fact, the adoption of such parallel measures is surely consistent with, or even required by, the principle of cross-pillar consistency across a 'single institutional framework' set out in Article 3 EU,[54] and the EU's objective to 'maintain and develop the Union as an area of freedom, security and justice' set out in Article 2 EU. The latter objective not only crosses over the first and third pillars but also implies a commitment to secure and guarantee human rights, for surely there is little chance of maintaining and developing such an area without also ensuring effective human rights protection. Logically, when considering the existence of human rights powers in the third pillar, we must also take account of the cross-pillar application of Articles 6(1), 6(2), 7 and 49 EU. Since the powers concerning policing and criminal law cooperation conferred by Article 30(1) and 31(1) EU appear to be non-exhaustive (each states that Union powers 'shall include' the listed powers),[55] it can surely be argued in light of the above that the non-exhaustive powers of the Union in these areas can be used to adopt a measure establishing a Human Rights Agency with monitoring powers concerning EU third pillar law and its implementation by Member States. It would be easy to accomplish this in practice, by means of a third pillar Decision parallel to the EC Regulation creating the agency, which would simply extend the Agency's remit into the third pillar.[56]

In the alternative, if the legal issues concerning the extension of the Agency's remit to the third pillar are considered to be overwhelming for now, there seems no convincing legal argument to prevent the extension of the Agency's remit to such matters after the EU Constitution enters into force. The current Articles 285 and 308 EC would then certainly apply to the current third pillar[57]; moreover, the latter would be revised to apply 'within the framework of the policies defined in Part III' of the Constitution, including, inter alia, all aspects of Justice and Home Affairs law in a single Title. The EU political institutions, when the

[53] See the *Framework Decision and Directive on facilitation of illegal entry* (OJ 2002 L 328); the *Regulation and Decision on management of the SIS II project* (OJ 2001 L 328); and the Convention *and Regulation establishing the CIS* (OJ 1995 L 316/33 and Reg 515/97, OJ 1997 L 82/1).

[54] Stating: 'The Union shall be served by a single institutional framework which shall ensure the consistency and the continuity of the activities carried out in order to attain its objectives while respecting and building upon the *acquis communautaire*.'

[55] This interpretation is confirmed, at least as regards criminal law, by the Opinion in *Pupino*, n 37 above.

[56] A Framework Decision would not be suitable since the creation of the Agency would not involve harmonisation of national law, while the adoption of third pillar Conventions has fallen into desuetude (on third pillar instruments, see Art 34 EU).

[57] See Arts III–429 and I–18 of the Constitutional Treaty, respectively.

Council adopts the Regulation establishing the EC Human Rights Agency, could declare their political commitment to extending the Agency's role to the issues of policing and criminal law as soon as possible after the Constitution takes effect. Given the time lag to adopt the Regulation and then to establish the Agency in practice, there might only be a short period or no period at all during which the Agency has no third pillar role—assuming that the Constitution is indeed ratified by 1 November 2006 as planned.[58]

The third key issue is the extent to which the Agency could play a role ensuring the protection of civil and political rights *outside* the EU. In principle, there is an obvious case for tasking an independent Agency with the collection and analysis of objective data relating to these rights, in particular because the independent nature of the Agency might help to address concerns that the EU institutions' external human rights policy is too inconsistent and politically motivated. However, given the size of such an undertaking, it would be advisable to give the Agency a purely 'domestic' role first; this would in any event be implicitly in accordance with the Paris principles, which do not envisage giving national human rights institutions the competence to examine the level of protection of human rights in other States. The potential extension of the Agency's role to protection of human rights outside the EU could be examined after several years of operations. For its part, the Commission appears to rule out any application of the Agency to external cases.[59]

Having said that, there are areas where EU policies touching on important civil and political rights to be guaranteed within the Union are affected by matters external to the EU. The most obvious cases arise in the spheres of extradition and asylum law, where the key question to be answered is whether a person would face persecution as defined in the Geneva Convention on the Status of Refugees, or a real risk of torture or persecution or a flagrant denial of justice (and arguably violations of other rights) in a non-Member State.[60] The same considerations apply to movement of asylum-seekers between Member States, as the European Court of Human Rights has ruled that before moving an asylum-seeker to another Member State pursuant to EU (and presumably now EC rules), each Member State must consider the argument that another Member State would return that asylum-seeker to a third State in breach of Article 3 ECHR, and so cannot rely automatically on the EC or EU arrangements in place to justify that removal.[61] Also, the EC's intention to adopt a common list of third countries which all Member States must regard as 'safe' countries of origin for asylum-seekers should be assessed in light of these rules.[62] There could be parallel issues regarding the removal of irregular migrants (some of whom may be failed asylum-seekers, who have arguably not been given

---

[58] Art IV–447 of the Constitutional Treaty.
[59] See n 45 above.
[60] *Soering v UK* Series A no 161 (1985) 11 EHRR 439.
[61] Decision in *TI v UK* (Reports of Judgments and Decisions 2000–III).
[62] See latest draft of the asylum procedures (Council doc 14203/04, 9 November 2004).

sufficient procedural rights to plead their case before removal).[63] Furthermore, the EC and EU have entered into close cooperation with non-Member States in this field, in particular Norway, Iceland and Switzerland,[64] along with extradition and mutual assistance treaties with the United States and many treaties between Europol and third States or non-EU bodies.[65] The application of the rules on data transfer from the EU to non-EU countries in the EC data protection Directive has also been a highly contested issue.[66] In light of all this, it would be desirable to confer upon the EU Human Rights Agency the power to examine human rights protection in third countries to the extent that such protection is integral to the protection of civil and political rights within the Union.

The fourth and final issue of scope is whether the Agency should have a role examining the *positive obligations* of the EU/EC and Member States when they implement or derogate from EC or EU law, to the extent that such obligations exist in connection with civil and political rights. Such obligations exist in the context of the ECHR,[67] and so logically must exist within EC/EU law to the extent that the general principles of EC law are inspired particularly by the ECHR and to the extent that the provisions of the Charter correspond to it. The possibility that the general principles confer positive obligations has been recognised by the Court of Justice,[68] and the potential that the Charter imposes them is recognised by the explanations to it.[69] There seems no good reason to exclude the Agency from having a role regarding positive obligations as well as negative ones, although it is probably not necessary to set out the Agency's role in this respect expressly.

IV. POWERS OF THE AGENCY

Let us assume that the Agency will have the scope of activity as outlined in Parts 2 and 3: dealing with all civil and political rights set out in the Charter and the

[63] See the second thematic report of the EU Network of Independent Experts, available at: http://www.europa.eu.int/comm/justice_home/cfr_cdf/index_en.htm#.

[64] See treaties on association with Schengen and asylum responsibility rules (OJ 1999 L 176/35; OJ 2000 L 15/1; OJ 2001 L 93/38; and COM (2004) 593, 14 September 2004).

[65] See the EU/US treaties at OJ 2003 L 181; discussion of the Europol treaty powers in C Rijken, 'Legal and Technical Aspects of Cooperation Between Europol, Third States and Interpol' in V Kronenberger (ed), *The European Union and the International Legal Order: Discord or Harmony?* (The Hague, Asser, 2001) p 577; and discussion of Europol's external practice in S Peers, 'Governance and the Third Pillar: The Accountability of Europol' forthcoming in DM Curtin and RA Wessel (eds), *Good Governance and the European Union: some reflections on conceptual, institutional and substantive frameworks* (Antwerpen, Intersentia, 2004).

[66] See Cases C–317/04 *EP v Council*, C–318/04 *EP v Commission* and *Opinion 1/2004*, all pending.

[67] For a recent analysis, see A Mowbray, *The Development of Positive Obligations under the European Convention on Human Rights by the European Court of Human Rights* (Oxford, Hart Publishing, 2004).

[68] Case C–68/95 *T Port* [1996] ECR I–6065.

[69] See the explanations to the Charter set out in a Declaration to the Constitution Treaty, commenting on Art 51(2) (document IGC 87/04 add 2, 6 August 2004).

general principles of EC law; covering action by the EU and its Member States when implementing or derogating from EC/EU law; extending its activities to the third pillar and to the protection of rights in non-Member States when directly linked to EU or EC law; and examining the positive obligations of the EU and its Member States within that scope. What powers should the Agency then have in order to make an effective contribution to the protection of civil and political rights within its scope of activity?

The best way to answer this question is to examine two existing models: the EU's current Monitoring Agency on racism, xenophobia and anti-Semitism, and the 'Paris Principles' for national human rights institutions adopted by the General Assembly of the United Nations.[70]

If we look at the existing Regulation establishing the EU Monitoring Agency, the principal objective of the Agency is to 'provide' the EC and its Member States with:

> objective, reliable and comparable data at European level [. . .] in order to help them when they take measures or formulate courses of action within their respective spheres of competence.[71]

Also:

> the Centre shall study the extent and development of the phenomena and manifestations of racism, xenophobia and anti-Semitism, analyse their causes, consequences and effects and examine examples of good practice in dealing with them.[72]

To these ends, the Centre must[73]:

a) 'collect, record and analyse information and data';
b) 'build up cooperation between the suppliers of information and develop a policy for concerted use of their databases in order to foster[. . .]the wide distribution of their information';
c) 'carry out scientific research and surveys, preparatory studies and feasibility studies';
d) 'set up documentation resources open to the public, encourage the promotion of information activities and stimulate scientific research';
e) 'formulate conclusions and opinions for the Community and its Member States';
f) 'develop methods to improve the comparability, objectivity and reliability of data at Community level by establishing indicators and criteria that will improve the consistency of information';
g) 'publish an annual report on the situation regarding racism and xenophobia in the Community, also highlighting examples of good practice, and on the Centre's own activities';
h) 'set up and coordinate a European Racism and Xenophobia Information Network';
i) 'facilitate and encourage the organization of regular round-table discussions or meetings of other existing, standing advisory bodies within the Member States.'

---

[70] See Reg 1035/97 (OJ 1997 L 151/1) and n 52 above, respectively.
[71] Art 2(1), Reg 1035/97, *ibid*.
[72] *Ibid*.
[73] Art 2(2) Reg 1035/97, *ibid*.

The second and third powers apply 'where appropriate' at the request of the EP, Council or Commission. In the Commission's view, the Agency (after its expanded mandate) should focus upon the gathering of information and the drafting of opinions.[74]

As for the Paris principles, they specify first of all that the national institutions 'shall be vested with competence to promote and protect human rights.'[75] They 'shall' have seven 'responsibilities':

a) to submit 'opinions, recommendations, proposals and reports on any matters concerning the promotion and protection of human rights', which 'shall relate to':

    (i) '[a]ny legislative or administrative provisions, as well as provisions relating to judicial organizations, intended to preserve and extend the protection of human rights'; this entails examination of existing and proposed measures, and the institution 'shall make such recommendations as it deems appropriate to ensure that these provisions conform to the fundamental principles of human rights; it shall, if necessary, recommend the adoption of new legislation, the amendment of legislation in force and the adoption or amendment of administrative measures'

    (ii) 'any situation of violation of human rights which it decides to take up';

    (iii) issuing reports on general or specific matters concerning the 'national situation' of human rights;

    (iv) drawing the attention of the government to human rights situations in the country and proposing initiatives to the government to end that situation;

b) to promote and ensure harmonization of national legislation and practice with international human rights treaties which the State is a party to, and the effective implementation of such treaties;

c) to encourage ratification of those treaties, and ensure their implementation;

d) to contribute to national reports to human rights treaty monitoring bodies, and to express an opinion on the subject;

e) to cooperate with international and other national institutions competent in the area of human rights;

f) to assist in developing and execution of human rights education and research; and

g) to publicise human rights and efforts to combat discrimination, particularly race discrimination, 'by increasing public awareness,' inter alia, through the media.

In addition, they 'may' have the power 'to hear and consider complaints and petitions concerning individual situations.' Although this is only an option under the Paris Principles, it is considered to be an 'important' power by analysts of the operation of national human rights institutions.[76]

Which model would enable the Agency to play a bigger contribution as regards the protection of civil and political rights? There is some overlap between the powers, particularly the power to issue opinions (point (a) of the

---

[74] See n 45 above.

[75] Point 1 of the Annex to the General Assembly Resolution, n 52 above.

[76] International Council on Human Rights Policy, *Performance and Legitimacy: International Human Rights Institutions* (2000), pp 112–113.

Paris principles and point (e) of the Regulation) and reports (point (a) of the Paris principles and point (g) of the Regulation), to assist in research (point (f) of the Paris principles and points (d) and (h) of the Regulation), and to publicise the relevant issues (point (g) of both the Paris principles and the Regulation). However, the Paris Principles clearly imagine a fuller role as regards issuing opinions to the government and public awareness, envisage a particular role concerning the ratification and implementation of international human rights treaties, and provide for a role in education and (optionally) individual complaints. In contrast, the focus of the existing Agency is the collection and analysis of information in order to provide that information to public bodies.

If we compare a model for the Agency based on the provision of information to a model based on a competence to promote and protect human rights, the latter model is surely far more likely to enable the Agency to make a significant contribution to the protection of civil and political rights within the scope of its activities. The reason for this conclusion is that in most cases, the protection of civil and political rights does not depend upon the provision of data to public authorities, for provision of data alone is not likely to play a decisive role in preventing human rights breaches, resolving human rights complaints and encouraging a culture concerned with ensuring effective human rights protection. Racism, anti-Semitism and xenophobia issues are in some ways distinct, as the chief source of acts of violence and discrimination in the European Union today is likely to be private individuals and companies—notwithstanding the racist, anti-Semitic or xenophobic attitudes or behaviour of some political officials or institutions and the implicit racist, anti-Semitic or xenophobic aspects which arguably are present in EU or Member States' public policies. On the other hand, it is public authorities which will wholly or largely be responsible for breaches of, for instance, the right to liberty or the right to private life.

It is true that as far as immigration and asylum is concerned, the Agency could play a valuable role as a neutral disseminator of information, given that public arguments about asylum and immigration are often fuelled by inaccurate perceptions of its extent. But any role in this area could end up overlapping with the role of Eurostat in producing public statistics on this issue.[77]

Applying the second model to the scope of the Agency's activities, how could it be adapted to the particular activities of the Agency in light of the particular features of the EU legal order? Taking the Paris principles in order, the Agency could obviously play a particularly important role as regards legislation and administrative measures. This would entail examining existing or proposed acts by the EU, or by the Member States when implementing or derogating from EU law, relevant to civil and political rights. It would be necessary to specify that

---

[77] The Commission is planning to propose a Regulation on this issue in December 2004, according to its rolling work programme, available at: http://www.europa.eu.int/comm/off/work_programme/rolling_programme/agenda_planning_3_month_forecast.pdf, accessed 16 November 2004.

the Agency would have to take account of the principles of subsidiarity and proportionality when exercising all its activities, particularly when suggesting the adoption of new EU measures or the amendment of existing measures. This role (as well as some or all of the other 'legal' tasks of the Agency) could be wholly or partly delegated to the existing EU Network of Independent Experts. But (as in the case of monitoring Member States to ensure the effective application of Article 7 EU), if the Network is abolished or its role curtailed in future for legal or political reasons, the Agency (or another entity linked to it) should be assigned such tasks.

As regards situations of violations of human rights, the Agency could take these up whenever such violations have allegedly been committed by the Union or by the Member States when implementing or derogating from Union law. The release of reports on general or specific human rights matters could also take place within the same scope. For example, the Agency could examine the specific issue of the right to asylum within the context of EU measures and national implementation or derogation, although in areas such as freedom of expression, which are less comprehensively affected by EU measures, it would have a lesser role to play. The same applies to the power to draw attention of the EU and the Member States to human rights situations within the EU which could fall within the scope of EU law and which could be addressed by means of EU law or national initiatives implementing or derogating from it.

Next, the Agency could play a particular role contributing to the EU's planned accession to the ECHR (presuming that the EU Constitution enters into force), assisting with analyses of the procedural aspects of accession and advising on whether any changes to the substantive law of the EU (or of the Member States implementing or derogating from EU law) would be necessary. Adapting the Paris Principles to the EU's legal framework, the Agency could also play a role in ensuring that EU law and national measures implementing or derogating from it are consistent with other international treaties which the EU has *not* acceded to, but which are sources of the general principles of EU law or which also concern some of the rights set out in the Charter, particularly (for our purposes) the ICCPR. If there is political will and legal competence for the EU to accede to other existing or future international human rights treaties besides the ECHR, then of course the Agency could have an important role to play in that process.

Unless the EU accedes to a Convention with a monitoring procedure, the Agency would have no role to play therein; but it could be argued that there should be some EU-wide coordination of national reports to human rights treaty monitoring bodies, where the issues in question fall at least in part within the scope of EU law. Alternatively or additionally, the EU institutions could develop a useful practice of drafting and publishing regular reports on the extent to which EU law, and national implementation or derogation from it, affects Member States' obligations under various international human rights treaties. These reports could be annexed to national reports to treaty monitoring bodies.

In either case, the Agency could have a role to play contributing to national reports and expressing an opinion on them.[78]

The Agency could have a particularly important role to play regarding on issues distinct to the EU legal system (and therefore not addressed in the Paris Principles): the role of the constitutional traditions of the Member States on the development of EU general principles and the interpretation of the Charter. It could be tasked with the role of researching and analyzing national constitutional traditions in particular areas, presenting that information to the public, and making any necessary recommendations about changes to or development of EU law. Of course, conversely, it would not be appropriate to task the Agency with the role of making criticisms of or suggesting changes to national constitutions.

Another role for the Agency based on the distinct features of EU law would be the task of examining the extent and effectiveness of non-judicial remedies, including ombudsmen, national human rights institutions, and other measures, which are available within the Member States as regards the protection of rights within the scope of EU law within the national legal order. This could supplement and enhance the effectiveness of the work of the network of national ombudsmen created within the framework of the EU Ombudsman's office.[79] There may be a particular need for the development of such measures in the area of free movement of persons. The Agency might be asked to examine whether there is a case for developing soft law or hard law at EU level recommending or requiring the creation of such bodies, at least in certain areas such as free movement of persons, and if so, what the content of that law should be.[80]

Next, the Agency could obviously be assigned the task of cooperating with relevant national and international institutions; it should also be given the task of cooperating with relevant EU bodies (the EU Ombudsman, the Data Protection Supervisor and the Data Protection working party), in particular because while the activities of the Agency should exclude any direct overlap with the activities of these pre-existing bodies, there would be an overlap between the general human rights role of the Agency and the specific roles of the pre-existing bodies.[81] As for education and research, the Agency would obviously have a role to play in educating sections of the public about the general principles of law and particularly the Charter (including not only the substantive rights, but the limits on their scope of application and their relationship with national and international law). It could also inform the public about the

---

[78] On the role of the Agency and monitoring by international bodies, see the second report of the EU Network of Independent Experts, p 20.

[79] On the work of this network, see pp 223–224 of the EU Ombudsman's Annual Report for 2003.

[80] The requirement that Member States create national bodies with the task of ensuring protection for human rights within the scope of EU law is not new; see Art 8a of Dir 76/207 sex discrimination (OJ 1976 L 39/40), as inserted by Dir 2002/73 (OJ 2002 L 269/15), Art 13 of Dir 2000/43 on race discrimination (OJ 2000 L 180/22) and Art 28 of Dir 95/46 on data protection (OJ 1995 L 281/1).

[81] On the latter two bodies, see Reg 45/2001 (OJ 2001 L 8/1) and Art 29 of Dir 95/46, see n 80 above.

extent to which EU law impacts upon human rights matters, the planned accession of the EU to the ECHR and the general issue of the relationship between national courts, the European Court of Human Rights and the EU courts. The potential research role of the Agency has in part been set out above; but the Agency could also be involved in research as to how EU laws with a particular impact on human rights are being implemented or derogated from by the Member States, above and beyond the analysis which the Commission is able to carry out. This would not (and could not) impinge upon the Commission's first pillar infringement powers (which would extend to the current third pillar if the Constitution is ratified), but it could feed into the possibility of the Commission using those powers, just as the European Parliament's petitions procedure feeds into the possible use of infringement powers.

Finally, the Agency could obviously play a role publicizing the EU's role in human rights—including the limits of that role—to the public, in particular the media. As for the existing remit of the Agency, nothing in the above analysis is meant to suggest that its role and activities regarding the fight against racism, anti-Semitism and xenophobia should be reduced or sidelined. On the contrary, it may be opportune to consider whether that role should be strengthened along with the widening of scope of the Agency's activities—although that is an issue beyond the scope of this chapter.

This brings us to the *optional* power for national human rights institution, the power to receive complaints regarding individual violations. Of course such a role is vitally important in the purely national context, but there seems no reason to give an EU body a parallel role, as long as the EU Ombudsman (and Data Protection Supervisor) is able to offer sufficient non-judicial protection against human rights violations directly by the EU institutions, and national bodies are able to offer sufficient non-judicial protection against human rights violations by the Member States implementing or derogating from EU law. If protection at one or both of these levels is lacking, it is surely easier to improve the protection at that level, if necessary by means of EU measures creating an obligation for the Member States to create non-judicial bodies or enhance their powers, than create a substantial additional task for the EU Agency, given the importance and extent of the other tasks it should have, as outlined above.

V. CONCLUSION

An EU Human Rights Agency would have little or no impact if its tasks are essentially confined to the collection and presentation of statistical data. But neither should the EU aim to create an agency with anything like the full range of powers or scope of activities of 'classic' national human rights institutions. The complex system of multi-level governance within the European Union and the distinct structure of the EU legal system call for the creation of a *sui generis* entity, which should be carefully adapted to its unique legal and political environment. An

Agency tasked with addressing all civil and political rights which are set out in the Charter and in the international and national sources of the EU general principles of law, enjoying competences within the entire scope of the first and third pillars, and examining actions both of the EU institutions and of the Member States when they implement or derogate from EU law, can play an important role as regards examining existing, proposed or potential legal measures, issuing reports, ensuring compatibility of EU and relevant national measures with national and international human rights standards, and in contributing to education, research and publicity related to the EU's role in human rights. Of course, the Agency could not by itself ensure that those human rights are fully protected, without the political will to support human rights at the EU and national level and the maintenance and further development of judicial protection for human rights at various levels. Certainly, the Agency would not be a substitute for improving the role of the Court of Justice in justice and home affairs matters or for strengthening the legal and constitutional protection for human rights by means of enhancing the legal status of the Charter and ensuring EU accession to the ECHR. But, if the Agency is given sufficient powers and a sufficient scope of activity, and a budget commensurate to carry out its tasks, it could play a modest but significant role in ensuring the protection of civil and political rights within the EU.

6

The Contribution of the EU Fundamental Rights Agency to Combating Discrimination and Promoting Equality

I. INTRODUCTION

CREATING A NEW EU Fundamental Rights Agency ('FRA' or 'Agency') by extending the remit of the European Monitoring Centre on Racism and Xenophobia raises 'delicate questions.'[1] The Communication in October 2004 from the Commission of the European Communities initiating the public consultation on the functions and structure of the FRA identifies several such issues, including the 'definition of its field of action' and 'problems concerning the adaptation of the existing structure to ensure that the Agency is effective.'[2] However, one thing is clear. Even if the Agency's remit is confined to the narrowest remit envisages in the Commission's Communication, dealing with those fundamental rights within the scope of Community (or Union) law, and the Agency's role is limited to help ensure compliance with fundamental rights in Community law by the Community institutions (and the Member States when implementing Community law) within the Community, issues of status equality and non-discrimination will be a central feature of the Agency's work, particularly after the Constitutional Treaty ('Constitution') comes into force.

* Professor of Human Rights Law, Oxford University; Overseas Affiliated Professor of Law, University of Michigan Law School. The author has acted as an advisor to the Equality Commission for Northern Ireland, and was a former member of the Standing Advisory Commission on Human Rights. He is currently a member of the European Commission's network of legal experts on the application of Community law on equality between women and men, and the network of legal experts on non-discrimination. This chapter is written in a personal capacity.

[1] Commission of the European Communities, *The Fundamental Rights Agency: Public consultation doc*, SEC(2004)1281, Brussels, 25 October 2004, COM(2004) 693 final ('Communication'), p 3.

[2] *Ibid.* p 3.

Article I–2 of the Constitution will set out the Union's values, incorporating various aspects of status equality explicitly among them.[3] Article I–3 will set out the Union's objectives and give a prominent place to combating social exclusion and *discrimination*, and promoting social justice and protection, *equality between women and men*, solidarity between generations and protection of the rights of the child, among these objectives. When this provision is considered alongside two further provisions, Article III–116 and Article III–118, the mainstreaming of equality and non-discrimination in carrying out functions under Part III appears likely to become an obligation for Union institutions, if it is not such already.[4] Equally, the Union's *competences* in the area of equality are, and will remain, broad. Article III–124 will set out the general competence of the Union in legislating against discrimination, equivalent to Article 13 under the existing Treaty. The Constitution's provisions regarding social policy will also clearly be of considerable importance for gender equality. Article III–209 will set out the basic objectives of the social policy provisions of the Constitution. 'With a view to achieving the objectives' of Article III–209, Article III–210 will provide that, 'the Union shall support and complement the activities of the Member States' in a range of fields, including 'equality between women and men with regard to labour market opportunities and treatment at work.' Article III–214 will provide for equal pay and equal opportunities in employment; it states that:

> Each Member State shall ensure that the principle of equal pay for female and male workers for equal work or work of equal value is applied.

It is the equivalent of Article 141 of the existing Treaty. Several provisions in Part III will deal specifically with trafficking of women and children and their sexual exploitation.[5]

So too, the Charter of Fundamental Rights includes extensive provisions on equality and non-discrimination, of course. There are several particularly relevant provisions. Article II–80 provides that 'Everyone is equal before the law.' Article II–81 on non-discrimination provides that:

> Any discrimination based on any ground such as sex, race, colour, ethnic or social origin, genetic features, language, religion or belief, political or any other opinion, membership of a national minority, property, birth, disability, age or sexual orientation shall be prohibited.

---

[3] 'The Union is founded on the values of respect for human dignity, freedom, democracy, *equality*, the rule of law and respect for human rights, *including the rights of persons belonging to minorities*. These values are common to the Member States in a society in which pluralism, *non-discrimination*, tolerance, justice, solidarity and *equality between women and men* prevail.'

[4] Art III–116 will provide that 'In all the activities referred to in this Part, the Union shall aim to eliminate inequalities, and to promote equality, between women and men.' Art III–118 provides further that 'In defining and implementing the policies and activities referred to in this Part, the Union shall aim to combat discrimination based on sex, racial or ethnic origin, religion or belief, disability, age or sexual orientation.'

[5] Art III–267, Art III–271.

Article II–82 requires the Union to 'respect cultural, religious and linguistic diversity.' Article II–83 specifically addresses quality between women and men. It provides, in the first paragraph: 'Equality between women and men must be ensured in all areas, including employment, work and pay.' Article II–84 provides for certain rights of the child. Article II–85 makes provisions regarding the rights of the elderly. Under Article II–8, the Union:

> recognises and respects the right of persons with disabilities to benefit from measure designed to ensure their independence, social and occupational integration and participation in the life of the community.

Article II–93 on family and professional life provides that: 'The family shall enjoy legal, economic and social protection.' Paragraph 2 continues:

> To reconcile family and professional life, everyone shall have the right to protection from dismissal for a reason connected with maternity and the right to paid maternity leave and to parental leave following the birth or adoption of a child.

Whilst issues of equality and non-discrimination will thus be central to the Agency's work, the precise role of the Agency in this context is an issue at the centre of the current debates about the FRA. The representatives of the Member States meeting within the European Council in Brussels in December 2003 decided to:

> extend the remit of the European Monitoring Centre on Racism and Xenophobia in order to convert it into a Fundamental Rights Agency,'[6]

but otherwise left the place of equality and discrimination within any new Agency uncertain.

The Communication sketches out various different models that might be created, with different implications for the role that equality and discrimination issues might play in the Agency's mandate. Under the first model, the Agency would be asked to monitor all the fundamental rights protected by Community law and included in the Charter. Equality and non-discrimination would be a sub-set of the range of fundamental rights. This, the Communication notes:

> would [. . .] give the Agency an extremely broad field of action, especially if its activities were to include respect for fundamental rights in relations between the individual and the EU institutions or States, but also in all social relations between individuals, as is currently the case in respect of racism and xenophobia.[7]

Under a second model, the Agency would be asked to focus on only certain 'thematic areas having a special connection with Community policies or the Union.' Several are mentioned as possibilities, including 'immigration, asylum, non-discrimination, ethical questions, guarantee of criminal proceedings, violence, etc.' Among these areas, 'racism and xenophobia would continue to be given

---

[6] Communication, p 3.
[7] *Ibid*, p 7.

priority by the Agency.'[8] Without indicating directly which of these options it prefers, the Commission's Communication insists that a 'balance between a potentially vast area of intervention and the effectiveness of the Agency' must be ensured.[9]

This chapter seeks to contribute to the debate about the role of the FRA in equality and non-discrimination by drawing on experiences at the national level (focusing on the United Kingdom) to illuminate this debate. Before turning to this experience, however, it is worth drawing attention to an issue that the Communication appears largely to ignore, namely the relationship between the Agency and equality and non-discrimination bodies at the Community level. Although the Communication does draw attention to the establishment of the European Gender Institute,[10] and notes that the aims of the Agency must take account of its creation, it does not draw attention to several other relevant bodies, in particular two with which this author is currently associated: the network of legal experts on the application of Community law on equality between women and men,[11] and the network of legal experts on non-discrimination (which considers the implementation of the race and framework employment directive).[12] Whilst the Communication rightly says that it:

> will be necessary to identify the synergies which the Agency could develop with the *network of independent experts on fundamental rights,*

equivalent issues are likely to arise in connection with these other expert networks.

II. INSPIRATION FROM NATIONAL INSTITUTIONS?

The Commission's Communication states that the European Union can and should learn from the experience of the operation of national human rights institutions. These, it says:

> can serve as a source of inspiration when establishing the Agency, even though care should be taken to avoid simply transposing these examples, given the specificity of the EU.[13]

What, more precisely, might those lessons be?

The growth of national human rights institutions has been extraordinary in the past decade, not only in the old and new European Union Member States,[14]

---

[8] Communication, p 7.

[9] *Ibid.*

[10] Conclusion 43 of the presidency of the European Council of Brussels (17 and 18 June 2004).

[11] Available at: http://europa.eu.int/comm/employment_social/equ_opp/rights/experts_en.html.

[12] Available at: http://www.humanconsultancy.com/projects.htm.

[13] Commission of the European Communities, *The Fundamental Rights Agency: Public consultation doc*, SEC(2004)1281, Brussels, 25 October 2004, COM(2004) 693 final ('Communication'), p 4.

[14] EU Network of Independent Experts on Fundamental Rights (CFR-CDF), Opinion of the EU Network of Independent Experts in Fundamental Rights Regarding the Role of National Institutions for the Protection of Human Rights in the Member States of the European Union, March 2004, CFR-CDF.Opinion1.2004.

but worldwide. This has occurred not least because of the activities of the United Nations Office of the High Commission for Human Rights, in particular during the 1990s, in seeking to have states establish such bodies using the Paris Principles[15] as a basis for their powers and functions.[16] These bodies are often seen as particularly important in the context of tackling discrimination and promoting equality. The Committee on the Elimination of Racial Discrimination (CERD), for example, has adopted General Recommendation No 17 on *Establishment of national institutions to facilitate the implementation of the Convention*.[17] The Committee recommends States parties to establish national commissions or other appropriate bodies, taking into account the Paris Principles, to serve such purposes as: the promotion of respect for the enjoyment of human rights without discrimination, the review of government policy towards protection against racial discrimination, the monitoring of legislative compliance with the provisions of the Convention, the education of the public about the obligations of States parties, and assisting the Government in the preparation of reports to CERD.

In the European context, the recommendations developed by the Council of Europe's European Commission against Racism and Intolerance (ECRI) have also proved influential in this respect. ECRI's second General Policy Recommendation, on *Specialised bodies to combat racism, xenophobia, anti-Semitism, and intolerance at national level*,[18] recommends that the governments of the Member States, consider carefully the possibility of setting up a specialised body to combat these problems, if such a body does not already exist. In examining this question ECRI recommended that states make use of a set of basic principles annexed to the recommendation 'as guidelines and a source of inspiration presenting a number of options for discussion at national level.'[19] The preamble recognises that:

> the form such bodies might take may vary according to the circumstances of member States and may form part of a body with wider objectives in the field of human rights generally.[20]

[15] Endorsed by the 85th plenary meeting of the United Nations General Assembly, 20 December 1993: UN doc A/RES/48/134.

[16] International Council on Human Rights Policy, Performance and Legitimacy: National Human Rights Institutions (International Council on Human Rights Policy, Geneva, 2000); C Flinterman and M Zwamborn, *From Development of Human Rights to Managing Human Rights Development, Global Review of the OHCHR Technical Cooperation Programme, Synthesis Report*, Netherlands Institute of Human Rights (SIM) in partnership with MEDE European Consultancy, September 2003. In addition, the CESCR has also adopted an important General Comments of relevance to this study on 'The role of national human rights institutions in the protection of economic, social and cultural rights.'

[17] CERD, 42nd Session, 1993. Available at: http://www.unhchr.ch/tbs/doc.nsf/0/4872085cc3178e3bc12563ee004beb99?Opendocument.

[18] ECRI general policy recommendation No 2, 13 June 1997 (CRI (97) 36).

[19] *Ibid*. para 1.

[20] ECRI general policy recommendation No 2, 13 June 1997 (CRI (97) 36), Preamble, indent 15.

More recently, both the Race Directive and the amended Equal Treatment Directive provide that a national body or bodies must be designated for the promotion of equal treatment and that this national body should be empowered to assist individual victims.[21]

Arising in part from these initiatives, there is now an extensive array of national institutions, but they differ extensively in how equality and non-discrimination issues are treated. Some have a mandate that includes equality and non-discrimination amongst the range of human rights issues that the institution has within its jurisdiction. Others have a mandate that is limited to equality and non-discrimination issues. Within the latter category, some national equality bodies deal with discrimination on the basis of several grounds (gender, race, and disability, etc), whilst others deal only with one ground of discrimination (such as gender or race).

Information about the operation of the various equality bodies at the national level is growing steadily. The European Union now has extensive experience of the operation of these bodies, and indeed of assessing their effectiveness.[22] The relatively recent establishment of national human rights institutions has meant that independent assessments of the operation of these bodies are only now becoming more widespread, but here too information is steadily building.[23] Much of that assessment is critical of the operation of these bodies,[24] leading some to call into question the emphasis placed on such bodies.[25] We are now entering a phase where the role of such national institutions can be viewed in a somewhat more balanced way, perhaps with less unalloyed enthusiasm, but with more realism.

Much of the utility of emerging assessments of national human rights institutions emphasises the importance of context specificity in determining whether such institutions have been successful or not.[26] There is much work to be done

---

[21] Council Dir 2000/43/EC implementing the principle of equal treatment between persons irrespective of racial or ethnic origin, OJ L 180/22, 19 July 2000, art 13; Dir 2002/73/EC of the European Parliament and of the Council of 23 September 2002 amending Council Dir 76/207/EEC on the implementation of the principle of equal treatment for men and women as regards access to employment, vocational training and promotion and working conditions, OJ L 269/15, 5 October 2002, Art 8a. There is no equivalent requirement in Council Dir 2000/78/EC establishing a general framework for equal treatment in employment and occupation, OJ L 303/16, 21 February 2003.

[22] See the European Commission report 'Specialised bodies to promote equality and/or combat discrimination,' 2002. Available at: http://europa.eu.int/comm/employment_social/fundamental_rights/index_fr.htm.

[23] C Flinterman and M Zwamborn, *From Development of Human Rights to Managing Human Rights Development, Global Review of the OHCHR Technical Cooperation Programme, Synthesis Report*, Netherlands Institute of Human Rights (SIM) in partnership with MEDE European Consultancy, September 2003.

[24] International Council on Human Rights Policy, *Performance and Legitimacy: National Human Rights Institutions* (International Council on Human Rights Policy, Geneva, 2000); See also: V Sripati, 'India's National Human Rights Commission: A Shackled Commission?' (2000) 18 *Boston University International Law Journal* 1.

[25] LC Relf, 'Building Democratic Institutions: The Role of National Human Rights Institutions in Good Governance and Human Rights Protection' (2000) 13 Harvard Human Rights Journal 1.

[26] International Council on Human Rights Policy, *Performance and Legitimacy: National Human Rights Institutions* (International Council on Human Rights Policy, Geneva, 2000).

in the future in pulling together these national assessments, seeing to what extent general lessons can be drawn. What I will do in this chapter, however, is provide a more limited case study of the debate in the United Kingdom over national human rights institutions in the context of equality issues specifically,[27] and attempt to draw out some issues that arise from that experience, as a contribution to the debate over the establishment of an EU Fundamental Rights Agency, with an equality and non-discrimination mandate.

III. THE EXPERIENCE OF THE UNITED KINGDOM IN THE ESTABLISHMENT OF EQUALITY AND HUMAN RIGHTS BODIES

There is a long tradition in the United Kingdom of establishing agencies (or 'Commissions' as they are usually termed in the United Kingdom) in the context of efforts to tackle discrimination and promote status equality. By the end of the 1990s, Commissions had been established dealing with race, sex, and disability in Britain (the Commission for Racial Equality, the Equal Opportunities Commission, and the Disability Rights Commission respectively). Separate Commissions, with similar names, had also established in Northern Ireland on each of these issues, in addition to one specifically dealing with equality between the two religio-political communities in Northern Ireland (the Fair Employment Commission for Northern Ireland). The United Kingdom experience may be of particular relevance to the EU debate because it has involved relatively recent consideration of the relationship between a new human rights commission, and its role vis-à-vis these existing Commissions responsible for anti-discrimination issues, raising somewhat similar issues to that between the new EU Fundamental Rights Agency and the existing monitoring centre on racism and xenophobia. The United Kingdom example is perhaps particularly interesting, since two markedly different models of possible relationships have been developed, one in Northern Ireland, the other in the rest of the United Kingdom.

1. Initial Proposals for a Human Rights Commission in Britain

The first relevant discussions took place in the United Kingdom before and during the passage of the Human Rights Act 1998, which (effectively) incorporated the European Convention on Human Rights into United Kingdom law. Among the many issues this incorporation raised was whether a human rights commission should be established to play a role similar to that played by the existing equality commissions.

---

[27] Another contributor to this book (Manfred Nowak) considers the relationship between the EU Human Rights Agency and the national human rights institutions in ch 4.

In Britain (as opposed to Northern Ireland, which I consider subsequently), the issue was raised in the context of the incorporation into United Kingdom law of the European Convention on Human Rights ('ECHR'), when the Independent Public Policy Research ('IPPR'), a think tank close to the Labour Party, announced prior to the General Election that it was considering recommending the amalgamation of the British CRE and EOC into a British Human Rights Commission. Following the victory of the Labour Party in the General Election and the decision to incorporate the ECHR, the issue of a Human Rights Commission was considered within government in the context of the drafting of the Human Rights Bill, but the Government announced that a decision had been taken not to establish such a body for the time being, pending further consultation with the statutory equality commissions. The White Paper, *Rights Brought Home*, noted that:

> before a Human Rights Commission could be established [. . .] more consideration needs to be given to how it would work [. . .] and there needs to be a greater degree of consensus on an appropriate model among existing human rights [meaning essentially *equality*] bodies.[28]

However, the Government considered that at some stage in the future, in the light of practical experience of the working of the new legislation, the issue might be reconsidered.

2. The Northern Ireland Equality and Human Rights Commissions

The second major development involved the separate discussions in Northern Ireland surrounding the establishment of a separate Human Rights Commission for Northern Ireland, and the possible amalgamation of the then existing Northern Ireland equality bodies into one body. We have seen that in Northern Ireland there existed equality bodies separate from those in Britain, and separate from each other. There had also existed, since the early 1970s, a statutory Standing Advisory Commission on Human Rights, which had the function of advising government on the human rights implications of its policies and proposals in Northern Ireland. It had no enforcement powers. There was no equivalent body in Britain.

The possibility of an amalgamation of the statutory equality commissions into one equality commission had a long history. In brief, a proposal to this effect had first been made by government in a Consultation Paper on the revision of the fair employment legislation in the mid-1980s.[29] The suggestion that the Fair Employment Agency (as it was called before becoming the Fair

---

[28] White Paper, *Rights Brought Home: The Human Rights Bill*, Cm 3782, October 1997, paras 3.8 to 3.11.

[29] Department of Economic Development, *Equality of Opportunity in Northern Ireland: Future Strategy Options* (1986).

Employment Commission) should be amalgamated with the Equal Opportunities Commission for Northern Ireland,[30] received a hostile response from many commentators. The proposal was not endorsed by the government's Standing Advisory Commission on Human Rights ('SACHR') in its 1987 report on fair employment,[31] and was not adopted by government.[32] Instead, it recommended that the issue be kept under review. SACHR had again considered the issue in the context of its 1997 report on employment equality,[33] and again concluded that the equality agencies should not be amalgamated but that the issue should again be kept under review. In 1998 however, the Government proposed, subject to public consultation, to create a new unified statutory authority bringing together the then existing Northern Ireland equality agencies.[34]

A crucial development changed the debate over the advantages to be gained from the amalgamation of the equality bodies. During the 1990s, as part of its review of equality issues, the government proposed to introduce an equality mainstreaming duty in Northern Ireland.[35] This was subsequently confirmed by the Belfast Agreement, and implemented in section 75 of the Northern Ireland Act 1998. This provides that each 'public authority' is required, in carrying out its functions relating to Northern Ireland, to have 'due regard' to the need to promote equality of opportunity between certain different individuals and groups. The relevant categories between which equality of opportunity is to be promoted are between persons of different religious belief, political opinion, racial group, age, marital status, or sexual orientation; between men and women generally; between persons with a disability and persons without; and between persons with dependants and persons without. This equality duty represented an important shift away from relying on the operation of traditional anti-discrimination law to address structural inequalities. Without prejudice to these obligations, a public authority in Northern Ireland is also, in carrying out its functions, to have regard to the desirability of promoting good relations between persons of different religious belief, political opinion or racial group.

It appeared from the government's White Paper to be clear that the major reason in favour of the establishment of a unified Equality Commission was the need to find some institutional mechanism for the monitoring and enforcement of this statutory duty on public bodies to promote equality of opportunity. The

---

[30] The Fair Employment Agency and the Equal Opportunity Commission were the only two equality bodies then in existence.

[31] *Religious and Political Discrimination and Equality of Opportunity in Northern Ireland: Report on Fair Employment*, 1987, Cm 237 (London, HMSO).

[32] Northern Ireland Office, *Fair Employment in Northern Ireland* (Cm 380), 1988 (London, HMSO)

[33] Standing Advisory Commission on Human Rights, *Employment Equality: Building for the Future*, 1997, Cm 3684.

[34] White Paper, *Partnership for Equality*, 1998, Cm 3890. The Northern Ireland equality agencies then in existence were the Fair Employment Commission, the Equal Opportunities Commission, the Commission for Racial Equality, and the Northern Ireland Disability Council.

[35] *Ibid.*

reason given for the establishment of a body external to the civil service for carrying out these functions was the need for external assistance to enable the public bodies to implement the duty effectively. 'It is doubtful whether public sector bodies would have the expertise to implement effectively these proposals without external assistance.'[36] But because the necessary expertise was already to some extent present in the existing equality agencies, and a new equality body set up solely to monitor and enforce the new public sector duty 'could not hope to duplicate this expertise,'[37] 'the most rational organization solution would be the creation of a unified Equality Commission, bringing together the existing statutory bodies.'[38] The 'main purpose' of the amalgamation would be to enable their work to be greatly extended into a new area, a positive engagement with the public sector to promote equality of opportunity in a broad sense.[39]

The White Paper envisaged this unified Equality Commission possibly operating 'on the basis of separate directorates for fair employment, gender, race and possibly [. . .] disability.'[40] Other directorates could implement the new functions associated with the new public sector equality duty: setting standards for statutory schemes, validating specific schemes, monitoring their implementation and investigating complaints that schemes had not been appropriately applied by public bodies.[41]

This issue was then thrown into the negotiations for a peace settlement, alongside the additional issue of the establishment of a new human rights commission, replacing the existing Standing Advisory Commission on Human Rights. The Belfast Agreement provided that a new Northern Ireland Human Rights Commission would be established, with membership from Northern Ireland 'reflecting the community balance' and with some investigatory powers, although not ones that would have satisfied the standards set down in the Paris Principles. This Commission would be established 'independent of Government, with an extended and enhanced role beyond that currently exercised by the [SACHR].' This role would include keeping under review the adequacy and effectiveness of laws and practices, making recommendations to Government, providing information and promoting awareness of human rights, considering draft legislation referred to it by the new Assembly, and 'in appropriate cases,' bringing court proceedings or providing assistance to individuals doing so.[42] The new Human Rights Commission would be tasked specifically with consulting and advising:

---

[36] White Paper, *Partnership for Equality*, 1998, Cm 3890. The Northern Ireland equality agencies then in existence were the Fair Employment Commission, the Equal Opportunities Commission, the Commission for Racial Equality, and the Northern Ireland Disability Council, para 4.11.

[37] *Ibid*, para 4.12

[38] *Ibid*.

[39] *Ibid*.

[40] *Ibid*, para 4.13.

[41] *Ibid*, para 4.11.

[42] *Ibid*; Belfast Agreement, Rights, Safeguards and Equality of Opportunity, Human Rights, New Institutions in Northern Ireland, p 5.

on the scope for defining, in Westminster legislation, rights supplementary to those in the European Convention on Human Rights, to reflect the particular circumstances of Northern Ireland, drawing as appropriate on international instruments and experience. [. . .] Among the issues for consideration by the Commission will be [. . .] a clear formulation of the rights not to be discriminated against and to equality of opportunity in both the public and private sectors.[43]

The Agreement noted that the British Government proposed to create a new statutory Equality Commission to replace the Fair Employment Commission, the Equal Opportunities Commission (Northern Ireland), the Commission for Racial Equality (Northern Ireland), and the Disability Council. Such a unified Commission would 'advise on, validate and monitor the statutory equality obligation and will investigate complaints of default.' But this proposal was not agreed by the negotiating parties or by the Irish Government, being 'subject to the outcome of public consultation currently underway.' The responses about the proposal to create a unified Equality Commission displayed a high level of interest. About 98 out of the 123 submissions commented positively or negatively. Only eighteen could be said to have been unambiguously in favour of the amalgamation proposal. Of those expressing a view, the government estimated that 55 were broadly against.[44] Several expressed concern that a single equality commission would create a hierarchy of discrimination. In particular, many of these specifically indicated their concern that religious discrimination issues might get disproportionate attention. Many wrote of the risk of losing expertise accumulated over many years in the field of fair employment and gender equality, and the risk that relatively new initiatives in the field of race and disability rights might be undermined.

A campaign to modify the Government's proposals on amalgamating the equality Commissions into a new single Equality Commission was unsuccessful. In an attempt to meet the various criticisms of the proposal that had been made (in particular that religious equality would dominate the working of the new body) the announcement indicated that the legislation would require the Equality Commission to devote appropriate resources to gender, race, and disability issues. It would also allow the Commission to establish consultative councils on these issues. A working party would be established, including representatives of the existing Commissions, and representatives of the groups most affected by the statutory duty (who were ultimately not included, in fact) to consider a new internal structure for the Commission.

Alternative proposals that would have delayed the establishment of the unified Commission were rejected by the Government. The possibility that the

---

[43] Belfast Agreement, Rights, Safeguards and Equality of Opportunity, Human Rights, New Institutions in Northern Ireland, p 4.

[44] This section is adapted from an analysis of the responses by the Committee on the Administration of Justice. Committee on the Administration of Justice, *Preliminary Analysis by the Committee on the Administration of Justice of Responses to the White Paper* Partnership for Equality (30 September 1998).

new Human Rights Commission should consider the future of the existing equality Commissions, perhaps even absorbing them into a single human rights and equality body was rejected on the ground that the Government saw 'value in distinguishing between the functions of a Human Rights Commission and the executive responsibilities of an Equality Commission.'[45] A more gradualist approach to amalgamation such as bringing the existing bodies together only for certain purposes, or sharing common services, was rejected as contributing to uncertainty. Finally, the need for a single body, which would be able to respond to complaints of failure by public authorities to apply the statutory equality duty, was seen as crucial. The alternative of providing that the 'primary' means of redress should be through the courts was thought likely to carry the:

> risk of creating disruption to efficient government at a time when the new adminis-
> tration will be finding its feet and attempting to develop innovative ways of working
> together.[46]

Many bodies, particularly the Equal Opportunities Commission for Northern Ireland, continued to resist and argue that the decision should be reversed. It was implemented, however, in the Northern Ireland Act 1998, which established a new Equality Commission for Northern Ireland, and a separate Northern Ireland Human Rights Commission, together with the new statutory equality duty, which introduced equality mainstreaming, as discussed above.

Whilst the Equality Commission has handled the difficult issues of creating one body out of several with commendable skill, the operation of the Northern Ireland Human Rights Commission since its establishment is a telling example of what may go wrong with such bodies. It is a sad story, in which almost all that can go wrong with such bodies did go wrong, with allegations of collusion by some members of the Commission with government bodies casting doubt on their independence, lack of any real progress on its main statutory function of recommending a Bill of Rights for Northern Ireland, several well-publicised resignations by prominent members of the Commission, leading eventually to a decision by government not to reappoint virtually the whole of the existing Commission and replace them with new members.[47] It is, therefore, a salutary tale for others contemplating the establishment of a human rights commission.

---

[45] 'Secretary of State Announces Equality White Paper Decisions,' Northern Ireland Information Service, 10 July 1998.

[46] *Ibid.*

[47] Joint Committee on Human Rights, Fourteenth Report, *Work of the Northern Ireland Human Rights Commission*, HL 132, HC 142, 15 July 2003; Response to the 14th Report of the Joint Committee on Human Rights in the Session 2002–03—*On the Work of the Northern Ireland Human Rights Commission*, March 2004.

3. A British Human Rights Commission Revisited

A third development involved the decision by the British government to revisit the establishment of a human rights commission for the rest of the United Kingdom. The occasion for this was the initiation of a debate within government during 2000 over the bringing together of the existing (non-Northern Ireland) equality commissions into one body. Unlike in Northern Ireland, the principle reason motivating the government's decision was not the implementation of mainstreaming. In Britain, unlike Northern Ireland, there is no *general* statutory duty on public authorities to adopt mainstreaming across a wide range of equality grounds, but (at that time) only in the context of racial equality. The Race Relations (Amendment) Act 2000, which established this more limited duty, differs from the Northern Ireland duty in several respects. First, the duty applies only to racial and ethnic equality, rather than covering a broad range of grounds. The Act requires that each of a specified list of public bodies must, in carrying out its functions, have due regard to the need to eliminate unlawful racial discrimination, and to promote equality of opportunity and good relations between persons of different racial groups.[48] The Secretary of State has made an order that imposes certain specific duties on a more limited group of public bodies and other persons who are also subject to the general duty.[49]

Since there was no general statutory duty across several grounds, the argument that amalgamation was necessary to ensure 'joined-up' enforcement of the duty, as in Northern Ireland, was not possible. Instead, the motivating factor in amalgamation in Britain appears to have been the adoption of the EC directives prohibiting discrimination on the basis of race, age, religion, sexual orientation, and disability. The British government was opposed to establishing separate enforcement bodies for each 'new' ground (ie, the grounds not already legislated for in the United Kingdom: age, religion and sexual orientation). Merely adding these grounds to one of more of the existing Commissions, whilst possible, was equally unattractive.

In December 2001, the Government announced that it had decided in principle to move towards the establishment of a 'single equality body,'[50] which would combine the functions of the three existing anti-discrimination commissions (the Equal Opportunities Commission, the Commission for Racial Equality and the Disability Rights Commission). The new body would have responsibilities relating to the three new 'strands' of antidiscrimination legislation (relating to age, sexual orientation and religion or belief).[51] However, the government sought more public discussion of whether this was appropriate and,

---

[48] S 71.

[49] Race Relations Act 1976 (Statutory Duties) Order 2001.

[50] See *Towards Equality and Diversity: Implementing the Employment and Race Directives*, Cabinet Office, Department of Trade & Industry, Home Office and Department for Work and Pensions, December 2001. See also: Twenty-second Report, Session 2001–02, paras 7 to 12.

[51] Following implementation of the 'Employment' and 'Race' Dirs 2000/43/EC and 2000/78/EC.

if so, how it should be accomplished. In October 2002, the government launched its consultation on equality institutions in Great Britain.[52]

Those advocating the establishment of a human rights commission in Britain (it will be remembered that one had only been established in Northern Ireland by this time) took advantage of the opportunity of this debate to urge that the mandate of any new equality commission should be broadened to incorporate an additional human rights function. In particular, the Joint Committee on Human Rights of the House of Commons and House of Lords examined the issue during the first few months of 2003. In March 2003 the Committee published its report on *The Case for a Human Rights Commission*.[53] It found that the development of a culture of respect for human rights in Britain was in danger of stalling, and that there was an urgent need for the momentum to be revived and the project driven forward. It concluded that this task could not be undertaken by the courts alone, or developed solely by an agency within government.[54] It found the case for the establishment of an independent human rights commission in Great Britain compelling. It concluded:

> an independent commission would be the most effective way of achieving the shared aim of bringing about a culture of respect for human rights.[55]

On 30 October 2003, the Government announced that it had decided to proceed with a single equality body, *and* to give it a human rights dimension as well as an equality remit. This body was given the provisional title of the 'Commission for Equality and Human Rights' ('CEHR'). The government's statement announced that, alongside its equality functions, the new commission would promote a culture of respect for human rights, especially in the delivery of public services.[56] Beyond that, the government left open to further discussion the issue of what powers the new body should have, and what its structure should be. The Parliamentary Joint Committee on Human Rights, in May 2004, welcomed the broad decision,[57] and considered in more detail the functions, powers and structure of the proposed commission so far as they related to human rights.[58]

A few days later, in May 2004, the Government announced its more detailed proposals in a White Paper.[59] The government confirmed that the existing

---

[52] *Equality and Diversity: Making it happen*, Cabinet Office, Department of Trade & Industry, Home Office and Department for Work and Pensions, October 2002, available at: http://164.36.253.98/equality/project/making_it_happen/cons_doc.htm.

[53] Sixth Report, Session 2002–03, *The Case for a Human Rights Commission*, HL Paper 67–I and II, HC 489–I and II; see also Twenty-second Report, Session 2001–02, *The Case for a Human Rights Commission: Interim Report*, HL Paper 160, HC 1142, n 50 above.

[54] Sixth Report, Session 2002–03, n 53 above, para 99.

[55] *Ibid.*

[56] HC Deb, 30 October 2003, cols 18–20WS.

[57] Joint Committee on Human Rights, Eleventh Report of Session 2003–04, Commission for Equality and Human Rights: Structure, Functions and Powers (HL 78, HC 536, HMSO, 2004), 5 May 2004.

[58] *Ibid.*

[59] White Paper, *Fairness For All: A New Commission for Equality and Human Rights*, May 2004, Cm 6185.

equality bodies would be amalgamated into one new body, and that that body would retain the existing investigatory and enforcement functions and powers of these bodies as regards anti-discrimination law. In the context of its human rights mandate, however, its functions would be largely promotional and advisory. It would not, for example, have even the limited investigatory and litigation powers that the Northern Ireland Human Rights Commission had. Instead, the new body would play an important role in promoting a culture of respect for human rights through providing systematic advice and guidance to public bodies. It would help public bodies move forward from bare compliance, to using good human rights practice to encourage better public services. It regarded it as appropriate that there should be greater powers regarding the promotion of equality and non-discrimination than the promotion of human rights generally.[60] As regards the issue of positive duties, there was an undertaking in the White Paper to introduce public sector duties, similar to that in the Race Relations (Amendment) Act, in relation to equality of opportunity for disabled people and between men and women, but not as regards other strands of prohibited discrimination, and not as regards human rights generally.[61]

IV. LESSONS FROM THE UNITED KINGDOM EXPERIENCE

1. Powers of Human Rights Institutions

What, then, can be drawn from this case study of the United Kingdom developments? One issue facing the Community in the establishment of the EU Human Rights Agency that might be illuminated by considering the UK experience is the issue of the appropriate powers to give to a human rights commission, in particular whether enforcement powers should be provided to the Agency, and of what type. One of the major issues in the operation of the Northern Ireland Human Rights Commission relates to the adequacy of its statutory powers. The question of what powers relating to human rights are appropriate to the new CEHR has also been a central issue in recent British discussions.

In the case of the Northern Ireland Human Rights Commission, the issue involved, inter alia, the Commission's inability to compel the production of information from any source and by its lack of access *as of right* to premises. Although recommendations had been made by both the Commission and the House of Commons Northern Ireland Affairs Committee on this issue, no amendments have been forthcoming for the government, up to the time of writing.[62] Most recently, however, the Commission was granted leave to take judicial review proceedings against the Secretary of State, challenging the decision

---

[60] *Ibid*, para 1.24.
[61] *Ibid*.
[62] See Northern Ireland Human Rights Commission, *A Supplementary Review on the Commission's Powers*—submitted to Government, 1 April 2004.

of the government to refuse the Commission access to a Juvenile Justice Centre. In March 2002 the Commission had published research reviewing the conditions under which children and young people were detained in the criminal justice system in Northern Ireland, and making recommendations. From 2003, the Commission had attempted to secure permission to visit a particular Centre to carry out research on how those recommendations have been implemented. The relevant government department refused the Commission access, claiming it has no right of access under its powers and that other, more appropriate bodies had the responsibility to inspect the Centre. The Northern Ireland High Court granted leave for the Commission to judicially review the Secretary of State based on two key points: firstly, that the Commission has a legitimate expectation of co-operation from the Government given its previous commitment to co-operation, clearly stated to Parliament and, secondly, that the NIO has wrongly assumed that the Commission's powers in this case may only be exercised where no other statutory provisions exist for the type of work proposed by the Commission.[63]

Nor has the issue of the human rights enforcement powers of the British CEHR been resolved satisfactorily. In its May 2004 report,[64] the Joint Committee recommended that the new body should have a widely drawn remit in respect of the promotion of a culture of respect for human rights, going beyond the Convention rights incorporated into United Kingdom law by the Human Rights Act. It recommended that the Commission should have a role in reporting on the UK's discharge of its international human rights obligations. The Commission's role should be focused on achieving strategic change through promotion, advice, the spreading of best practice and the raising of public awareness. It should not, for the most part, be directly involved in the resolution of individual cases. The key role of the new Commission will be working with the public sector to give practical effect to a culture of respect for human rights in the policy and practice of providers of public services. The Committee recommended that this should be achieved through close co-operation with the bodies charged with regulating, auditing and inspecting the quality of public services. The Commission should also be able to guide and advise the private sector on the development of a culture of respect for human rights. It also proposed a general statutory duty on public authorities to promote human rights. The Committee recommended that the Commission should have a duty to build the capacity of the private and voluntary sectors to advise and assist individuals in understanding and asserting their rights. It recommended that the Commission should promote alternative dispute resolution as a way of avoid-

---

[63] See Northern Ireland Human Rights Commission, Press Release, *Human Rights Commission Granted Leave in Case against the Secretary of State*, Wednesday 7 July 2004.

[64] Joint Committee on Human Rights, Eleventh Report of Session 2003–04, *Commission for Equality and Human Rights: Structure, Functions and Powers* (HL 78, HC 536, HMSO, 2004), 5 May 2004.

ing litigation and pre-empting violations of rights. The Commission should have a general duty to promote good relations between communities and groups within Great Britain based on respect for the values of human rights so as to encourage the peaceful resolution of disputes.

The Committee recommended that the Commission should be able to conduct public inquiries into matters of public policy relating to human rights. It recommended ancillary powers needed to make these inquiries effective. It proposed that the Commission, in addition to the power to assist as a friend of the court or to intervene as a third party in significant cases raising questions of public interest relating to human rights, should have an exceptional power to seek judicial review on compliance by public authorities with their duties under the Human Rights Act. The Commissioners should be appointed with the involvement of Parliament, and should not be chosen as 'champions' of particular strands of the Commission's responsibilities. The Committee recommended special arrangements to guarantee the independence of the Commission as a constitutional watchdog, while also securing its democratic accountability. These include a special relationship between the Commission and Parliament.

Following the White Paper, the Committee noted that there is agreement between it and the Government on most of the fundamental principles of the design of the Commission.[65] However, the Committee identified the following areas of divergence and raises questions in relation to them: the precise nature of the general duty to be placed upon the CEHR in relation to the promotion and protection of human rights; the details of the power of the Commission to conduct 'general inquiries' into matters connected with human rights; the case for introducing a public sector duty in relation to human rights; the details of the scope of and restrictions on the power of the Commission to support individual cases in the courts in which discrimination and human rights issues are raised; the facilitation of alternative dispute resolution in human rights cases by the Commission; the case for giving the Commission power to seek judicial review of the policies, actions and omissions of public authorities under the Human Rights Act; institutional and funding arrangements to secure the independence and accountability of the new body. These will continue to be issues of debate in the run up to the introduction of legislation to implement the White Paper proposals, and in Parliament itself during consideration of draft legislation.

The conclusion from this experience seems to be that in the absence of a clear alternative mechanism for resolving complaints and conducting investigations, the establishment of a human rights agency raises significant expectations that are unlikely to be satisfied if the body does not have effective powers, and that this will lead to continued pressure to provide such powers where they have not

---

[65] Joint Committee on Human Rights, Sixteenth Report of Session 2003–04: *Commission for Equality and Human Rights: The Government's White Paper*, HL 156; HC 998 (HMSO, London, 2004), 4 August 2004.

been initially accorded to the commission on its establishment. This casts an interesting light on the discussion in the Communication on the powers of the Agency. The Communication is relatively unspecific but it is made clear that, although the FRA may have:

> consultative, informative and monitoring functions and be able in particular to formulate opinions and draw up studies and reports and education and information schemes,[66]

the Commission does not envisage that the Agency will be 'accorded other powers given to national human rights institutions in particular "quasi-judicial" powers (dealing with complaints and petitions),' since the Treaty has:

> already conferred them on the [Community] institutions: the Commission's role of supervising the proper application of Community law must be respected.[67]

Not giving the Agency independent investigatory powers is likely to throw the spotlight back on the Commission to be more active in pursuing its enforcement functions in the equality context.

2. Single or Multiple Equality Bodies

A second issue raised by the UK experience that may also be relevant for the debate on the role of the FRA is the appropriateness of joining all the equality strands together in the context of a single body. In several jurisdictions which have adopted an agency regulation approach, the issue has arisen as to whether the preferable approach is to establish a *single* agency which is responsible for equality across a range of different groups, including race, gender, disability, sexual orientation, etc, or have several different agencies responsible.

One common argument in favour of a single agency approach covering all the separate equality strands is that particular equality agendas may gain in strength from being associated with other equality agendas. Two separable arguments recur. The first is that equality and non-discrimination are indivisible and that it strengthens each dimension of equality ideologically for it to be seen as part of a wider, broader movement. The second is that it strengthens those dimensions of equality that do not have the political priority of some other dimensions of equality for them to be associated with those dimensions that do have strong political support. In some jurisdictions, it is said, the movement against disability discrimination might have stronger political weight if it were associated with gender equality, which is perceived to be given greater political priority at the present time, and therefore benefit from greater financial resources. A more pragmatic argument in favour of a single agency is that, particularly from

---

[66] Communication, p 4.
[67] *Ibid.*

the point of view of organisations subject to regulation, a 'one-stop-shop' is desirable where advice on equality and discrimination across all grounds can be obtained and co-ordinated. This, it is said, saves time, money, and aggravation. It also avoids the perception of potentially inconsistent signals being sent on similar issues by different agencies. A similar argument, it is said, obtains in the context of victims of discrimination: it is not infrequent that a complainant comes to an equality body with a relatively broad sense of grievance which spans several possible areas of discrimination (for example, a complaint by an Afro-Caribbean woman) and it would be useful to be able to handle these issues in a co-ordinated way, dealing with the allegations in a way which recognises the overlapping nature of the jurisdictions involved.

The Government's justification for its decision to amalgamate the different equality commissions into one reflects these arguments. It is best summed up in the White Paper issued in 2004.[68] A single body would be a strong and authoritative champion for equality and human rights. The CEHR would be well positioned to drive change, making dignity and respect, fair treatment and social justice core values. The CEHR would incorporate a depth of expertise on specific areas of discrimination, while also being able to cast a wide net across all equality and human rights issues. Through a cross-cutting approach, a single organisation would be better able to tackle barriers and inequalities affecting several groups, and identify and promote strategic solutions. A single organisation would benefit individuals seeking advice and support on all discrimination issues and information on human rights, in an accessible and user-friendly way. Providing a single point of contact, for individuals and for the agencies and organisations to which they turn for advice, would deliver real benefits for everyone. In its policies and approach, a single organisation would be better equipped to address the reality of the many dimensions of an individual's identity, and therefore tackle discrimination on multiple grounds. A single organisation would be better able to meet the needs of employers and service providers, providing a single access point to information, advice and guidance on the full breadth of equality and human rights issues. A single organisation would be more effective at promoting improvements to the delivery of public services. It would provide guidance and support on human rights good practice and compliance, and can take a cross-cutting seamless approach on the full breadth of equality issues on a sector by sector basis with, for example, health authorities, local government and education providers. A single organisation would also provide an opportunity to pursue a more coherent approach to enforcing discrimination legislation. The CEHR could ensure, for example, that when it takes action to tackle unlawful discrimination in one equality area it also takes the opportunity to ensure improvements in the other areas of discrimination. A single organisation would be able to work to promote good

---

[68] White Paper, *Fairness for All: a New Commission for Equality and Human Rights*, May 2004, Cm 6185, para 1.16.

relations among different communities, building trust and understanding that will contribute to a more cohesive society. A single organisation would combine the strengths of the existing Commissions with the expertise from key organizations representing the new equality strands, identifying and promoting creative responses to the challenges and opportunities it will face.

There are four reasons for injecting a degree of caution, however, into this debate. The first is that the argument in favour of a single equality body covering many grounds assumes a relative degree of harmony in the allocation of resources within the single enforcement body. To the extent that the distribution of scarce resources involves tensions and conflicts, this harmony cannot be guaranteed. Indeed, experience from some countries has shown that agencies with such broad remits are not infrequently riven with in-fighting between the different 'constituencies.' One or other type of discrimination may be regarded by some as 'special':

> in the sense that the issue cannot be treated operationally as something that is submerged in the generality of [the] day to day work [of the body].[69]

So, for example, the Vice Chair of ECRI has argued that there are three reasons for regarding racial discrimination as 'special' in this way:

> First, racial discrimination is at the root of a large proportion of human rights abuses. Second, the handling of such cases calls for a high level of expertise. Third, these sorts of cases tend to involve the most vulnerable groups in society; and fourth, they are frequently the most politically charged.

Against this background, he says:

> it seems inconceivable to us in ECRI that any national body, irrespective of its precise form and remit, should not have within it at least a section dedicated to dealing with problems of discrimination on the grounds of race as defined in the International Convention.[70]

This issue might be addressed in the context of the FRA by the allocation of earmarked budgets, and separate policy-making functions, for each area within the single agency.

A second reason for some caution regarding amalgamation is that part of the strength of *separate* agencies is the extent to which they are perceived as serving the needs of a *specific* group: women, or ethnic minorities, for example. This identification with the organisation may be a source of strength in the inevitable political disputes that arise, over funding for example. If these separate constituencies are seen as being submerged in some larger entity, there is a danger that this source of strength may be lost. Thirdly, the benefits of a 'one-stop-

---

Summing up of the colloquy by Mr Michael Head, Vice Chair, European Commission against Racism and Intolerance (ECRI), in ECRI, *The Place and Role of National Specialised Bodies in Combating Racism*, Lausanne, Switzerland 22–24 October 1998, Summary of the Proceedings, Council of Europe, Strasbourg, 1998, p 8.

Ibid, p. 8

shop' are largely illusory if there are significantly different statutory provisions dealing with race, gender, religion, disability, and so on. At the moment there are considerable differences in requirements between race, gender and disability discrimination legislation in the United Kingdom. Until there is greater harmonisation of the various substantive requirements, the benefits of a single agency, at least in terms of their being a one-stop-shop may prove difficult to establish. In both Northern Ireland and Britain, pressure has grown for legislation (often termed a 'Single Equality Act') that would harmonise the different pieces of existing equality law into a more coherent whole. In the context of the EU, a single equality body is likely also to increase the already existing pressure for harmonisation of the Community's equality and non-discrimination directives.

3. Human Rights Institutions and Equality Bodies

The third issue that arises from the UK debate is how to combine the establishment of a new human rights body with an existing equality-related body, and how, in particular, to ensure that the existing functions of the equality body are continued effectively after the establishment of the new body. Should the extension of the EUMC's remit to include human rights more broadly be seen as a threat to the effective pursuance of EU action in combating racism and xenophobia, as some would fear? Or instead, to the extent that the concern for racial discrimination will now be joined with that of discrimination as part of a general mandate to fulfil fundamental rights, should we see this as a positive evolution for the development of an anti-discrimination policy for the EU?

The appropriateness of introducing a human rights mandate into a body focusing on the eradication of discrimination and the promotion of equality has been a central issue in the British discussions.[71] The Parliamentary Joint Committee on Human Rights considered that where, as increasingly there must be, there is a focus by the new body on access to public services, the human rights dimension (for example the right to life, the right to education, the right of access to information, the right to privacy, the right to be free from degrading treatment) would be fundamental. It also noted that disadvantaged and marginalised groups were among the people whom the Human Rights Act was supposed most directly to benefit. While some issues that any new body would confront would principally engage discrimination issues, others would clearly engage human rights questions, and many would engage both. In light of this, the Committee considered the options for the institutional relationship between a human rights commission and the proposed new equality body, and expressed

---

[71] See S Spencer, 'Partner Rediscovered: Human rights and equality in the UK' in C Harvey (ed), *Human Rights in the Community*, British Institute of Human Rights (Oxford, Hart Publishing, forthcoming in 2004).

a preference for there to be an integrated human rights and equality commission.[72] The new commission, the Committee believed, would have the ability to adopt a more holistic approach where human rights would provide a framework within which to persuade public authorities to promote and protect human rights standards and treat all people with dignity, fairness and respect.

Against this, two arguments have predominated. The first is institutional, based on the British experience of the development of human rights and equality thinking. Based on this experience, it is argued, there is the danger that in amalgamating 'human rights' and 'equality' issues in Britain, where they have largely grown and developed separated from each other, often with different institutions and different actors, there will be a 'capture' of the new Commission by the proponents of one or other issue, leading to the creation of a de-facto hierarchy between the two issues. This is an essentially institutional argument and may be addressed with institutional tools.

A second concern is more based on concerns about the compatibility of the underpinnings of equality and human rights. The Joint Committee recognised that where the work of the new commission was focused on legal remedies for discrimination in employment and the advancement of the economic status of disadvantaged groups, the relevance of human rights dimension to its work 'might be only peripheral.' To put the matter more crudely, if human rights is thought to be predominantly about liberty *from* government, and equality is thought to be in part about redistribution *by* government, then the two agendas may be on a collision course, and status equality may be undermined by an overly libertarian, negative conception of human rights.

One implication of this analysis is the importance of giving a mandate to any body amalgamating human rights and equality agendas that ensures that the redistributive elements within equality, and the solidarity-based elements in human rights, are both adequately recognised and valued. A mandate for the EU Fundamental Rights Agency based on *all* the rights and principles set out in the EU Charter of Fundamental Rights (including in particular the rights included under 'solidarity') would be an essential part of ensuring that the equality and human rights aspects of the mandate could be brought together in a way which emphasised their commonalities, rather than those aspects in which they may diverge.

4. Mainstreaming Equality and Human Rights

The fourth issue that arises in the UK context that may have relevance for the development of the mandate of the EU Human Rights Agency involves the issue of 'mainstreaming.' Mainstreaming originally grew up in the context of equality implementation, particularly gender equality, but is now increasingly used as

---

[72] Sixth Report, Session 2002–03, n 53 above, para 203.

a technique for the effective implementation of equality across several strands in the Community.[73] It involves attempting to ensure that equality is made central to the construction and delivery of the policies and practices of all public bodies. We have seen already the adoption in the United Kingdom of two varieties of mainstreaming: that arising from the public sector equality duties in Northern Ireland under section 75 of the Northern Ireland Act 1998, and in Britain under the Race Relations (Amendment) Act 2000.

Underlying the Northern Ireland and British attempts at equality mainstreaming is an important perception: that unless special attention is paid to equality in policy-making, it will become too easily submerged in the day-to-day concerns of policy makers who do not view that particular policy preference as central to their concerns. The motivation for mainstreaming equality lies not only, therefore, in the perception that anti-discrimination law, positive action initiatives, and even traditional methods of constitutional protection of equality, are limited, but also in the perception that questions of equality and non-discrimination may easily become sidelined. Mainstreaming, by definition, attempts to address this problem of sidelining directly, by requiring all government departments to engage directly with equality issues. Has this any relevance for human rights implementation in the EU, in particular the debate about the functions of the Agency?

A particularly important technique has been developed to make this idea of equality mainstreaming effective in Northern Ireland.[74] There is a requirement that 'impact assessments' be carried out as part of the process of considering proposals for legislation or major policy initiatives. (There is somewhat less emphasis in practice on impact assessment under the racial equality mainstreaming model.) Put simply, the idea of an impact assessment involves an attempt to try to assess what the effect of the legislation or policy is, or would be, on particular protected groups, such as women or minorities. Mainstreaming should, thereby, encourage greater resort to evidence-based policy making and greater transparency in decision-making, since it necessitates defining what the impact of policies is at an earlier stage of policy making, more systematically and to a greater extent than is currently usually contemplated. And, to the extent that mainstreaming initiatives can develop criteria for alerting policy makers to potential problems before they happen, it is more likely that a generally reactive approach to problems of inequality can be replaced by pro-active early-warning approaches. Current government policy in many countries in the area of equality has often been criticised as tending to be too reactive to problems that might well have been identifiable before they became problems.

---

[73] See J Shaw, Mainstreaming Equality in European Union law and policy-making' (European Network against Racism, July 2004). See also: O De Schutter, ch 2 of this volume.

[74] C McCrudden, 'Mainstreaming Equality in the Governance of Northern Ireland' (1996) 22 Fordham International Law Journal 1698; C McCrudden, 'Equality' in CJ Harvey (ed), *Human Rights, Equality and Democratic Renewal in Northern Ireland* (Oxford, Hart Publishing, 2001), p 75.

As importantly, impact assessment and the duty to promote equality combine to produce an approach that encourages a more positive approach to equality, rather than the negative approach often adopted hitherto. In the equality context, this leads to an examination of how far the public body can and should exercise its discretion in such a way as to advance rather than retard equality. This involves examining alternative ways of delivering policies, and examining ways of moderating any adverse effects that may occur. This approach of emphasising the effect of policies on the human right in question and what the public body can do about it, rather than one that narrowly concentrates on the direct responsibility of the public authority for any breach of human rights seems particularly well suited as a method of addressing the obligations of promoting and protecting human rights.

A second important feature of the mainstreaming experience in Northern Ireland is the extent to which groups inside and outside the mainstream political process has attempted to use impact assessment as part of a strategy to construct a more participatory approach to public policy debate. In short, groups have used the mainstreaming process to become involved in influencing governmental decision-making. From this perspective, mainstreaming should not only be a technical mechanism of assessment within the bureaucracy, but an approach that encourages the participation of those with an interest. It is true, of course, that good decision-making should require policy-makers to seek out the views of those potentially affected by the decisions. Unlike more traditional mechanisms of consultation, however, mainstreaming in Northern Ireland does this by requiring impact assessments of a degree of specificity that establishes a clear agenda for discussion between policy makers and those most affected. We can see, therefore, the inter-linked nature of the two crucial features of mainstreaming: impact assessment and participation. One of the most far-reaching by-products of mainstreaming becomes the development of a crucial link between government and civil society. This development encourages greater participation in decision-making by marginal groups, thus lessening the democratic deficit. The requirements in Northern Ireland of extensive consultations throughout equality mainstreaming processes aim to empower individuals collectively to engage with public authorities to address equality issues of relevance to the public authority.

We have seen that the Parliamentary Joint Committee on Human Rights proposed a general statutory duty in the United Kingdom on public authorities to promote human rights. This was a major reversal of the previous assessment by the Committee. In a report published in 2003, the Committee had considered whether it would be appropriate to impose a positive obligation on public authorities to promote human rights, comparable to the positive duty to promote race equality imposed on public authorities by section two of the Race Relations (Amendment) Act 2000, it had decided that, on the evidence then available to it, it was unlikely to be useful. In its May 2004 report, the Committee revisited the issue in the light of new evidence which showed both the limited extent to which public authorities have proactively engaged with human rights in their decision-making processes and of the apparent success of the positive duty to promote race equality in improving the quality of decision-making and service delivery.

The Committee concluded:

> We are now persuaded by the evidence that imposing a 'positive' or 'general' duty on public authorities to promote human rights will be an effective way of advancing this. It would provide a firm statutory foundation for the framework within which the new commission would operate, giving it a very clear role in the articulation of guidance for the implementation of the duty. Requiring public authorities to assess all of their functions and policies for relevance to human rights and equality, and in the light of that assessment to draw up a strategy for placing human rights and equality at the heart of policy making, decision making and service delivery, would be an effective way of achieving the mainstreaming of human rights and equality which will be one of the commission's principal purposes.[75]

The government responded to this proposal in July 2004, in which it announced that it was:

> not persuaded that positive statutory duties in relation to human rights, going beyond those contained in the Human Rights Act, are needed.[76]

The Joint Committee clearly considers the issue should be pursued. In August 2004, it noted that the Government's White Paper did not deal with the introduction of a public sector duty relating to human rights, but it recommended that the legislation should do so.[77]

There are, however, both practical and more theoretical objections to mainstreaming in the human rights context. The Northern Ireland experience demonstrates that the use of impact assessment is not unproblematic, even in the context of equality. It is clear that there needs to be greater organisational learning on the part of government, and an end to being seen to constantly 'reinvent the wheel' by periodically asking the same people the same questions. Furthermore, with respect to collecting data there does seem to be a danger of the 'best becoming the enemy of the good.' The purpose of impact assessment is not to engage in a purely academic exercise. The purpose ought to be to produce information on which public policy makers can assess whether there is likely to be an issue or a problem. There needs to be greater recognition that perfect data just does not exist. Policy makers make decisions all the time on the basis of data that is second best—the same principle must apply in relation to promoting

---

[75] *Ibid*, para 32.

[76] Government Response to Joint Committee on Human Rights, Eleventh Report of Session 2003–04: *Commission for Equality and Human Rights: Structure, Functions and Powers*, Cm 6295 (HMSO, London, 2004) July 2004, p 3.

[77] Joint Committee on Human Rights, Sixteenth Report of Session 2003–04, *Commission for Equality and Human Rights: The Government's White Paper*, HL 156; HC 998 (HMSO, London, 2004), 4 August 2004.

greater equality. Data is relevant only insofar as it is useful in ensuring greater equality; data should not be gathered simply for more and more analysis. An equivalent danger exists if impact assessment becomes incorporated more generally in human rights mainstreaming.

If there is a significant absence of effective NGO activity, mainstreaming of the type envisaged in the Northern Ireland model will not work. Even if there are such NGOs in existence, that the involvement of such groups is unproblematic, since their participation raises issues regarding the competence of such groups, including their access to information and resources. In principle, however, a major argument in favour of mainstreaming is that it may contribute to increased participatory democracy. This aspect of the Northern Ireland equality mainstreaming process has, however, stimulated much debate. Several issues have been identified that need to be addressed if mainstreaming along these lines were to be applied in the human rights context more broadly. There is the problem of those encouraged to participate becoming overwhelmed by the sheer number of consultations that they are drawn into. Indeed some have recently complained of 'consultation fatigue.' Undoubtedly there is a major problem with the form consultation appears to be taking. Better *targeting* of consultation is required. So too is providing funding to those consulted to enable them to participate effectively.

'Mainstreaming' human rights is, in many ways, an attractive additional mechanism for ensuring greater compliance with human rights obligations, particularly those requiring the 'protection' and 'promotion' of human rights. As manifested in the Northern Ireland model of equality mainstreaming, it addresses several of the problems that mainstreaming might be said to involve. However, there are several as yet unresolved aspects of the operation of the Northern Ireland approach even in the context of equality that mean that adopting the Northern Ireland model is potentially problematic. In addition, the implications of the differences between mainstreaming equality and mainstreaming human rights generally need more thought. We have seen that there may be differences in the level and type of civil society involvement in the two issues, that there may be differences in the attitudes of government to the two agendas, and in the institutional arrangements for promoting compliance. In particular, the somewhat more focussed nature of the equality guarantee may enable mainstreaming to be more effective in that context than in the general human rights context. Some thought, then, needs to be given to how best to incorporate the potential benefits of human rights mainstreaming, which are considerable, whilst avoiding the problems that too quick a resort to adapting existing methods of equality mainstreaming to human rights might lead to. We need to ensure that human rights are advanced, rather than retarded, by mainstreaming.

V. CONCLUSION

In conclusion, whilst one should be cautious about assuming that any of the 'solutions' determined in the UK context is easily transferable to the EU context, my suggestion is that the United Kingdom experience is illustrative of several important issues that are likely to confront EU policy makers in determining the shape and structure of any new EU Human Rights Agency, and that it does provide a useful source from which inspiration may be drawn in considering how to think about several of the issues flagged up in the Commission's Communication.

7

The Contribution of the EU Fundamental Rights Agency to the Realization of Economic and Social Rights

PHILIP ALSTON*

INTRODUCTION

BROADLY STATED, THE Fundamental Rights Agency will have a mandate to monitor respect for fundamental rights within the EU. Since the list of rights reflected in the EU Charter of Fundamental Rights includes certain economic and social rights it can reasonably be assumed that these rights will constitute at least part of the new Agency's mandate. But, as noted below, this proposition cannot in fact be taken for granted. Assuming, however, that the Agency will concern itself to some extent with these rights, then a number of important issues must be addressed. Thus the main focus of the present chapter is on the following questions: which economic and social rights should be included within the new Agency's mandate; what role will economic and social rights standards contained in international instruments other than the EU Charter play; how should the role of the FRA be conceptualized, and more specifically what is involved in 'monitoring'; what, if anything, can the FRA learn from the experience of the other principal international procedures which already play a role in monitoring the enjoyment of economic and social rights in Europe; and what are the main considerations which should guide the Agency in shaping its approach to these rights.

* Professor of Law and Faculty Director, Center for Human Rights and Global Justice, New York University School of Law. Special Rapporteur of the UN Commission on Human Rights in relation to Extrajudicial, Summary or Arbitrary Executions, and former Chairperson of the UN Committee on Economic, Social and Cultural Rights (1991-98).

1. THE INCLUSION OF ECONOMIC AND SOCIAL RIGHTS WITHIN THE AGENCY'S MANDATE

Before turning to address specific questions as to how the Agency might address economic and social rights it must be noted that the assumptions implicit in the opening lines of this chapter should not be taken for granted. In other words, it cannot automatically be assumed that the EU's Fundamental Rights Agency (FRA) will concern itself with social and economic rights, or at least not in any systematic or comprehensive way. The Communication presented by the Commission in relation to the FRA poses the question of which rights should be addressed in the Agency's work. The response offered is that while the Agency could be asked to monitor all of the fundamental rights included in the EU Charter of Fundamental Rights, such an approach would result in giving it 'an extremely broad field of action', a prospect which, the document seems to imply, might be unwelcome. An alternative is then offered which would avoid such an outcome. The Agency's work could instead be focused on (i.e. limited to) 'thematic areas having a special connection with Community policies or the Union' and these areas are illustrated by reference to subjects such as 'immigration, asylum, non-discrimination, ethical questions, guarantee of criminal proceedings [sic], violence, etc.'[1]

While most readers would assume that this second option is little more than a formality put forward in order to ensure that there is some discussion, the Commission nonetheless goes on to emphasize the need to 'ensure a balance between a potentially vast area of intervention and the effectiveness of the Agency'. There is no guarantee that the flexibility thereby sought could not be used as a reason to resurrect arguments to the effect that economic and social rights, far from being justiciable, are essentially programmatic.[2] In line with such arguments, these rights should be viewed more in terms of 'principles' than 'rights', and as such they are already adequately dealt with by a myriad of technical and economic arrangements already in place within the EU's structures. They are, in brief, not the type of issues in relation to which the Agency could be expected to be very effective.

Such an outcome would represent a stunning reversal of many years of evolving EU human rights policies, both internally and externally, in which the relevance of social rights has frequently been acknowledged. It would also amount to a repudiation of the hard-fought gains to ensure the presence of at

---

[1] Communication from the Commission, The Fundamental Rights Agency: Public Consultation Document (COM(2004)693 final, of 25 October 2004.

[2] It should be noted that 'programmatic' in this context is usually intended to convey the sense that the rights in question can only be the focus of broad programs which do not convey any necessary sense of individual or group entitlement or of strong governmental obligation. For a very different interpretation intended to give some authentic rights-based consent to programmatic approaches see G McKeever and F Ni Aolain, 'Thinking Globally, Acting Locally: Enforcing Socio Economic Rights in Northern Ireland', [2004] *European Human Rights Law Review* 158, 165–67.

least certain key social and economic rights in the EU Charter of Fundamental Rights. And it would strike a major blow against the principle of indivisibility of all human rights to which the EU and its Member States have long subscribed in international forums. Most importantly, as will be argued below, it would put in doubt the EU's commitment to social rights and would diminish the level of protection which the citizens of Europe are entitled to expect.

2. DEFINING ECONOMIC AND SOCIAL RIGHTS FOR THE AGENCY'S PURPOSES

One of the most complex and problematic issues involves determining what constitute the 'economic and social rights' in the EU Charter. They are nowhere defined as such, and indeed as noted below one of the major achievements of the document is that it does not classify rights as falling into the traditional categories of civil, cultural, economic, political, or social.

There are several sources of confusion in relation to the definitional aspect of these rights. The first is that even in the UN context, the question of classification is problematic in a number of respects. In the first place, it is not entirely clear why some rights such as freedom of association, are recognized as being within both of the major categories and thus included in the International Covenant on Economic, Social and Cultural Rights as well as the International Covenant on Civil and Political Rights. At the same time, the right to education, which is so closely linked to the enjoyment of both civil rights and political rights and is accepted as falling within one or other of those categories in the US context (the great majority of State constitutions within the US contain some form of a right to education) is treated exclusively as an economic, social and cultural right.[3] Secondly, while it is often asserted that the three categories of economic, social and cultural can readily be distinguished from one another, it is in fact rather invidious to classify the right to work as an economic rather than also a social right, the right to culture as a cultural rather than also a social right, the right to education as a social rather than an economic or cultural right, and so on.

In the EU context the debate is equally confusing but for a significantly different reason. The term economic rights was originally interpreted as referring to rights such as the freedom of movement, the freedom to pursue a trade or profession, or the right to property. The emphasis was often upon the need to treat the citizen of another Member State as well as one's own citizens in relation to economic matters. In this respect, the early history of the emergence of a concept of fundamental rights within the jurisprudence of the European Court of Justice reflected more closely the approach contained in the German

---

[3] For an excellent analysis of the difficulty of categorizing the right to education see M Nowak, 'The Right to Education', in A Eide et al (eds), *Economic, Social and Cultural Rights: A Textbook* (2nd ed, Dordrecht, Nijhoff, 2001) 245.

GrundGesetz than any conception of economic rights which would be recognizable from the perspective of international human rights law.

Finally, the debate over the justiciability of certain rights in the Charter context led to the introduction of another distinction which has further muddied the waters in terms of any attempt to identify which rights should be thought of as economic and social rights. As noted earlier, the Charter refrains from characterizing any particular right as being economic, social or otherwise but instead uses different chapter categories of dignity, freedoms, equality, solidarity, citizens' rights, and justice. These categories do not, however, track neatly any known way of categorizing different rights and the implications of putting a right under one chapter as opposed to another appear not to be especially significant. Even the solidarity chapter, for example, which appears to contain most (but by no means all) of the rights which might be categorized as being economic and social if one were to use a UN-type approach, contains a number of rights which are clearly political in nature, such as the right to strike and the right to consultation.

In what is generally explained as a last ditch effort by those who lost the debate during the drafting of the Charter in 2000 to classify economic and social rights as non-justiciable, a provision was added to the text in the context of the subsequent Convention debates over the EU Constitution. The result was the inclusion of Article 52(5), which is examined in more detail below.[4] In addition, an explanatory note was drafted in relation to this provision by the Council Secretariat. It was then amended following the conclusion of the Inter-Governmental Conference which adopted the draft Constitution. The Updated Explanations are now included in Declaration 12 to the Treaty Establishing a European Constitution.[5]

The Declaration explains that Article 52(5) clarifies the distinction between 'subjective rights' and 'principles'. According to Article 51(1), the former 'shall be respected', and the latter 'shall be observed'. The UK representative in the Charter negotiations was one of the strongest proponents of this differentiation and he explained that 'principles only give rise to rights to the extent that they are implemented by national law or by Community law when it is competent to do so.'[6] The Declaration, based on the earlier explanatory memorandum, seeks to justify this approach by reference, inter alia, to the case law of the European Court of Justice in relation to the 'precautionary principle' and to the principles of agricultural law. It is at best surprising to a human rights lawyer that an analogy could be drawn between, on the one hand, a determinedly soft and still much contested principle of international law (the precautionary principle) and a set of general policy considerations (agricultural policy) and, on the other

---

[4] See text following n 33 below.

[5] Declarations to be annexed to the Final Act of the Intergovernmental Conference and the Final Act, doc. CIG 87/04 ADD 2 REV 2 (25 Oct. 2004), p 93.

[6] Lord Goldsmith QC, 'A Charter of Rights, Freedoms and Principles' (2001) 38 *CMLRev* 1201, 1213.

hand, the long-established norms of international human rights law expressed in a range of treaties accepted by and applicable to all EU Member States. Nevertheless, this is the approach suggested in the explanatory Declaration.

A further issue raised by the last minute changes to the Charter concerns the statement that rights are to be respected, while principles are (only?) to be observed. It is true that the term 'respect' has a long and venerable lineage within international human rights law.[7] In contrast the term 'observe' is not commonly used and its meaning is unclear. The context would seem to suggest that it denotes a significantly lower level of obligation. It could not however be reduced to a commitment to take some account of the principles or to more or less respect them, to the extent possible, etc. What the drafters presumably had in mind is an obligation not to take positive steps to violate the principles. But even if a positive obligation to take all available measures to promote the realization of a right is considered to be going too far (although that is in effect the obligation in force under the International Covenant on Economic, Social and Cultural Rights) this would still not rule out the need for positive measures to be taken to remedy violations or to prevent other actors from violating the relevant rights. The role of the Agency in contributing to an informed understanding of the implications of the term 'observe' should thus not be under-estimated.

The next question that arises is which of the Articles in the Charter deals with principles and which with rights? Despite the potential significance of this purported distinction no clear answer is provided in either the Charter itself or in the Declaration emerging from the constitutional Convention. The latter does however contain the following statement:

> For illustration, examples for [sic] principles recognised in the Charter include e.g. Articles 25, 26 and 37. In some cases, an Article of the Charter may contain both elements of a right and of a principle, e.g. Articles 23, 33 and 34.

But as Gráinne de Búrca has pointed out, this comment only adds to the 'fuzziness' by listing 'the rights of the elderly' (Art. 25) and 'the rights of the disabled' (Art. 26) as examples of 'principles' recognised by the Charter', even though each of them is clearly expressed in the Charter in terms of human rights.[8]

The confusion is further compounded by the inconsistent ways in which the Charter itself uses the term 'principles'. Thus, in the second preambular paragraph, it is proclaimed that 'the Union is founded on the indivisible, universal values of human dignity, freedom, equality and solidarity; it is based on the

---

[7] For a recent exposition of the approach adopted in this respect by the Human Rights Committee see General Comment No. 31 (2004) on Art 2 The nature of the general legal obligation imposed on States Parties to the Covenant, UN doc. CCPR/C/74/CRP.4/Rev.6 (2004).

[8] Art 25: the EU recognises and respects 'the rights of the elderly to lead a life of dignity and independence and to participate in social and cultural life'; Art 26: the EU recognises and respects 'the right of persons with disabilities to benefit from measures designed to ensure their independence, social and occupational integration and participation in the life of the community'. See G de Búrca, 'Beyond the Charter: How Enlargement has Enlarged the Human Rights Policy of the EU', (2004) 27 *Fordham International Law Journal* 679.

principles of democracy and the rule of law'. In other words the importance of 'principles' in this context is clearly acknowledged but at the same time they are distinguished from the universal values of human dignity etc. and the preamble goes on to talk about the need to strengthen the protection of fundamental rights. There are several other points at which reference is made to principles, including the principle of subsidiarity,[9] 'democratic principles',[10] 'the principle of equality',[11] the 'principle of sustainable development',[12] and the principle of proportionality.[13] Of this group only sustainable development would seem to fit in the category of non-rights which the explanatory memorandum was apparently seeking to create. In contrast, the principle of 'equality between men and women' recognized in Article 23 has been the subject of a range of directives, and has long been treated as a fundamental right by the European Court of Justice. It is also a central pillar of international human rights law, embodied in many treaties binding upon all of the Member States of the EU such as Article 3 of the International Covenant on Civil and Political Rights.[14] Presumably therefore this is one 'principle' which should not be treated as a 'principle' in the sense intended by the explanatory memorandum.

On the other hand, some of those issues which are generally assumed to constitute 'principles' as opposed to 'rights' are expressly formulated in human rights terms. The provision relating to health, for example, begins by proclaiming that 'Everyone has the right of access to preventive health care and the right to benefit from medical treatment . . .'.

Another unanswered puzzle which emerges from the curious attempt to defuse British concern over economic and social rights by the inclusion of placating terminology in an explanatory memorandum rather than in the Charter itself is what precisely is meant in this context by the term 'subjective right'[15] and how such rights relate to human rights or fundamental rights in general. Should the Charter have been renamed the EU Charter of Fundamental Subjective Rights and Principles, or even just the Charter of Rights and Principles? Since these questions go well beyond the scope of the present analysis it must suffice just to flag them in this context.

Three major points emerge from this section of the chapter. The first is that defining which rights are economic and social rights and which are not is by no

---

[9] Charter of Fundamental Rights, preambular para 5, and Art 51.

[10] *Ibid*, Art 14(3) on the right to education recognizes: 'The freedom to found educational establishments with due respect for democratic principles and the right of parents . . ..

[11] *Ibid*, Art 23.

[12] *Ibid*, Art 37.

[13] *Ibid*, Art 52.

[14] See for example the Human Rights Committee's General Comment No. 28 (2000), Art 3: The equality of rights between men and women, UN doc. HRI/GEN/1/Rev 6 (2003), p 179.

[15] While the term 'subjective right' is well-known to various European administrative law traditions, meaning a right that an individual can invoke directly, it is not one that fits easily or well into any international human rights lexicon given the extent to which that body of law acknowledges a diverse range of means by which rights can be claimed without distinguishing between subjective and other types of rights.

means as easy as most observers would assume. This also means that any attempt by the FRA to downplay or even exclude these rights from its purview, or at least to give them only a minor role, would itself be fraught with difficulty precisely because there is so much overlap and genuine interdependence among the different types of rights recognized in the Charter. The second point is that the lack of clarity highlighted above does not mean that there is no such thing as an economic or social right, nor does it change the fact that some aspects of the Charter can appropriately be considered to be non-self-executing. What it does mean, however, is that broad general categorizations are not the way to make the necessary determinations and that instead a more nuanced case-by-case analysis is required according to the context in question.

The third point is probably the most important in terms of the approach to be adopted by the FRA. It is that neither the Agency, nor others involved in the promotion and monitoring of the Charter,[16] will be well served by an approach which gives credibility to the incoherent distinction between 'principles' and 'subjective rights'. The Charter should instead be approached on its merits and it should be assumed that each of the rights contained in the Charter of Fundamental Rights is just that—a fundamental right. That approach does not prejudge issues of the self-executing status of the norm, nor the question of whether particular aspects of the right are best approached through an emphasis on the role of the courts, of administrative action, or of some other appropriately tailored measures.

3. THE ROLE OF ECONOMIC AND SOCIAL RIGHTS IN THE EU CONTEXT

The history of social rights in the EU context is a chequered one. The Treaty of Rome contained several important provisions relating to social rights, but these were determinedly secondary to the overall goal of economic integration. Articles 117 and 118 proclaimed the goals of achieving better working conditions and improved living standards for workers but these remained largely hortatory, in contrast to Article 119 which firmly committed the Community to the principle of equal pay for equal work for men and women. The latter provision assumed particular significance in the mid-1970s when the Equal Pay and Equal

---

[16] It is a little surprising in this regard to see that the Network of Independent Experts begins its analysis of health rights with the heading 'The "principle" of health care', and then goes on to indicate that 'Art 35 of the Charter on health care should undoubtedly be classed among the provisions that establish "principles" rather than "subjective rights"—within the meaning of this distinction which the reviews of Art 52 of the Charter carried out by Working Party II of the European Convention were meant to establish.' See EU Network of Independent Experts on Fundamental Rights, *Report on the Situation of Fundamental Rights in the European Union in 2003*, Doc CFR-CDF rep EU 2003 (Jan 2004) [referred to hereinafter as EU Network Report (Jan 2004)], p 123. Since the Declaration which seeks to clarify the intention of Art 52 in this respect makes no mention of Art 35, it seems unnecessary for commentators to go out of their way to characterize it in such unequivocal terms.

Treatment Directives were adopted as part of a Social Action Programme launched in 1974. But this burst of social rights activism was short-lived and it was not until 1989 that new impetus was breathed into the process by the adoption of the Community Charter of the Fundamental Social Rights of Workers. The 1992 Maastricht Protocol and Agreement on Social Policy was subsequently made part of the EC Treaty under the Amsterdam Treaty of 1997, which also included an Employment Chapter (obligating the Community to 'contribute to a high level of employment') to be promoted through the 'open method of coordination'. At the same time the Treaty expressly reserved a number of important labour rights issues to the Member States and excluded EU competence. Despite the gradual advances made towards the embrace of social rights policies the bottom line throughout this period was, as Poiares Maduro has observed, that 'the internal logical of market integration . . . prevailed even where conflicts with social rights arose.'[17]

It was against this rather inauspicious, but not entirely negative, background that the debate over the inclusion of social rights in the EU Charter of Fundamental Rights took place. Primarily because of the less statist and more broadly based composition of the Convention that drew up the Charter, as well as because of its initially unresolved or ambiguous status, it proved possible to transcend the deep and abiding reluctance of governments to undertake firm commitments in relation to social rights. Before looking briefly at the debates leading up to the adoption of the Charter it is appropriate to note that, despite the ambivalent place accorded to social rights in the EU's internal policies during this period, there was no doubt about the EU's formal position in relation to these rights in terms of its external human rights policies. In both the development and accession contexts, the EU consistently made clear that economic and social rights were an important part of the equation. Thus, to take one of many examples in relation to the former context, the Council's 1999 Regulation on human rights in development activities asserted that Community action was firmly 'rooted in the general principles established by the Universal Declaration of Human Rights [which includes extensive provisions on economic and social rights], the International Covenant on Civil and Political Rights and the International Covenant on Economic, Social and Cultural Rights.'[18] Similarly, in negotiating the accession of new members, economic and social rights issues also enjoyed 'a significant presence in the assessment of the political criteria for each applicant', both as separate political criteria and as part of the *acquis communitaire*.[19]

But it was the adoption of the EU Charter in 2000 that affirmed, in especially strong terms, the EU's commitment to social rights. Although Bruno de Witte

[17] M Poiares Maduro, 'Striking the Elusive Balance between Economic Freedom and Social Rights in the EU', in P Alston (ed) *The EU and Human Rights* (Oxford, OUP, 1999) 468.

[18] Council Reg 975/1999, preambular para 6 [1999] OJ L120/1.

[19] A Williams, *EU Human Rights Policies: A Study in Irony* (Oxford, Oxford University Press, 2004) pp 72–73.

has argued that the relevant provisions of the EU Charter do not amount to a major innovation by comparison with pre-existing law unless one adopts a narrow definition of the latter as being restricted to primary EU law, he also concedes the importance of the Charter in raising the profile of social rights. Thus he acknowledges that as soon as the reference point is broadened out to include all the individual rights granted by secondary Community law 'the harvest of social rights is much more important'.[20]

While the EU Charter was being drafted the UN Committee on Economic, Social and Cultural Rights took the unusual step of urging the Convention to ensure that economic and social rights were included 'on an equal footing with civil and political rights'. If this result was not achieved, the Committee suggested that it 'would have to be regarded as a retrogressive step contravening the existing obligations of Member States of the European Union under the International Covenant on Economic, Social and Cultural Rights'.[21] It based this analysis on the obligation contained in the Covenant to take progressive measures to promote the relevant rights. The Committee's intervention was no doubt well advised, even if its legal analysis is eminently disputable. Its case would have been strengthened if the ECJ had interpreted EU law as requiring Member States to adopt positive obligations in relation to social rights within the context of its case law on the general principles of EU law but this has not so far been the case.

4. THE PLACE OF ECONOMIC AND SOCIAL RIGHTS IN THE EU CHARTER

During the process of drafting the Charter economic and social rights were one of the major sources of controversy. These debates have been adequately analyzed elsewhere and will not be recounted here.[22] Suffice it to note that the strategy pursued by the main proponents of the rights was built on three pillars.[23] The first was to recognize the principle of solidarity, both in the preamble and as a separate chapter heading. The second was to ensure that a range of individual economic and social rights were included and the third was to include a non-regression or horizontal rights protection provision which became Article 53.[24]

The result, it has been suggested, is that the 'EU Charter makes no distinction between civil and political rights of the kind protected under the ECHR, and

---

[20] B de Witte, 'The Social Rights "Acquis" of the European Union', paper presented to International Conference on Social Rights in Europe, University of Leiden, 2000.

[21] Doc CHARTE 4315, CONTRIB 182, of 24 May 2000.

[22] See generally T Hervey and J Kenner (eds) *Economic and Social Rights Under the EU Charter of Fundamental Rights: A Legal Perspective*, (Oxford, Hart Publishing, 2003)

[23] See M Lerch, 'European Identity in International Society: A Constructivist Analysis of the EU Charter of Fundamental Rights', Constitutionalism Web-Papers, ConWEB No 2/2003, available at http://les1.man.ac.uk/conweb, p 17.

[24] See Section 8 below for a discussion of Art 53.

economic, social and cultural rights . . .'.[25] At one level this is an accurate description. At a deeper level, however, it can be seen that some of the economic and social rights are accorded significantly different treatment. We have already noted the purported distinction between 'principles' and 'subjective rights' which is aimed at marginalizing economic and social rights. Despite its clumsiness and lack of clarity it nonetheless serves to highlight the qualified status sought to be accorded to these rights. A second aspect supporting the contention that economic and social rights are treated differently is the extent to which many of them are made subject to national laws and practices, in a way that is less true of civil and political rights. This issue is analysed in more detail below.[26]

A third aspect is the use of extremely broad and somewhat open-ended language in relation to some of the rights that might be classified as being economic or social in nature. Several examples shall suffice to illustrate this point. Article 13 provides that 'The arts and scientific research shall be free of constraint', Article 17(2) says that 'Intellectual property shall be protected', Article 22 states that 'The Union shall respect cultural, religious and linguistic diversity', and Articles 37 and 38 respectively call upon the EU to ensure 'a high level of environmental protection' and 'a high level of consumer protection'.

In addition to these various ways in which at least some economic and social rights formulations appear not to be as strong as some of their civil and political rights counterparts, we must also take into account the continuing hostility towards economic and social rights which has not been put to rest as a result of their inclusion in the Charter. Indeed that development continues to draw fire from commentators on diverse grounds. One is that they undermine democracy since it should be up to legislators and not judges to decide on 'societal issues'. Turning them into 'legal or technical issues' undermines popular sovereignty by restricting the capacity of the majority to choose to ignore such rights.[27] Similarly, in evidence to the UK Parliament's House of Commons, Professor Richard Plender argued that economic and social rights should not be equated with civil and political rights partly because of their resource implications and partly because of their unsuitability for judicial determination.[28] The Commons

---

[25] A Ward, 'Access to Justice', in S Peers and A Ward (eds), *The EU Charter of Fundamental Rights: Politics, Law and Policy* (Oxford, Hart, 2004) 123 at 132.

[26] See Section 8 below.

[27] P de Hert, 'John Rawls on Constitutionalism and the Charter of Fundamental Rights of the European Union', in W Heere (ed), *From Government to Governance: The Growing Impact of Non-State Actors on the International and European Legal System* (Proceedings of the Sixth Hague Joint Conference held in The Hague, The Netherlands 3–5 July 2003) (The Hague, TMC Asser Press, 2004) 443, 449.

[28] 'Assessment of the content of a right to education or a right to fair wages seems to me to involve quite a different kind of mental exercise from assessment to the right to liberty or to a fairness of trial. It involves much more an assessment of relative resources within a population. These matters are not, I think, ideally suited to judicial settlement ...'. See Committee on European Scrutiny of the House of Commons, 36th Report, available at http://www.publications. parliament.uk/pa/cm199900/cmselect/cmeuleg/23-xvii/2302.htm, para 142.

Committee on European Scrutiny agreed with this assessment and expressed 'serious reservations' about the inclusion of economic and social rights in the Charter.[29] The UK subsequently played the crucial role in efforts to ensure that the economic and social rights contained in the Charter would be differentiated from the others and that they would not be justiciable. Before turning to the latter question, it is worth noting in this respect that the UK's *Human Rights Annual Report 2004* devotes an entire chapter to economic, social and cultural rights, laments the fact that it has proven difficult to make these rights directly enforceable, and insists that 'in reality, the different categories of rights cannot be separated.'[30]

All of these factors point to the need for the FRA to pay special attention to the relevant provisions of the Charter but also underscore the complexity of some of the tasks that await it.

5. THE JUSTICIABILITY OF THE ECONOMIC AND SOCIAL RIGHTS CONTAINED IN THE EU CHARTER

Another of the major challenges which the Agency will face in promoting the realization of the social rights provisions of the Charter relates to the age-old debate over the justiciability of these rights.[31] The history of the drafting of the relevant provisions has been recounted elsewhere[32] and it must suffice here to note that a distinction was inserted, at the last stage of the process of revising the final provisions of the Charter, to distinguish between the 'principles' and 'rights' contained in the Charter.[33] This has generally been referred to in the literature as distinguishing between justiciable and non-justiciable provisions but that terminology is actually misleading in this context and its use risks locking in hard and fast distinctions that have long been advocated by the opponents of

---

[29] *Ibid*, para 144.

[30] *Human Rights Annual Report 2004* (London, Foreign and Commonwealth Office, 2004), p 157. Available at http://www.fco.gov.uk/Files/kfile/FINALversion2edited%20Complete.pdf

[31] For one of the most recent such accounts see D Stewart and M Dennis., 'Justiciability of Economic, Social and Cultural Rights: Should There be an International Complaints Mechanism to Adjudicate the Rights to Food, Water, Housing, and Health?', (2004) 98 *American Journal of International Law* 462. For counter arguments see F Michelman, 'The Constitution, Social Rights and Liberal Political Justification', (2002) 1 *International Journal of Constitutional Law* 13; A Sachs, 'Social and Economic Rights: Can they be Made Justiciable?', (2000) 53 *Southern Methodist University Law Review* 1381; C Sunstein, 'Social and Economic Rights? Lessons from South Africa', (2001) 11 *Constitutional Forum* 123; I Koch, 'The Justiciability of Indivisible Rights', (2003) 72 *Nordic Journal of International Law* 3; and K L Scheppele, 'A Realpolitik Defense of Social Rights', (2004) 82 *Texas Law Review*) 1921.

[32] G de Búrca, n 8 above.

[33] Art 52(5): states: 'The provisions of this Charter which contain principles may be implemented by legislative and executive acts taken by institutions and bodies of the Union, and by acts of Member States when they are implementing Union law, in the exercise of their respective powers. They shall be judicially cognisable only in the interpretation of such acts and in the ruling on their legality.' For a defence of the distinction sought to be achieved through the insertion of this provision see Lord Goldsmith, n 6 above.

economic and social rights but which were notably rejected in the drafting of the EU Charter. More precisely, the distinction established by Article 52(5) is that 'principles' shall only be 'judicially cognizable' in the context of interpreting EU legislative or executive acts or acts taken by Member States when implementing EU law. But the principal significance of this qualification is that it requires some legislative or executive act to give specific content to the relevant right before a court can seek to make use of the Charter provision.

Seen in this light the provision is closer to the principle, well-known to international lawyers, that domestic courts will consider certain formulations to be 'non-self-executing' in the sense that they are unable to make use of them as freestanding principles to be applied directly. Instead they require the intermediate step of implementing legislation.[34] But the important point is that it is not only economic and social rights but also civil and political rights (as well as a great many other treaty formulations) that could be deemed non-self-executing. Indeed the US Government has taken the much contested step of declaring the provision of every international human rights treaty ratified in recent years to be non-self-executing.

The analysis adopted by the Network of Independent Experts reflects this distinction although it does not use the term non-self-executing. It notes instead that:

> This distinction, however, does not mean that such a 'principle' is not [justiciable]. At the most, it is the mode of [justiciability] that differs, rather than the actual possibility of invoking the provision before a judicial authority.[35]

The Network's opinion goes further than this in seeking to give legal significance to the 'principles' by arguing that neither the EU nor a Member State, acting within the scope of EU law, would be permitted to adopt a measure which is clearly inconsistent[36] with any of the principles recognized in the Charter.[37]

Another reason to avoid applying the term non-justiciable to any of the economic and social rights in the Charter is that the non-discrimination aspects of those rights will certainly be justiciable in so far as they are read in conjunction with the equality provisions of the Charter or the non-discrimination clause in Article 21(1) which prohibits 'any discrimination based on any ground such as

---

[34] For an analysis of this issue see Committee on Economic, Social and Cultural Rights, General Comment No 9 (1998): Domestic application of the Covenant, UN Doc E/1999/22, Annex IV, para 10. The Committee concludes its analysis by suggesting that '[t]he adoption of a rigid classification of economic, social and cultural rights which puts them, by definition, beyond the reach of the courts would thus be arbitrary and incompatible with the principle that the two sets of human rights are indivisible and interdependent. It would also drastically curtail the capacity of the courts to protect the rights of the most vulnerable and disadvantaged groups in society.'

[35] See EU Network Report (Jan 2004), n 16 above, para 123. The actual text uses the terms 'justifiable' and 'justifiability' but this is an extremely common typographical error, facilitated by the fact that the term justiciable is never used in common parlance.

[36] The phrase used is 'a sufficiently obvious infringement of those principles', *Ibid*.

[37] For this purpose reference is made to Arts 26, 35, 37 or 38, *Ibid*.

sex, race, colour, ethnic or social origin, genetic features, language, religion or belief, political or any other opinion, membership of a national minority, property, birth, disability, age or sexual orientation.'

For present purposes, however, it must suffice to draw two conclusions from this part of the analysis. The first is that the term non-justiciable should not be embraced either by the FRA or by other commentators when dealing with any of the provisions of the Charter, since it is at best misleading and at worst undermines the importance of the social rights recognized in the document. The second is that the real significance of Article 52(5), from the perspective of the Agency, is that there is a need to promote the adoption of legislation and the taking of executive acts by EU institutions and bodies which would give effect to the relevant rights and would trigger an element of justiciability to the extent that the measures taken are considered, as a matter of law, to be justiciable. This conclusion thus identifies a task of major importance which should be addressed systematically by the new Agency if it is to give a serious impetus to the enjoyment of economic and social rights.

6. THE RELEVANCE OF OTHER INTERNATIONAL INSTRUMENTS RECOGNIZING ECONOMIC AND SOCIAL RIGHTS

The EU as such is not a party to any of the major human rights treaties which recognize economic and social rights, such as the European Social Charter, the International Covenant on Economic, Social and Cultural Rights, or the various ILO conventions dealing with labour rights. Despite various proposals that it should accede to the European Social Charter,[38] and strong arguments that have been developed in favour of such a course of action,[39] there seems no immediate prospect that this will happen.

The preamble to the Charter notes that the Charter 'reaffirms . . . the rights as they result, in particular, from the constitutional traditions and international obligations common to the Member States, . . . the Social Charters adopted by the Union and the Council of Europe . . .'. This statement, combined with the non-regression approach embodied in Article 53, have been interpreted by most observers as clearly underscoring the relevance, in the process of interpreting Charter provisions, of international formulations of human rights to the extent that they are reflected in the common constitutional traditions or constitute common international obligations.

Marika Lerch has noted that a great many of the submissions made to the Convention which drafted the Charter invoked and relied explicitly upon a

---

[38] P Alston and J H H Weiler, 'An 'Ever Closer Union' in Need of a Human Rights Policy: The European Union and Human Rights', in P Alston, with M Bustelo and J Heenan (eds), *The EU and Human Rights* (Oxford, OUP, 1999) p 32.

[39] O De Schutter, *L'adhésion de l'Union européenne à la Charte sociale européenne révisée*, European University Institute Working Paper LAW No. 2004/11.

broad range of international obligations. It can reasonably be assumed that the European Court of Justice will, in relation to the Charter, continue its practice of referring to these other treaties in its judgments under the rubric of the 'sources of inspiration' from which it derives general principles of EU law. Thus for example in *Defrenne v Sabena III*,[40] the Court reinforced its reasoning by observing that 'the same concepts are recognized by the European Social Charter . . . and by [ILO] Convention No 111 . . . concerning discrimination in respect of employment and occupation'.[41] An earlier case had also made reference to social security as an internationally recognized principle based on ILO Convention No 48 on the Maintenance of Migrants' Pension Rights.[42] The other relatively frequently cited human rights treaty is the International Covenant on Civil and Political Rights. It is true, however, that the examples are not legion but, for present purposes, it is the principle that counts.

Since several of the other contributions to this volume have given careful consideration to the role that should be played by international standards generally it is unnecessary for this chapter to go over that ground. Suffice it to add that the argument for the Agency to make strong and effective use of those standards in relation to economic and social rights is especially strong in view of the very valuable jurisprudence that has emerged within the context of the ESC, the ICESCR and the ILO. None of this is to downplay the complexities of making use of those standards. They relate to the complex issue of the EU's competences in some areas such as health and the absence of rights-based approaches to social issues within much of the social sectoral activity of the Union.[43] But such complexity is appropriate and inevitable and it should not be used as an argument against the use of the jurisprudence emerging from other mechanisms to shed light on the issues arising out of the EU Charter and on the potential approaches which might be adopted.

7. CONCEPTUALIZING THE ROLE OF THE FRA

As other contributors to this volume have noted, and as the Introduction also underlines, there has been a significant evolution in the way in which the possible functions of the FRA are viewed. In particular, the way in which the Commission communication recounts the background to the proposal gives a rather inadequate account. It is thus necessary to retrace the steps that led to the present situation in order to understand the roles that were envisaged for the Agency by those who had identified the need for one, and then to contrast those with the orientation of the Commission's proposals which are under review here.

---

[40] Case 149/77, *Defrenne v Sabena* [1978] ECR 1365.
[41] *Ibid*, para 26.
[42] Case 6/75, *Horst v Bundesknappschaft* [1975] ECR 823, at 836.
[43] See eg T Hervey, 'The Right to Health in EU Law', in Hervey and Kenner, n 22 above, p 193.

The establishment of an Agency of this type was first proposed in 1998 in a study that Joseph Weiler and the present author prepared for the *Comité des Sages* which issued the report entitled *Leading by Example: A Human Rights Agenda for the European Union for the Year 2000*.[44] It called upon the European Council to adopt a statement 'confirming its overall commitment to ensuring effective action to promote respect for human rights by recognizing that a monitoring mechanism is not only a desirable, but also an essential, Community contribution.' The conclusion drawn was that the objectives of the European Monitoring Centre on Racism and Xenophobia in Vienna 'should be expanded and adapted to enable it to perform the necessary tasks'. It is important to recall, however, that this was not an isolated proposal, nor one which was assumed to be capable of shouldering the entire burden of ensuring respect for human rights within the EU. Indeed, in terms of only the recommended institutional arrangements alone, the expanded Agency was seen as one element in a four-part overall scheme. The package consisted of (i) 'a Directorate-General with responsibility for human rights, to be headed by a separate Member of the Commission'; (ii) the monitoring agency; (iii) 'a specialist human rights unit' within the office of the High Representative for the Common Foreign and Security Policy; and (iv) a mainstreaming approach in which 'all other institutions of the European Union should be called upon to enhance their human rights functions and sensibilities'.[45]

The 1998 report containing these recommendations was launched at a major conference in Vienna, opened by the then Deputy Chancellor of Austria, Wolfgang Schüssel. In a twist of fate which took place less than two years later, Mr Schüssel was to become Chancellor in a Government which included representatives of a political party whose views were considered by some observers to call into question the common European values in areas such as the rights of immigrants and minorities. The controversy that erupted as a result within the EU was resolved on the basis of a report by a group of *sages* who made a number of recommendations, including some addressed to the need for a stronger set of monitoring arrangements within the EU as a whole.[46] These included a reference to the need for an Agency.

The relevant recommendations in each of these reports were largely ignored in official circles until the European Council meeting in December 2003 decided to establish a 'Human Rights Agency'.

The October 2004 Communication from the Commission gives only a rather partial and not especially accurate picture of this background. It begins by observing that the Council called for the creation of a 'Fundamental Rights

---

[44] P Alston and J H H Weiler, above n 38, p 3.

[45] *Ibid*, pp 41–42.

[46] *Report by Martti Ahtisaari, Jochen Frowein and Marcelino Oreja, adopted in Paris on 8 September 2000.* Curiously, the Report did not have a separate title although it is indicated in the table of contents that the main focus is on 'the commitment of the Austrian Government to the common European values, in particular relating to the rights of minorities, refugees and immigrants'.

Agency', which of course it did not.[47] The divergence from the Council's actual call for a 'Human Rights Agency' is explained in a casual footnote which says that 'for the purposes of this text, the expressions 'fundamental rights' and 'human rights' carry the same meaning'. Even if that were really the case, and I have suggested above that it is not necessarily so, the onus would then be on the Commission to explain why there is a need to change the title when the two expressions have the same meaning. It is clear, as Manfred Nowak has also argued in this volume,[48] that there are strong policy reasons underlying the Commission's decision to unilaterally change the terminology.

The Commission then explains that the European Council's 2003 decision 'ended a long debate in which support for setting up such an Agency was widely expressed.' While the text itself gives no indication of the nature of that debate or the sources, a footnote makes a reference to the 2000 report, although not to the 1998 report. That footnote states that the *sages* had 'recommended the creation of an EU Agency on Human Rights in order to contribute to the establishment of a mechanism within the EU to monitor and evaluate the commitment and performance of individual Member States with respect to common European values'. But this quotation gives only a very limited indication of what the *sages* had in mind. It must be conceded that the sages did not elaborate in great detail upon their proposal, despite the importance that they accorded to it, and nor was it entirely clear how the monitoring arrangements would work. Nevertheless, their report does make two things clear. The first is that the monitoring mechanism would 'allow an open and non-confrontational dialogue'[49] with any Member State in relation to which serious concerns had been voiced, thus implying an operational role of some kind. The second is that it followed the 1998 report almost exactly in recommending the need for a range of institutional arrangements which:

> may include the creation of a Human Rights Office within the Council reporting to the European Council; the appointment within the Commission of a Commissioner responsible for human rights issues; and particularly the extension of the activities, budget and status of the existing [Racism Observatory] . . . in order to make possible the establishment of a full EU Agency on Human Rights.[50]

Finally, the *sages* called for a 'system of prevention' to be put into place 'which would react through information and educational measures' to the problems of racism and xenophobia.[51]

---

[47] In the Presidency Conclusions of the Brussels European Council Meeting of 12–13 December 2003 the Council stressed 'the importance of *human rights* data collection and analysis with a view to defining Union policy in this field, agreed to build upon the existing European Monitoring Centre on Racism and Xenophobia and to extend its mandate to become a *Human Rights Agency* to that effect.' (emphasis added). Precisely the same formulation appears again in the conclusions of the European Council of 4–5 November 2004 (The Hague Programme).

[48] See chapter 4 above.

[49] *Ibid*, para 117.

[50] *Ibid*, para 119.

[51] *Ibid*, para 118.

The relevance of this review of the historical record is twofold. The first is to underscore the fact that the Agency called for by the two major reports issued in recent years was in no sense a 'lightweight' one, to use the Commission's characterization of its proposal.[52] Indeed the sages talked of a 'full EU Agency on Human Rights'. This is relevant because these two reports are commonly referred to as having provided the impetus and even the rationale for the creation of such an Agency. The second reason for reviewing the historical record is that both of the relevant reports placed the Agency in the context of a broader set of human rights structures with which it would interact. In such a setting it was considered appropriate for the Agency's functions to be limited so as not to overlap with those performed by the other component parts of the overall structure. In the event, however, there is no specialist human rights Commissioner and, as yet, no human rights office in the High Representative's structure although proposals to this effect were made in December 2004 by the European Council.

One of the consequences of this is that the Agency will be called upon to perform a wider range of functions than would otherwise have been the case. This, of course, has a range of implications in terms of resources, staffing, and strategy. To the extent that the Commission's Communication plays down all of these aspects and bases itself on the assumption that a very substantially enlarged, and in some ways much more diverse, mandate can be performed without a major review of the functions and approach to be adopted by the Agency, there is good reason for concern.

8. THE AGENCY'S ROLE IN RELATION TO NON-REGRESSION

As noted above, the principle of non-regression was one of the three pillars on which the Charter's economic and social rights proponents relied heavily. It will thus be important for the Agency to play a role in relation to economic and social rights of ensuring that the phrase 'in accordance with national law and practice' is not interpreted in such a way as to nullify the rights in relation to which it is used. The enjoyment of a good many of the rights in the Charter is made subject to such a provision. This is the case for example in relation to the right to marry and to found a family (Article 9), the right to conscientious objection (Article 10(2)), the freedom to found educational establishments (Article 14(3), the freedom to conduct a business (Article 16), workers' right to information and consultation (Article 27) the right to collective bargaining and to strike (Article 28), the right to protection against unjustified dismissal (Article 30), the entitlement to social security benefits and social services (Article 30), the right to social and housing assistance (Article 30), the right of access to preventive health care and the right to benefit from medical treatment (Article 35) and access to services of general economic interest (Article 36).

---

[52] Communication, section 8, p 10.

While not all of these rights could be classified as economic or social rights, it is nonetheless true that the majority would fall into that category. In contrast, the recognition of most civil and political rights is formulated in the Charter in terms of 'everyone has the right to . . .', and no caveat relating to national laws and practices is added. It is important that the FRA should acknowledge in its work on economic and social rights that while such a caveat is clearly relevant to any interpretation of the right involved, such national laws will need to be read down to the extent to which they are inconsistent with the right itself as it has been generally interpreted or as it is formulated or applied in other international norms which are applicable to the situation. This position is formally protected by the non-regression clause in Article 53 of the EU Charter which states that the Charter cannot be used to justify a lower level of protection than that recognized by 'Union law and international law and by international agreements to which the Union or all the Member States are party . . .' including the ECHR. It will be important to ensure that this clause is applied in its fullness so as to take account of all relevant international human rights obligations.

Article 9, to take one example of a right which might or might not be classified as a social right, is short and succinct. It provides that 'The right to marry and the right to found a family shall be guaranteed in accordance with the national laws governing the exercise of these rights.' Of particular importance in interpreting this provision so as to ensure that national laws do not deprive it of its strength would be Article 23(2) of the International Covenant on Civil and Political Rights and the jurisprudence which has been generated in relation to that provision.[53]

9. THE 'MONITORING' FUNCTION

One of the key issues confronting the FRA is to define the term 'monitoring', which has been used as a sort of shorthand to define its functions. Before looking at the specific recommendations contained in the Commission's communication it is useful to recall the details provided in the 1998 report prepared for the *sages* and to consider, in a more general context, what the term monitoring means or might mean in a context such as this. Consideration will then be given to the meaning attributed to the term by the EU in other settings and to the implications of suggesting an analogy between the functions of the Agency and those of a national human rights institution. Although these issues have been considered in greater or lesser detail by some of the other contributors to this volume none of those chapters looks at the issue specifically in terms of economic and social rights.

---

[53] This provision states that 'The right of men and women of marriageable age to marry and to found a family shall be recognized.' As to its interpretation see in particular Human Rights Committee General comment No 19 (1990) on Art 23, UN doc HRI/GEN/1/Rev 6 (2003), p 149.

Although the 1998 report by Alston and Weiler called for a monitoring agency it did not go into extensive detail as to what this might involve. The main explanatory comment was the following:

> While there is a great deal of unsystematic information which suggests lacunae and gaps in the vindication of human rights in the field of application of Community law, no observer can have a comprehensive picture in this regard because there is no agency which is empowered to provide or collect such information in a regular, ongoing and systematic fashion. As a result, the Community lacks the necessary information base upon which it should make decisions as to the identification of legislative and policy priorities and the allocation of administrative and budgetary resources in the field of human rights.[54]

There were, of course, strong reasons at that time for keeping the proposal at a level of generality. The most important was a concern that any detailed indication of the functions to be performed might simply deter governments from taking the proposal seriously. But a great deal has changed in the intervening six years. While the 1998 report spoke of an incoherent and very patchy internal EU human rights policy, the situation today has been transformed by the open discussion of a range of initiatives, the adoption of the EU Charter, the agreement to accede to the ECHR, the creation of the Network of Independent Experts, the preparation of an annual report, and a range of other initiatives designed to contribute to a comprehensive human rights policy. It is thus necessary to go beyond the analysis contained in the 1998 report and to examine more carefully the sort of approach that is called for in relation to the new FRA.

(i) Some general considerations as to terminology

Monitoring is a commonly used term within the framework of international law,[55] but it is by no means the only one used to denote the type of activities that might be undertaken in order to establish the element of accountability, which is what each of the different terms has in common with the other. Other chapters in this volume have contrasted monitoring with supervision. In addition to these two terms international organizations also engage in follow-up, verification and surveillance and it is helpful to briefly consider how each of the five terms is used in order to get a better sense of the interpretation that should be applied to monitoring in the context of the FRA. A brief digression in this direction also serves to underscore the extent to which all governments, including those of the EU, are already subject to extensive accountability procedures under international law. This helps to put the role of the FRA into its broader context and to make clear to those who object to a systematic monitoring role

---

[54] Alston and Weiler, n 38 above, p 13.
[55] See generally P Alston and J Crawford (eds), *The Future of UN Human Rights Treaty Monitoring*, (Cambridge, CUP, 2000).

for the FRA that such monitoring is very much par for the course in terms of an array of existing mechanisms.

Follow-up is a much-favoured term within the UN system to refer to the measures that will be taken to give effect to the provisions of international declarations, programs of action, etc. It is especially popular in relation to some aspects of women's rights such as the Beijing Platform of Action. Its appeal, however, is also its weakness. It is appealing to governments because it is usually non-specific and rarely targeted to specific country situations. It might, however, be sufficient to embrace some weak versions of the tasks envisaged as being performed by the FRA.

Verification is a term much favoured in the area of weapons control and disarmament (such as the 1992 Chemical Weapons Convention).[56] According to the Oxford English Dictionary it signifies '[t]he action of establishing or testing the truth or correctness of a fact, theory, statement, etc., by means of special investigation or comparison of data.' It thus has the connotation of being an occasional rather than a continuing process and of assuming that their is a single truth which, as a factual matter, is capable of being definitively ascertained, or verified.

Supervision is the term used in the European Convention on Human Rights and that has long been favoured by the International Labour Organization (ILO) in relation to international labour standards. The ILO does not, however, proffer any technical definition of this term which would help us to ascertain the parameters of such supervisory activities. *Oxford English Dictionary* definitions of the term include: '[g]eneral management, direction, or control; oversight, superintendence' and '[t]he action of reading through for correction, revision by a superior authority'. Some of the elements in these definitions, such as 'control' or 'correction by a superior authority' would almost certainly be rejected by States if put forward by way of explanation of the principles underlying the ILO's supervisory process. The conclusion to be drawn is that the content of 'supervision' within the ILO context is something that must be deduced on the basis of what the Organization actually does (or, less charitably, is able to get away with), rather than of any pre-agreed definition.

Surveillance is the activity undertaken by the International Monetary Fund (IMF) in order to ascertain the extent of governmental compliance with agreed policies. More specifically, under Article IV of its Articles of Agreement the IMF is mandated to 'exercise firm surveillance over the exchange rate policies of members' and to adopt 'specific principles for the guidance of all members with respect to those policies'. The principal *Oxford English Dictionary* definition of 'surveillance' is the: '[w]atch or guard kept over a person etc., esp. over a suspected person, a prisoner, or the like; often, spying, supervision; less commonly,

---

[56] The following analysis draws in part upon P Alston, 'Establishing Accountability: Some Current Challenges in Relation to Human Rights Monitoring', in E Verhellen (ed), *Monitoring Children's Rights*, (The Hague, Nijhoff, 1996) p 21.

supervision for the purpose of direction or control, superintendence'. While many of these terms would be considered to be too strong by Fund officials, the IMF's own analyses certainly do not seek to portray the exercise as merely one of dialogue and an exchange of views.

And finally we come to the term monitoring. The *Oxford English Dictionary* definition captures rather well the essence of the concept as currently applied in the human rights area. A monitor is '[o]ne who admonishes or gives advice or warning to another as to his conduct'. 'Also *(rare)*, one who advises another to do some particular action, an instigator'. The general usage of the term to monitor is said to be: 'to observe, supervise, or keep under review; to measure or test at intervals esp. for the purpose of regulation or control'. This definition seems quite accurate, at least until the final phrase which moves us closer to the assumptions that seem to underlie some of the other concepts, perhaps even including 'supervision'.

One predictable response to this survey on the part of an international lawyer would be to conclude that the nature of the accountability function inevitably varies with the subject-matter and does little more than reflect the objective requirements that apply in relation to each area (distrust in relation to armaments; the overriding exigencies of economic cooperation in the monetary area, etc.). Hence the foregoing survey of the different terminology employed in different contexts would be seen to be no more than a re-statement of the obvious. What I wish to suggest, however, is that such a response takes far too much for granted in terms of assuming that the status quo has a clear, appropriate and perhaps even inevitable logic to it. In fact, we should not assume that there are 'natural' or 'inevitable' limits to either the extent and reach, or to the form and methods, of holding States to account in relation to their human rights obligations.

The more important conclusion to be drawn is that our principal focus should not be on trying to find a free-standing definition of the term 'monitoring', but rather on the underlying question of how best to ensure respect for the principle of accountability in relation to the fundamental rights recognized in the EU Charter. At a minimum this will require the Agency to review the data which it amasses with a view to undertaking evaluations of the extent to which the obligations contained in the Charter are being met by the various authorities responsible. In this sense the 'opinions' which the FRA is envisaged to adopt will need to be evaluative and critical, albeit constructively so.

(ii) External guides to the content of monitoring

In addition to the foregoing survey of the different terminologies used in relation to human rights accountability, two other reference points are important in considering the approach which the FRA might take: (i) the approach of the EU in its external relations; and (ii) the approach adopted by national human rights institutions.

In terms of the first of these reference points it is worth noting that the term 'monitoring' is regularly used in relation to the work being funded by the European Union and undertaken in various international human rights trouble spots. In Kosovo, for example, a 1999 Decision by the Organization for Security and Co-operation in Europe (OSCE) mandated its Mission in Kosovo to undertake 'monitoring, protection and promotion of human rights, including, inter alia, the establishment of an Ombudsman institution . . .'. [57] The resulting 'monitoring' role has been interpreted generously to include:

— Monitoring the legal system in Kosovo and assisting in its development
— Providing assistance and support to victims of high-risk crimes, such as trafficking
— Ensuring an individual's right to property
— Investigating cases of discrimination and working to find solutions
— Monitoring human rights related to security and law enforcement
— Promoting and raising awareness of human rights.[58]

The EU Monitoring Mission (EUMM) in the Western Balkans, which is now a full-fledged instrument of the CFSP and is financed entirely from the EC budget, defines its mandate to include the following elements:

> Monitoring of political and security developments in the area of responsibility;
> Giving particular attention to border monitoring, inter-ethnic issues and refugee return;
> Providing analytical reports on the basis of tasking received;
> Contribution to the early warning of the Council and to confidence- building, in the context of the policy of stabilisation conducted by the Union in the region.[59]

This is not to suggest that any 'monitoring' function performed by the FRA is directly analogous to the functions performed by such external monitoring missions. There are, of course, many distinctions to be drawn between the two. The point I wish to make, however, is that use of the term monitoring does give rise to at least certain minimal expectations of the extent to which the performance of the target to be monitored measures up to the objective normative standards which are laid down, as well as certain levels of analytical specificity in terms of the outcome of the monitoring.

The same point can be reinforced by reference to the practice of national human rights institutions which the Commission itself suggests as a 'source of inspiration' and the rather extensive functions of which are examined elsewhere in this volume. It must suffice in the present context to note that 'data collection and analysis and the drafting of opinions'[60] would be likely to be criticized as

---

[57] Organization for Security and Co-operation in Europe, Permanent Council, Decision No 305, 1 July 1999, available at http://www.osce.org/docs/english/pc/1999/decisions/pced305.pdf

[58] See 'Protecting and Promoting Human Rights in Kosovo', available at http://www.osce.org/kosovo/human_rights/

[59] http://europa.eu.int/comm/external_relations/cfsp/fin/actions/eumm03.htm. For an analysis of its role see UK House of Commons, Committee on European Scrutiny, 36th Report, available at http://www.publications.parliament.uk/pa/cm200304/cmselect/cmeuleg/42-xxxvi/4218.htm

[60] The main tasks identified by the Commission for the FRA. See Communication, n 1 above, p 8.

being too minimal if suggested by the government of many developing countries which the EU has urged to set up appropriate national human rights mechanisms.

10. LESSONS LEARNED FROM OTHER INTERNATIONAL ENDEAVOURS TO MONITOR SOCIAL RIGHTS

In light of the conclusion reached above to the effect that international standards relating to economic and social rights should be taken into account by the FRA it is also appropriate to consider what lessons, if any, might usefully be learned by the FRA on the basis of the experience gained in other international human rights contexts in relation to the monitoring and promotion of these rights. The two principal contexts which are relevant are the European Social Charter (ESC) and the International Covenant on Economic, Social and Cultural Rights (ICESCR). European states have very extensive experience in engaging with the monitoring mechanisms set up under these treaties, in particular the European Committee of Social Rights (ECSR) under the ESC and the Committee on Economic, Social and Cultural Rights (ESCR Committee) under the ICESCR. For the purposes of the present chapter we will have to content ourselves with a very impressionistic survey of a complex set of procedures, but this will nonetheless be sufficient to enable us to draw some conclusions of relevance to the FRA.

The main technique used by both of these bodies is the examination of reports submitted by governments on a regular basis according to pre-established formats. In neither case has the experience of reporting been a particularly rewarding one. The hope that government agencies will be willing to present self-incriminating information has been shown to be a forlorn one. Both committees spend a great deal of time searching for other sources of information and it could well be argued, although it goes far beyond the scope of the present paper, that the time and effort put into the preparation of such reports would be better spent in other ways. The Commission Communication distinguishes between active and passive approaches to data collection. The latter is indeed premised on requesting regular reports from EU institutions and Member States while the former would involve more selective, and pro-active approaches. Based on the experience of the ESC and the ICESCR there are good reasons to eschew the passive approach. And in any event, the reports submitted to those two bodies are already available even if they are not precisely tailored to the terms of the formulations used in the EU Charter. In addition there will be a great deal of information available in other EU contexts (for example, information generated by exercises involving the open method of coordination etc). Given the strength of the reporting arrangements already in place under the auspices of the Network of Independent Experts it would seem to make much more sense either to augment that or to supplement it in specified and complementary ways.

The second major technique now used by the ESC, and which the ESCR Committee would very much like to emulate, concerns the examination of complaints, a function also performed by a significant number of national human rights institutions. The Commission's Communication on the FRA is adamant that 'the Agency will not have similar powers as the Treaty has already conferred them on the institutions'.[61] Without needing to challenge the assumptions implicit in this assertion, it would be difficult to argue that the experience of either the ESC or the national institutions, in terms of economic and social rights, has been so positive as to warrant a major struggle to ensure that a complaints function is attributed to the FRA.[62]

A third technique used by the ESCR Committee, but not the ESC ECSR, is the elaboration of carefully reasoned statements of interpretation relating to specific rights or issues arising in the context of the Committee's work in developing the jurisprudence of the Covenant. These 'General Comments' have, in some cases at least, had a major impact on interpretations adopted by other bodies and some have been relied upon heavily by national courts. The clearest such example is General Comment No 3 on the nature and scope of States Parties obligations[63] which has been examined at length in the path-breaking judgments in this area adopted by the South African Constitutional Court.[64] While there is no potentially direct analogy between these General Comments and any approach which the FRA might take, the capacity to produce 'opinions' which is foreseen for the Agency could serve a comparable function in terms of spelling out the issues which should be addressed in any actions by the EU or the Member States designed to give substance to the economic and social rights provisions of the Charter.

Another major approach to economic and social rights which has been strongly promoted by the ESCR Committee is mainstreaming. This approach has been explored very effectively by Olivier de Schutter in this volume and it will suffice for present purposes to say that the UN experience in this regard has been relatively positive.

A final lesson to emerge from the work of UN supervisory bodies, and in particular the ESCR Committee and the Committee on the Rights of the Child,[65] is the importance which these bodies have explicitly attached to the role to be played by national institutions. In 1998 the former committee adopted a General

---

[61] The main tasks identified by the Commission for the FRA. See Communication, n 1 above, p 4.

[62] For an assessment that is at best mixed see R Churchill and U Khaliq, 'The Collective Complaints System of the European Social Charter—An Effective Mechanism for Ensuring Compliance with Economic and Social Rights?' (2004) 15 *European Journal of International Law* 417.

[63] Committee on Economic, Social and Cultural Rights, General Comment No 3 (1990): The nature of States parties' obligations (Art 2, para 1, of the Covenant). UN doc HRI/GEN/1/rev 6 (2003), p 14.

[64] See various analyses cited in n 32 above.

[65] Committee on the Rights of the Child, General Comment No 2 (2002): The role of independent national human rights institutions in the protection and promotion of the rights of the child, UN doc HRI/GEN/1/rev 6 (2003), p 289.

Comment on 'the role of national human rights institutions in the protection of economic, social and cultural rights'.[66] It urged all such institutions to pay particular attention to these rights and suggested the following indicative list of possible functions in relation to these rights:

(a) promoting educational and informational programmes;
(b) scrutinising existing and draft laws for compliance with the ICESCR;
(c) providing technical advice, or undertaking surveys;
(d) identifying national level against which the realization of economic and social rights could be measured;
(e) conducting research or holding inquiries;
(f) monitoring compliance with the ICESCR and issuing reports; and
(g) examining complaints.

This list raises several possibilities which should be considered by the FRA. One is educational. While it need not perform the functions itself it could catalyse and monitor training at the national level to educate public officials, the judiciary, and other key groups in relation to economic and social rights, the implications of which are rarely well understood.

Another function which has been used to excellent effect by some national institutions is the holding of public inquiries into respect for a specific right, either in general, in a particular region, or by a given group within the community. If properly organized the benefits to be derived from the consultative process itself can be as useful as the outcome.

But the major issue to be resolved in relation to the FRA is what exactly it will do with the data that it will be authorized to collect. The Communication says that the main aim will be to form the basis for opinions for the institutions and the Member States. A great deal then turns on what is envisaged by 'opinions' in this context. Ideally the Agency will go well beyond the techniques used by the Vienna Racism Monitoring Centre, of which the Commission's own assessment has been strongly critical.[67]

11. DRAWING CONCLUSIONS AS TO THE PLACE OF ECONOMIC AND SOCIAL RIGHTS IN THE FRA'S WORK

(i) The need for an effective Agency

As noted earlier, the reports by the two groups of *sages*, from which the Agency proposal sprang, envisaged a strong set of monitoring arrangements and assumed that they would be only one part of a more comprehensive institutional response to human rights within the emerging structures of the EU. One of the consequences of the fact that the EU has chosen not to designate a dedicated Human Rights

---

[66] General Comment 10 (1998), UN doc E/C 12/1998/25.
[67] See the comments on this issue in the chapter in this volume by G de Búrca.

Commissioner and has not yet set up a human rights office in the High Representative's structure is that the Agency will need to perform a wider range of functions than would otherwise have been the case. This has various implications in terms of resources, staffing and strategy. To the extent that the Commission's Communication plays down all of these dimensions and bases itself on the assumption that a very substantially enlarged, and certainly much more diverse, mandate can be performed without a major review of the functions and approaches to be adopted by the Agency, there is certainly reason for concern.

Indeed one commentator, assuming that the FRA will be given only rather soft functions to perform, has concluded that it should instead be named the EU 'Fundamental Rights Observatory'.[68] Other commentators have also predicted that the functions to be undertaken by the Agency will be rather modest. These fears serve to underscore that there is a significant risk that the FRA will not be treated as a full-fledged EU Agency and, more importantly, will not be given the sort of remit that it will need if it is to live up to its name. If the functions are so modest that they lack credibility it would not be the first time that a human rights agency or commission had been established in bad faith (this is, of course, not to suggest any possible parallel with the establishment of human rights commissions by, for example, Haiti's Baby Doc Duvalier or Zaire's Mobutu Sese Seko). A more likely outcome is that the Agency will be given a minimalist set of functions designed to satisfy at least some of the constituencies that had called for the establishment of an effective EU human rights monitoring mechanism. But an ill-equipped, overly constrained, and ineffectual FRA will in fact only harm the EU's standing, both within Europe and more broadly. It will seem odd to the residents of Europe, and offensive to those living outside, that the EU which so regularly calls upon developing countries to ensure that they have authentic, effective, and adequately-resourced mechanisms in place to monitor and report on human rights, has opted not to establish such machinery for itself.

It is to be hoped, however, that the fears expressed by various observers will prove to be unjustified. Viewed in that more positive light it is appropriate to show why it is important to reject several arguments that have been invoked in favour of a minimal role for an EU Agency in this area.

One such criticism of according a broad role to the Agency is that if it were empowered 'to review the general state of human rights within the Member States' this would 'fundamentally change the nature of the EU, bringing it closer to a human rights organization'.[69] In an unintended fashion, such a criticism goes to the heart of the problem. The assumption that institutions for European governance can be divided up into those which are quintessentially 'human rights organizations' and those that presumably do relatively little in relation to such issues is profoundly mistaken. The whole thrust of mainstreaming human

---

[68] M Heim, *Discussion Paper on the Proposed European Union Human Rights Agency* (Brussels, The Centre, 2004) available at http://www.thecentre.eu.com/site_26/fil/dsk_340_2.pdf, para 31.

[69] *Ibid*, para 13.

rights which is widely accepted within the EU and increasingly even within the UN context is to ensure that all such organizations have a basic human rights mandate. Some element of monitoring and evaluating actual situations is unavoidable if such endeavours are to be effective. While there is ample room for debate as to the appropriate form which such functions should take in any given situation, the suggestion that any such role would bring about a fundamental change in the EU's role is certainly going too far.

Another argument often relied upon to justify a minimalist role for the FRA is that comprehensive monitoring of the human rights situation in the EU already takes place under the procedures and mechanisms established by the Council of Europe and the UN. This is linked to a concern that the proliferation of additional monitoring mechanisms will enhance the risk of diverging human rights standards which would cause confusion and diminish the effectiveness of all of the relevant arrangements.[70] The most obvious response to this objection is that under neither of the principal existing international procedures is the EU itself subject to monitoring. Even in relation to the Member States, such concerns need to be taken into account but in order to do so it is essential to undertake a careful review of the functions that really are being performed by such mechanisms. A comprehensive review of that type goes well beyond the scope of the present chapter but it is instructive to consider more precisely what the critique actually involves in relation to economic and social rights. The brief review undertaken above of the functions performed by the different human rights agencies already monitoring these rights in relation to EU Member States has shown that they are far from being adequate for this purpose.

Finally, it has been argued that, in order to avoid the unnecessary proliferation of international arrangements, no new EU monitoring procedures should be established. In addition to the point above which goes to the efficacy of those existing arrangements, this argument is undermined by considerations of subsidiarity. Apart from being a principle of EU law it is also an empirical reality in relation to international human rights arrangements. In the vast majority of instances such mechanisms can play only a secondary or backup role, and should not be seen as the first line of defence. It is thus always preferable for action to be taken at the national level, and failing that, at the regional level, before reliance is placed upon international mechanisms. It is thus inconsistent with this scheme of things to argue that since some UN mechanisms are monitoring human rights performance it would be inappropriate for the FRA to do so. In reality, the UN is not only a last resort. It is also less well placed than a regional grouping to ensure that nuanced and carefully tailored steps are taken to remedy situations in which human rights are not being adequately respected. Of course, if the regional mechanism is ineffectual or is applying standards that are too weak, there is no option but for the international level to step in. But this

---

[70] *Ibid*, para 14.

is hardly a good argument for the FRA to refrain from doing all it can to monitor and expose human rights problems as they arise.

(ii) The way forward for the FRA on economic and social rights

Assuming that a strong Agency structure will emerge, it is appropriate to draw some conclusions from the foregoing analysis as to the considerations which the FRA should take into account in devising its approach to economic and social rights.

Economic and social rights should be a full and essential part of the FRA's remit. In this respect the Agency should treat all of the provisions of the Charter as relating to fundamental rights and not approach its work by seeking to distinguish between subjective rights and principles. Apart from the fact that such a distinction remains dubious at best and almost impossible to apply in the abstract, it is of marginal relevance to the reporting and monitoring functions to be performed by the Agency.

Similarly, the Agency should avoid in its work use of the term 'non-justiciable' in relation to these rights. The Charter provides simply that certain 'principles' are not judicially cognizable until appropriate legislative or other action has been taken. But once it has, the rights are clearly justiciable. This point serves to highlight the fact that the Agency has an especially important role to play in identifying areas in which legislative and other acts are required in order to give substance and meaning to relevant principles. If instead the Agency were to confine itself to the identification of situations involving violations it will play a much less constructive role and one not likely to be appreciated by any of its constituencies.

The FRA should adopt an approach to economic and social rights which puts them in their broader international normative context and pays due regard to the approach adopted under treaties such as the ESC and the ICESCR, and, to the extent that they have been widely ratified by EU Member States, ILO Conventions.

Non-discrimination is a very revealing lens through which to view these rights and one which would fit very readily into the model developed by the Vienna Racism Centre. By the same token, a strategy which focuses exclusively on non-discrimination is clearly not an adequate response to the much more broad-ranging and demanding set of economic and social rights contained in the Charter.[71]

The emphasis of the new Agency should be on playing a catalytic role. This approach will be consistent not only with the principle of subsidiarity and with the limited available resources, but will also maximize its effectiveness. That in turn means building networks, relying on groups such as the Network of

---

[71] This is sometimes misleadingly called the 'violations approach' but a more useful term is the minimal enforcement model. See G McKeever and F Ni Aolain, n 2 above, at 162–63.

Independent Experts, and building the capacity to capitalize effectively on work being done elsewhere.

The Agency will also need to build constituencies which support its work, certainly in general, but especially in relation to economic and social rights. Without the strong and active support of key constituencies the Agency's work will not get the inputs, the support, the attention, the funding, or the publicity that it needs in order to succeed. If it relies only upon traditional human rights partners it will not succeed in building the necessary constituencies.

By the same token it will need to make an effort to prompt its traditional partners (NGOs, national institutions, observatories, etc) to take a more broad brush approach which gives full recognition to economic and social rights as fundamental rights in their own work. Those partners must themselves acknowledge that traditional legal and court-focused techniques will not be sufficient in relation to these rights. As has been observed in a different context, 'partnerships for social justice cannot be technical but, rather, must involve attention to power issues'.[72]

These challenges also underscore the need for appropriately trained staff for the Agency. Indeed one of the principal lessons that emerges, both from the experience of the various international mechanisms and also from efforts to date in relation to some of the key social rights contained in the EU Charter, is the need for specialist expertise to undertake the technical assessments of problems affecting rights such as labour rights and the rights to health and housing. A good example of this, which is by no means unusual, is provided by the detailed reports prepared by the EU's Network of Independent Experts on the EU Charter. These reports, which are generally of a very high quality, are considerably more detailed and insightful in relation to the more traditional rights than they are in relation to many of the social rights that have been the subject of monitoring. In the Network's report on the situation in 2003, for example, Article 22 dealing with cultural, religious and linguistic diversity is not addressed directly or in the fullness of its implications but only in terms of nondiscrimination in relation to the ground of membership of a national minority.[73] In relation to several other articles, such as Article 24 on the rights of the child, Article 25 on the rights of the elderly,[74] Article 27 on worker's right to information and consultation within the undertaking, Article 28 on the right of collective bargaining and action, Article 29 on the right of access to placement services,[75] Article 32 on the prohibition of child labour and protection of young people at work, and Article 33 on family and professional life,[76] the report contains the following annotation:

---

[72] P Stubbs, 'International Non-State Actors and Social Development Policy', Globalism and Social Policy Programme, *Policy Brief No 4* (2003) 8.
[73] EU Network Report, n 16 above, p 108.
[74] *Ibid*, p 111.
[75] *Ibid*, p 117.
[76] *Ibid*, p 122.

> There is no new significant development to be reported under this provision of the Charter, for the period under scrutiny.

While this could conceivably be the case in relation to one or another right, the fact that, to take an example almost at random, the report devotes ten pages to Article 8 on the protection of personal data[77] would seem to confirm that the experts write in depth about the issues on which they are knowledgeable and find little if anything to say on the issues which are not traditionally within their remit. This is not intended as a criticism of the report of the Independent Network but serves to highlight two tasks which should be prominent on the agenda of the FRA. The first is to ensure that it taps into the expertise of individuals working in the areas covered by all of the diverse social rights. And the second is that it should acknowledge a responsibility to help to put meat on the bones of those social rights which have not yet been elaborated in the same detail as the more traditional or familiar rights.

In concluding this chapter the most central point to be made is that if the promise of the EU Charter in terms of the indivisibility of all fundamental rights, including economic and social rights, is to be fulfilled it will require a deliberate and carefully tailored strategy on the part of the FRA.

---

[77] *Ibid*, pp 57–67.

8

The Contribution of the EU Fundamental Rights Agency to the Realization of Workers' Rights

BRIAN BERCUSSON*

I. INTRODUCTION

THE PROPOSED CREATION of a Fundamental Rights Agency at EU level[1] is driven by the adoption of the EU Charter of Fundamental Rights at Nice in December 2000 and its incorporation into the proposed Constitutional Treaty for Europe.[2] The EU Charter includes provisions which are at the heart of labour law in Europe.[3] It has the potential to renew labour law in the Member States and at EU level.[4]

In both the Convention which drafted the Charter and the Convention on the Future of Europe which proposed its incorporation into the Constitutional Treaty, debates raged over economic and social rights in general, and workers'

---

* Professor of European Social and Labour Law, King's College, University of London; Guest Professor, Swedish National Institute for Working Life (Arbetslivsinstitutet), Stockholm (1997–); Visiting Professor, l'Institut d'Etudes Politiques, Paris (2002).

[1] *The Fundamental Rights Agency, Public consultation document*, (SEC(2004) 1281) Communication from the Commission, COM(2004) 693 final, Brussels, 25 October 2004.

[2] *Ibid*, fn 6: 'The Charter of Fundamental Rights [. . .] has been included in part II of the Treaty establishing a Constitution for Europe, with binding legal force. It constitutes an authentic expression of the fundamental rights protected by the Community legal framework.'

[3] Freedom of association (Art 12), right of collective bargaining and collective action (Art 28), workers' right to information and consultation within the undertaking (Art 27), freedom to choose an occupation and right to engage in work (Art 15), prohibition of child labour and protection of young people at work (Art 32), fair and just working conditions (Art 31), protection of personal data (Art 8), non-discrimination (Art 21), equality between men and women (Art 23), protection in the event of unjustified dismissal (Art 30).

[4] There has been extensive commentary on the labour law dimension of the EU Charter. See B Bercusson (ed), *European Labour Law and the EU Charter of Fundamental Rights* (Brussels, European Trade Union Institute, 2003) summary version. Full version forthcoming: (Baden-Baden, Nomos, 2005).

rights in particular.[5] Much depends on what emerges by way of mechanisms for the enforcement of the fundamental rights of labour proposed by the EU Charter.[6] This chapter considers the potential contribution of the Fundamental Rights Agency to the realisation of the fundamental rights of workers in the EU.

The chapter begins by addressing the potential role for the Fundamental Rights Agency as regards fundamental rights of workers in the general context of EU labour regulation, which has experienced a variety of legal strategies (Section II). In particular, realisation of the fundamental rights of workers is examined in the wider context of mechanisms of implementation, application and enforcement of the rights of workers and their organisations through judicial, administrative and industrial relations mechanisms (Section III). However, against this background, the Fundamental Rights Agency will be operating in the new EU constitutional context; in particular, the adoption of the EU Charter of Fundamental Rights (Section IV).

The overall objective of the chapter is to identify *substantive obstacles* and *procedural solutions* to realisation of the fundamental rights of workers (Section IV). The substantive obstacles (a) identified include: (1) the potential conflict of EU fundamental rights with limited EU competences; (2) the distinction between 'rights' and 'principles' and the implications for justiciability; (3) the relation of EU fundamental rights to national laws and practices; (4) the significance of the 'Explanations' to the Charter; and (5) the role of international labour standards.

The procedural solutions (b) proposed in the chapter begin by considering (1) the current economic context of the Lisbon Strategy; (2) the legal context of the amendments to the EC Treaty by the Treaty of Nice; and (3) the Commission's Social Policy Agenda. Analysis of (4) the 'open method of coordination' (OMC) and the social dialogue focuses in particular on the Commission's Communications of 26 June 2002 (a) and 12 August 2004 (b), and then addresses the possible engagements of these processes (c). The role envisaged for the Fundamental Rights Agency (5) acknowledges the central role of labour in the European social model (a), and aims to engage with the OMC and social dialogue (b) to promote a process for realisation of fundamental labour rights (c). This process is outlined as 'mainstreaming' fundamental rights of workers (6) by specifying minimum procedural standards (a), an obligation on the social partners to engage in a 'spirit of cooperation' (b), and detailed requirements regarding the process of information (c) and consultation (d) in concluding agreements elaborating the fundamental rights of workers. The proposed

---

[5] B. Bercusson, 'Episodes on the Path towards the European Social Model: The EU Charter of Fundamental Rights and the Convention on the Future of Europe' in C Barnard, S Deakin, G Morris (eds), *The Future of Labour Law, Liber Amicorum Sir Bob Hepple* (Oxford, Hart, 2004).

[6] It should be noted that (i) not all workers' rights are fundamental, (ii) not all workers' rights are in the EU Charter, and (iii) workers' rights, whether or not fundamental and whether or not in the EU Charter, may be affected by the emergence of a European Constitution.

procedural solution is summarised (e) and conclusions are presented as to how the Fundamental Rights Agency can contribute (VI).

II. FUNDAMENTAL RIGHTS OF WORKERS IN THE GENERAL CONTEXT OF EU LABOUR LAW

The significance of the creation of a Fundamental Rights Agency at EU level and its potential contribution to the protection of fundamental rights in the field of employment and industrial relations should be assessed in the specific context of labour regulation in the EU. And EU labour regulation is best understood in the context of the evolution of the European Communities since their foundation with the European Coal and Steel Community (ECSC) in 1951. Throughout more than half a century, the Community has experienced a variety of often competing legal strategies for the formulation and implementation of labour law and social policy.[7]

The earliest strategy is that which characterised the founding of the ECSC: active labour market policy and labour involvement in regulation. In complete contrast, the following period was characterised by a strategy of neo-liberal laissez-faire, reflected in the almost total absence of social policy and labour law provisions in the Treaty of Rome of 1957. This strategy was contested by an ambitious Social Action Programme adopted in 1974, which sought to harmonize labour legislation in the common market. This strategy was brought to a halt by the opposition of a Conservative Government elected in the United Kingdom in 1979 with a domestic strategy of deregulation of labour markets. The result was the EU exploring a non-legislative strategy in the form of indirect financial instruments and the launching of the European social dialogue in 1985.

The 1992 objective of the European Single Market led to pressures for a strategy to achieve a social dimension through fundamental social and economic rights in a non-binding Community Charter of the Fundamental Social Rights of Workers of 1989. The social dialogue strategy was formally institutionalised in the Maastricht Protocol and Agreement on Social Policy of 1992, now incorporated into the EC Treaty by the Treaty of Amsterdam of 1997. The Treaty of Amsterdam also introduced a new Employment Chapter into the Treaty of Rome, with a novel regulatory mechanism: the 'open method of coordination.'

On 7 December 2000, an EU Charter of Fundamental Rights, including many social and labour rights, was unanimously approved by the European Parliament, Commission and Council. Initially limited to a political declaration, it is to be given a formal legal status through incorporation in the Constitutional Treaty drafted by the Convention on the Future of Europe and adopted by the Intergovernmental Conference meeting in Brussels on 17–18 June 2004. It has been repeatedly cited before the European Court of Justice.

---

[7] B Bercusson, *European Labour Law* (London, Butterworths, Law-in-Context Series, 1996) pt II, 'History and Strategies of European Labour Law' chs 3–6, pp 43–94.

This history reveals the extraordinary range of competing legal and institutional strategies which have characterised attempts to construct a European labour law, and the engagement of Member States, Community institutions and interest groups, primarily organisations of employers and trade unions, in the course of developing these strategies.[8]

III. FUNDAMENTAL RIGHTS OF WORKERS IN THE GENERAL CONTEXT OF ENFORCEMENT OF LABOUR LAW

Specifically, therefore, a role for a Fundamental Rights Agency should be analysed *in the general context of mechanisms of implementation, application and enforcement of the rights of workers and their organisations in the EU*. Further, to understand the role of fundamental workers' rights at EU level, it is necessary to understand the *national* context of such rights in the Member States, not least as regards the mechanisms of their implementation and enforcement.

One account of the application of labour law in *national* jurisdictions identified three principal mechanisms: through the administration, through the courts and through the social partners (*administrative, judicial* and *industrial relations* mechanisms of enforcement).[9] There are differences in the effectiveness and in the importance attached to each of these mechanisms of enforcement among the

---

[8] Institutional struggles over regulatory territory in the sphere of employment and labour relations are emblematic of international regulatory competition and coordination. The institutions involved, the legal strategies adopted, and the political tactics used offer many lessons for international labour regulation on a wider global scale. B Bercusson, 'Regulatory Competition in the EU System: Labour' in D Esty and D Geradin (eds), *Regulatory Competition and Economic Integration: Comparative Perspectives* (Oxford, Oxford University Press, 2000) pp 241–62. To take just one illustration, rich in irony: the United Kingdom's government's stance from 1979 in preventing the adoption at Community level of labour legislation by blocking the requisite unanimity in the Council of Ministers was dictated by its domestic policy. It is, therefore, ironic that it was this United Kingdom blockage of labour legislation at EU level which provided the critical stimulus to a transformation in legal strategy for workers' rights at EU level: the emergence of a competing regulatory strategy in the form of dialogue between the social partners at European level. The doubtless unintended consequence of the United Kingdom government policy of de-collectivisation of industrial relations at domestic level was the huge advance in collectivisation of industrial relations at EU level. Deregulation of collective bargaining in the United Kingdom produced regulation through social dialogue at EU level. While the British trade unions (TUC) and employers (CBI) were ignored in London, they were engaged in the process of negotiating EU level collective agreements in Brussels! The framework agreements on parental leave (1996) and part-time work (1997) are examples. These became EU legislation in the form of legally binding Directives, at a time when the United Kingdom government had excluded itself from participating in the legislative process through the 1992 Maastricht 'opt-out.' Council Dir 96/34/EC of 3 June 1996 on the Framework Agreement on parental leave concluded by UNICE, CEEP and the ETUC; OJ L 145/4 of 19 September 1996. Council Dir 97/81/EC of 15 December 1997 concerning the Framework Agreement on part-time work concluded by UNICE, CEEP and the ETUC; OJ L 14/9 of 20 January 1998.

[9] A Supiot, '*L'application du droit du travail en Europe*' (1991) 47 *Travail et Emploi, Ministère des affaires sociales, du travail et de la solidarité*, France. A similar framework has been applied to enforcement of EU labour law; see B Bercusson, *European Labour Law* (London, Butterworths, 1996) pt III, 'Enforcement of European Labour Law' chs 7–11, pp 97–163.

labour law systems of the Member States. Various mechanisms interact and overlap in different ways within each national jurisdiction.[10]

Although there is controversy about the particular efficacy of one or other mechanism in a specific national context, one axiom of labour law should be remembered. The effectiveness of labour law rules is in inverse proportion to the distance between those who make the rules and those who are subjected to them: the greater the distance, the less their effectiveness; the lesser the distance, the greater their effectiveness. The presumption is that rules originating from social partners engaged in collective bargaining, being closest to those subject to these rules, achieve a higher level of effectiveness. Conversely, those emerging from legislative or administrative processes, distant from employers and workers, will have relatively less efficacy. Whatever the national equilibrium among the various mechanisms of enforcement, the argument is that those systems in which the social partners are more prominent in rule making will be those in which the effectiveness of enforcement is greater.

This axiom should be borne in mind when considering the potential contribution of a Fundamental Rights Agency to the realisation of workers' rights in the sphere of employment and industrial relations. Moreover, the Fundamental Rights Agency is likely to operate in a new constitutional context. The Constitutional Treaty will affect the profile and activities of the Agency with respect to the enforcement of fundamental rights of workers through judicial, administrative and industrial relations processes.

IV. THE NEW EU CONSTITUTIONAL CONTEXT

The Fundamental Rights Agency (FRA) is being proposed in a new constitutional context. This new constitutional context includes a number of specific qualities concerning labour which favour a definitive role for the FRA. In Part I of the Constitutional Treaty, the Title on 'The Democratic Life of the Union,' in Article I–48 provides:

> The European Union recognises and promotes the role of the social partners at Union level, taking into account the diversity of national systems; it shall facilitate dialogue between the social partners, respecting their autonomy. The Tripartite Social Summit for Growth and Employment shall contribute to social dialogue.

In Part II, the EU Charter includes fundamental rights of labour. In Part III, 'The Policies and Functioning of the Union,' 'The Union and the Member States shall

---

[10] J Malmberg (ed), *Effective Enforcement of EC Labour Law* (Uppsala, Iustus Forlag, 2003). Foreword by B Bercusson, pp 17–25. Within each Member State, equilibrium among the different mechanisms has been established. This is not to say that all such national equilibria are functionally equivalent. That in some Member States the administrative, judicial or industrial relations mechanism is predominant does not imply that the overall equilibrium in each Member State assures equally effective enforcement. Specifically, the presence or absence of strong mechanisms of judicial enforcement is not determining.

[. . .] work towards developing a coordinated strategy for employment [. . .] with a view to achieving the objectives defined in Article I–3)' (Article III–97). The social partners at EU level (Articles III–105–106) and in the Member States (Article III–104(4)) are acknowledged as active participants in the formulation and implementation of EU social and labour policy.

The EU model of employment and industrial relations is determined by the organisational forms of workers and employers at EU and national levels; specifically, their interactions in a variety of ways and at different levels, often characterised as 'social partnership.' Perhaps the most familiar is collective bargaining between an employer and a union at *sectoral* level in most countries, though also at company or enterprise level. But in the EU, this is only one of three institutional forms of interaction. The other two are processes at *national* level (macro-level) and at the *workplace* (micro-level). It is the existence of all three levels and their inter-relationship which define the specific character of the European model of employment and industrial relations.[11]

Critical to the success of this specific EU model of employment and industrial relations is collective organisation in the form of organisations of workers and employers, the central actors in a 'social partnership' model. This defining feature of the European model implies substantial trade union membership, a pre-condition for the emergence of social partnership, and is recognised in Article I–48 of Part I of the Constitutional Treaty.

As important as this institutional safeguard of the social partners in the European constitutional model are the rights enshrined in Part II of the Constitution, the Charter of Fundamental Rights. The EU Charter, breaks new constitutional ground by including in a single list of fundamental rights not only traditional civil and political rights, but also a long list of social and economic rights, among them fundamental rights of workers. During the process of drafting the Constitutional Treaty in the Convention on the Future of Europe, some Member States made strenuous attempts to downgrade the legal effects of the Charter. The Convention itself made some 'adjustments' to the final provisions of the Charter, but insisted these were not changes, merely 'clarifications.'

Similarly, the Praesidium of the Convention which drafted the EU Charter had prepared 'explanations' to the Charter. These were stated categorically to 'have no legal value and are simply intended to clarify the provisions of the Charter.' In Part II of the Constitutional Treaty, the Convention on the Future of Europe added to the Preamble of the Charter a sentence that:

---

[11] Contrasting the presence and role of trade unions and workers' representative organisations in the United States with European experience illustrates the singularity of the European model of employment and industrial relations. Its manifestation, in all its diversity, at both EU and Member State levels, in the form of macro-level *national* dialogue, collective bargaining at *intersectoral* and *sectoral* levels, and collective participation in decision-making at the *workplace* is the most salient quality distinguishing the European model of employment and industrial relations.

the Charter will be interpreted by the courts of the Union and the Member States with due regard for the explanations prepared at the instigation of the Praesidium of the Convention which drafted the Charter.

In the final negotiations over the Constitution at the summit of 17–18 June 2004, this sentence was amended to include a reference to explanations 'updated under the responsibility of the Praesidium of the European Convention.' In addition, another paragraph 7 was added to Article II–52 of the EU Charter:

> The explanations drawn up as a way of providing guidance in the interpretation of the Charter of Fundamental Rights shall be given due regard by the courts of the Union and of the Member States.[12]

Finally, in various Articles of the Charter, reference is made to 'national laws and practices,' including in relation to the fundamental trade union and workers' rights in Articles 27, 28 and 30 of the Charter.

V. SUBSTANTIVE OBSTACLES AND PROCEDURAL SOLUTIONS TO THE REALIZATION OF THE FUNDAMENTAL RIGHTS OF WORKERS

The potential contribution of the FRA to the realisation of fundamental rights of workers engages specific difficulties raised by the EU Charter's provisions. The Charter left open many substantive questions of law which are central to the effective realisation of the fundamental rights of workers. The FRA, comprising a body of experts, could greatly alleviate the tensions resulting from these outstanding issues. In particular, the FRA could seek to promote solutions negotiated by the 'social partners' (organisations of employers and trade unions), without prejudicing the ultimate authority of the European Court of Justice to resolve these questions: 'bargaining in the shadow of the Court.'

The following sections analyse some outstanding substantive legal problems to the solution of which the FRA could contribute and the procedural solutions proposed to resolve these problems.

a) Substantive Obstacles

Substantive legal problems of the EU Charter's provisions on the fundamental rights of workers which remain to be resolved include five issues: the potential conflict of EU fundamental rights with limited EU competences; the distinction between 'rights' and 'principles' and the implications for justiciability; the relation of EU fundamental rights to national laws and practices; the significance of the 'Explanations' to the Charter; and the role of international labour standards.

---

[12] As regards the legal status of the Explanations, this outcome seems, contrary to the Preamble, to have diluted the legal force of the explanations and makes no reference to updated explanations.

1. EU Fundamental Rights versus EU Competences

The EU Charter, by including fundamental labour standards, sets up a specific political dynamic. Failure to make the promised fundamental rights effective will create bitter disillusionment, especially among those who are promised specific labour rights, and will undermine their loyalty to the European integration project. The values of the Charter are a declared part of the construction of Social Europe. Its objectives are to be secured through the exercise of the competences allocated under the Union's Constitution. Perhaps the most sensitive issue arising from the Charter's labour rights is their potential impact on EU competences.[13] Incorporating the Charter in a Constitutional Treaty entails a review of the respective competences of Member States and the EU.[14]

The competences of the Community and the Union are frequently a subject of litigation between those seeking to extend, or to limit them. If there is a potential conflict between the scope of Union competences and some Charter rights, the solution should be to reinforce the status of fundamental rights, not abandon them or allow their violation in order to protect the Treaty. At least, it should be left to the European Court of Justice (ECJ) to resolve this conflict. The ECJ has played a cautious but essential role in protecting fundamental rights. It has done this in the interests of protecting the Treaty from national constitutional courts which would reject it precisely because the Treaty appeared to contradict fundamental rights in national constitutions. By recognising fundamental rights as not conflicting with the Treaty, thus giving way to the objections of these national constitutional courts, the ECJ has preserved the Treaty.

One example will serve to highlight both the importance and the sensitivity of this issue. Freedom of association and the right to take collective action are

---

[13] In the Convention on the Future of Europe, Working Group II was given the task of formulating proposals regarding the EU Charter. The most notable aspect of the Working Group's report was its unanimous recommendation that the EU Charter be incorporated into the Constitutional Treaty. Less noted, however, was the heated debate in Working Group II on the potential impact of incorporation of the Charter on the division of competences between the EU and the Member States, particularly as this would affect social and labour competences. The Final Report of Working Group II proposed a number of contentious 'adjustments.' In the discussion in the Plenary, a number of Members of the Convention from the European Parliament criticized the Working Group's proposed 'adjustments' to the horizontal clauses. Sylvia-Yvonne Kaufmann referred to the dangers of the proposed 'adjustments' introducing new elements by the back door. Elena Paccioti warned that 'adjustments' to the horizontal clauses evinced an attempt to water down the Charter. However, the Member of the Convention representing the German Parliament, Jürgen Meyer, argued that the new clauses were mere clarifications which did not change the substance of the Charter. Professor Gráinne de Búrca wrote one of 'Ten Reflections on the Constitutional Treaty for Europe' prepared by the European University Institute, a contribution submitted to the Convention by Giuliano Amato (CONV 703/03 of 28 April 2003). Professor de Búrca analysed Working Group II's proposed 'adjustments' and recommended that, with one minor exception, they should be rejected.

[14] Arguably, whatever the division of competences, effective implementation of the Charter must be guaranteed, whether by the EU or the Member States.

explicitly guaranteed in Articles 12 and 28 of the Charter.[15] But Article 137(5) of the EC Treaty[16] appears explicitly to exclude the right of association and the right to strike. A potential conflict with Article 137(5) therefore emerges when the EU Charter is incorporated into the Constitutional Treaty.[17] For example, a measure adopted by the Community on the right to strike or freedom of association, central issues of workers' fundamental rights, might be challenged as outside EU competences. Would the European Court uphold the measure where it can be linked with a Charter provision, particularly if the measure has the explicit objective of implementing a fundamental right guaranteed by the EU Charter? The proclamation of fundamental rights in a Constitutional Treaty confronts an Article 137(5) EC which appears to deny the Union competence to implement those rights. This contradiction undermines both these rights and the Union.

The FRA could scarcely ignore this explosive situation. Indeed, it could assist in the promotion of fundamental rights of association and collective action by addressing this apparent contradiction. To do so it could draw on its reputation as an objective body with undisputed expertise in the field of fundamental rights, including fundamental rights of workers. Specifically, it could seek to resolve the contradiction through the procedural mechanism of encouraging the

---

[15] Art 12 of the EU Charter (re-numbered Art II–72 of the Constitutional Treaty) provides for 'freedom of association at all levels, in particular in [. . .] trade union [. . .] matters [. . .], which implies the right of everyone to form and to join trade unions for the protection of his or her interests.' Art 28 of the Charter (re-numbered Art II–88 of the Constitutional Treaty) provides for 'the right [. . .] in cases of conflicts of interest, to take collective action to defend their interests, including strike action.'

[16] Before the Treaty of Nice, Art 137(6) EC. Inserted as Art III–104(6) of the Constitutional Treaty: 'The provisions *of this Article* shall not apply to pay, the right of association, the right to strike or the right to impose lock-outs.' In the Constitutional Treaty, Art III–104(6): '*This Article* shall not apply to pay, the right of association, the right to strike or the right to impose lock-outs.'

[17] One argument is that there is no contradiction between the Charter and Art 137(5) EC, since the Charter in Art 51(1) states: 'The provisions of this Charter are addressed to the institutions and bodies of the Union [As amended in the Provisional consolidated version of the draft Treaty establishing a Constitution for Europe, CIG 86/04, Brussels, 25 June 2004: "The provisions of this Charter are addressed to the Institutions, bodies, offices and agencies of the Union"] with due regard to the principle of subsidiarity and to the Member States only when they are implementing Union law.' It is argued that by virtue of Art 137(5) EC, freedom of association and the right to strike fall *exclusively within Member State competence*. The EU Charter affects 'Member States *only when they are implementing Union law*.' As there can be no Union law on these matters, there is no contradiction between the EU Charter and Art 137(5) EC. In other words, *if* Art 137(5) EC provides that such action falls outside Community competence, the EU Charter does not affect the position, as Art 51(2) states: 'This Charter does not extend the field of application of Union law beyond the powers of the Union or establish any new power or task for the Union, or modify powers or tasks defined in other Parts of the Constitution.' However, this argument is based on the questionable assumption that there is *no* EU competence over the matters listed in Art 137(5) EC. Art 137(5) EC begins: 'The provisions *of this Article* shall not apply to pay, the right of association, the right to strike or the right to impose lock-outs.' There is nothing which excludes Community competence as regards these matters being exercised under *any other Art* of the Treaty. The incorporation of the *EU Charter* in the Constitutional Treaty would provide *another possible legal basis* for Community action. It can be argued that the Community *could* take action to achieve the rights of association and collective action in the EU Charter if these rights were not being sufficiently achieved by the Member States, according to the principle of subsidiarity defined in Art 5 EC.

social partners, authors of the relevant provision in Article 137(5) EC,[18] to negotiate a solution. Failure to negotiate a solution would inevitably entail litigation
culminating in the European Court of Justice deciding the issue. The FRA's task
is to facilitate this 'bargaining in the shadow of the Court.'

2. *'Principles' and Justiciability*

Working Group II of the Convention on the Future of Europe added an additional paragraph to Article 52 (Article 52(5)):

> The provisions of this Charter which contain principles may be implemented by leg-
> islative and executive acts taken by the institutions and bodies of the Union, and by
> acts of Member States when they are implementing Union law, in the exercise of their
> respective powers. They shall be judicially cognisable only in the interpretation of
> such acts and in the ruling on their legality.

This new limitation aims to prevent 'principles' being interpreted in future as
containing elements of positive rights for individuals. This proposal was vainly
resisted by members of Working Group II, who complained that it resurrected
the distinction between rights and principles which had been rejected by the
drafting Convention.[19]

By re-asserting the distinction between 'rights' and 'principles,' with the
implication that the latter have lesser legal effects, Working Group II was trying
to open the door to transforming some 'rights' into mere 'principles.' The
Working Group even admitted that it was aiming at social rights when it
stated:[20]

> This is consistent both with case law of the Court of Justice and with the approach of
> the Member States' constitutional systems to 'principles' *particularly in the field of
> social law*.

Moreover, this interpretation of the amendment in Article 52(5) is repeated in
the 'updated' Explanations to 'clarify' the Charter.[21]

---

[18] Art 137(5) EC was in the agreement concluded by the EU social partners on 31 October 1991,
which subsequently became the Agreement on Social Policy annexed to the Protocol on Social Policy
of the Treaty on European Union, later integrated into the EC Treaty by the Treaty of Amsterdam.

[19] In criticising the Working Group's amendments during the Convention Plenary's debate on the
Final Report of Working Group II, Olivier Duhamel, a Member of the Convention from the
European Parliament, stated they were 'unnecessary and retrograde' and singled out the alleged distinction between 'rights and principles,' as did Anne Van Lancker, who specifically identified the distinction between rights and principles as attempting to limit the Charter. The French Government
representative, Pierre Moscovici, warned that the distinction between rights and principles could
limit the interpretation of those principles.

[20] S A.II.6, p 8 of the Final Report of Working Group II.

[21] 'Paragraph 5 clarifies the distinction between "rights" and "principles" set out in the Charter.
According to that distinction, subjective rights shall be respected, whereas principles shall be
observed (Art 51(1)). Principles may be implemented through legislative or executive acts (adopted
by the Union in accordance with its powers, and by the Member States only when they implement
Union law); accordingly, they become significant for the Courts only when such acts are interpreted
or reviewed. They do not however give rise to direct claims for positive action by the Union's

However, the 'adjustment' may not have the effect claimed for it. It does not appear to apply to most of the provisions regarding employment and industrial relations in Chapter IV: 'Solidarity,' of the Charter.[22] The field of social and labour law as understood by the 'updated' Explanations is far from coherent.[23] The alleged distinction between rights and principles is far from clear and the 'updated' Explanations do nothing to clarify it. They only add to the confusion. This distinction was rejected by the Convention which drafted the Charter. The attempt by the Praesidium of the Convention in its 'updated' explanations to revive the distinction between rights and principles, to be used against rights 'particularly in the field of social law,' is unlikely to recommend itself to the European Court of Justice, least of all in the field of labour law. There is an urgent need for clarification. Again, the Fundamental Rights Agency could play an important role by using its expertise to elaborate the concept of the justiciability of fundamental social rights in general and to clarify the justiciability of the fundamental rights of workers in particular.

The fundamental social and economic rights in the EU Charter go beyond those of workers and trade unions to include others of a more programmatic nature. Implementation of the Charter aims to build a bridge between *programmatic* (social and economic rights) and *justiciable* (civil and political) rights. Justiciable rights equate to effective and enforceable rights. The challenge is to *establish* clearly *justiciable rights of workers and trade unions*, for example, trade union rights of association, information and consultation, collective bargaining and collective action, and, further, to *develop* implementation of *programmatic* social and economic rights, for example, to health, education, etc.

---

institutions or Member States authorities. This is consistent both with case law of the Court of Justice [two cases are cited: Case T–13/99 and Case C–265/85] and with the approach of the Member States' constitutional systems to "principles" particularly in the field of social law. For illustration, examples for principles recognised in the Charter include eg Arts 25, 26 and 37. In some cases, an Art of the Charter may contain both elements of a right and of a principle, eg Arts 23, 33 and 34.' Provisional consolidated version of the Declarations to be annexed to the Final Act of the Intergovernmental Conference, CIG 86/04, ADD 2, Brussels, 25 June 2004, pp 64–65.

[22] Art 27: 'Workers' right to information and consultation within the undertaking,' Art 28: 'Right of collective bargaining and action,' Art 29: 'Right of access to placement services,' Art 30: 'right to protection against unjustified dismissal,' Art 31: 'right to working conditions which respect his or her health, safety and dignity.'

[23] The illustrations given as 'examples for principles recognised in the Charter' include Art 25, entitled 'The rights of the elderly,' and Art 26, which begins: 'The Union recognises and respects the right of persons with disabilities.' However, in many factual situations, both of these provisions are easily capable of being translated into positive and justiciable rights. The other example given is clearly remote from established rights in labour law; Art 37: 'Environmental protection,' which refers to 'the principle of sustainable development.' Illustrations said to contain 'both elements of a right and of a principle' were Art 23: 'Equality between men and women,' perhaps the field with the most extensive and established positive rights in EU social and labour law; Art 33: 'Family and professional life,' which includes the 'right to protection from dismissal for a reason connected with maternity,' and Art 23 'Social security and social assistance,' which refers to 'entitlements' and 'rights.'

The tasks of an implementation strategy are three-fold. First, with respect to *justiciable* rights, the task is to develop effective implementation, looking to effective sanctions, preventing regressions, removing qualifications, thresholds, exclusions and modifications. Secondly, the task is to *move more social and economic rights towards justiciability*; formulating them as positive and enforceable rights; and including effective sanctions. Thirdly, with respect to *programmatic* rights, the task is implementation through effective monitoring of government policy and actions, with possible judicial review of consistency and powers of nullification. The FRA can play an important role in ensuring that the EU Charter acquires the character of a *dynamic* instrument, and that Member States have to actively accommodate the new fundamental social rights.[24]

3. National Laws and Practices

Working Group II of the Convention on the Future of Europe added an additional paragraph to Article 52 (Article 52(6)): 'Full account shall be taken of national laws and practices as specified in the Charter.' There is little doubt that certain fundamental rights of workers were the target of this 'adjustment.' The references in the Charter to 'national laws and practices' are concentrated in Chapter IV, 'Solidarity,' including many fundamental social rights.[25] Working Group II's Final Report merely observed that 'it seems appropriate to the Group to include a clause in the Charter recalling [the references to national laws and practices].'[26]

The precise legal consequences of the Charter's references to 'national laws and practices' are far from clear and raise a number of problems. The Fundamental Rights Agency could address these problems and elaborate solutions in light of basic principles of EU law. For example, would the fundamental principle of the supremacy of Community law be undermined if Charter rights, incorporated into the Constitutional Treaty, were limited by national laws and practices? Could national courts adjudicating on a dispute over

---

[24] A form of 'dynamic subsidiarity.' See 'Subsidiarity and Solidarity,' ch 4, pp 63–74, in B Bercusson, S Deakin, P Koistinen, Y Kravaritou, U Muckenberger, A Supiot, B Veneziani, *A Manifesto for Social Europe*, (Brussels, European Trade Union Institute, 1996).

[25] The Charter's references to national laws and practices affect the trade union and labour rights in Arts 27 (Workers' right to information and consultation within the undertaking), 28 (Right of collective bargaining and action) and 30 (Protection in the event of unjustified dismissal). In contrast, *no* restrictions of this character are expressed in other Arts of the Charter, including Art 12 (Freedom of assembly and of association), Art 15 (Freedom to choose an occupation and right to engage in work), Art 21 (Non-discrimination), Art 23 (Equality between men and women), and Art 30 (Fair and just working conditions).

[26] The 'updated' Explanations shed little light by commenting: 'Paragraph 6 refers to the various Arts in the Charter which, in the spirit of subsidiarity, make reference to national laws and practices.' The Convention which drafted the Charter did not regard this added para as an appropriate horizontal clause and the repeated mantra of the Convention and its Working Group II was that no substantive changes were to be made to the Charter; the 'adjustments' are only 'clarifications.'

violation of fundamental rights in the Charter override the Charter if it conflicted with national laws and practices? Would the European Court of Justice, called upon to give a preliminary ruling, give priority to national laws and practices over fundamental rights in the EU Constitutional Treaty? Or, where national laws and practices restrict the rights granted, rule that the supremacy of Community law requires that the *objectives* of the Community in prescribing these rights should allow for an interpretation *overriding* limitations in national laws and practices?

If Charter rights are limited to 'national laws and practices,' the national standard becomes not the minimum, but the maximum standard. This eliminates any added value of the Charter. The added value of the Charter will only be realised if the references to national standards in the Charter are treated as fixing the minimum standards on which Charter rights may improve. The most important justification for the Charter is that it establishes a common set of fundamental rights guaranteed to all citizens of the EU. This is lost if fundamental rights are subject to national laws and practices. The danger of national laws providing different minimum fundamental rights will only be avoided if the Charter is interpreted as establishing a common set of fundamental rights which may go beyond national laws and practices.

The FRA's expertise would be particularly valuable because 'national laws and practice' appear to be less national than international standards. Article 52(3) states that corresponding Charter rights, including those referring to national laws and practices, are to be the same as those in the European Convention for the Protection of Human Rights (ECHR). National laws and practices must not conflict with the ECHR, since all Member States have ratified the ECHR. Article 53 similarly binds the Charter to a level of protection not less favourable than various international standards. Again, national laws and practices must comply with these international standards. In effect, the EU Charter's reference to 'national laws and practices' means no more than compliance with these international standards.

Finally, the references to national laws and practices are in some twelve different Articles of the Charter and include six different formulations. This diversity should be ignored as much as possible in favour of a common interpretation. Interpretation of the Charter is complex enough without having to ascertain the precise meaning of the different references to national laws and practices. For reasons of supremacy, uniformity, EU objectives and maximum standards of human rights, the differences in the formulations should be interpreted to produce a *minimum* of diversity among and deference to national standards. The ultimate decision on these matters is, of course, for the European Court of Justice. However, the Fundamental Rights Agency, with acknowledged expertise in fundamental rights at both national and international levels, could contribute to resolving the apparent conflicts between fundamental rights in the EU Charter and limitations imposed by national laws and practices on the scope of these rights.

4. *The 'Explanations' to the Charter*

The Commission's Communication on the Fundamental Rights Agency refers to the 'Explanations' to the Charter when stating that 'It might be worth asking the Agency to monitor all the fundamental rights protected by Community law and included in the Charter.'[27] Footnote 19 observes that:

> The provisions of the Charter have a clear basis for interpretation in the 'Explanations relating to the complete text of the Charter,' a document drawn up under the responsibility of the Praesidium of the Convention which drafted the Carter, not having any legal effect and intended simply for clarifying the provisions of this document. Although these explanations do not have in itself [sic] any legal effect, they constitute a valuable interpretation tool intended to clarify the provisions of the Charter.

This is perhaps to underestimate the problems posed by these 'Explanations,' not least to the realisation of the fundamental rights of workers in the EU.

The Praesidium of the Convention which drafted the EU Charter submitted a final text of 28 September 2000,[28] accompanied by another explanatory text of 11 October 2000,[29] to the European Council at Biarritz on 13–14 October 2000. This latter document comprised 'explanations' to accompany the text of the Charter. These 'explanations' were unambiguously not drafted or approved by the Convention which prepared the Charter, a fact repeatedly emphasised by the Praesidium itself. The EU's website reproduces the Charter alongside these explanations of the Praesidium. There it is stated categorically twice in footnotes to the text of the Charter:

> These explanations have been prepared at the instigation of the Praesidium. They have no legal value and are simply intended to clarify the provisions of the Charter.

Nonetheless, the Praesidium of the Convention on the Future of Europe made an 'adjustment' to the Preamble to the EU Charter, now Part II of the Constitutional Treaty. This was the only substantive alteration made to the Charter's Preamble. It reads ('adjustment' in italics):[30]

> The Charter reaffirms, with due regard for the powers and tasks of the Union and the principle of subsidiarity, the rights as they result, in particular, from the constitutional traditions and international obligations common to the Member States, the European Convention for the Protection of Human Rights and Fundamental Freedoms, the Social Charters adopted by the Union and by the Council of Europe and the case law of the Court of Justice of the European Union and of the European Court of Human Rights. *In this context, the Charter will be interpreted by the Courts of the Union and*

---

[27] COM(2004) 693 final, Brussels, 25 October 2004, p 7.

[28] CONVENT 50, CHARTE 4487/00, Brussels, 28 September 2000 (OR fr).

[29] CONVENT 49, CHARTE 4473/00, Bruxelles, 11 October 2000 (in French).

[30] CONV 802/03, 12 June 2003. Draft Constitution, Vol II, Draft revised text of Pts Two, Three and Four. Reproduced in the draft Constitutional Treaty of 18 July 2003.

the Member States[31] *with due regard for the explanations prepared at the instigation of the Praesidium of the Convention which drafted the Charter.*

The 'adjustment' appears intended to attribute a legal value to the explanations disclaimed by their authors.[32]

The final outcome of the European Council summit which met on 17–18 June 2004 to decide on the draft EU Constitution reflected the dispute manifested in the Working Party of Legal Experts established to review the draft Treaty. The Preamble to the EU Charter was amended adding the phrase suggested by the Chair of the Working Party referring to the explanations of the Praesidium which drafted the Charter: 'and updated under the responsibility of the Praesidium of the European Convention.'[33]

In addition, there was also added another paragraph 7 to Article II–52 of the EU Charter (Scope and interpretation of rights and principles):

> The explanations drawn up as a way of providing guidance in the interpretation of the Charter of Fundamental Rights shall be given due regard by the courts of the Union and of the Member States.

---

[31] It is worth noting here that the reference to Courts of the Member States is further evidence of the expectation that the Charter will be accorded legal status in disputes before national courts as well as the European Court of Justice.

[32] Further, the Intergovernmental Conference of the EU Member States established a Working Party of IGC Legal Experts to undertake editorial and legal adjustments to the draft Treaty establishing a Constitution for Europe. In its Report of 25 November 2003 (CIG 50/03) the Working Party refers to 'five footnotes drafted on the responsibility of the Chairman of the Working Party, on particular legal points.' One of these is attached to the Preamble to the EU Charter following the sentence added by the Praesidium of the Convention on the Future of Europe. The fn reads as follows: 'The Legal Adviser to the IGC [is of the opinion that] suggests adding at the end of this sentence, for reasons of legal certainty and transparency, a phrase to point out that the explanations mentioned here have been updated on the responsibility of the Praesidium of the European Convention; if this were not done, the existing text would be inaccurate. The following addition is supported by the great majority of delegations (with the German, Austrian, Belgian, Luxembourg and French delegations opposing it, because they feel that it raises issues of political desirability): "the explanations prepared at the instigation of the Praesidium of the Convention which drafted the Charter and updated on the responsibility of the Praesidium of the European Convention." Also, since the text explicitly states that the Charter will be interpreted by the courts of the Union and of the Member States *"with due regard to"* those explanations, it would be legally inconceivable that the text of the explanations should not be available to those courts and to the Union's citizens. The Legal Adviser therefore suggests that they be made universally accessible, by ensuring that they are published in the "C" series of the Official Journal of the European Union.' See also: the report of the Chairman of the Working Party, Mr. Jean-Claude Piris, Director-General of the Council Legal Service, CIG 51/03 of 25 November 2003, which replicates the substance of this text. Differences include that the objections of the five delegations are put down to 'political expediency'; the amendment suggested reads 'and updated *under* the responsibility of the Praesidium of the European Convention.' The reference to explanations 'updated on the responsibility of the Praesidium of the European Convention' adds to concerns about the legal status of these explanations, since that Praesidium had no authority to undertake such updating and did not even refer to it in the sentence it added to the Preamble. The opposition expressed by five Member States to this 'technical' amendment highlights these concerns.

[33] CIG 85/04. Brussels, 18 June 2004. PRESID 27, Annex 10. See now the Provisional consolidated version of the draft Treaty establishing a Constitution for Europe, CIG 86/04, Brussels, 25 June 2004.

As regards the legal status of the Explanations, this outcome seems, if anything, to have diluted their legal force. The authority seemingly attributed to the explanations by the Preamble's apparent mandatory requirement that that Charter '*will* be interpreted by the courts of the Union and the Member States *with due regard* to the explanations' is reduced in new Article 52(7) of the Charter. Instead, the explanations are merely '*a way of providing guidance* in the interpretation of the Charter' and 'shall be given *due regard* by the courts of the Union and of the Member States.' So 'will be interpreted' becomes 'shall be given due regard.' Article II–52(7) takes precedence over the Preamble.[34]

To these amendments, the European Council added a 'Declaration for incorporation in the Final Act concerning the explanations relating to the Charter of Fundamental Rights':[35]

> The Conference takes note of the explanations relating to the Charter of Fundamental Rights prepared under the authority of the Praesidium of the Convention which drafted the Charter and updated under the responsibility of the Praesidium of the European Convention, as set out below.[36]

However, the updating itself highlights one obvious and outstanding problem of the Explanations. Both the original Explanations and those added by the Convention on the Future of Europe will rapidly become outdated as new legislation is adopted and new decisions of the ECJ are added to the corpus of EU law. The inadequacy of the explanations as an interpretative instrument will soon be apparent.

There are also serious questions about the quality of the updating exercise. An example is selectivity: the 'updated' Explanation to Article 30 of the Charter refers to the consolidated Directive 2001/23/EC on the safeguarding of employ-

---

[34] Moreover, perhaps reflecting the reservations of the five Member States expressed in the fn attached by the Chairman of the Working Party to the amendments to the Preamble suggested by the Legal Adviser to the IGC, the text of new Art II–52(7) of the Charter makes *no reference* to the updated explanations.

[35] See n 32 above.

[36] This Declaration, to be incorporated in the Final Act, (emphatically) merely 'takes note' both of the original explanations and the update. The Explanations are not incorporated into the Charter, which is Pt II of the EU Constitution. Rather the Explanations are to be attached to this Declaration. The Declaration includes the following para at p 15: 'These explanations were originally prepared under the authority of the Praesidium of the Convention which drafted the Charter of Fundamental Rights of the European Union. They have been updated under the responsibility of the Praesidium of the European Convention, in the light of the drafting adjustments made to the text of the Charter by that Convention (notably to Articles 51 and 52) and of further developments of Union law. Although they do not as such have the status of law, they are a valuable tool of interpretation intended to clarify the provisions of the Charter.' The reference to updating 'in light of [. . .] further developments of Union law' is reflected in a number of references to legislation adopted after December 2000. For example, the 'updated' Explanation to Art 8, 'Protection of personal data,' refers to Reg No 45/2001 on the protection of individuals with regard to the processing of personal data. The 'updated' Explanation to Art 27, 'Workers' right to information and consultation within the undertaking,' now includes a reference to Dir 2002/14/EC (general framework for informing and consulting employees in the European Community). There are citations of post-2000 decisions of the ECJ in the Explanations to Arts 1 and 3 (the same case).

ees rights in the event of transfers of undertakings, and Directive 80/987 on the protection of employees in the event of the insolvency of their employer, as amended by Directive 2002/84/EC. However, Article 23 refers to Directive 76/207/EC on the implementation of the principle of equal treatment for men and women as regards access to employment, vocational training and promotion, and working conditions, but does not mention that this Directive was revised by Council Directive 2002/73/EC.[37]

Selectivity is likely to be even more of a pitfall with respect to citation of decisions of the European courts. The original Explanations contained references to 31 court decisions scattered very unevenly among the Articles of the Charter.[38] The 'updated' Explanations added four decisions which were decided post- December 2000: one to each of Articles 1, 45, 50 and 52 (the last of these referring to the new Article 52(4) inserted by the Convention). Additional 'updated' Explanations to the new Article 52(4) also included references to three pre-December 2000 decisions.

There is clearly an urgent need for a procedure for regular updating of the Explanations, engaging a body of eminent authorities. The Fundamental Rights Agency would be a suitable choice. There will inevitably be a potential overlap with the interpretative jurisdiction of the European Court of Justice. The FRA will have to be sensitive to this.

5. *International Standards*

The Preamble states that the EU Charter reaffirms:

> rights as they result, in particular, from the [. . .] international obligations common to the Member States, the European Convention for the Protection of Human Rights and Fundamental Freedoms, the Social Charters adopted by the Union and by the Council of Europe[39] and the case law of the Court of Justice of the European Union and of the European Court of Human Rights. In this context, the Charter will be interpreted by the Courts of the Union and the Member States with due regard for the explanations.

This provision makes use by the courts of the Praesidium's explanations more difficult because the Praesidium's explanations are not always comprehensive or consistent in referring to, for example, those 'international obligations common

---

[37] OJ 2002 No L269/15.

[38] Only 10 Arts cited decisions:

Article:	11	15	16	19	20	41	47	50	51	52
No of Decisions:	1	3	4	1 Eur. Ct. of HR	3	7 (1 cited twice)	4 plus 1 Eur. Ct. of HR	2	4	1

[39] The 'updated' Explanations include 22 references to the European Social Charter and Revised European Social Charter and 15 references to the Community Charter of the Fundamental Social Rights of Workers. See Provisional consolidated version of the Declarations to be annexed to the Final Act of the Intergovernmental Conference, CIG 86/04, ADD 2, Brussels, 25 June 2004.

to the Member States' which are explicitly the interpretative context, the inspiration and source of the EU Charter's provisions. In particular, in the case of those provisions referring to individual employment and collective labour rights, the absence in the Praesidium's Explanations of references to the core ILO Conventions which bind all Member States is noticeable, and regrettable. A couple of examples will illustrate this point.

The Praesidium's 'Explanations' to Article 12 (Freedom of assembly and of association) state that: 'Paragraph 1 of this Article corresponds to Article 11 of the ECHR [European Convention for the Protection of Human Rights]' and further asserts that:

> The meaning of the provisions of paragraph 1 is the same as that of the ECHR, but their scope is wider since they apply at all levels, including European level.

This wider scope, which applies to all levels from the workplace up to the EU level, could have immense implications for the exercise of freedom of association going beyond the ECHR provisions.

The Praesidium's Explanations go on to add: 'This right is also based on Article 11 of the Community Charter of the Fundamental Social Rights of Workers.' The precise scope of Article 11 of the Community Charter ('Freedom of association and collective bargaining') has also been the subject of scrutiny and could extend beyond the confines of the provision in the ECHR.[40] The Praesidium's 'Explanations' to Article 28 (Right of collective bargaining and action) state:[41]

> This Article is based on Article 6 of the European Social Charter and on the Community Charter of the Fundamental Social Rights of Workers (points 12 to 14). The right of collective action was recognised by the European Court of Human Rights as one of the elements of trade union rights laid down by Article 11 of the ECHR [. . .] *The modalities and limits for the exercise of* collective action, including strike action, come under national laws and practices, including the question of whether it may be carried out in parallel in several Member States.

There is an obvious contradiction between requiring respect for the ECHR and the assertion that collective action 'comes under national laws and practices.' The contradiction is evident when the European Court of Rights finds a Member State's law to be in violation of the ECHR, as was recently the case

---

[40] B Bercusson, *European Labour Law* (London, Butterworths,1996), ch 37, pp 585–89, see n 7 above.

[41] The eight words in italics were not in the Explanations provided by the Praesidium of the Convention which drafted the Charter. They were added by the Praesidium of the Convention on the Future of Europe. They cannot be characterised as 'updating,' the ostensible justification for changes in the Explanations adverted to in the additional phrase attached to the Preamble by the IGC on 18 June 2004 (though not mentioned in the new Art 52(7) of the Charter). This additional phrase rather confirms the view as to the political calculations which underlie the attempt to foist the 'Explanations' as an interpretive framework on the courts. It is tantamount to a suggestion that Member State laws which restrict strike action do not violate the right to strike, but merely limit the modalities of its exercise.

with the UK in respect of Article 11.[42] In addition, collective action 'carried out in parallel in several Member States' engages precisely the trans-national dimension of collective action in the European single market. Confining it to national laws and practices contradicts a fundamental right of European collective action. It is inevitably addressed at EU level,[43] not least by the European Court of Justice.[44]

Moreover, apart from these references to European and international instruments, there are other international obligations binding EU Member States. These are not always mentioned by the Praesidium's Explanations, though the Preamble emphatically states that the Charter reaffirms these obligations.[45] This indicates the incompleteness of the Praesidium's Explanations, which no doubt explains the admirable caution expressed by that Praesidium with respect to the use to be made of its Explanations. It would seem that, under pressure from some Member States anxious to restrict the ambit of the EU Charter's rights, the amendment was attempting to elevate the Explanations to a status never intended by its authors, the Convention which drafted the Charter, or even the Convention's own Working Group II, which did not include any such recommendation its own list of 'adjustments.'

This last amendment to the EU Charter's Preamble begins, after the reaffirmation 'in particular [of] international obligations common to the Member States,' with the phrase '[i]n this context.' The Explanations should be read, and the EU Charter interpreted, with full weight attached to this context of the international obligations of the EU and its Member States. The Fundamental Rights Agency, with expertise in the protection of the fundamental rights of workers in international labour standards, is particularly well suited to provide the necessary elaborations and updating of the Explanations. The many references in the Explanations to international human rights measures and the explicit reference to international instruments are an invitation for the expertise of the FRA to be demonstrated.

---

[42] *Wilson and the National Union of Journalists; Palmer, Wyeth and the National Union of Rail, Maritime and Transport Workers; Doolan and others v United Kingdom*, [2002] IRLR 128, decided 2 July 2002. For a detailed discussion of the potential impact on British labour law of what has been called 'probably the most important labour law decision for at least a generation,' see K Ewing, 'The implications of *Wilson and Palmer*' [2003] 32 *Industrial Law Journal* 1–22.

[43] See Council Reg (EC) No 2679/98 of 7 December 1998 on the functioning of the internal market in relation to the free movement of goods among the Member States. OJ L337/8 of 12.12.98 (the 'Monti Reg').

[44] See Case C–112/00 *Schmidberger* [2003] ECR I-5659.

[45] The Preamble's reference to international obligations could have important consequences for the interpretation of the EU Charter. For example, trade union collective action has often been restricted, allegedly to protect public and/or essential services. The ILO's Freedom of Association Committee has established international standards on collective action in public/essential services. Relying on Art 28 of the EU Charter (right to collective action), trade unions could promote challenges to more restrictive national laws. Again, Art 12(1) of the Charter on freedom of association could be interpreted as guaranteeing rights which go beyond what is provided in some national laws, for example, regarding interference in a union's internal affairs, rights to representation, recognition by an employer, access to union members at the workplace, or to take part in union activities.

In conclusion, the FRA is not an agency of judicial enforcement of workers' rights. However, it may contribute to, and has a potentially valuable role to play in the realisation of workers' rights in the EU by attempting to clarify in an authoritative manner some of the outstanding substantive legal issues left open following the adoption of the EU Charter: 1) potential conflicts between EU fundamental rights and EU competences in the fields of employment and industrial relations, 2) the distinction between 'principles and rights' and the 'justiciability' of fundamental rights of workers, 3) the relation of EU fundamental rights to national laws and practices in employment and labour relations, 4) the significance and elaboration of the 'Explanations' to the Charter, and 5) the role of international labour standards. There remains to explore how the Fundamental Rights Agency could contribute to the resolution of these substantive problems.

b) Procedural Solutions

In light of the dynamic history of European labour law and the many legal and institutional strategies adopted for the realisation of workers' rights, it will come as no surprise that yet another permutation is emerging, one which has produced a series of what I have called 'hybrids.'[46] In particular, the past decade has witnessed dramatic changes in the EU's methods of labour regulation. The traditional approach of *judicial enforcement* of labour standards laid down in EU legislation (directives) is constantly under the pressure of new doctrinal developments.[47] In addition, there has emerged a new *industrial relations* mechanism, the process of social dialogue and European framework agreements between the social partners.[48] There is also a new *administrative* mechanism, the 'open method of coordination' (OMC), applied to the European Employment Strategy (EES).[49]

The so-called 'Lisbon Strategy' is the context which has produced a new approach to administrative application and enforcement of workers' rights. The Treaty of Nice provided the legal framework for the changes signalled by the Lisbon Strategy, which took shape in the Commission's Social Policy Agenda 2000–2005.

---

[46] B Bercusson, '*Droit du travail: les interactions entre droit national et droit communautaire*' (2004) 100 *Travail et Emploi, Ministère des affaires sociales, du travail et de la solidarité*, France.

[47] See, eg: *Bernhard Pfeiffer et al v Deutsches Rotes Kreuz Kreisverband Waldshut eV*, Joined Cases C–397/01 to C–403/01. Opinions of Advocate-General MD Ruiz-Jarabo Colomer, 6 May 2003 and 27 April 2004; decision of the European Court of Justice, 5 October 2004.

[48] Maastricht Treaty, now Arts 138–139 EC.

[49] Art 128 of the EC Treaty in the Title on Employment introduced by the Treaty of Amsterdam, now Arts 125–130 EC.

1. The Context: the Lisbon Strategy

The Lisbon European Council of 23–24 March 2000 articulated a new strategic goal for the EU:

> to become the most competitive and dynamic knowledge-based economy in the world capable of sustainable economic growth with more and better jobs and greater social cohesion.[50]

As well as a new strategic goal, the Lisbon Council highlighted the 'open method of coordination' as a principal process through which this goal was to be achieved.

In its Social Policy Agenda 2000–2005, the Commission confirmed the Lisbon Strategy.[51] Reflecting the approach favoured by the Lisbon Council, the Commission stated:

> This new Social Policy Agenda does *not seek to harmonise social policies*. It seeks to work towards common European objectives and increase *co-ordination of social policies* in the context of the internal market and the single currency.

2. The Treaty of Nice: from Judicial Enforcement to Administrative Process

The approach emphasising *coordination* is reflected in the changes to the Social Chapter of the EC Treaty adopted by the Treaty of Nice in December 2000. Article 137(2) EC was amended by the Treaty of Nice in two apparently minor ways. First, it *added* to Article 137(2) EC's provision encouraging cooperation between Member States the phrase '*excluding any harmonisation of the laws and regulations of the Member States.*' Secondly, this phrase *replaced* the former Article 137(2) EC's provision limiting cooperation measures solely '*in order to combat social exclusion.*' Instead, the reference to 'combating of social exclusion' is inserted into the Treaty of Nice's new Article 137(1)(j) EC.

The replacement in Article 137(2) EC of the phrase 'in order to combat social exclusion' by the insertion of the new phrase 'excluding any harmonisation of the laws and regulations of the Member States' has two very significant implications. The first is that *coordination/cooperation* is an approach which may henceforth be applied to *all* the social policy areas listed in the revised Article 137(1) EC (not only 'in order to combat social exclusion'). Secondly, in social policy generally, as in the case of employment policy (Article 129 EC), the process of cooperation/coordination *excludes* 'any harmonisation of the laws and regulations of the Member States.'

These amendments to Article 137 EC by the Treaty of Nice mark the new departure in EU social policy signalled by the Lisbon Strategy. EU social policy is *not* primarily to be implemented through the adoption by means of *directives*

---

[50] Lisbon Presidency Conclusions, para 5.
[51] COM(2000) 379 final, Brussels, 28 June 2000, s 1.2, p 5.

of minimum requirements (Article 137(2)(b) EC, formerly 137(2)) in the fields listed in Article 137(1)(a–i). Rather, in all these fields there is the *alternative* of measures designed to encourage *cooperation* between Member States in all social policy fields (Article 137(2)(a) EC), no longer restricted to combating social exclusion (ex Article 137(2) of the EC Treaty), and explicitly '*excluding any harmonisation of the laws and regulations of the Member States.*'

3. The Social Policy Agenda 2000–2005: Legislation, Social Dialogue and Administrative Processes

The European Council at Nice in December 2000, in adopting the Commission's Social Policy Agenda 2000–2005 of 28 June 2000, declared that in its implementation:

> all existing Community instruments bar none must be used; the open method of co-ordination, legislation, the social dialogue, the Structural Funds, the support programmes, the integrated policy approach, analysis and research.[52]

The Commission's Social Policy Agenda 2000–2005 also stated that: 'To achieve these priorities, an adequate combination of all existing means will be required.' Although a *variety* of means were listed, the *scope* of application allocated to each was significant.

The *first* was 'The open method of co-ordination, inspired by the Luxembourg Employment Process and developed by the Lisbon and Feira Councils.' There was *no limit* specified to the scope of matters suitable for the application of this method. The *third* was stated as follows:

> The Social Dialogue as the most effective way of modernising contractual relations, adapting work organisation and developing adequate balance between flexibility and security.

The role of social dialogue is strictly *limited* to work relationships within the enterprise. In contrast, the *second* means listed was:

> *Legislation*: Standards should be developed or adapted, *where appropriate*, to ensure the respect of *fundamental social rights* and to respond to *new challenges*. Such standards can *also* result from *agreements* between the social partners at European level.

The scope of legislation required to achieve the European social model embraces fundamental social rights and new challenges. There is scope for judicial enforcement primarily where the EU adopts legislative measures. However, there is no sign of such a legislative programme. On the other hand, there is a clearly unlimited scope for the open method of coordination as an instrument for achieving the Lisbon strategy. The Lisbon strategy, and the Social Policy Agenda 2000–2005, may succeed or fail depending on the efficacy of its chosen instrument.[53]

---

[52] Nice European Council, 7–9 December 2000, Annex 1, para 28.
[53] See 'EU in danger of missing key employment targets' (2004) 363 *European Industrial Relations Review* 37–40.

4. *The Open Method of Coordination and Social Dialogue*

a. *The Commission's Communication of 26 June 2002: the Problem of Effectiveness.* In its Communication of 26 June 2002 on the role of social dialogue in European labour law, entitled 'The European social dialogue, a force for innovation and change,'[54] the Commission noted, under the heading 'Improving monitoring and implementation,' that:

> The European social partners have adopted joint opinions, statements and declarations on numerous occasions. More than 230 such joint sectoral texts have been issued and some 40 cross-industry texts [. . .][55] However, in most cases, these texts did not include any provision for implementation and monitoring: they were responses to short-term concerns. They are not well known and their dissemination at national level has been limited. *Their effectiveness can thus be called into question.*

On the question of the perceived lack of effectiveness, the Commission noted that:[56]

> Special consideration must be given to the question of how to implement the texts adopted by the European social partners. The recommendations of the High-Level Group on Industrial Relations and Change see the use of machinery based on the open method of coordination as an extremely promising way forward. The social partners could apply some of their agreements (where not regulatory) by *establishing goals or guidelines* at European level, through regular *national implementation reports* and regular, systematic *assessment of progress* achieved.

To that end, the Commission recommended:

> The social partners are requested to: adapt the open method of coordination to their relations in all appropriate areas; prepare monitoring reports on implementation in the Member States of these frameworks for action; introduce peer review machinery appropriate to the social dialogue.

b. *The Commission's Communication of 12 August 2004: 'Process-oriented' Texts.* In the first section of its latest Communication on the social dialogue, the Commission asserts that:[57]

> In recent years the social partners have wished to pursue a more autonomous dialogue and are adopting a diverse array of initiatives, including an increasing number of 'new generation' joint texts, characterised by the fact that they are to be followed-up by the social partners themselves. This requires *greater interaction between the different*

---

[54] COM(2002) 341 final, 26 June 2002.

[55] These figures are updated in Annex 1 of the Commission's Communication, *Partnership for change in an enlarged Europe—Enhancing the contribution of European social dialogue*, COM(2004) 557 final, Brussels, 12 August 2004: 'over 40 joint texts by the cross-industry social partners and approximately 300 by the sectoral social partners.'

[56] *Ibid*, s 2.4.1, p 18.

[57] Partnership for change in an enlarged Europe—Enhancing the contribution of European social dialogue, COM(2004) 557 final, Brussels, 12 August 2004, s 1, p 3.

levels of industrial relations, including effective industrial relations systems and social partner capacities at national level.

This is elaborated in Section 3.2.1, at p 7:

The Commission has identified two main categories of texts which could qualify as 'new generation' texts: autonomous agreements, and process-oriented texts which make recommendations of various kinds (frameworks of action, guidelines, codes of conduct, and policy orientations). The essential difference is that agreements are to be implemented and monitored by a given date, whereas the second kind entail a more *process-oriented approach*, involving regular reporting on progress made in following-up the objectives of the texts.[58]

In the category of 'process-oriented texts,' three main types of instrument are listed: 'frameworks of action' (1 example provided), 'guidelines and codes of conduct' (20 examples listed) and 'policy orientations' (5 examples listed). All three are characterised by '(Regular) follow-up and (annual) reporting by the social partners.'

The predominant form of 'new generation' texts is clearly the latter so-called 'process-oriented texts,' the implementation of which follows the 'open method of co-ordination.' Anxieties as to the efficacy of this method of implementing policy were already expressed in the Commission's Communication of 26 June 2002. Yet over two years later, the Commission can do no more than exhort the social partners: 'Improving the impact and follow-up of the European social dialogue' (Section 4.3, p 9):

It encourages the social partners to make greater use of peer review techniques inspired by the open method of coordination for following-up these texts, for example by setting targets (quantitative, where feasible) or benchmarks, and regularly reporting on progress made towards achieving them.

It remains to be seen whether the OMC, hitherto criticised as to its effectiveness when implemented by Member States' administrations in the field of employment policy, is an appropriate mechanism for the social partners. If joint opinions and other non-regulatory instruments continue to be ineffective, their failure may imply other, more rigorous steps towards effectiveness, including regulatory social dialogue agreements and/or legislation.

---

[58] Annex 2 describing these 'new generation' texts is revealing. The first category, 'autonomous agreements,' appears under the rubric in Annex 2: 'Agreements implemented in accordance with Article 139(2): minimum standards.' Of these, it is said: 'Effective implementation and monitoring is important in the case of agreements of this kind, particularly if they have been negotiated subsequent to a Commission consultation under Art 138. Art 139(2) states that the Community level agreements *'shall* be implemented' (emphasis added), which implies that there is an obligation to implement these agreements and for the signatory parties to exercise influence on their members in order to implement the European agreement' (emphasis added) (at p 16). The category of autonomous agreements has a grand total of three: the framework agreement on telework of July 2002, a second agreement on work-related stress of May 2004, not yet formally approved by the social partners, and an Agreement on the European licence for drivers carrying out a cross-border interoperability service.

c. *A Delicate Engagement: OMC and Social Dialogue.* There have been earlier, but different, proposals to engage the mechanism of the OMC with that of the social dialogue so as to draw on their different strengths to achieve the realisation of workers' rights.[59] The social partners were early called upon to play a major role in the OMC process of the EES: 'The social partners need to be more closely involved in drawing up, implementing and following up the appropriate guidelines.'[60]

The EU's most significant institutional contribution to social policy—the creation and development of EU social dialogue—is at risk of being marginalised *in* the OMC, just as the EU social dialogue risks becoming marginalised *by* the OMC. The emphasis so far has been on the (disappointing) role of the social dialogue in the OMC. If the social partners become marginalised in the OMC, the scenario of a withering away of the EU social dialogue becomes more likely. On the other hand, a revival of the EU social dialogue may serve not only to assist the success of the OMC, but also assist the evolution of EU social and labour law, a vital component of the EU social dimension.

It might have been assumed that the EU social dialogue (intersectoral or sectoral) would be a, if not *the*, primary contribution of the social partners to the EES. After all, the EU intersectoral framework agreements on part-time and fixed-term work (and sectoral agreements on working time in the sectors excluded from the Working Time Directive) demonstrated the potential of the social partners to regulate the labour market, with the Community's objectives on employment explicitly in mind.

However, it appears that the primary, if not only, social partner engagement in the EES is at national or sub-national levels. This is evident in the way implementation of the Employment Guidelines is perceived as being primarily at national, local or enterprise level. Employers' organisations (UNICE) emphasise the impact of what is being done voluntarily, usually at enterprise level. This outcome reduces the EU-level social dimension by emphasising action at national, local or enterprise level. It is suggested that the OMC offers an institutional framework that could reinforce EU social dialogue, which, in turn,

---

[59] See, eg: B Bercusson, 'Institutional reform and social and labour policy' in U Mückenberger (ed), *Manifesto for Social Europe* (Brussels, ETUI, 2001) pp 101–128. See also: B Bercusson, 'The role of the EU Charter of Fundamental Rights in building a system of industrial relations at EU Level' (2003) 9 *Transfer: European Review of Labour and Research* 209–228.

[60] Lisbon Presidency Conclusions, para 28. This was reinforced at the Feira Council which invited the social partners 'to play a more prominent role in implementing and monitoring the Guidelines which depend on them.' See the Commission Proposal for a Council Decision on guidelines for Member States' employment policies for the year 2001, Explanatory Memorandum, p 3. The social partners within the Member States, called upon to play an important part in the European Employment Strategy, are, in many cases, also the protagonists of analogous strategies adopted on a tripartite basis at national level. The social partners could attempt, where possible, to link up and co-ordinate aspects of the EES which are complementary with national social or employment pacts. The European Council and the Commission, in formulating the Guidelines under the EES, could seek to co-ordinate the Guidelines with national experience and ensure that review of the application of specific Guidelines takes into account the development of social pacts in a particular national context.

would assist the success of the EES. The challenge is to develop an institutional design which would graft on to the OMC process the social partners' involvement in various forms (EU-level intersectoral and sectoral dialogue).[61] The OMC could be institutionally accommodated to the EU social dialogue with a view to their mutual reinforcement. To posit one scenario: guidelines could emerge from an EU-level social dialogue between EU social partners with mandates from affiliated social partners drawing on experience of national employment pacts, or following on from proposals by the Commission. Affiliated social partners at Member State level could produce National Action Plans to implement the Guidelines embodied in EU framework agreements. The Commission and Council could review and report on implementation and supplement this with recommendations in the form of EU legislative proposals where implementation was inadequate.[62]

---

[61] A number of suggestions could be put forward by way of illustration. First, the institutional structure could easily accommodate the EU social partners' involvement in the elaboration and implementation of Guidelines. Art 128(2) EC currently gives them no role whatsoever in the elaboration of the Guidelines formulated at EU level. Yet the Social Chapter, in Art 138(2), requires the Commission 'before submitting proposals in the social policy field [to] consult management and labour on the possible direction of Community action.' Such consultation would be mandatory if this was a proposal related, for example, to 'the integration of persons excluded from the labour market' (Art 137(1)). It is not at all clear that proposals concerning Employment Guidelines are exempt from this requirement. If this vital procedural requirement has been ignored, the whole process could be at risk of judicial nullification. Secondly, Member States' elaboration and implementation of the National Action Plans envisaged by Art 128(3) do not refer at all to the social partners. Yet this would seem to be an obvious requirement, evident in the numerous tripartite social or employment pacts negotiated in Member States. The inter-action of these national experiences with the EES is obvious: their success (in Denmark, the Netherlands, and Ireland) were one of the inspirations for the EES. By institutionally engaging the social partners in the formulation of National Action Plans, the EES could inspire social pacts on employment. The existing articulation between the social partners at national level with their EU-level organisations would greatly benefit the process of implementation of Guidelines formulated with the participation of the EU-level organisations and implemented with the participation of their affiliates in the Member States. Thirdly, the Employment Guidelines could go well beyond their existing modest remit in encouraging social partners' involvement. The Guidelines could include procedural as well as substantive targets; for example, along the lines of requirements of information and consultation at enterprise level already in the *acquis communautaire*. The role of incentive measures envisaged by Art 129 could be influential. On 25 July 2000, the Commission adopted a cooperation incentive package to boost the employment strategy. This aims to provide financial incentives by creating the legal basis for funding in the area of mainstreaming equal opportunities across the employment field. The role of Commission funding in developing and spreading the organisation of European works councils is a reminder of the potential of such funding.

[62] Another proposal combining OMC and social dialogue appeared in the Final Report of the Convention's Working Group XI on Social Europe. This specified (para 41): 'that the [OMC] can be applied *only* where no Union legislative competence is enshrined in the Treaty and in areas *other than* those where the coordination of national policies is governed by a special provision in the Treaty defining such coordination (in economic matters (Art 99) and in the area of employment (Art 128) in particular).' The result is that the scope for the OMC in labour policy, under these conditions, is extremely limited. Arts 137–139 of the EC Treaty provide for EU legislative competence in most areas of employment and industrial relations. Employment is explicitly excluded as covered in Art 128 of the EC Treaty. The areas remaining for OMC are marginal to labour, though perhaps more relevant to general social policy: trans-European networks, enterprise policy and research and technological development. The Working Group's Report went on to recommend that 'The Treaty provision on the OMC should be embodied in the Constitutional Treaty, within the chapter on

The question is whether the process of realisation of the *fundamental* rights of workers can engage with the mechanisms of the OMC and of social dialogue. Can the Fundamental Rights Agency make a specific contribution to the application of these mechanisms to resolve the problems of implementation and enforcement of fundamental rights of workers?

5. A Role for the Fundamental Rights Agency

a. *The Role of Labour in the European Social Model.* The inclusion in the EU Charter of social and economic rights related to working life confirmed that these are to be considered fundamental to the EU social model, what it means to be an EU citizen. A, if not *the*, defining feature of the European social model is engagement of organisations of workers and employers.[63]

Organisations of employers and trade unions play a major role in most Member States.[64] Their institutional forms and interactions at various levels reflect the European social model of working life, a central component of social citizenship. The day to day working life of most people in the office, shop or factory is subject to a myriad of decisions concerning, for example, working practices (performance), conduct at work (disciplinary matters), health and safety, and many others. Rather than these decisions being taken unilaterally by

---

Union instruments which constitute non-legislative measures' (para 42). Despite this constitutional status, the most important point is that the Working Group states unequivocally that the OMC has *no* application in the sphere of employment and labour relations where legislative measures are applicable or in employment policy where the Treaty specifies procedures. These limitations on the operation of the OMC are repeated again in para 43 of the Final Report of Working Group XI. But there is one slight, and very important difference: after excluding areas where the Union has legislative competence or specific provision is made, the Working Group adds: 'or where the Union *has competence* only for defining *minimum* rules, in order to go *beyond* these rules.' This is significant both in expanding the scope and defining the standards which can be established through the OMC. As to *scope*: Art 137(2)(b) EC (post-Nice) specifies that the Council: 'may adopt, in the fields referred to in paragraph 1(a) to (i), by means of Directives, *minimum* requirements.' Working Group XI *seems* to open the door for the OMC to operate in the fields of employment and labour relations referred in Art 137(1)(a)–(i). However, the OMC can *only* be used to 'go *beyond* these minimum rules.' This means that the OMC *cannot* operate where there are *no* rules. Where EU legislative competence has not been exercised, there are no rules beyond which the OMC can go. As to *standards*: where legislative competence exists, and *has* been exercised to establish minimum rules, the OMC *cannot* establish inferior or even equal standards. It must operate to promote *higher* standards. The practical consequence is that the OMC *cannot* become a *substitute* for legislation on social, employment and labour standards. It cannot replace legislation, including that resulting from social dialogue framework agreements. The Member States are precluded from using the OMC in those fields, except to improve on established standards.

[63] B Bercusson, 'EU Citizenship and Fundamental Social Rights: Community Law—European Law—National Law' in P Rodière (ed), *European Union Citizenship in the Context of Labour and Social Law*, (Academy of European Law, Trier, Bundesanzeiger, Koln, 1997) pp 9–18; B Bercusson, 'The Institutional Architecture of the European Social Model', paper delivered at the WG Hart Workshop, Institute of Advanced Legal Studies, London, 25–27 June 2003, published in Tridimas and Nebbia (eds) *European Union Law for the 21st Century* (Oxford, Hart, 2004).

[64] For a useful survey, see the European Foundation for the Improvement of Living and Working Conditions, Dublin; European Industrial Relations Observatory (EIRO) on-line; comparative overview of 'Industrial relations in the EU, Japan and USA, 2000.'

management, there has developed in the Member States of the EU a mandatory system of participation by workers in such decisions through representative structures of 'works councils,' 'enterprise committees,' trade union bodies and similar forms. These exist in almost all the 'old' Member States (Austria, Belgium, Denmark, Finland, France, Germany, Greece, Italy, Luxembourg, the Netherlands, Portugal, Spain and Sweden).

The representative structures established by legislation or by generally applicable collective agreements in these countries provide for bodies to receive information and be engaged in consultation, or even co-determination, on a range of matters relating to the company's economic position having implications for the workforce, as well as on decisions affecting the day to day working life of employees. Only in Ireland and the United Kingdom is such a general and permanent system lacking. In Directive 2002/14/EC, EC law took a decisive step towards establishing the practice of information and consultation of employee representatives as part of the European social model.[65]

Information and consultation of workers or their representatives in the enterprise is a fundamental right under the EU Charter (Article 27). The Constitutional Treaty provides that the EU 'recognises and promotes the role of the social partners [and] shall facilitate dialogue between the social partners' (Article I–48). This process, which underpins the European social model, can and should be reinforced by the Fundamental Rights Agency. The current trend in EU labour regulation is to focus on the 'soft law' administrative mechanism of the OMC and the autonomous industrial relations mechanism of the social dialogue. However, neither of these mechanisms is delivering the goods.[66] The question is, in this current context, how can the FRA contribute to the realisation of the fundamental rights of workers?

b. *The Fundamental Rights Agency, Social Dialogue and the OMC. As regards the social dialogue*, the problem with the social dialogue is that there is no prescribed end, so failure to reach agreement is acceptable. Yet fundamental rights are not negotiable. So failure is not an option; agreement must be reached. It is known that when an outcome is mandatory, negotiations tend to succeed. Parties will be forced to compromise for fear of imposition of a solution by others. The Maastricht Agreement on Social Policy reflected this logic of 'bargaining in the shadow of the law.'

The FRA can contribute as follows. First, the bare outline of procedures required of the Commission under the consultative clause of Article 138 EC

---

[65] The initial draft proposals signalled a fundamental change in EU social policy: the objective was not harmonisation of national law, but 'to make the essential changes to the existing legal framework [. . .] appropriate for the new European context' (Preamble, Recitals 15–16) COM/98/612, 11 November 1998. See the Preamble to the final Dir, particularly Recital 17: 'the object is to establish a framework for employee information and consultation appropriate for the new European context described above [in Recitals 6–16]').

[66] See *Facing the challenge: The Lisbon strategy for growth and employment*, Report from the High Level Group chaired by Wim Kok, November 2004.

needs to be extensively elaborated. Secondly, given the paucity of results in the form of social dialogue agreements, a requirement to 'work in a spirit of cooperation' could be imposed to put pressure on the social partners to engage in social dialogue in a constructive manner. Thirdly, the FRA plays a role where failure to reach 'agreements' produces other 'texts,' for which the Commission recommends an implementation and enforcement procedure analogous to the OMC.

As regards the OMC, the problem is the process whereby administrative guidelines are formulated at EU level by the Commission and Council, and implemented through the OMC process prescribed in Article 128 EC. The problem is not failure to reach policy conclusions, but ineffective implementation of them. This reflects a lack of engagement of key players: the social partners. There are lessons to be learned from the social partners' desire for autonomous agreements. The problem of enforcement of 'non-binding' texts is resolved by increasing the engagement of the social partners at all levels, not only at EU level, so that their commitment to ('ownership' of) the outcome will guarantee effective implementation.

What these processes of OMC and social dialogue have in common is the engagement of various institutional actors at EU level: EU institutions and the EU social partners. They are to produce outcomes in the form of agreements, guidelines or other 'process-oriented' texts. Here the axiom of effective labour law enforcement formulated earlier (effectiveness as a function of the proximity of norm creators to their subjects) should be recalled. This axiom is reflected in the Commission's most recent Communication on the role of the social partners:[67]

> The evolution of the social dialogue is consistent with the Commission's more general efforts to improve European governance. The social dialogue is indeed a pioneering example of improved consultation and the application of subsidiarity in practice and is widely recognised as making an essential contribution to better governance, as a result of the proximity of the social partners to the realities of the workplace. Indeed, the social partners are different in nature from other organisations, like pressure or interest groups, because of their ability to take part in collective bargaining.

It is to the processes of OMC and social dialogue that the Fundamental Rights Agency could provide crucial assistance.[68] The main task envisaged for the

---

[67] *Partnership for change in an enlarged Europe—Enhancing the contribution of European social dialogue*, Communication from the Commission, COM(2004) 557 final, Brussels, 12 August 2004, s 3.1, p 6.

[68] Before analysing this more closely below, it is worth pointing out the functional equivalence between various aspects of the OMC procedure and the so-called 'mainstreaming' policy being promoted in various contexts, including those for other fundamental rights in this volume (see the chapters by O De Schutter and C McCrudden). The aspect which both the OMC and mainstreaming have in common is procedural in nature: the procedure whereby specified objectives (eg, a high level of employment, fundamental rights of workers) are to be achieved in both cases involves a specific process of decision-making. In mainstreaming, the authorities responsible are to take into account the fundamental rights through a variety of mechanisms (eg, information, impact assessments, action plans, etc). In OMC, the process is minimally outlined in Art 128 EC. In what follows the procedure proposed for the realisation of the fundamental rights of workers expands this to incorporate a role for the social partners, and to elaborate a more detailed process of decision-making.

Agency is to flesh out these processes of OMC and social dialogue by playing an active role. How? The Communication outlines 'Tasks to be entrusted to the Agency.'[69]

c. *Promoting a Process for Realisation of Fundamental Labour Rights.*   As applied to realisation of the fundamental rights of workers, the starting point is the EU Charter's fundamental rights of collective bargaining (Article 28) and information and consultation in the enterprise (Article 17), supported by EC Treaty Articles 138–139 and reinforced now by Article I–48 of the Constitutional Treaty: promoting social partners and facilitating social dialogue. Given the very wide scope of the fundamental rights of workers prescribed in the EU Charter (eg, fair and just working conditions (Article 31), protection against unjustified dismissal (Article 30), etc), the Agency has a legitimate interest in securing their effectiveness. It cannot usurp the European Court's role in ultimately interpreting the Charter. Nor should it attempt by itself to flesh out the substantive standards. Its role should be, in accordance with long experience (and the above-mentioned axiom of labour law) *to promote agreement between the social partners on the content of these rights, such a process being that best suited to effective enforcement.*[70]

The problem is that the process of decision-making by way of social dialogue which could produce such agreements or texts is scarcely known outside a narrow circle of practitioners,[71] and little exists by way of guidance, with the Commission not going beyond exhortation. Yet there is a body of EU law which could be drawn upon: EU directives on *information and consultation* are concerned with fundamental rights of workers in specific situations such as collective dismissals, acquired rights in the event of transfers of undertakings and European Works Councils; more generally, the procedure has been elaborated in a framework Directive 2002/14/EC of 2002.[72] And, of course, the process itself is declared a fundamental right in Article 27 of the EU Charter.

---

[69]   COM(2004) 693 final, Brussels, 25 October 2004, ss 5: 1) data collection and analysis, 2) opinions and views intended for the EU institutions and the Member States, 3) a communications and dialogue strategy with various members of civil society.

[70]   For an earlier essay along these lines, directed towards the earlier Community Charter of the Fundamental Rights of Workers of 1989, see B Bercusson, 'Fundamental Social and Economic Rights in the European Community' in A Cassese, A Clapham, JHH Weiler (eds), *Human Rights and the European Community: Methods of Protection*, Vol II of European Union—The Human Rights Challenge, (Baden-Baden, Nomos, 1991) pp 195–294, and especially at pp 206–11, 217–18, 226–30, 284–85.

[71]   There is a brief description by K Ahlberg in 'The negotiations on fixed-term work' in K Ahlberg, C Vigneau, B Bercusson, and N Bruun, *Fixed-term Work in the EU: A European agreement against discrimination and abuse*, (Stockholm, National Institute for Working Life, 1999) pp 13–38. A more detailed study of the social dialogue which concluded the agreement on fixed-term work is forthcoming, to be published by the European Trade Union Institute, Brussels.

[72]   Council Dir 75/129/EC of 17 February 1975 on the approximation of the laws of the Member States relating to collective dismissals, OJ L 48/29, as amended by Dir 92/56 of 24 June 1992, OJ L 245/92; consolidated in Council Dir 98/59/EC of 20 July 1998, OJ L 225/16. Council Dir 77/187/EC of 14 February 1977 on the approximation of the laws of the Member States relating to the safeguarding of employees' rights in the event of transfers of undertakings, businesses or parts of

These directives indicate a procedure to be followed in the field of fundamental rights of workers analogous to the 'mainstreaming' procedure advocated in other fields. The Fundamental Rights Agency can draw on this to propose, then apply procedures to encourage agreement, and ultimately promote outcomes to realise the EU Charter's fundamental rights of workers.

6. *'Mainstreaming' Fundamental Labour Rights*

The Fundamental Rights Agency should be responsible for securing the operationalization of this process at EU level in the context of the OMC and the EU social dialogue.[73] The processes of mainstreaming, information and consultation and social dialogue aim at decision-making. They seek to proceduralise decision-making in such a way as to secure outcomes that take account of specified policy objectives affected by fundamental rights. In the sphere of the OMC, the decision-makers are governments or EU institutions. The question is how to integrate the social partners into that decision-making process. In the sphere of the *social dialogue*, the challenge is to secure outcomes which take account of and are consistent with the requisite fundamental rights of workers. The process itself engages the social partners; the problem is failure to engage and agree.

What, more precisely, is this process? As a model, we can draw on the elements outlined in greatest detail in Directive 2002/14/EC. Specifically, we can seek inspiration from this instrument in order to identify the objectives and principles underlying the process of decision-making and what is required, substantively and procedurally, by way of information and consultation. The key point here is that this process aims to ensure outcomes which secure the fundamental rights of workers. In this way, the process is akin to 'mainstreaming.' The difference is that mainstreaming in the area of fundamental rights of workers requires a process engaging not only, or even primarily, the public authorities. Rather, the objective is to ensure that the process engages to the fullest extent the social partners at relevant levels.

a. *Minimum Requirements.*   The Fundamental Rights Agency would need to set out the 'minimum' requirements for the process whereby the social partners engage in the OMC and the EU social dialogue. At the moment, there is less than

---

businesses, OJ L 61/26, as amended by Dir 98/50/EC of 29 June 1998, OJ L 201/88 of 17 July 1998; consolidated in Dir 2001/23/EC of 12 March 2001, OJ L/82/16. Council Dir 94/45/EC of 22 September 1994 on the establishment of a European Works Council or a procedure in Community-scale undertakings and Community-scale groups of undertakings for the purposes of informing and consulting employees, OJ L 254/64 of 30 September 1994. Council Dir No 2002/14 establishing a framework for informing and consulting employees in the European Community, OJ 2002, L80/29.

[73] Given the delicacy of its tasks, a major issue concerns the composition of the FRA, or that part of it responsible for dealing with fundamental labour rights. For example, as in many Member State bodies, its composition may be tripartite, including representatives of the social partners as well as experts.

a minimal skeleton of requirements in Article 128 EC (OMC) and Articles 138–139 EC (EU social dialogue). It is essential that this process be elaborated.

Article 1(1) of Directive 2002/14/EC provides that it sets out 'minimum' requirements. In interpreting this phrase in the context of the Working Time Directive, the European Court of Justice emphasised that it did not imply the lowest common denominator among the standards prevailing in Member States, but rather specified a Community minimum standard to be complied with by all Member States.[74] Article 1(1) refers to 'the right to information and consultation of employees,' the same right declared in Article 27 of the EU Charter of Fundamental Rights.[75] Article 1(2) mandates that the 'practical arrangements for information and consultation,' must be such 'as to ensure their effectiveness,' a criterion with particular resonance in EC law (*effet utile*).[76]

b. *'Spirit of Cooperation'.*   Failure to agree, in the case of the EU social dialogue, is attributable to the social partners' acting in their sectional interests alone. This is not the only model available. Article 1(3) of Directive 2002/14/EC provides:[77]

> When defining or implementing practical arrangements for information and consultation, the employer and the employees' representatives shall *work in a spirit of cooperation* and with due regard for their *reciprocal* rights and obligations, taking into account the interests *both* of the undertaking or establishment and of the employees.

By virtue of covering *both* 'defining *or* implementing practical arrangements for information and consultation,' the obligation to 'work in a spirit of cooperation' applies not only in the definition of practical arrangements, but during their application. The principle is of general application to any and all practical arrangements for information and consultation. The FRA could elaborate such an obligation for the EU social partners in the social dialogue. It could provide more detailed guidance regarding procedures, resolving impasses, etc

c. *Information.*   An essential basis for decision-making is information. 'Information' is defined in Article 2(f) of Directive 2002/14/EC by reference to

---

[74] *United Kingdom of Great Britain and Northern Ireland v Council of the European Union*, Case C–84/94 [1996] ECR I–5755.

[75] 'Workers' right to information and consultation within the undertaking. Workers or their representatives must, at the appropriate levels, be guaranteed information and consultation in good time in the cases and under the conditions provided for by Community law and national laws and practices.'

[76] As regards the OMC, the minimum requirements for procedures engaging the social partners would apply to the EU institutions (Commission and Council) responsible for formulating the Guidelines. They would apply to procedures whereby the Member State authorities responsible for formulating the national action plans engaged with the social partners. In the *social dialogue*, the minimum requirements would apply to the behaviour of the social partners negotiating agreements through the social dialogue.

[77] Art 1(3) may be compared with similar provisions in the European Works Councils Dir, Arts 6(1) and 9.

process ('transmission'), nature ('data') and purpose ('to acquaint [. . .] and to examine'). Other provisions supplement both the substantive content of the information to be disclosed and the process by which it is to be disclosed. Article 4(3) prescribes the practical arrangements for information which are to be determined by the Member States:

Information shall be given at such time, in such fashion and with such content as are appropriate to enable, in particular, employees' representatives to conduct an adequate study and, where necessary, prepare for consultation.

Moreover, Article 4(1) stipulates that these practical arrangements must accord with the principles set out in Article 1, which includes the general injunction that the practical arrangements 'be defined and implemented in such a way as to ensure their effectiveness.' The FRA could prescribe more detailed provisions regarding the substantive content and the process of information needed for the OMC or the social dialogue process. For example, a key issue is the timeliness of information provided. The effectiveness of the procedure can be compromised by late provision of information.[78] Again, using the odd English phrase 'in such fashion' ('*d'une façon*'), Directive 2002/14/EC refers to how the information is to be presented, its quantity and quality. To achieve the purpose of the exercise, it must not smother the social partners in paper, and it must serve to enable them to study and prepare.

The essential criterion for assessment of each aspect of the practical arrangements for information is whether they achieve the purpose stipulated. In the words of Directive 2002/14/EC: 'to enable, in particular, employees' representatives to conduct an adequate study and, where necessary, prepare for consultation.' There is, at least, a double task at the 'information' stage. The first task is to 'conduct an adequate study'; hence, the need for proper timing, 'fashion' and content of the information.[79] Then the task is to 'prepare for consultation,' which is prior to the actual consultation itself.

d. *Consultation.* Although the Collective Dismissals and Acquired Rights Directives did not define 'consultation,' both directives specify the obligation to 'consult [. . .] with a view to reaching an agreement.'[80] This phrase is found in Article 4 of Directive 2002/14/EC, and specifically in Article 4(4)(e). Article 4 of Directive 2002/14/EC prescribes that 'Member States shall determine the practical arrangements for exercising the right to information and consultation.' Article 4(4) provides:

---

[78] In the case of the OMC, the information collected by the EU institutions and Member States should be made available to the social partners. In the social dialogue, the employers will be under an obligation to provide the requisite information, as current directives already provide, 'in good time.'

[79] The phrase implies that conducting a study is preparatory to consultation.

[80] Acquired Rights Dir 1977, Art 7(2); Collective Dismissals Dir 1975, Art 2(1).

Consultation shall take place: while ensuring that the timing, method and content thereof are appropriate; at the relevant level of management and representation, depending on the subject under discussion; on the basis of information supplied by the employer [...] and of the opinion which the employees' representatives are entitled to formulate; in such a way as to enable employees' representatives to meet the employer and obtain a response, and the reasons for that response, to any opinion they might formulate; and with a view to reaching an agreement on decisions.'

Article 4(1) enjoins the Member States to determine that consultation takes place 'at the appropriate level in accordance with this Article,' and Article 4(4)(b) specifies that '[c]onsultation shall take place [...] at the relevant level of management and representation.' The directive mentions some explicit criteria for determining 'relevance,' but these leave much room for dispute.[81]

If consultation is intended to influence decisions, it must be with the employer who makes the decision at the relevant level, whether the contractual employer or, for example, the employer in the form of a parent company.[82] As to the 'relevant level of [...] representation' of the workforce, although phrased in the singular, there is no reason to confine the obligations to one level of employees' representatives. The impact of the decision may be felt at many levels, and practical arrangements should require information and consultation at these relevant levels.[83]

As regards timing, previous directives required the consultation to be 'in good time,'[84] if not 'as soon as possible.'[85] What is 'appropriate' timing may vary

---

[81] In the social dialogue context, the relevant levels have been intersectoral in some cases (Agreements on Part-Time Work and Fixed-Term Work, Parental Leave, Telework, Work-Related Stress). In other cases, they have been sectoral (Working Time Dir), though in fact these have engaged subsectors of the transport sector. In still other cases, the level has been that of multi-national enterprises (European Works Councils). The application of fundamental rights may, in some cases, allow for them to be the subject of social dialogue at different levels, as adjusted to different contexts (as in the case of health and safety). The case of OMC is much more diverse, with guidelines appropriate to a myriad of contexts. Again, the engagement of the social partners should resolve this issue by agreement on the relevant level.

[82] This was the purpose of the 1992 amendments to the Collective Dismissals Dir which provided for the information and consultation obligations to 'apply irrespective of whether the decision regarding collective redundancies is being taken by the employer or by an undertaking controlling the employer,' and rejected any 'defence on the part of the employer on the ground that the necessary information has not been provided to the employer by the undertaking which took the decision leading to collective redundancies' (Art 2(4)). See also: the Acquired Rights Dir, Art 7(4).

[83] An excellent study undertaken by researchers at Ruskin College emphasised that coordination among levels of representatives was crucial to successful engagement of employees' representatives in decision-making in the enterprise. See the study undertaken by Ruskin College, Oxford, for the Commission. Final Report presented to the Directorate General for Internal Market and Industrial Affairs and the Directorate General for Employment, Social Affairs and Education of the European Commission, *The Control of Frontiers: Workers and New Technology: Disclosure and Use of Company Information* (Ruskin College, Oxford, 1984). See also: Appendix to Final Report: Summaries of Case Studies. The conclusions of the Final Report are reproduced in (1984) 134 *European Industrial Relations Review* 22.

[84] Collective Dismissals Dir, Art 2; Acquired Rights Dir, Art 7.

[85] European Works Councils Dir, Annex, para 3: 'This information and consultation meeting shall take place as soon as possible.'

according to circumstances: the nature of the decision and its impact, the organ-isation of employees' representation, etc.[86] A crucial issue for the Fundamental Rights Agency is to make clear that the process of information and consultation is to take place *prior* to a decision being made or agreement reached.

The 'method' of consultation, in light of Article 4(4)(d) and (e), obviously includes, eg, meetings, feedback, and advice from experts. The reference in Article 4(4)(d) to 'meet the employer' is not limited to one meeting.[87] Article 4(4)(c)) provides for 'the opinion which the employees' representatives are entitled to formulate' on the basis of the information supplied by the employer, and Article 4(4)(d) fleshes out the element of 'establishment of dialogue' in the definition of 'consultation' in Article 2(g) by specifying the employer's 'response, and the reasons for that response.' This 'reasoned response' is not an explanation for management's decision; this has not yet been taken. Rather, it is the employer's response to the opinion of the employees' representatives on the employer's proposals. If that opinion puts forward options, the employer needs to respond to them and justify any rejection of these options.

The method of consultation envisages a pro-active approach by employees' representatives; not only to react to the employer's proposals, but to formulate their own. Article 4(3) qualifies their activity in terms of conducting an adequate study in preparation for consultation. The ensuing 'opinion' is not the end of the process, but only its beginning; it requires a reasoned response by the employer, which is only another element in the process of consultation 'with a view to reaching an agreement.'

e. *Summary.* To summarise: the procedure envisaged for mainstreaming fun-damental rights of workers incorporates the following nine sequential stages derived from the information and consultation process established in EU labour law and proclaimed as a fundamental right in Article 27 of the EU Charter:[88]

1. transmission of information/data (Article 2(f));
2. acquaintance with and examination of data (Article 2(f));
3. conduct of an adequate study (Article 4(3));
4. preparation for consultation (Article 4(3));
5. formulation of an opinion (Article 4(4)(c));
6. meeting (Article 4(4)(d));
7. employer's reasoned response to opinion (Article 4(4)(d));

---

[86] The Ruskin College study emphasised the importance of early access to the decision-making process and a predetermined decision-making procedure (as well as co-ordination of the structures of employees' representation); See n 83 above.

[87] Again, unlike the subsidiary requirements in the European Works Councils Dir, Annex, para 2, which specify 'once a year,' but also envisage further meetings (para 3) 'Where there are excep-tional circumstances [which] shall take place as soon as possible.'

[88] The references are to Arts in Dir 2002/14/EC. This summary of the preceding analysis of Dir 2002/14/EC is drawn from B Bercusson, 'The European Social Model Comes to Britain' (2002) 31 *Industrial Law Journal* (September) 209–244.

8. 'exchange of views and establishment of dialogue,' (Article 2(g)), 'discussion' (Article 4(4)(b)) 'with a view to reaching an agreement on decisions' (Article 4(4)(e));

9. 'the employer and the employees' representatives shall work in a spirit of cooperation and with due regard for their reciprocal rights and obligations, taking into account the interests both of the undertaking or establishment and of the employees' (Article 1(3)).

This defines, in a pragmatic way, the process required for the effective implementation of the fundamental rights of workers. It goes beyond exhortation and becomes a legally structured process. It is the definitive description of the process of participation by the social partners in decision-making, here the elaboration of the fundamental rights of workers. The implementation and enforcement of the fundamental rights of workers are to be secured through this process.[89]

The importance of the process cannot be overstated. It is the pressure exerted by engagement in these mandatory processes that is crucial to both achieving agreement through the social dialogue, and effective enforcement of OMC policies. The engagement of the social partners through these processes reflects the labour law axiom highlighted above.

The effective enforcement of non-binding texts reached through the social dialogue (eg, the agreements on telework and work-related stress) is a function of the degree of engagement of the social partners at national level. The more dense the process of engagement in concluding the agreements, the more effectively they will be enforced. The answer to complaints regarding the lack of effect of agreements implemented through the 'practices and procedures of labour and management' (Article 139(2) EC)) is for the Fundamental Rights Agency to secure the requisite engagement of the social partners at all relevant levels. This can be done by formulating the procedures and processes securing participation by all those affected ('mainstreaming'). Similarly, the Commission's concerns at the ineffectiveness of 'process-oriented' texts can be met by increasing the intensity of engagement of the social partners.

One objection is that fundamental rights are *a priori* not open to negotiation. However, given vagueness of definition and infinite variety of contexts, they need further specification. The procedures of specification are all important. Judicial and administrative specification is the traditional method. However, in

---

[89] For *social dialogue*, where agreement is the central criterion of success, everything is bent on enforcing procedures, in the expectation that they will produce agreement (though ultimately agreement cannot be enforced, because of the principle of autonomy of the social partners). The task of the Fundamental Rights Agency is to promote active engagement in the procedures to the maximum. It is different for the OMC: it is not so much agreement reached as some other process-oriented text (eg, a guideline), engaging EU and Member State authorities. The key then becomes enforcing the outcome (usually non-binding). To this end, the maximum engagement of the parties in the process may enhance the effectiveness of the ultimate text reached, since they will have committed themselves actively to achieving it.

the field of fundamental rights of workers, the labour law axiom looks rather to the social partners. The task of the Fundamental Rights Agency is to operationalise this axiom and secure its effectiveness.

Again, the parallel with 'mainstreaming' may be drawn. But instead of specifying a policy objective to be taken into account by a procedure re-aligned to facilitate that outcome (eg, obligatory impact assessments, action plans, etc), the emphasis in the labour law field is on procedures engaging the social partners.

VI. CONCLUSION

Despite the experience in many Member States of active engagement by social partners in processes of information and consultation and social dialogue, the Fundamental Rights Agency cannot alone create the necessary culture of engagement in elaborating fundamental rights of workers. Nonetheless, it is suggested that it can contribute to the fostering of such a culture on the basis of the following propositions:

First, the legal basis of FRA policy in the labour field is the fundamental right in Articles 27 and 28 of the EU Charter (information and consultation and collective bargaining, now renumbered as Articles II–87 and II–88 of the Constitutional Treaty) and Article I–48 of the Constitutional Treaty (recognising and promoting the social partners and facilitating the social dialogue). Second, the premise underlying FRA policy is that safeguarding fundamental rights in the employment and industrial relations sphere is most effectively achieved through the processes of information, consultation and social dialogue engaging the social partners at appropriate levels.

Third, however, realism about resources dictates that FRA should focus on the transnational dimension. At the level of the multinational enterprise, the role of European works councils in safeguarding fundamental rights should be promoted.[90] At sectoral level, sectoral social dialogue committees should be engaged in the formulation and implementation of fundamental rights of workers.[91] At the EU level, fundamental rights should be promoted through the EU social dialogue and the OMC.[92]

Fourth, the FRA needs to play a proactive role, especially given the absence of any detailed definition of the processes involved. Directive 2002/14/EC provides a framework of principles. Fifth, in light of experience at Member State level, where the social partners lack the ability to enforce their rights, the FRA should step in. Various methods may be used: codes of practice, benchmarking, active presence on relevant bodies, *locus standi* before tribunals, mandatory default standards.

---

[90] To date, European works councils have been established in less than one half of those multinational enterprises eligible to have them.

[91] A small number of the 30 sectoral social dialogue committees established to date have adopted texts elaborating core fundamental rights of workers in their sector.

[92] See the two proposals indicated above, nn 61 and 62.

One should not be deluded into thinking that institutional design is the answer; without political will, such proposals are sand castles. But fundamental rights are not a luxury. Not least, information and consultation is not only a fundamental right of workers, it is also critical to the successful management of economic and social change. The successful economic integration of Europe is dependent on management of necessary change. Respect for the fundamental right of information and consultation and the constitutional commitment to social dialogue are essential conditions for this success. Labour law experience indicates that these processes offer the best chance for realisation of the fundamental rights of workers. The Fundamental Rights Agency can best fulfil its mandate by supporting these processes of autonomous engagement of the social partners.

Part III

The EU Fundamental Rights Agency in a Wider Context

9

The Contribution of the Agency to the Implementation in the EU of International and European Human Rights Instruments

RICK LAWSON*

I. INTRODUCTION

WHICH STANDARDS SHOULD the Fundamental Rights Agency apply? Should the EU Charter of Fundamental Rights be its lodestar? Or should the Agency be guided by the European Convention of Human Rights and other international instruments in the field of human rights? Or should it engage in comparative legal analysis of the constitutional traditions of its Member States in order to identify common principles? Should it do all?

These questions appear to be superfluous in the light of the Commission's Public Consultation document on the Fundamental Rights Agency, which asserts:

> The Charter of Fundamental Rights, which was proclaimed in Nice in December 2000, and which forms Part II of the Constitutional Treaty with legally binding effect, brings together a package of rights, freedoms and principles which will, when the Constitutional Treaty enters into force, bind the EU institutions and the Member States when they apply EU law. The Commission considers that, although it is not legally mandatory as matters stand, it already constitutes an authentic expression of the fundamental rights protected by Community law as a set of general principles. As such, it constitutes an essential reference document in the discussion on the definition of the Agency's areas of intervention.[1]

So the picture seems clear: the Charter shines as bright as Polaris; it will guide the Agency. A closer look, however, reveals a certain ambiguity. The EU

---

* Professor RA Lawson, Europa Instituut, Department of Public Law, Faculty of Law, University of Leiden, The Netherlands.

[1] COM (2004) 693 final of 25 October 2004, p 7.

Charter is '*an* essential reference document,' but is it also the Agency's *sole* reference? Should it be? An exclusive focus on the Charter would perhaps be difficult to reconcile with the fact, noted by the Commission in the same document, that the Agency 'is to operate in a global environment,' so that it 'must ensure that it is receptive to it.'[2] This suggests that the Agency should also take into account the international bill of rights. The Commission, however, actually hints in the opposite direction—perhaps the Agency should limit itself to only *some* of the Charter's rights:

> It might be worth asking the Agency to monitor all the fundamental rights protected by Community law and included in the Charter. This would provide an overall view of the rights on which the Union is based [. . .] A reference to the Charter would, however, give the Agency an extremely broad field of action.[3]

Against this background, the present contribution will explore the standards that the Fundamental Rights Agency (FRA) should use.

Three preliminary points must be made. Firstly, it is still uncertain which tasks will be entrusted to the FRA. This complicates a discussion of the standards that the Agency should apply: the 'proper' standards may differ depending on the scope of the Agency's functions. A reference to the international bill of rights, for instance, would be appropriate for a body that is involved in the formulation of foreign policy; an emphasis on the EU Charter is conceivable if the body were to monitor the institutions of the Union.

The Commission's Public Consultation document is not extremely generous in assigning tasks to the FRA:

> the Agency's principal tasks can be defined as the collection and analysis of objective, reliable and comparable data at European level,

which 'should be targeted on the drafting of opinions for the institutions and the Member States.'[4] This does not bring us much further: should opinions be based on the Charter or on the European Convention of Human Rights (ECHR)? In an attempt to overcome this problem, we will take the present significance of fundamental rights to the EU as a starting point. The current situation will be analysed along three axes or 'dimensions': *self-restraint* (where the Union institutions accept that they are bound by a self-defined set of fundamental rights; section II (a)), *external review* (where the question is raised to what extent EU action may be reviewed under existing international standards; section II (b)), and *imposition on third parties* (where the Union advocates compliance with fundamental rights by third countries and Member States; section II(c)). It is submitted that each of these dimensions has its own characteristics and sensitivities; they offer 'lessons learned' that may be useful when determining the terms of reference for the FRA.

---

[2] COM (2004) 693 final of 25 October 2004, p 4.
[3] *Ibid*, p 7.
[4] *Ibid*, pp 8 and 9.

Secondly, it should be noted that this contribution is written—and indeed, the shape of the FRA will have to be determined—at a point in time where we do and yet do not have a European Constitution. The text of the Treaty establishing the Constitution of Europe has been adopted by the Intergovernmental Conference, but no one can predict whether it will actually enter into force. A series of referenda and parliamentary procedures may lead to the conclusion that in the final analysis our heads of State or Government are actually not the *Herren der Verträge*. As a result we have to limit ourselves at this stage to the observation that Article I–9 of the Constitution provides for Union accession to the ECHR and that part II incorporates the Charter of Fundamental Rights— but we do not know whether these provisions will ever become binding. One may try to avoid this reality by asserting, as the Commission's Public Consultation document does, that the Charter 'already constitutes an authentic expression of the fundamental rights protected by Community law'—but it is difficult to deny that the future of the Constitution is a uncertain factor with a major impact on the legal and political environment in which the FRA will have to function.

Thirdly, assuming that the Constitution will enter into force, there is another hurdle to be taken. Article I–9 of the Constitution asserts that the Union 'shall' accede to the ECHR, but this formulation[5] conveniently ignores that accession will require agreement from the other side as well: the Council of Europe and its 46 Member States. Admittedly, the Council of Europe has repeatedly indicated that it would welcome EU accession, and the new Protocol 14 to the ECHR contains a clause to this end: 'The European Union may accede to the Convention.'[6] The explanatory memorandum to the latter provision, however, warns us that this is not the whole story:

> It should be emphasised that further modifications to the Convention will be necessary in order to make such accession possible from a legal and technical point of view [. . .] At the time of drafting of this protocol, it was not yet possible to enter into negotiations—and even less to conclude an agreement—with the European Union on the terms of the latter's possible accession to the Convention, simply because the European Union still lacked the competence to do so. This made it impossible to include in this protocol the other modifications to the Convention necessary to permit such accession. As a consequence, a second ratification procedure will be necessary in respect of those further modifications, whether they be included in a new amending protocol or in an accession treaty.[7]

---

[5] As in doc CIG 87/04 of 6 August 2004. Interestingly, the Draft Treaty as presented by the Convention had used more cautious terms: 'the Union *shall seek* accession' (doc CONV 850/03, 18 July 2003). The very first draft of this provision (Art 5 as it then was) was even less enthusiastic: 'the Union *may* accede' (doc CONV 528/03, 6 February 2003).

[6] Protocol 14 to the Convention for the Protection of Human Rights and Fundamental Freedoms, amending the control system of the Convention (adopted 13 May 2004), Art 17, amending the existing Art 59 ECHR.

[7] Explanatory Memorandum, ss 101–102, available at: http://conventions.coe.int/Treaty/EN/Reports/Html/194.htm.

It remains to be seen how this 'second ratification procedure' will proceed. It will be interesting to watch the negotiations that will precede EU accession: some non-EU Member States may believe that they have an interesting bargaining chip here.

For present purposes, however, we leave these issues aside and concentrate on the significance of fundamental rights to the EU.

II. THE EU AND FUNDAMENTAL RIGHTS: A DYNAMIC RELATIONSHIP IN THREE DIMENSIONS

a) First Dimension: Self-constraint

If one analyses the position of fundamental rights in the legal order of the Union (which for the sake of convenience will be equated with the Communities), it becomes clear that three interrelated but distinguishable developments have taken place and continue to take place. The first one of these, also in chronological terms, is one of self-constraint.

1. *General Features*

Ever since the ECJ's landmark judgments in the cases of *Handelsgesellschaft* and *Nold*[8] in the early 1970s, the Union has been in a process of accepting and acknowledging that it is bound by fundamental rights. The case-law is well-known[9] and may be summarised as follows:

> according to settled case-law, fundamental rights form an integral part of the general principles of law, whose observance the Court ensures. For that purpose, the Court draws inspiration from the constitutional traditions common to the Member States and from the guidelines supplied by international treaties for the protection of human rights on which the Member States have collaborated or to which they are signatories. The ECHR has special significance in that respect.[10]

---

[8] ECJ, Case 11/70, *Internationale Handelsgesellschaft* [1970] ECR 1125, s 4; Case 4–73, *Nold* [1974] ECR 491, s 13.

[9] For an overview, see B de Witte, 'The Past and Future Role of the European Court of Justice in the Protection of Human Rights' in P Alston (ed), *The EU and Human Rights* (Oxford, Oxford University Press, 1999), pp 859–897.

[10] ECJ, Joined Cases C–20/00 and C–64/00, *Booker Aquaculture ao* [2003] ECR I–7411, s 65; references to earlier case-law omitted. Note that the use of the words 'international treaties' goes back to the English translation of the *Nold* judgment, which indeed used the term 'treaties.' This is similar to the German version, the official language of that case, which referred to 'die internationale Verträge.' By contrast, the French text, used in the internal deliberations of the Court, referred to '*les instruments internationaux*' and the Dutch version to '*internationale wilsverklaringen.*' The English/German translation seems to exclude non-binding instruments such as the Universal Declaration of Human Rights, the texts adopted in the frame work of the OSCE and recommendations of, for instance, the Committee of Ministers of the Council of Europe. Since there are no a priori reasons why the ECJ should be unable to take the principles enshrined in non-binding texts into account, it would be preferable to retain the more extensive French version of *Nold*.

Recent decisions show that this is still a very dynamic branch of case-law. Take for instance *Baustahlgewebe* in which the Court found a Community violation of fundamental rights for the first time in history, or *Connolly* on the freedom of expression of EU civil servants, or again *Roquette Frères* where the Court accepted that the Commission must comply with the requirements of the right to respect for private life when searching business premises. [11]

Although the common constitutional traditions were the first source of fundamental rights to be recognised by the ECJ, its importance seems to have diminished over the years.[12] Instead the ECJ has increasingly referred to the ECHR and to the jurisprudence of the European Court of Human Rights. It should be added that the ECJ has also based itself on other human rights instruments, albeit to a lesser extent.[13]

The principles established in the Court's case law were reaffirmed in the preamble to the Single European Act, then incorporated in the Treaty of Maastricht (Article F(2) EU) and then in the Treaty of Amsterdam (Article 6(2) EU). The only difference is that the reference to *other* human rights instruments, which has always been maintained in the Luxembourg case-law, never made it to the treaty texts. The explanation will probably be that the drafters preferred a shorter reference to the sources of fundamental rights. Be that as it may, Article I–9 (3) of the Constitutional Treaty provides:

> Fundamental rights, as guaranteed by the European Convention for the Protection of Human Rights and Fundamental Freedoms and as they result from the constitutional traditions common to the Member States, shall constitute general principles of the Union's law.

Our first conclusion should therefore be these two sources of fundamental rights—the ECHR and common constitutional traditions—will be still alive when the Constitution enters into force.

Yet it is also true that the Court has always been careful to state that it only draws 'inspiration' from the 'guidelines' supplied by human rights treaties. Clearly the Court did not and does not consider itself bound by these treaties, as the following quote illustrates:

[11] ECJ, Case C–185/95 P, *Baustahlgewebe* [1998] ECR I–8417, s 29; Case C–274/99 P, *Connolly v Commission* [2001] ECR I 1611, s 37; Case C–94/00, *Roquette Frères* [2002] ECR I–9011, s 25.

[12] It is a telling detail that the 'Black Monday' draft treaty presented by the Dutch presidency in 1991 (which was subsequently vetoed) did not refer to constitutional traditions at all. Draft Art G (2) provided: 'The Union shall respect the rights and freedoms as recognised in the European Convention for the Protection of Human Rights and Fundamental Freedoms' (see *Europe Documents* No 1746/1747 of 20 November 1991). Compare: ECJ, Case 379/87, *Groener* [1989] ECR 3967, and Case C–36/02, *Omega Spielhallen* (judgment of 14 October 2004, not yet reported), as examples of cases in which considerable weight was given to constitutional values (albeit without any comparative analysis and with a different purpose—ie, not to find general principles of Community law binding the institutions, but to justify national policies that might otherwise be deemed incompatible with EC law).

[13] For a reference to the ESC, see ECJ, Case 24/86, *Blaizot* [1988] ECR 403 s 17. For references to the ICCPR, see ECJ, Case 374/87, *Orkem* [1989] ECR 3351, s 31, and C–249/96, *Grant* [1998] ECR I–650, s 44. For a reference to an ILO Convention, see ECJ, Case 43/75, *Defrenne* [1976] ECR 474, s 20.

Article 6(1) of the EHRC provides that [. . .] everyone is entitled to a fair and public hearing [. . .] *The general principle of Community law* that everyone is entitled to fair legal process, *which is inspired by those fundamental rights* [. . .] is applicable in the context of proceedings brought against a Commission decision imposing fines on an undertaking for infringement of competition law.[14]

Likewise the ECJ keeps some distance when it refers to individual judgments of the Strasbourg Court:

the reasonableness of such a period must be appraised in the light of the circumstances specific to each case and, in particular, the importance of the case for the person concerned, its complexity and the conduct of the applicant and of the competent authorities (see, *by analogy*, the judgments of the European Court of Rights).[15]

Meanwhile the Charter of Fundamental Rights of the EU was adopted, as a political document, in Nice in December 2000.[16] As is well-known, the Charter contains a wide variety of rights: civil and political rights, economic, cultural and social rights. Its text reveals a certain amount of ambiguity: some provisions are expressly directed to the EU; others are not addressed to any authority in particular but relate to policy areas where the Union has little or no competence. Be that as it may, the Charter combines classic and innovative provisions, from the prohibition of slavery to the right to good administration—in short, it is an attempt to formulate the 'state of the art' in human rights.

Following the Charter's proclamation, the Commission announced that it would take the Charter into account when drafting legislation.[17] Yet in the Luxembourg case-law the Charter's role is less than prominent. Presumably because of its soft law nature, the ECJ has refrained from applying it, although the Court of First Instance and a number of Advocates General had no difficulty in doing so.[18] But it is quite predictable that the incorporation of the Charter into the Constitutional Treaty will change the status quo. Once the Constitution enters into force, there is nothing to prevent the ECJ from applying the Charter. Likewise it will be even more difficult than it is today to ignore the Charter in the legislative process.

---

[14] ECJ, Case C–185/95 P, *Baustahlgewebe* [1998] ECR I–8417, ss 21–22 (emphasis added; references to earlier case-law omitted).

[15] *Ibid*, s 29 (emphasis added).

[16] OJ 2000, C 364. On the Charter, see J-Y Carlier and O De Schutter, *La Charte des droits fondamentaux de l'Union européenne* (Brussels, Bruylant, 2002); W Heusel (ed), *The Charter of Fundamental Rights and Constitutional Development in the EU* (Trier, Bundesanzeiger, 2002); P Eeckhout, 'The EU Charter of Fundamental Rights and the Federal Question' (2002) 39 *CML Rev* pp 945–994; JW Sap, *Het EU-Handvest van de Grondrechten—De opmaat voor de Europese Grondwet* (Deventer, Kluwer, 2003); J Meyer (Hrsg), *Kommentar zur Charta der Grundrechte der Europäischen Union* (Baden-Baden, Nomos, 2003).

[17] See SEC (2001) 380/3: 'any proposal for legislation and any draft instrument to be adopted by the Commission will therefore, as part of the normal decision-making procedures, first be scrutinised for compatibility with the Charter.'

[18] Compare, eg: the Opinion of AG Léger with the Court's ruling in *Hautala*: C–353/99 P, *Council v Hautala* [2001] ECR I–9567 and I–9594.

This raises a number of questions. One set of questions is of a substantive nature. Will the 'new' Charter have a real impact on EU law? For instance, will the right of access to documents 'benefit' from its inclusion as a 'fundamental' right in the Charter? What contents will be given to 'new' rights, such as the right to good administration? To what extent will the 'constitutionalisation' of fundamental rights affect the balance between individual freedom and collective security in the 'Area of Freedom, Security and Justice'? Many similar questions could be raised; the point is that we do not know how many of these rights will be interpreted and applied.

A second set of questions is of a procedural nature. It is one thing to accept that the institutions are bound by fundamental rights, but what about the agencies and entities such as Europol and Eurojust? Article 51 of the Charter (Article II–111 of the Constitution) asserts, inter alia, that the provisions of the Charter 'are addressed to the institutions, bodies, offices and agencies of the Union.' But how will one ensure in practice that these bodies respect the rights and freedoms of the Charter? Will rights be accompanied by effective remedies? Will the inclusion of the right to an effective remedy in the Charter entail an improvement of the individual's standing before the ECJ in 'classic' annulment actions?[19]

Thirdly, it will be interesting to see if the institutional balance within the EU will change as a consequence of the incorporation of the Charter into the EU Constitution. Will the ECJ assume more control over EU policies through the application of fundamental rights? It would seem that the Member States, when negotiating the Constitution, have taken several measures in order to prevent just that development. Two examples will be mentioned here, since they may or may not have an impact on the FRA's future activities.

On the one hand, the scope for judicial interpretation is limited by the explanations of the Charter provisions.[20] The Member States increasingly underlined the importance that they attach to these explanations. During the final negotiations on the Constitution, an express stipulation was inserted that the explanations 'shall be given due regard by the courts of the Union and of the Member States.'[21] It remains to be seen whether what 'due regard' means in practice and whether the explanations are as helpful as the Member States believe.

On the other hand, a clause was inserted (Article II–52 (5); Article II–112 (7) of the Constitution), clearly designed to keep the courts out of the area of policy decisions in cases about socio-economic rights:

---

[19] Art 47 of the Charter; Art II–107 of the Constitution. On this issue, compare: CFI Case T–177/01, *Jégo-Quéré v Commission* [2002] ECR II–2365, with ECJ, Case C–263/02 P, *Commission v Jégo-Quéré* (judgment of 1 April 2004, not yet reported).

[20] These were prepared by the Praesidium of the 'first' Convention (which drafted the Charter) and updated by the Praesidium of the 'second' Convention (which drafted the Constitution).

[21] Art 52 (7) of the Charter; Art II–112 (7) of the Constitution. See also the declaration contained in Annex 10 to doc CIG 85/04 (18 June 2004).

> The provisions of this Charter which contain principles may be implemented by legislative and executive acts [. . .] They shall be judicially cognisable only in the interpretation of such acts and in the ruling on their legality.

The explanation asserts:

> Principles may be implemented through legislative and executive acts [. . .], accordingly, they become significant for the Courts only where such acts are interpreted or reviewed. They do not however give rise to direct claims for positive action by the Union's institutions or by the Member States.

One cannot help noticing, however, that the conceptual difference between 'rights' and 'principles' is rather foggy. Many provisions contain a bit of both. In addition one cannot help noticing that neither Charter itself nor legal practice are consistent in their terminology. As to the Charter: no one will deny that Article II–23 (equality of men and women) contains 'rights'—but the provision itself refers to the 'principle' of equality! As to the ECJ: its famous *Bosman* judgment referred to:

> the *principle* of freedom of association [as] enshrined in Article 11 ECHR and resulting from the constitutional traditions common to the Member States

which was 'one of the fundamental *rights* which [. . .] are protected in the Community legal order.'[22] And even in 2004, after the distinction between rights and obligations had been introduced in the EU Charter, the ECJ referred in *Karner* to the '*principle* of freedom of expression' which is 'expressly recognised by Article 10 ECHR.'[23] All in all, it is most likely that the distinction between rights and principles will be a source of confusion.

2. Meaning for the FRA

Which lessons for the Fundamental Rights Agency can be drawn from the above? I believe that there may be three.

First, it is understandable that political and academic attention tends to go to the EU Charter. In this context it does not come as a surprise that the Commission, in its Public Consultation document on the FRA, refers to the EU Charter as 'an essential reference document.' One could even argue that the FRA, irrespective of the way in which its mandate is formulated, will be *under an obligation* to take into account the Charter. After all, the FRA will be an 'agency' of the EU and this implies, according to Article 51 of the Charter (Article II–111 of the Constitution), that the provisions of the Charter are 'addressed' to it!

In the second place, it may be true that the EU Charter provides for an appealing, up-to-date human rights catalogue—or, as the Commission puts it, 'an authentic expression of the fundamental rights protected by Community law.'

---

[22] ECJ, Case C–415/93, *Bosman* [1995] ECR I–4921, s 79 (emphasis added).
[23] ECJ, Case C–71/02, *Karner* (judgment of 25 March 2004, not yet reported), s 50 (emphasis added).

But we have also seen that the interpretation and application of many Charter provisions is still uncertain; that it is not clear how these rights will be enforced in practice; and that a somewhat artificial distinction between 'rights' and 'principles' has been introduced.

To what extent do these factors diminish the usefulness of the Charter for the FRA? One advantage that the FRA would have when compared to the ECJ, is that there are no procedural obstacles to extending its activities to *all* institutions, bodies, offices and agencies of the Union. The limitations that surround the individual's access to the ECJ, and that may diminish the degree of protection that the Charter can offer in reality, simply do not apply to the FRA when collecting data or when formulating policy recommendations.

Another advantage is that the FRA may be in a less awkward position than the judiciary to deal with the 'principles' laid down in the EU Charter. The proposition that 'principles' do not give rise to direct claims for positive action by the Union's institutions or by the Member States, should in no way bother the FRA in its advisory and supervisory functions.

The fact remains, however, that the practical implementation of many of the Charter's vague provisions is likely to raise a number of questions. What weight should the FRA give to the official explanations? Should it give them 'due regard,' just as the courts are supposed to—or could we argue, *a contrario*, that the FRA, since it is not a court, is free to take a more liberal approach to them? Whatever the answer is, it would seem that the Charter's light is probably too diffuse to serve as a reliable lodestar to the FRA.

Thirdly, one should not overlook that the Charter is not the only source of fundamental rights. As we have seen, Article I–9 (3) of the Constitution expressly states that the ECHR and common constitutional traditions will continue to be general principles of EU law. There is no reason why the FRA should ignore these sources. Of course it may be complicated and time-consuming to compare the constitutional traditions of 25 EU Member States in order to identify common principles. Quite often the outcome may simply be in line with the EU Charter. But one cannot exclude that the EU Charter, extensive as it is, contains lacunae or vague provisions that require clarification. Nor can one exclude that the constitutional traditions evolve in a way not anticipated by the Charter.

Likewise international instruments for the protection of human rights 'on which the Member States have collaborated or to which they are signatories,' as the famous phrase of the ECJ runs, may offer additional protection. The ECHR is the obvious example, but it is by no means the only relevant treaty. Thus, the EU Network of Independent Experts on Fundamental Rights pointed out that the rights of minorities are not guaranteed, as such, in the EU Charter, whereas several international instruments do protect minority rights.[24] It is inconceivable that the FRA were to overlook minority rights for the sole reason that they are not expressly guaranteed by the EU Charter. Likewise, the UN Convention

---

[24] EU Network, *Fundamental Rights in the EU in 2003*, p 11.

on the Elimination of All Forms of Racial Discrimination (CERD) would be an obvious reference text for the FRA when dealing with racism and xenophobia.

b) Second Dimension: the EU and External Standards

The conclusion from the previous paragraph must be twofold: (a) the EU Charter will be a major source of inspiration to the FRA, but (b) EU law also points to other sources, notably the ECHR and common constitutional traditions, which the FRA should take into account.

That conclusion, and especially the second leg of it, is amplified if one takes into account the international context in which the Union operates. In our discussion so far, we have conveniently ignored the possibility that the EU, in interpreting and applying fundamental rights, adopts views that differ from those of the international bodies that are specifically charged with the supervision of compliance with human rights. In practice such differences may occur. It is one thing for the EU to assert that it is bound by fundamental rights; it is quite another thing to have that claim tested by external bodies.

This issue has been addressed in the literature. Most attention goes, quite naturally, to the question whether there are divergences between Luxembourg and Strasbourg.[25] In practice the risk of divergences is diminishing since the ECJ is increasingly prepared to refer to the Strasbourg jurisprudence; recent judgments illustrate this trend.[26] But the risk of divergences continues to exist, as we will see below. It will be interesting to take a brief look at this issue: it can provide us with an idea of the consequences of the hypothetical situation where the FRA loses sight of international minimum standards and issues opinions that fail to reflect the practice of international human rights bodies.

1. General Features

The Convention that was established to prepare the EU Charter received hundreds of letters, proposals, reactions and suggested amendments from civil society. From the *Lega italiana dei Diritti dell'Animale (LIDA)* to the *European Bureau for Lesser Used Languages (EBLUL)* and from the *Confederation of British Industry (CBI)* to the *Executive Committee of the Leuenberg Church Fellowship (LCF)*: they all tried to persuade the Convention to do something.

---

[25] See, eg: RA Lawson, 'Confusion and Conflict? Diverging Interpretations of the European Convention on Human Rights in Strasbourg and Luxembourg' in RA Lawson and M de Blois (eds), *The Dynamics of the Protection of Human Rights in Europe—Essays in Honour of HG Schermers* vol III (Boston, Martinus Nijhoff, 1994), pp 219–252; D Spielmann, 'Human Rights Case Law in the Strasbourg and Luxembourg Courts: Conflicts, Inconsistencies, and Complementarities' in P Alston (ed), *The EU and Human Rights* (Oxford, Oxford University Press, 1999) pp 757–780.

[26] See, eg: Case C–185/95 P, *Baustahlgewebe* [1998] ECR I–8417, s 29; Case C–7/98, *Krombach* [2000] ECR I–1935, s 39; Case C–465/00, *Österreichischer Rundfunk* (judgment of 20 May 2003, not yet reported), s 73 et seq.

Contribution No 182 came from the United Nations Committee on Economic, Social and Cultural Rights. The UN Committee applauded the attempts to draft the Charter and to incorporate both civil and political rights *and* economic, social and cultural rights. The Committee nevertheless pointed out that:

> if economic and social rights were not to be integrated in the Draft Charter on an equal footing with civil and political rights, such negative regional signals would be highly detrimental to the full realization of all human rights at both the international and domestic levels, and would have to be regarded as a retrogressive step contravening the existing obligations of Member States of the European Union under the International Covenant on Economic, Social and Cultural Rights. In such a case, *the Committee might have to raise this issue when examining reports by States parties, as a violation of the obligation under article 2(1) ICESCR* 'to achieving progressively the full realization of the rights recognised in that Covenant,' ie taking measures geared to progressively realise and promote economic, social and cultural rights.[27]

This passage squarely raises the issue of the relation between existing international human rights treaties and the EU Charter. What happens if the EU offers a lower level of protection than other instruments, or if it fails to 'progressively realise and promote' these rights? Most human rights treaties provide for complaints procedures, but applications could not be brought against the EU itself: it is not a contracting party to any of these instruments. The UN Committee, however, suggested that the *Member States* might be held accountable if the EU were to adopt a Charter that fall short of their own obligations. Is this bluff? Is it a realistic scenario?

An answer might be found in Strasbourg, where a similar argument was raised several times. The fact that the EU was not and still is not, a party to the ECHR did not prevent claims about the Union from being brought against the Member States instead. Two groups of cases may be distinguished: (a) complaints addressed against all Member States, the argument being that the Member States may be held collectively responsible for violations of the Convention by Union institutions, and (b) complaints addressed against a particular Member State which acted as *longa manus* of the Union.

Interestingly, in one of its very first decisions—in 1958!—the European Commission of Human Rights observed that if a State party to the ECHR concludes another international agreement which disables it from performing its obligations under the Convention, it will be answerable for any resultant breach of its obligations thereunder.[28] Since there is no reason to assume that this principle does not apply to international agreements establishing an international organisation, the Commission's decision seemed to open the door to 'Member State responsibility' for the conduct of international organisations.

---

[27] Doc CHARTE 4315, CONTRIB 182, of 24 May 2000 (emphasis added).
[28] ECommHR, 10 June 1958, *X & X. v FRG* (Appl No 235/56), *Yearbook ECHR* vol 2 (1958–1959), p 300.

Indeed, in the 1980s the Commission dealt with a series of cases in which it expressly left open the possibility that the Member States are answerable for violations of the ECHR by Community institutions. All cases were rejected, however, on other grounds.[29]

In 1990 the Commission changed its position. In the well-known case of *M & Co,* it found that the transfer of powers to an international organisation is not incompatible with the Convention provided that within that organisation fundamental rights receive an 'equivalent protection.'[30] The ECJ was considered to offer this 'equivalent protection.' The principle established by *M & Co* was later applied to a fairly large number of cases concerning alleged Community violations: all these complaints were rejected without much ado. Apparently the Strasbourg Commission did not want to force domestic authorities to review Community measures prior to their implementation—which would, of course, be a serious obstacle on the road of European integration. Likewise in *Pafitis,* a case concerning the reasonable-time requirement of Article 6 ECHR, the Court refused to take into consideration the time needed by the ECJ for delivering a preliminary ruling. The Court observed that:

> to take it into account would adversely affect the system instituted by Article 177 of the EEC treaty and work against the aim pursued in substance in that Article.[31]

Thus judicial restraint characterised the Strasbourg decisions in this area in the 1990s. In 1999, however, the European Court took a more assertive approach. In *Matthews* the Court observed that:

> The Convention does not exclude the transfer of competences to international organisations provided that Convention rights continue to be 'secured.' Member States' responsibility therefore continues even after such a transfer.[32]

The facts of the *Matthews* case were rather specific, though, and a more straightforward decision of the Strasbourg Court was needed. An opportunity was offered by the case of *Guérin,* where a French company brought a complaint against the 15 Member States for a judgment delivered by the ECJ; but the application was rejected as manifestly ill-founded.[33] Then the case of *Senator Lines* seemed destined to become the leading case in this area; it was assigned to the Grand Chamber of the European Court of Human Rights. The applicant in the case was a German company that complained of a breach of the right to a fair trial (Article 6 ECHR) by the Court of First Instance and the European

---

[29] See, eg: ECommHR, 9 December 1987, *Tête v France* (Appl No 11123/84), DR 54, p 76; ECommHR, 19 January 1989, *Dufay v EC and its Member States* (Appl No 13539/88).

[30] ECommHR, 9 February 1990, *M & Co v FRG* (Appl No 13258/87), DR 64, p 144; *Yearbook ECHR* vol 33 (1990), p 51.

[31] ECtHR, 26 February 1998, *Pafitis ao v Greece* (Reports 1998, p 457; Appl No 20323/92), s 95.

[32] ECtHR, 18 February 1999, *Matthews v the UK* (Reports 1999–I, p 251; Appl No 24833/94), s 32.

[33] ECtHR, 4 July 2000, *Guérin Automobiles v les 15 Etats de l'Union Européenne* (Appl No 51717/99). The Court considered the application inadmissible, without deciding whether it was competent *ratione personae* to hear the complaint.

Court of Justice. Unfortunately the case was declared inadmissible in March 2004 on factual grounds.[34] Also in the case of *Bankovic,* concerning military actions by NATO, the issue of collective Member State responsibility was touched upon, but left unresolved.[35]

With respect to the second group of cases, which concerns complaints addressed against specific Member States which implement EU law, the Strasbourg case-law is ambiguous too. On the one hand a straightforward approach is adopted when Contracting Parties act in order to execute international obligations, for instance under an extradition treaty with a third country:

> Under Article 1 of the Convention the member States are responsible for all acts and omissions of their domestic organs allegedly violating the Convention regardless of whether the act or omission in question is a consequence of domestic law or regulations or of the necessity to comply with international obligations.[36]

This means that the rule whereby a State is accountable for human rights violations by its own authorities, also applies where these authorities implement EU law. Indeed, in *Cantoni* the Strasbourg Court reviewed the quality of French rules relating to the sale of medicinal products, without attaching any significance to the fact that these rules had been adopted in order to implement an EC directive.[37] Yet the Strasbourg bodies failed to follow that line in the cases of *M & Co* and *Pafitis* mentioned above. Clarification may be expected from two cases that are currently pending before the Strasbourg Court: *Bosphorus Airlines v Ireland* and *Emesa Sugar v the Netherlands*. Both raise the question to what extent an individual Member State may be held responsible for the implementation of an ECJ ruling by its domestic courts.

The case of *Bosphorus Airlines* concerns the seizure by the Irish authorities of an aircraft which Bosphorus had leased from Yugoslav Airlines JAT. When the aircraft was in Ireland for maintenance, in 1993, it was seized under an EC Regulation which implemented the UN sanctions against the Federal Republic of Yugoslavia (Serbia and Montenegro). When Bosphorus challenged the retention of the aircraft, the Irish Supreme Court referred a preliminary question to the ECJ on whether the aircraft was covered by the relevant Regulation. The answer was in the affirmative: the ECJ considered that the general interest outweighed the individual rights of Bosphorus.[38] Subsequently the Supreme Court applied the decision of the ECJ and rejected Bosphorus's appeal. The aircraft was the only one ever seized under the relevant EC and UN regulations.

---

[34] ECtHR, 10 March 2004, *Senator Lines GmbH v Austria ao* (Appl No 56672/00).

[35] ECtHR, 21 December 2001, *Bankovic ao v Belgium ao* (Reports 2001–VII, p 333; Appl No 52207/99), s 83.

[36] ECommHR, 9 February 1990, *M & Co v FRG* (Appl No 13258/87), DR 64, p 144; *Yearbook ECHR* vol 33 (1990), p 51.

[37] ECtHR, 15 November 1996, *Cantoni v France* (*Reports* 1996, p 1617), s 30. See also: the British position in *Watson & Belmann* [1976] ECR p 1207, at p 1191, quoted in s II(c)(1).

[38] ECJ, Case C–84/95, *Bosphorus* [1996] ECR I–3953.

Bosphorus then brought a complaint in Strasbourg under Article 1 of Protocol No 1 (protection of property), arguing that it had to bear an excessive burden resulting from the manner in which the Irish State applied the sanctions regime and that it suffered significant financial loss. Four years later, in September 2001, the Strasbourg Court held a hearing on the admissibility and merits of the application, following which the case was declared admissible.[39] More than two years later the Chamber relinquished jurisdiction in favour of the Grand Chamber. In May 2004 the President of the Court gave the European Commission leave to intervene as a third party, and in September 2004 the Court decided to devote a *second* hearing to the case. The unusual length of the procedure suggests that the case is considered as highly sensitive.

The case of *Emesa Sugar* relates to the way in which the procedure before the ECJ is organised. Emesa was a party in proceedings before a Dutch court which referred questions to the ECJ for a preliminary ruling. When the case was pending before the ECJ, after the Advocate General had delivered his Opinion, Emesa sought leave to submit written observations in order to respond to the AG's submissions. The Statute of the ECJ and its Rules of Procedure make no provision for this. However, Emesa based its request on Article 6 ECHR and the well-established case-law of the Strasbourg Court according to which the concept of a fair hearing implies the right to adversarial proceedings. This requires that the parties to criminal or civil proceedings must have the opportunity to have knowledge of and comment on all evidence adduced or observations filed, with a view to influencing the court's decision.[40] The Strasbourg Court has consistently held that this principle also applies to the submissions of the Advocates General before the highest national jurisdictions.[41] Emesa took the view that this case-law also applies to the Opinion delivered before the ECJ by the AG and accordingly sought leave to reply to it.

In deciding on this request, the ECJ first reiterated its adherence to fundamental rights and confirmed the special significance of the European Convention. It then examined the status and role of the AG within the Community's judicial system. The ECJ concluded that the case-law of the European Court of Human Rights 'does not appear to be transposable to the Opinion of the Court's Advocates General.'[42] It remains to be seen whether the grounds advanced by the ECJ are convincing,[43] but in any case Emesa's application was dismissed.

---

[39] ECtHR, 13 September 2001, *Bosphorus Airways v Ireland* (Appl No 45036/98).

[40] See, eg: ECtHR, 18 March 1997, *Mantovanelli v France* (Reports 1997, p 436; Appl No 21497/93), s 33; 3 March 2000, *Krcmár v Czech Republic* (Appl No 35376/97), s 40.

[41] See, eg: ECtHR, 30 October 1991, *Borgers v Belgium* (Series A, vol 214–B; Appl No 12005/86), ss 26–29, and 20 February 1996, *Vermeulen v Belgium* (Reports 1996, p 224), ss 29–30.

[42] ECJ, Case C–17/98, *Emesa Sugar (Free Zone) NV v Aruba* (Order) [2000] ECR I–665.

[43] For a more detailed discussion, see the author's annotation in (2000) 37 *CML Rev* pp 983–990, and D Spielmann in (2000) *Revue trimestrielle des droits de l'homme* No 43. See also: the later case of *Kress,* following which it seems difficult to support the ECJ's position in *Emesa* (ECtHR, 7 June 2001, *Kress v France* (Appl No 39594/98)).

Following the preliminary ruling of the ECJ, the Dutch court decided the case accordingly. Emesa then brought a complaint in Strasbourg against the Netherlands. Its main argument is that the Netherlands is responsible for the fact that the Dutch court, in applying the ECJ's ruling, relied on a judgment delivered in breach of Article 6.[44]

2. Meaning for the FRA

Which lessons for the Fundamental Rights Agency can be drawn from the above? Clearly the FRA is not likely to become involved in individual cases. But our brief discussion of cases like *Cantoni, Senator Lines, Bosphorus Airlines* and *Emesa Sugar* leads to three conclusions that are also relevant to the future mandate of the FRA.

First, the consistent acknowledgement by the ECJ of the importance of the ECHR is not, in itself, an absolute guarantee that ECJ rulings will always be in line with the Strasbourg case-law. Different interpretations may occur; the balancing of competing interests may lead to different outcomes. *Bosphorus Airlines* and *Emesa Sugar* may serve as illustrations: although one cannot predict their outcome, the least we can say is that arguable claims are brought in Strasbourg. Of course this is not to suggest that the ECJ acted in bad faith when deciding cases such as *Bosphorus*; the domestic courts too arrive at conclusions which are not always shared in Strasbourg. This is the reason why one should not expect too much from Article 52 (3) of the Charter (Article II–112 (3) of the Constitution), which states that insofar as the Charter contains rights that correspond with rights guaranteed by the ECHR, the meaning and scope shall be the same. The idea behind it is excellent, but there is no guarantee that this will work in practice.

Secondly, a perceived failure of the Union institutions to live up to the standards of the ECHR may easily lead to procedures before the European Court of Human Rights—even in the absence of EU accession to the ECHR. It is true that the case-law in this area is still unsettled. An unambiguous doctrine of 'Member State responsibility' is yet to be developed. But the trend in the Court's case-law is clear: at the very least a State is responsible where its own authorities, in implementing EU law, violate the ECHR. This prospect in itself should be enough to persuade the FRA to do what Article I–9 of the Constitutional Treaty already demands: take the ECHR seriously. Needless to add that this analysis should not be limited to the ECHR: exactly the same line of reasoning can be followed with respect to other human rights treaties to which the EU Member States are bound.

Thirdly, as was noted in the introduction, Article I–9 of the Constitution provides that the Union shall accede to the ECHR. The good news is that

---

[44] *Emesa Sugar* (registered as Appl No 62023/00) has been 'communicated' to the Dutch government; the Commission intervened. An admissibility decision is expected in 2005.

accession will take away the need to bring cases against EU Member States about situations that are to a considerable extent beyond their control. The bad news, however, is the way in which Article I–9 has been formulated. It may give rise to *a contrario* arguments: the Union may accede to the ECHR, but it does not have the competence to accede to *other* human rights treaties. It should be stressed that this has never been the intention of the drafters of the Constitution. In its explanation of the draft text of 26 May 2003, the Praesidium of the Convention emphasised that there are no reasons at all for such a restrictive interpretation.[45] It is important to remember this and to realise that the door is open for EU accession to *other* human rights treaties. There are two reasons to make use of this possibility.[46] A 'positive' reason is that the EU, in acceding to international human rights treaties such as CERD, could strengthen the position of these instruments and demonstrate its commitment to international human rights standards. A 'negative' reason is that a failure to ratify may lead to a situation where EU Member States are held accountable for EU violations of these treaties, as was evidenced by Contribution No 182 from the United Nations Committee on Economic, Social and Cultural Rights.

So if the lesson of section II(a)(2) was that the Fundamental Rights Agency should take into account the EU Charter on the one hand and the ECHR and common constitutional traditions on the other—we can now add a fourth source: other human rights treaties.

c) Third Dimension: Promotion of Human Rights

In the two 'dimensions' discussed so far, the Union's role was essentially passive in the sense that the institutions accepted that they are bound by fundamental rights standards or that the Union is subjected, albeit indirectly, to external review. The third 'dimension' relates to the Union in an active role: advocating compliance with human rights. Since the Union's human rights policy vis-à-vis third countries is already dealt with elsewhere in this volume,[47] we will concentrate mainly on the way in which the Union seeks to promote human rights in the Member States—and what this means for the FRA.

---

[45] CONV 724/03, annex 2, p 58: 'This paragraph may ask that the Union *seek* accession only in the specific case of the ECHR; however this particular formula is not in any way intended to rule out the *possibility* of accession to other conventions. As the Praesidium has already pointed out, only the European Convention on Human Rights is mentioned in this paragraph because of the fact that a Court of Justice opinion in 1996 had rejected Community competence to accede to that Convention on the basis of considerations specific to it.' The opinion referred to is Opinion 2/94 [1996] ECR I–1759, indicating that accession to the ECHR warrants an unequivocal legal basis.

[46] See also, in this regard: the proposals made in the Report on the situation of fundamental rights in the European Union in 2003, EU Network of Independent Experts on Fundamental Rights, 2004, pp 20–21.

[47] See the contribution of MK Bulterman in ch 10 of this volume.

1. General Features

The position of the EU vis-à-vis its own Member States raises many interesting and sensitive questions of a constitutional nature.[48] Are the Member States obliged, *as a matter of EU law,* to respect fundamental rights? Which fundamental rights? Do the EU institutions have a role to play in supervising domestic compliance with these standards? Can they take measures, or should they be able to do so, if a Member States violates human rights? Should the EU actively promote human rights in the Member States? Should the capacity of the Union to involve itself with domestic human rights be limited to situations were violations threaten to disturb the internal market? Or should *any* violation of human rights be a concern to the Union? If so, how does this relate to the activities of the Council of Europe, and in what way will this affect the position of the European Court of Human Rights? What is the impact of the introduction of European citizenship, the creation of an 'Area of Freedom, Security and Justice,' and the adoption of the Charter?

Like in the 'first dimension' discussed above, it was the ECJ that initiated this discussion. The Court decided in the late 1980s that the general principles of Community law, including fundamental rights, do not only bind the institutions, but also the Member States where they implement Community law.[49] It later added that the same applies if Member States restrict the common market freedoms (free movement of workers, of services, of goods, of capital): any such restriction should be in conformity with human rights.[50] It later adopted a more general formula, as a result of which the present state of the case-law can be summarised as follows:

> according to the Court's case-law, where national legislation falls *within the field of application of Community law* the Court, in a reference for a preliminary ruling, must give the national court all the guidance as to interpretation necessary to enable it to assess the compatibility of that legislation with the fundamental rights whose observance the Court ensures.[51]

It is worth observing that it may be easier, and therefore more attractive, for individual applicants to try and get their human rights claim before the ECJ than before the European Court of Human Rights: any court, even at first instance, can refer preliminary questions to the Luxembourg Court, whereas Strasbourg can only be accessed after a lengthy process whereby all domestic remedies are exhausted. The individual may not be bothered too much by the fact that an *authentic* interpretation of the ECHR can only be obtained in Strasbourg: he

---

[48] See, eg: A von Bogdandy, 'The European Union as a human rights organization? Human rights and the core of the EU' (2000) 37 *CML Rev* pp 1307–1338.

[49] ECJ, Case C–5/88, *Wachauf* [1989] ECR p 2609, s 19.

[50] ECJ, Case C–260/89, *ERT* [1991] ECR p I–2925, s 43.

[51] ECJ, Case C–71/02, *Karner* (judgment of 25 March 2004, not yet reported), s 49, emphasis added.

will happily rely on any 'European' ruling in his favour. And if the ECJ happens to rule against him, he can always exhaust domestic remedies and try his luck in Strasbourg.[52] Accordingly the same case may be subsequently examined by the ECJ and the European Court of Human Rights—which in turn raises the issue of possibly diverging interpretations of human rights standards.

That risk was highlighted by the UK government already in the case of *Watson & Belmann* (1976). As to the question whether the ECJ should review if Italian rules relating to the registration of foreigners complied with the ECHR, the UK observed:

> Any exercise of overlapping jurisdiction by the institutions established by the Convention and by the Court of Justice of the European Communities could give rise to confusion and conflict. The generalised and somewhat imprecise language of the Convention and of the exceptions to which most of the rights set out in Section I thereof are subject can give rise to questions of construction which fall with the ultimate jurisdiction of the institutions created by the Convention. Similarly, it is for those institutions alone to make a ruling on a national measure which is contrary to the Convention but compatible with Community law.[53]

Behind this argument was a more general sentiment that the ECJ ought not to review national measures for their compliance with human rights standards. In response to this proposition Advocate General Trabucchi stated that the ECJ could not examine alleged infringements of fundamental rights by a State body 'to the same extent to which it could do so in reviewing the validity of Community acts.'[54] The issue was left undecided in *Watson & Belmann*. But some ten years later the ECJ did assume the power to review domestic measures from a human rights perspective, provided that they are 'within the scope of Community law.' The ECJ never adopted AG Trabucchi's suggestion that the fundamental rights test should not be equally demanding when national measures are under review.

The result is a constant flow of cases, usually through the preliminary rulings procedure, where it was alleged that national authorities violate human rights: *Demirel* on the German decision to expel the spouse of a Turkish worker, *Cinétèque* on the French restrictions of the sale of videotapes of films, *Grogan* on the Irish prohibition of information about abortion facilities abroad, *Konstantinidis* on the way in German authorities transcribed a Greek name, *Kremzow* on the consequences for a criminal conviction of the finding that the trial had been unfair—and more recently cases such as *Carpenter* and *Baumbast* on the free movement of persons and their family members, *Österreichischer Rundfunk* and *Lindqvist* on the right to privacy, *Booker Aquaculture* on the

---

[52] For an example (apart from *Bosphorus* etc, mentioned in section II(b)(1)), compare ECJ, case C–206/91, *Koua Poirrez* [1992] ECR p I–6685, with ECtHR, 30 September 2003, *Koua Poirrez v France* (Appl No 40892/98).

[53] ECJ, Case 118/75, *Watson & Belmann* [1976] ECR p 1207, at p 1191. Note that the quote offers support for the concept of 'Member State responsibility' discussed in s II(b)(1).

[54] Opinion in case 118/75, *Watson & Belmann* [1976] ECR p 1207.

absence of financial compensation following the destruction of fish infected by a contagious disease, and *Karner* on compatibility with the freedom of expression of Austrian restrictions on advertisement.[55]

The newest fashion in this branch of jurisprudence is that *Member States* invoke fundamental rights in order to justify policies which might otherwise be deemed incompatible with EU law. An early example was offered by the Dutch 'media cases' where the Netherlands government sought to rely on Article 10 ECHR in order to defend restrictions applying to broadcasting corporations.[56] More recently the Austrian Government successfully invoked its obligations under Article 11 ECHR in order to justify its permission for a demonstration on the public highway which hampered the free movement of goods.[57] And in October 2004 the ECJ accepted that German authorities prohibited the commercial exploitation of 'laser games' on the ground that these games, to the extent that they simulate the killing of human beings, are incompatible with human dignity, as protected by Article 1 of the German Constitution.[58]

Like in the first 'dimension' discussed above, the judicial interest in domestic compliance with human rights was gradually joined by political interest and legislative activities. In the early 1990s the European Parliament started to discuss human rights in the Union and adopted annual resolutions on this issue. Measures to fight discrimination and racism were adopted. Harmonisation occurred in areas where the internal market suffered from diverging national standards, for instance in the field of data protection.[59] The development of the 'Area of Freedom, Security and Justice' has led to wide-ranging discussions on issues as diverse as asylum, migration and border policies, the protection of national security, crime prevention, judicial cooperation in criminal matters and the approximation of procedural and substantive criminal law.[60] The potential impact of all these matters on fundamental rights is clear—and so is the need for

---

[55] ECJ, Case 12/86, *Demirel* [1987] ECR, p 1417; Joined Cases 60–61/84, *Cinétèque* [1985] ECR p 2627; Case 159/90, *Grogan* [1991] ECR p I–4741; Case C–168/91, *Konstantinidis* [1993] ECR p I–1191; Case C–299/95, *Kremzow* [1997] ECR 1997, p I–2629; Case C–60/00, *Carpenter* (judgment of 11 July 2002, not yet reported); Case C–413/99, *Baumbast* (judgment of 17 September 2002, not yet reported); Joined Cases C–465/00, C–138/01 and C–139/01, *Österreichischer Rundfunk* (judgment of 20 May 2003, not yet reported); Case C–101/01, *Lindqvist* (judgment of 6 November 2003, not yet reported); Joined Cases C–20/00 and C–64/00, *Booker Aquaculture ao* (judgment of 10 July 2003, not yet reported); Case C–71/02, *Karner* (judgment of 25 March 2004, not yet reported).

[56] ECJ, Case 353/89, *Commission v the Netherlands* [1991] ECR I–4097. See also: Case C–377/98, *Netherlands v Parliament and Council* [2001] ECR p I–7079. On the latter case see especially the Opinion of AG Jacobs, s 197: 'the rights invoked by the Netherlands are indeed fundamental rights, respect for which must be ensured in the Community legal order. The right to human dignity is perhaps the most fundamental right of all, and is now expressed in Art 1 of the Charter of Fundamental Rights . . .] It must be accepted that any Community instrument infringing those rights would be unlawful.'

[57] ECJ, Case C–112/00, *Schmidberger* (judgment of 12 June 2003, not yet reported).

[58] ECJ, Case C–36/02, *Omega Spielhallen* (judgment of 14 October 2004, not yet reported).

[59] See, eg: Dir 95/46, *OJ* L 281, 32.

[60] For the latest overview of what is now called the 'Hague Programme,' see the Presidency Conclusions of the Brussels European Council (4–5 November 2004), doc 14292/04.

mutual confidence in the level of human rights protection in each of the Member States.

Meanwhile the Treaty of Amsterdam introduced Article 7 EU. This provision allows for measures against Member States if there is a serious and persistent breach of the fundamental values on which the EU is based, notably human rights. The procedure of Article 7 EU was enhanced by the Treaty of Nice, following the crisis surrounding the participation of the right-wing *FPÖ* in the Austrian government. Action may now be taken if there is 'only' a serious risk that things may go wrong in a Member State. The arrangement of Article 7 EU returns in Article I–59 of the Constitutional Treaty. It remains to be seen how this procedure will be applied in practice, and which level of transparency and input by third parties (such as, possibly, the FRA and/or the Network of independent experts on fundamental rights) the Member States are willing to accept.[61]

If one examines the developments in this area so far, the overall trend would seem to be one of growing acceptance that the EU has a legitimate interest in securing adequate respect for human rights in its Member States—either through judicial procedures before the ECJ or through political pressure on the basis of, eventually, Article 7 EU. Yet the '*Watson & Belmann* sentiments' of the mid-1970s re-emerged when the EU Charter of Fundamental Rights was negotiated. Article 51 (1) of the Charter (Article II–111 (1) of the Constitution) provides:

> The provisions of the Charter are addressed to the institutions, bodies, offices and agencies of the Union with due regard to the principle of subsidiarity *and to the Member States only when they are implementing Union law*.

The formula 'when they are implementing Union law' reflects current practice only to a very limited extent. It is either a mistaken formulation, or a clear attempt to roll back the existing case-law of the ECJ: many of the cases mentioned above did not concern the implementation of EU law, but related to very diverse situations which were considered to fall 'within the field of application of Community law.' It remains to be seen if the ECJ will adapt its jurisprudence and follow the narrower wording of Article 51 (1) Charter. There is no legal obligation to do so: on the basis of Article I–9 (3) of the Constitutional Treaty the ECJ could simply continue to review national measures 'within the scope of Community law.'

The narrow formulation of Article 51 (1) Charter is also by-passed in another sense. The political mechanism of Article 7 EU (Article I–59 Constitutional Treaty) may be triggered by human rights violations that are unconnected to the functioning of the internal market. Rightly so: if respect for human rights and adherence to democracy are preconditions to membership, then it is only

---

[61] For a first exploration, see the Commission's *Communication on Art 7 EU—Respect for and promotion of the values on which the Union is based*, COM (2003) 606 final of 15 October 2003.

logical that continuing respect for these values is a legitimate cause of concern for the Union—even if the violations happen to occur in a situation where the authorities are not implementing Union law.

2. Meaning for the FRA

Which lessons for the Fundamental Rights Agency can we draw? It was noted in the introduction that the uncertainty surrounding the FRA's tasks complicates a discussion of the standards that it should apply. This is especially true here. If the FRA is to confine its activities, as far as the Member States are concerned, to situations where they are 'implementing Union law,' then the EU Charter of Fundamental Rights is an appropriate standard. Article 51 (1) of the Charter expressly confirms that the provisions of the Charter 'are addressed to' the Member States in this situation.

The next question is whether the Charter is also an appropriate standard—and even the most appropriate standard—if the FRA is going to monitor the human rights performance of the Member States *in general*, ie, also covering situations where the Member States are not 'implementing Union law.' To avoid misunderstandings: I do think that there is a strong argument to be made for such an 'overall monitoring.' If the Union is competent to take measures against Member States in case of serious and persistent breaches of human rights, then it has a legitimate interest in monitoring the quality of human rights protection in the Member States. As the Commission suggested in its Public Consultation document, the Fundamental Rights Agency may be involved in this process.[62] However, it is one thing to state that the Agency has a task here; it is another thing to decide which standards the FRA should use when collecting and analysing data on the domestic protection of human rights.

Here the FRA faces two options. One option would be to apply the EU Charter to all instances of Member State action, irrespective of whether they are 'implementing Union law' as Article 51 (1) Charter puts it. This is the approach which the Network of Independent Experts on Fundamental Rights has adopted, basing itself, in the final analysis, on Article 7 EU (Article I–59 Constitutional Treaty).[63] I am not well placed to comment on the quality of the Network's reports, but it seems difficult to deny that the Network's approach has several advantages: it applies a coherent set of standards to all areas of Member State action; its reports, due to their broad range, have an obvious added value to the work undertaken by other supervisory bodies.

The second option would be more cautious. Given the hesitation among Member States to accept EU human rights supervision in situations which are not about 'implementing Union law,' as evidenced by the formulation of Article 51 (1) Charter, the FRA might prefer, at this stage of development of EU law, to

---

[62] This is not the place to discuss the relationship between the FRA and the Network of Independent Experts on Fundamental Rights; see the contribution of M Scheinin to this volume, ch 3.
[63] EU Network, *Fundamental Rights in the EU in 2003*, pp 10–12.

use existing human rights treaties rather than the Charter as a reference. Admittedly the Charter was adopted at the highest political levels and may be seen as the most authoritative embodiment of the common values on which the EU is based, but at the same time Article 51 (1) Charter intended to limit its applicability. It could therefore be argued that, when it comes to domestic affairs, the legitimacy of the ECHR is stronger than that of the Charter. The dilemma is, however, that the EU institutions are not in a position to give *authoritative* rulings on the question whether the ECHR, or any other international instrument, has been violated—that is the competence of the European Court of Human Rights and the other supervisory bodies. Therefore, if the second option were chosen, the FRA should closely follow the jurisprudence of these bodies and base its own policies vis-à-vis the Member States on their pronouncements.

III. CONCLUSION: IN SEARCH OF POLARIS

It is clear that the EU Charter will be 'an essential reference document' for the FRA. Yet the Charter is not the only source of fundamental rights: Article I–9 (3) of the Constitution confirms that the ECHR and common constitutional traditions will continue to be general principles of EU law. There is no reason why the FRA should ignore these sources, also because the interpretation and application of many Charter provisions is still uncertain. As was noted above, the Charter's light is still too diffuse to serve as a reliable lodestar to the FRA.

Likewise other international instruments for the protection of human rights 'on which the Member States have collaborated or to which they are signatories' may offer additional standards. An extra incentive to take the ECHR and other human rights treaties into account is that a failure to do so may lead to procedures whereby the Member States are held accountable. The importance of case-law should be emphasised in this respect: to take into account ECHR means to take into account the Strasbourg jurisprudence.

Apart from legal arguments there are, of course, also policy arguments that support the view that the FRA should not limit its reference standards to the EU Charter. Like the EU, the FRA is to function in a global environment. It should not be perceived as an isolated structure that pays no attention to the international developments in the field of human rights. Moreover, if the FRA were to be involved in the formulation of the Union's human rights policy vis-à-vis third countries, it would be reasonable to base its activities on the international bill of rights rather than on the Charter alone. In a way the same argument might be made when it comes to monitoring the Member States in areas where they act autonomously: it might be sensible to rely on the ECHR and other treaties to which they themselves adhered. It may be true that the legitimacy of the Union is enhanced if its *institutions* are subjected to high and innovative standards in the field of human rights, as embodied in the Charter—but the same may not necessarily be the case if the EU attempts to subject *the Member States* to these standards. It would already be quite an achievement if the Union were to amplify the obligations that the Member States themselves have assumed under the ECHR and other treaties.

A final remark is that the Agency, in addition to applying existing standards, could also be involved in the development of new concepts. To mention one example: Europe is arguably in need of a new 'private international law of human rights.' To many, the essence of Europe is the diversity of its nations. Yet the co-existence of diverse cultures may give rise to legal problems, especially in an era characterised by mobility. Accordingly one of the challenges facing the Union and its Member States is to strike the right balance between preservation of national identity, also in the sphere of human rights, and securing overall compliance with minimum standards to an extent that the Union can actually function. Spouses who have contracted a same-sex marriage in the Netherlands may wish to travel to another Member State with the aim to continue their marital life there. Pregnant women who wish to obtain an abortion may travel from Ireland to Great Britain. Soft drugs which are freely available in one Member State may be sold to citizens from Member States that pursue a zero tolerance policy. The EU Constitution does not give guidelines on how to deal with these and other consequences of diversity. Perhaps the FRA could contribute to the development of new standards that can guide 21st century Europe.

10

The Contribution of the Agency to the External Policies of the European Union

MIELLE BULTERMAN*

I. INTRODUCTION

CAN THE FUNDAMENTAL Rights Agency (FRA) make a contribution to the commitment of the European Union to include human rights considerations in its external policies? It is tempting to speculate how, by the introduction of what new instruments or bodies, the European Union's external policies would be served best. The discussion here, however, is confined to examining the possibilities of the FRA as perceived by the European Council on Decision of 13 December 2003 to make a valuable contribution to the Union's external policies. For that purpose, two aspects of human rights as an element of the external policies of the European Union need to be distinguished.

On the one hand, the European Union has to make sure that its external action is not in violation of the human rights to which it is bound. This aspect of human rights as an element of the Union's external policies relates to the obligation for the EU itself to respect human rights and is addressed in section II. On the other hand, the promotion of human rights is a foreign policy objective of the European Union: through its external action it actively seeks to promote respect for human rights by third countries. This aspect of the Union's external human rights dimension[1] will be examined in section III. Subsequently,

* Senior Lecturer, Europa Instituut, Leiden University. The author would like to thank Rick Lawson and Olivier De Schutter for their valuable comments on earlier drafts of this article.
[1] The term 'EU's external human rights dimension' is used here to comprise both aspects of human rights as an element of the external policies of the European Union. It comprises on the one hand the obligation of the Union to respect fundamental rights when engaged in external action and on the other hand the commitment of the institutions of the Union to promote respect for human rights in third countries. The term 'EU human rights policy' is used when reference is made to the latter aspect of human rights: the promotion and protection of human rights as a foreign policy objective.

we will focus in section IV on the changes that the entry into force of the Treaty establishing a Constitution for Europe (Constitutional Treaty) would bring. Finally, the question whether the new FRA can make a contribution to the EU's external policies is addressed in section V.

II. THE OBLIGATION TO RESPECT HUMAN RIGHTS AND EXTERNAL EU POLICIES

Neither the EU Treaty nor the EC Treaty contains a provision in which the relevance of human rights in the Union's external relations is spelled out. Throughout both Treaties, however, various references to human rights can be found which have implications for the Union's external action.

First and foremost, the relevance of Article 6(2) EU and the EU Charter of Fundamental Rights for external EU action need to be addressed. Article 6(2) EU codifies the case law of the ECJ on the European Union's human rights obligations:

> The Union shall respect fundamental rights, as guaranteed by the European Convention for the protection of human rights and fundamental freedoms signed in Rome on 4 November 1950 and as they result from the constitutional traditions common to the Member States, as general principles of Community law.

Article 6(2) EU extends to all actions of the European Union, thus including external action of the Community and action undertaken within the framework of the CFSP and the third pillar. The fact that the Union's external action may produce effects, or even take place, outside the territory of the European Union does not exclude the fact that such action has to comply with Article 6(2) EU. The same is true for the EU Charter of Fundamental Rights. According to Article 51, the provisions of the EU Charter are addressed 'to the Institutions, bodies, offices and agencies of the Union with due regard of the principle of subsidiarity and to the Member States only when they are implementing Union law.'[2] The conclusion that the Union's external action has to be in conformity with the EU Charter of Fundamental Rights is by no means a revolutionary view: both the Commission and the Council have confirmed the relevance of the Charter for external EU action. In its 2001 Communication on the Union's external human rights policy, the Commission stated:

---

[2] For the same opinion see: J Wouters, 'The EU Charter of Fundamental Rights: Some Reflections on its External Dimension' (2001) *Maastricht Journal of European and Comparative Law*, pp 3–10. See also: *Thematic Comment no 2: Fundamental Rights in the External Activities of the European Union in the Fields of Justice and Asylum and Immigration in 2003* of the EU Network of Independent Experts on Fundamental Rights for a detailed analysis of the applicability of the Charter of Fundamental Rights to external action of the European Union, available at: europa.eu.int/comm/justice_home/ cfr_cdf/doc/thematic_comments_2003_en.pdf.

the Commission consistent with its commitment to respect the EU Charter will ensure that in the formulation of other policies, any negative effect on human rights and democratisation is always avoided, and wherever possible, policies are adapted to have a positive impact.[3]

In addition, the Council has made reference to the Charter in its Conclusions on the EU's Role in Promoting Human Rights and Democratisation in Third Countries of 25 June 2001.[4]

While it is clear that external EU action has to comply with Article 6 EU and the rights laid down in the EU Charter of Fundamental Rights, it is less obvious what this obligation means in practice. So far, the case law of the ECJ provides little guidance in this respect. An important restriction on the ECJ's control over EU external action, is the fact that the Court has no jurisdiction over the CFSP and only limited jurisdiction over Police and Judicial Cooperation in Criminal matters. However, as the ECJ has jurisdiction over European Community law, the EU's external policies do not escape its control completely. Thus the ECJ has ruled on the suspension of the EC agreement with Yugoslavia after the outbreak of hostilities in that country,[5] on EC measures implementing economic sanctions against Iraq[6] and on EC and national measures implementing the UN sanction regime against the Federal Republic of Yugoslavia.[7] The latter case concerned a dispute before an Irish court over the impoundment by the Irish authorities of an aircraft which was leased by the Turkish company Bosphorus. According to the Irish authorities the impounded aircraft fell under the EC legislation implementing the UN sanction regime[8] against Federal Republic of Yugoslavia since it was owned by the Yugoslav national airline JAT. Bosphorus claimed that the impoundment amounted to a breach of its fundamental rights, in particular its right to peaceful enjoyment of its property. In its ruling, the ECJ observed that according to established case law the fundamental right invoked by Bosphorus is not absolute and that its exercise may be subject to restrictions justified by objectives of general interest by the Community. It continued:

> Any measure imposing sanctions has, by definition, consequences which affect the right to property and the freedom to pursue a trade or business, thereby causing harm to persons who are in no way responsible for the situation which led to the adoption of the sanctions (Section 22).

---

[3] Communication from the Commission to the Council and the European Parliament, *The European Union's Role in Promoting Human Rights and Democratisation in Third Countries*, COM(2001) 252 Final, p 7.

[4] In the introductory part it is stated: 'The Proclamation of the Charter on Fundamental Rights of 10 December 2000 reflects the overriding importance of human rights for all policies and activities of the European Union.'

[5] Case C–162/96 *Racke v Hauptzollamt Mainz* [1998] ECR I–3655.

[6] Case C–124/95 *Centro-Com v Treasury and Bank of England* [1997] ECR I–81.

[7] Case C–85/95 *Bosphorus v Minister for Transport, Energy and Communications and others* [1996] ECR I–3953.

[8] Reg 990/93 of 26 April 1993 concerning trade between the European Economic Community and the Federal Republic of Yugoslavia (Serbia and Montenegro) [1993] L/102/14.

As compared with an objective of general interest so fundamental for the international community, which consists in putting an end to the state of war in the region and to the massive violations of human rights and humanitarian international law in the Republic of Bosnia-Herzegovina, the impounding of the aircraft in question, which is owned by an undertaking based in or operating from the Federal Republic of Yugoslavia, cannot be regarded as inappropriate or disproportionate (Section 26).

One could question whether in this case a right balance was struck by the ECJ between the right to property of Bosphorus and the general interest of putting an end to the war and the human rights violations in the Republic of Bosnia-Herzegovina. The ECJ's conclusion that the impounding of the aircraft of Bosphorus cannot be considered as inappropriate or disproportionate measure is based on a rather abstract test whether an infringement on the right to property can be justified by the general interest pursuit with the UN sanction regime. The ECJ does not pay any attention to the specific circumstances of the case, such as the fact that the agreement between Bosphorus and JAT was concluded bona fide before the outbreak of hostilities and that the payments for the lease were made into a blocked account in accordance with Turkish legislation implementing the UN sanction regime.[9] Whether this approach is compatible with the Strasbourg standard remains to be seen.[10]

While the measure at dispute in *Bosphorus* (the EU sanction regulation) has a clear foreign policy dimension, it affects persons and entities *within* the European Union. With respect to the European Union's obligation to respect the EU Charter of Fundamental Rights when undertaking action that has extra-territorial effect, a parallel may be drawn with the obligations of the Contracting Parties under the ECHR. According to the European Court of Human Rights (ECrtHR), 'The responsibility of Contracting Parties can be involved because of acts of their authorities producing effects outside their own territory.'[11] The obvious question arises as to in what circumstances external action entails responsibility.

This question does not have an easy answer, and the case law of the ECrtHR only provides limited guidance on this point. In the case of *Bankovic*, for example, the ECrtHR declared a complaint about the NATO bombardments on

---

[9] See for a critical analysis: I Canor, '"Can two walk together, except they've agreed?" The relationship between international law and European law: the incorporation of United Nations sanctions against Yugoslavia into European Community law through the perspective of the European Court of Justice' (1998) 35 *CML Rev*, pp 137–187.

[10] The case of *Bosphorus v Ireland* is currently pending before a Grand Chamber of the EcrtHR. The case was declared admissible on 13 September 2001.

[11] *Drozd and Janousek v France and Spain* Series A no 240 (1992), para 91; *Loizidou v.Turkey (preliminary objections)* Series A no 310 (1995), para 62. See for an analysis of state responsibility for acts that take place or have effect outside the territory of the State: RA Lawson, 'The concept of jurisdiction in the European Convention on Human Rights' in PJ Slot and M Bulterman (eds), *Globalisation and Jurisdiction* (Leiden, Kluwer Law International, 2004), pp 240–259. See also F Coomans and MT Kamminga (eds), *Extraterritorial Application of Human Rights Treaties* (Antwerp, Intersentia, 2004).

Belgadro inadmissible, because the applicants had not been 'within the jurisdiction' of the States concerned as is required by Article 1 ECHR to entail responsibility under the ECHR.[12] It seems, however, that the strict approach of the EcrtHR in *Bankovic* is the exception rather than the rule. In many other cases the Court has made it clear that a State is bound by its human rights obligations under the ECHR when it is engaged in extra-territorial action.[13] A recent example is the *Ilascu* judgement,[14] concerning claims against Moldavia and Russia about, inter alia, the detention circumstances in Transdniestria. The ECrtHR held:

> A State's responsibility may also be engaged on account of acts which have sufficiently proximate repercussions on rights guaranteed by the Convention, even if those repercussions occur outside its jurisdiction.

To support this view, the EcrtHR makes reference to its decision in *Soering* case.[15] In that case, the ECrtHR held that the extradition of an individual to a country in which he runs a real risk of treatment in breach of Article 3 ECHR (prohibition of torture or inhuman or degrading treatment or punishment) entails the responsibility of the extraditing state. Obviously, a contracting party cannot be held responsible under the ECHR for human rights violations committed by a third country. The responsibility under the ECHR is established by exposing the individual to the risk that he will be ill-treated in the receiving country.[16] The principles underlying the *Soering* case have also been applied by the Human Rights Committee with respect to the ICCPR.[17] Under both the ECHR and the ICCPR, the responsibility of the contacting party is established by the decision to extradite the individual, not by the treatment actually given to him in the receiving country.

When the external action of a state—or an international organisation—has a direct impact on individuals in third countries, it may be clear that this entails the responsibility of the state or international organisation concerned: 'facticity creates normativity'[18] or 'control entails responsibility.'[19] States and international organisations are thus obliged to take into account the foreseeable impact of their action on the human rights of individuals in third countries. But

---

[12] *Bankovic ao v Belgium and 16 other Contracting States*, 12 December 2001. The question to what extent individual Member States are accountable under the ECHR for acts of their organisation was not addressed by the ECrtHR.

[13] *Loizidou v Turkey* Series A, no 310.

[14] *Ilascu ao v Moldova and Russia*, 8 July 2004.

[15] *Soering v United Kingdom*, 7 July 1989, Series A no 161 (1985).

[16] See, eg: the comment on the *Soering* case in RA Lawson and HG Schermers, *Leading Cases of the European Court of Human Rights* (Nijmegen, Ars Aequi Libri, 1999), p 324.

[17] See, eg: *Ng v Canada*, Communication No 469/1991.

[18] M Scheinin, 'Extraterritorial Effect of the International Covenant on Civil and Political Rights' in F Coomans and MT Kamminga (eds), *Extraterritorial Application of Human Rights Treaties* (Antwerp, Intersentia, 2004), pp 73–82.

[19] RA Lawson, 'Life after Bankovic: On the Extraterritorial Application of the European Convention on Human Rights' in F Coomans and MT Kamminga (eds), *Extraterritorial Application of Human Rights Treaties* (Antwerp, Intersentia, 2004), pp 83–125.

what if the European Union is financially or technically supporting a regime which is violating the human rights of its citizens? Would this amount to a violation of Article 6(2) EU and the EU Charter?

This argument was raised before the ECJ by Bernard Zaoui, whose wife was killed in a Hamas terrorist attack on the Hotel Park in Netanya in Israel. According to Mr Zaoui the suicide attack on the hotel was caused by the Palestinian educational system, more in particular the handbooks which incite hatred towards Israelis. As the largest sponsor of the Palestine society—and thus the Palestinian educational system—the Union was held responsible for the terrorist attack on the hotel. Consequently, Zaoui brought an action on the basis of Article 288 EC (non-contractual liability) before the Court of First Instance (CFI). The CFI held that there was not sufficient evidence to establish a causal link between the Community's financing and the Palestine educational system or between the Palestine educational system and the terrorist attack.[20] The action was thus dismissed.

In Strasbourg a similar case was brought by an Iraqi who was seriously injured while he was working on clearing in Iraq by stepping on an anti-personnel mine of Italian origin. He alleged that the Italian Government sold or allowed to sell anti-personnel mines thus failing to secure his right to life as guaranteed by Article 2 ECHR. The Commission held:

> There is no immediate relationship between the mere supply, even if not properly regulated, of weapons and the possible 'indiscriminate' use thereof in a third country, the latter's action constituting the direct and decisive cause of the accident which the applicant suffered. It follows that the 'adverse consequences' of the failure of Italy to regulate arms transfers to Iraq are 'too remote' to attract the Italian responsibility.[21]

According to the Commission the injuries suffered by the applicant were exclusively attributable to Iraq and the complaint was declared inadmissible.

Both cases are dismissed on similar grounds: the absence of a sufficient link between the disputed act of the International Organisation/State and the human rights violations occurring in third countries. Whether a sufficient link exists requires an appreciation of the factual circumstances. The application of the 'causal link' test as applied by the Commission in the *Tugar* case is very strict, making it rather difficult to hold a State responsible for human rights violations occurring in third countries which were made possible through its (financial or technical) support. One could question whether the approach in *Tugar* is not to strict in view of the ECrtHR's recent case law: doesn't the supply of landmines to a country as Iraq have 'sufficiently proximate repercussions' on the human rights of the people living there?

In any event, it would be in conflict with the importance attached to the EU Charter by the Institutions themselves if this narrow approach was maintained

---

[20] Case T–73/03, *Zaoui ao v Commission*, 23 April 2003, Order of the CFI.
[21] *Rasheed Tugar v Italy*, 18 October 1995.

by the European Union. As was noted above, the Commission has observed with respect to the EU Charter that:

> any negative effect on human rights and democratisation is always avoided, and wherever possible, policies are adapted to have a positive impact[22]

Furthermore, it would be difficult to reconcile such a narrow approach with the importance of human rights as a foreign policy objective (see section III(a)). There thus are sufficient reasons for the European Union to take into account the implications of its external activities on the human rights situation in third countries, even if there would not be an obligation to do so from a strictly legal point of view.

III. HUMAN RIGHTS AS A FOREIGN POLICY OBJECTIVE

a) EU Competence to make Human Rights a Foreign Policy Objective

In Article 11 EU, fifth indent, the aim '[t]o develop and consolidate democracy and the rule of law, and respect for human rights and fundamental freedoms' is explicitly enumerated as one of the objectives of the Common Foreign and Security Policy. There is thus a general mandate for the CFSP to engage in human rights activities. The European Community is not endowed with a similar general competence in the field of human rights. So far, the question of external Community competence in the field of human rights has not been given much attention in practice and legal doctrine, with the exception of the Community's competence to accede to the ECHR. Most authors do not find any difficulty in assuming that the Community is competent to engage in external human rights activities. According to Touscoz, the activities of the Community to promote human rights in third countries '*reposent sur une base juridique solide*' ('are grounded on a solid legal basis').[23] Another author even refers to the competence in the field of the protection and promotion of human rights as a '*compétence naturelle*' ('natural power').[24] However, these views are difficult to reconcile with the fact that the European Community can only act where given the power to do so. Community competence may not be presumed, but requires a legal basis in the EC Treaty. These principles also apply to Community action in the field of human rights.

---

[22] Communication from the Commission to the Council and the European Parliament, *The European Union's Role in Promoting Human Rights and Democratisation in Third Countries*, COM(2001) 252 final, p 7.

[23] See J Touscoz, 'Actions de la Communauté européenne en faveur des droits de l'homme dans les pays tiers' in A Cassese, A Clapham and J Weiler (eds), *European Union: The Human Rights Challenge* (Baden-Baden, Nomos, 1991), pp 507–546, at p 509.

[24] J-M Rachet, 'De la compétence de l'Union européenne en matière de défense et de promotion des droits de l'homme' (1995) 2 *Revue du Marché Commun*, pp 256–260, at p 256.

A clear competence to make human rights a foreign policy objective can be found in the EC Treaty provisions on (development) cooperation with third countries (Articles 177 and Article 181a EC). These provisions contain the following reference to respect for human rights:

> Community policy in this area shall contribute to the general objective of developing and consolidating democracy and the rule of law, and to that of respecting human rights and fundamental freedoms.[25]

It can be maintained that this reference entails that there is an obligation—and not merely a competence—for the Community to include human rights considerations in its development and cooperation relations with third countries. Support for this view can be found in the ruling of the ECJ in the case *Portugal v Council*.[26] In that case AG La Pergola made a plea that the absence of a human rights clause in an agreement on development cooperation would compromise the legality of Community action, 'because compliance with the specific wording of Article 130u EC [now Article 177] would no longer be guaranteed.'[27] Although the Court was not as outspoken as the Advocate General on the consequences of the absence of a human rights clause, it also established an obligation on the European Community to make the promotion of human rights an important element of its development policy:

> The very wording of the latter provision [Article 177 EC] demonstrates the importance to be attached to respect for human rights and democratic principles, so that, amongst other things, development cooperation policy must be adapted to the requirement of respect for those rights and principles.
> [. . .] to adapt cooperation policy to respect for human rights necessarily entails establishing a certain connection between those matters whereby one of them is made subordinate to the other.[28]

In practice, the Articles 310 (association agreements) and 308 EC (implied powers) have also been used as a legal basis for external Community action in the field of human rights. In view of the importance of respect for human rights within the European Union, it could be argued that Article 310 EC provides a sufficient legal basis for human rights action towards third countries associated with the Community. Article 308 EC provides a legal basis whenever Community action is necessary to attain one of the objectives of the EC Treaty and the necessary competence to undertake this action cannot be found elsewhere in the EC Treaty. Consequently, a necessary condition for the use of Article 308 EC is that the promotion of human rights world-wide constitutes an

---

[25] Art 177 EC on development cooperation was introduced in the EC Treaty by the Amsterdam Treaty. Art 181a EC on economic, financial and technical cooperation with third countries was introduced by the Nice Treaty.

[26] Case C–268/94 *Portugal v Council* [1996] ECR I–6699.

[27] Opinion of AG La Pergola in case C–268/94, *Portugal v Council* [1996] ECR I–6699, para 29.

[28] Case C–268/94, *Portugal v Council*, paras 24 and 26.

objective of the European Community. However, in the absence of a clear reference to the promotion of human rights in the EC Treaty, it is questionable whether the promotion of human rights constitutes an objective of the Community. This question was not addressed by the ECJ in *Opinion 2/94*[29] when it denied Community competence to accede to the ECHR on the basis of Article 308 EC. The ECJ held Community competence to accede to the ECHR would have constitutional implications and consequently exceed the scope of Article 308 EC.

Notwithstanding the fact that it might be questioned from a formal legal perspective whether Article 308 EC provides a sufficient legal basis for external Community action in the field of human rights, in practice the use of this provision for such action seems to be undisputed. For instance, Article 308 EC was used for Council Regulation No 976/1999 concerning Community funding of human rights related action in third countries that are not development countries.[30] So far, the use of Article 308 EC for the adoption of this measure has not been challenged.

b) Main Policy Principles and Policy Instruments

One of the guiding principles of the European Union's external human rights policy is the existence of universally binding human rights.[31] Through its external human rights policy, the European Union does not aim to create new human rights obligations for third countries, but to promote that third countries respect their (pre-existing) human rights obligations under international law.[32] As regards these human rights norms, the Universal Declaration of Human Rights (UDHR)[33] is given special significance, as well as the main international (ICCPR and ICSCR) and regional human rights (ECHR) instruments.[34] Obviously, Article 6 EU and the EU Charter of Fundamental Rights are of little relevance for the Union's policy to promote respect for human rights by third countries.[35]

---

[29] Opinion 2/94 (Re European Convention on Human Rights), [1996] ECR I–1061, para 23.

[30] Council Regulation (EC) No 976/1999 of 29 April 1999 laying down the requirements for the implementation of Community cooperation operations, other than those of development cooperation, which, within the framework of Community cooperation policy, contribute to the general objective of developing and consolidating democracy and the rule of law and to that of respecting human rights and fundamental freedoms [1999] OJ L/120/8.

[31] See, eg: the 2003 EU Annual Report on Human Rights, p 6.

[32] See with respect to the Union's policy to include human rights clauses in external agreements: B Brandtner and A Rosas, 'Trade Preference and Human Rights' in Ph Alston, M Bustelo and J Heenan (eds), *The EU and Human Rights* (Oxford, Oxford University Press, 1999), pp 699–722, at p 707. See also: EU Annual Report on Human Rights, 1999, s 4.2.5.

[33] See Statement of the EU on the occasion of the 50th anniversary of the UDHR, *Bull EU* 12–1998, 1.3.22.

[34] Communication from the Commission to the Council and the European Parliament, *The European Union and the External Dimension: From Rome to Maastricht and beyond*, COM(95)567 Final, p 9.

[35] See also: O. De Schutter, *Ancrer les droits fondamentaux dans l'Union européenne*, pp 33–36 available at: http://www.cpdr.ucl.ac.be/cridho.

Priority is given to positive measures to improve the human rights situation in third countries. An open and constructive dialogue between the Union and the Member States on the one hand and third countries on the other is considered an important element of this positive approach.[36] The European Union has established formal relations with most third countries through the conclusion of international agreements. Since 1995, the inclusion of a so-called *human rights clause* in the Community's cooperation agreements with third countries constitutes a non-negotiable part of the Commission's negotiation mandate. The human rights clause governs Union relations with over 100 countries. There are no EU guidelines to determine how the human rights clause should be applied. Most external agreements also establish an institutional framework for *political dialogue* between the Union and the third country concerned. In the EU guidelines on Human Rights dialogues (adopted on 13 December 2001) it is reconfirmed that:

> the issue of human rights, democracy and the rule of law is incorporated into all meetings and discussions it has with third countries, at every level, including political dialogue.

It is, however, difficult to get information on the frequency with which human rights are put on the political agenda in practice.

Human rights considerations have increasingly been included in *financial instruments* available to provide assistance to third countries. These include regional regulations (such as TACIS Regulation,[37] the MEDA Regulation,[38] and the OBNOVA Regulation[39]) as well as the financial resources available under Chapter B7–70 of the Community Budget. Chapter B–7–70, entitled the European Initiative for Democracy and Human Rights (EIDHR), covers all budget resources explicitly earmarked for the promotion of human rights and democratic principles. With respect to the respective use of the budget of Chapter B7–70 and the geographical regulations, the Commission maintains that a distinction needs to be made 'not in terms of the theme but the nature of

---

[36] Resolution of the Council and the Member States meeting in Council on Human Rights, Democracy and Development, 28 November 1991, *Bull.EC* 11–1991, 122. See also Commission Communication, *The European Union's Role in Promoting Human Rights and Democratisation in Third Countries*, COM(2001)252 Final.

[37] Council Reg 1279/96 of 25 June 1996 concerning the provision of assistance to economic reform and recovery in the New Independent States and Mongolia [1996] OJ L/165/1.

[38] Council Reg 1488/96 of 23 July 1996 on financial and technical measures to accompany (MEDA) the reform of economic and social structures in the framework of the Euro-Mediterranean partnership [1996] OJ L/189/1.

[39] Council Reg (EC) No 1628/96 of 25 July 1996 relating to aid for Bosnia and Herzegovina, Croatia, the Federal Republic of Yugoslavia and the former Yugoslav Republic of Macedonia [1996] OJ L/204/1. Council Reg (EC) No 2666/2000 of 5 December 2000 on assistance for Albania, Bosnia and Herzegovina, Croatia, the Federal Republic of Yugoslavia and the former Yugoslav Republic of Macedonia, repealing Regulation (EC) 1612/96 and amending Regs (EEC) No 3906/89 and (EEC) No 1360/90 and Decisions 97/256/EC and 1999/311/EC [2000] OJ L/306/1.

the intervention':[40] the human rights regulations should primarily be used to support NGOS and international organisations; the geographical regulations for projects which require the involvement of the country concerned.

Within international organisations such as the United Nations, the Council of Europe and the Organization for Security and Cooperation in Europe (OSCE), both the Community and the Member States participate. Furthermore, the European Community *cooperates* with other international organisations in the field of human rights. For example, the European Community cooperates with the Council of Europe to support the democratic reform in the Central and Eastern European countries. As regards the political participation *in* international organisations, the Member State have coordinated their action since the establishment of the European Political Cooperation (EPC, the predecessor of the CFSP). Within the General Assembly and the Human Rights Commission of the UN this cooperation results in common statements and the joint introduction or support of resolutions. Statements are made both by the Presidency of the Council and a representative of the Commission.

When the Union's efforts to further respect for human rights through positive measures are unsuccessful, due to a lack of commitment on the part of the third country concerned to pursue change, the Union will consider the taking of restrictive measures.[41] In the taking of these restrictive measures the Community and the Member States 'are guided by objective and equitable criteria.'[42] What these objective and equitable criteria are is not further clarified. As to the 'appropriate measures,' it is stated that they will be proportional to the seriousness of the case and that they could go from confidential or public demarches to suspension of cooperation with the States concerned. In the application of restrictive measures the Union will avoid penalising the population for governmental actions. Humanitarian and emergency aid directly benefiting vulnerable populations will never be suspended.[43] So far, restrictive measures on the basis of the human rights clause have only been taken in response to human rights violations in one of the ACP countries.[44]

---

[40] Resolution of the Council and the Member States meeting in Council on Human Rights, Democracy and Development, 28 November 1991, *Bull EC* 11–1991, 122. Commission Communication, *The European Union's Role in Promoting Human Rights and Democratisation in Third Countries*, COM(2001)252 Final, p 9.

[41] Resolution of the Council and the Member States meeting in Council on Human Rights, Democracy and Development, 28 November 1991, *Bull EC* 11–1991, 122.

[42] *Ibid.*

[43] *Ibid.*

[44] For a more detailed analysis of the use of the human rights as a legal basis for restrictive measures in case of human rights violations, see MK Bulterman, *Human Rights in the Treaty Relations of the European Community: Real Virtues or Virtual Reality?* (Antwerpen, Intersentia/Hart, 2001).

c) From Rhetoric to Reality

While the necessary instruments and resources seem to be available, the European Union has not yet managed to establish a human rights policy that stands the test of criticism. On the one hand, it is possible to criticise the Union's response—or failure to respond—to specific instances of human rights violations in third countries. For instance, the Union could be criticised for failing to take action on the basis of the human rights clause in its agreement with Israel in response to the situation in the occupied territories; or for failing to take a clear stance on the situation of the detainees in Guantanamo Bay. For present purposes, however, it is not so important to list instances in which the Union failed to respond to the human rights situation in third countries in a satisfactory matter, assuming that it would be possible to get agreement on what would be a satisfactory response in a specific situation. Here, it is more important to focus on the shortcomings in the regulatory and institutional framework that may be the cause that the Union's human rights policy is so susceptible to criticism.

Criticism on the Union's human rights policies has been expressed not only by NGO's and scholars, but can also be heard from within the EU. Important impetus to this debate was provided by the Human Rights Agenda of the *Comité des Sages*.[45] The *Comité* observed that there is a discrepancy between the rhetoric and practice of the Union's human rights policy. Their agenda also contained concrete proposals for improvement, such as the appointment of a Commissioner for Human Rights, the establishment of a specialist Human Rights Office to support the CFSP High Representative, the development of balanced and objective surveys on the human rights situation world-wide and the adoption of criteria for the application of the human rights clause. While the Human Rights Agenda was adopted in 1998, so far only a few of the suggestions of the *Comité des Sages* have materialised.

Within the European Union, the European Parliament has repeatedly stressed the need for improvement of the European Union's external human rights policy.[46] But also the Commission and the Council recognise the fact that there is room for improvement: 'coherence and consistency,' 'mainstreaming,' 'transparency' and 'prioritisation' are recurrent themes in Commission[47] and

---

[45] *Leading by Example: A Human Rights Agenda for the European Union for the Year 2000. Agenda of the* Comité des Sages *and Final Project Report*, (Florence 1998). The *Comité des Sages* consisted of Antonio Cassese, Catherine Lalumière, Peter Leuprecht and Mary Robinson.

[46] See, eg: European Parliament resolution on Human Rights in the World in 2004 and the European Union's Policy on the matter, adopted on 22 April 2004.

[47] The Commission, in its 2001 Communication *The European Union's Role in Promoting Human Rights and Democratisation in Third Countries*, identified three areas in which it could play a more effective role: (i) the promotion of coherence and consistency between EC and EU policies in support of human rights and democratisation, (ii) in placing a higher priority on, and mainstreaming, human rights and democratisation in the Union's relations with third countries, (iii) the adoption of a more strategic approach to the EIDHR.

Council[48] documents on the Union's external human rights policies. These themes are thus not merely theoretical aspirations formulated by external observers, but they are recognised as important attributes of a successful EU human rights policy by the most important actors involved. Consequently they provide a useful starting point for an exploration of the challenges facing the European Union.

1. Coherence and Consistency

According to Article 3 EU:

> the Union shall be served by a single institutional framework which shall ensure the consistency and the continuity of the activities carried out in order to attain its objectives while respecting and building upon the *acquis communautaire*.

As to the meaning of the concept of consistency and the means to ensure it, the Treaty is silent. Article 3 EU only provides that the Council and the Commission are responsible and have to cooperate for ensuring the *consistency* of the external activities of the Union as a whole in the context of its external relations, security, economic and development policies.[49] Clapham distinguishes no less than eight different aspects of the quest for consistency in the European Union's external action in the field of human rights[50]:

— consistency between the Union's economic influence and its foreign policy
— consistency between the pillars
— consistency between the different EU bodies
— consistency with regard to different non-Member States
— consistency over time
— consistency between dealing with human rights at home and abroad
— consistency between the existing monitoring of Member States and the absence of international accountability for EU institutions
— consistency between ambitions and available funds

To this list should be added the quest for consistency between theory and practice, which can be considered as the challenge that comprises all aspects of

---

[48] In the Council Conclusion of 25 June 2001, the Council reconfirmed its adherence to (i) coherence and consistency between Community action and the CFSP as well as development policy through close cooperation and coordination between its competent bodies and with the Commission, (ii) mainstreaming of human rights and democratisation into EU policies and action, (iii) openness of the EU's human rights and democratisation policy through a strengthened dialogue with the European Parliament and the civil society (iv) regular identification and review of priority actions in the implementation of its human rights and democratisation policy.

[49] See in more detail, NA Neuwahl, 'Foreign Policy and the Implementation of the Requirement of "Consistency" under the Treaty on European Union' in D O'Keeffe and PM Twomey (eds), *Legal Issues of the Maastricht Treaty* (London, Wiley Chancery Law, 1994), pp 227–246.

[50] A Clapham, 'Where is the EU's Human Rights Common Foreign Policy, and How is it manifested in Multilateral Fora?' in Ph Alston, M Bustelo and J Heenan (eds), *The EU and Human Rights* (Oxford, Oxford University Press, 1999), pp 627–683, at pp 637–640.

consistency enumerated by Clapham. Whatever the exact definition of term consistency, it is clear that any measure of consistency in the European Union's external human rights action is not ensured by the 'single institutional framework' as such. Cooperation and coordination within and between the different institutions that are engaged in the European Union's external activities need to take place. Coordination and cooperation to a large extent take place on an *ad hoc* basis and have not been institutionalised.[51]

2. Mainstreaming of Human Rights

While 'mainstreaming' is perceived as an important element of the Union's human rights policies, there is no clear definition of what mainstreaming means and what steps need to be taken to achieve it.[52] In the Council Annual Report on Human Rights (2004) mainstreaming is defined as 'the process of integrating human rights into all aspects of EU policy decision-making and implementation, including external assistance.'[53] The examples enumerated in the Annual Reports make it clear that limited progress has been made in mainstreaming of human rights throughout EU policies. Reference is made, for example, to the practice of including human rights clauses in external agreements, to the budgetary resources to sponsor human right projects in third countries and to the training of staff. However, it is difficult to see how mainstreaming is realised through these initiatives, when there are no guidelines concerning the relevance of human rights for the various fields of Union external action (such as its development, trade and environmental policy).

As an example of successful mainstreaming of human rights the Community's Generalised System of Preferences (GSP) could be mentioned. Under this system, tariff preferences are granted to products originating from developing countries.[54] On the one hand, the system provides for an incentive arrangement for countries that have implemented the right to organise and to bargain collectively and have adopted rules on the minimum age of admission to employment. On the other hand, the Community's GSP provides for temporal withdrawal, in whole or in part, of the scheme of generalised preferences in case of, inter alia, export of goods made by prison labour and any form of forced labour. Information on the existence of circumstances which necessitate temporary withdrawal form the GSP may be brought to the attention of the Commission by the Member States or by any natural or legal persons, or associations not endowed with legal personality, which can show an interest in such withdrawal.

---

[51] See on the internal organisational arrangements within the different institutions, M Fouwels, 'The European Union's Common Foreign and Security Policy and Human Rights' (1997) 15 *Netherlands Quarterly of Human Rights*, pp 291–324.

[52] See the contribution of O De Schutter in ch 2 of this volume for a more general discussion of the mainstreaming of human rights in the European Union.

[53] EU Annual Report on Human Rights—2004, p 19.

[54] Council Reg 2501/2001 of 10 December 2001 applying a scheme of generalised tariff preferences for the period from 1 January 2002 to 31 December 2004 [2001] OJ L/346/1.

This information is examined by the Commission in consultation with the Generalised Preference Committee, in which the Member States are represented. If the Commission considers withdrawal necessary, it submits a proposal to the Council. The Council decides the issue acting by qualified majority vote. In March 1997, Myanmar's access to the tariff preferences previously granted for certain industrial and agricultural products was withdrawn in response to the use of forced labour in that country.[55]

3. *Transparency*

According to the Council Conclusions of 25 June 2001, greater transparency is to be achieved through 'a strengthened dialogue with the European Parliament and the civil society.' As is evidenced by the criticism expressed by EP in its human rights resolution, the interaction between the Council and the European Parliament still is far from satisfactory.[56]

As far as the dialogue with civil society is concerned, it is important to note the information made available to the general public on the internet and in the Human Rights Reports of the Council. These Reports, which have been adopted since 1999, are based on the Declaration of the European Union on the occasion of the 50th Anniversary of the Universal Declaration of Human Rights of 10 December 1998. The Human Rights report intends to enhance the transparency of the Union's human rights policies by explaining who the actors of the Union's human rights policies are and setting out their goals, methods and activities. The report does not aim to provide an exhaustive overview of all action undertaken by the European Union in the period covered, but addresses the instruments and initiatives that can be employed by the European Union in order to address human rights situations and promote human rights principles world-wide. Both the internal and external human rights dimension of the EU is addressed in the report. It is difficult, however, to draw any conclusions from this information on the failures and successes of the Union's human rights action. For example, the Union's practice to include human rights clauses in external agreements is mentioned as an important element of the Union's external human rights action. However, information on the (positive and negative) measures taken by the Union on the basis of these human rights clauses is only scarcely made available.

---

[55] Council Reg 552/97 of 24 March 1997, temporarily withdrawing access to generalised tariff preferences from the Union of Myanmar [1997] OJ L/85/8.

[56] See European Parliament resolution on human rights in the world in 2003 and the European Union's policy on the matter, as adopted on 22 April 2004. In s 16, the Parliament 'Reiterates its demand for more openness and transparency on the part of the EU institutions and on the part of the Council in particular; maintains its criticism that the calls made in its resolutions for the Council to report back on the outcome of specific human rights issues, in particular as these come up in international organisations, are systematically disregarded; insists that Parliament should be given a full explanation whenever its human rights recommendations are not followed by Council or Commission.'

The dialogue with civil society has been formalised through the establishment of the EU Human Rights Discussion Forum.[57] This Forum provides an opportunity for exchange of views on the Union's human rights action. It is difficult to see, however, to what extent the proposals made during these meetings are actually taken up—or even considered—by the Union Institutions. In short, there is no direct link between this Forum and the day-to-day practice of the Union's external human rights action.

4. Prioritisation

The theme of 'prioritisation' has been taken up by the Commission with respect to the allocation of the financial means available under the budget heading 'European Initiative for Democracy and Human Rights.' In the Commission 2001 Communication on the EU's role in promoting human rights and democratisation in third countries, four thematic priorities for the EIDHR were chosen and it was suggested to concentrate the EIDHR support to a limited number of focus countries.[58] The thematic priorities are:

— support to strengthen democratisation, good governance and the rule of law
— activities in support of the abolition of the death penalty
— support for the fight against torture and impunity and for international tribunals and criminal courts
— combating racism and xenophobia and discrimination against minorities and indigenous peoples.

In order to further the aim of a strategic approach, the EIDHR Programming Document 2002–2004 was adopted by the Commission and is updated yearly. In the Council Conclusions of 25 June 2001, the Council welcomed the priorities identified for the EIDHR. The Council:

> will focus on these and other key issues, such as the rights of the child, freedom of the media and strengthening of civil society, including through human rights education.[59]

IV. THE TREATY ESTABLISHING A CONSTITUTION FOR EUROPE

The current legal framework for the Union's external human rights action can be summarised as follows. Various Treaty provisions provide a legal basis for the Community/Union to make human rights a foreign policy objective (Article 11 EU, Articles 177, 181a, 308 and 310 EC). This means that the Community/Union is competent to undertake external action with the aim of

---

[57] Available at: http://europa.eu.int/comm/external_relations/human_rights/conf/forum1/.
[58] Commission Communication, *The European Union's Role in Promoting Human Rights and Democratisation in Third Countries*, COM(2001)252 Final.
[59] *Ibid.*

influencing a state or group of states so that they may improve their respect for human rights.[60] In the context of the Community's (development) cooperation policies, there is even an obligation to take account of the objective of promoting respect for human rights in third countries (Articles 177 and 181 EC). As to the applicable human rights standard, the European Union's action to promote human rights in third countries is based on the existing human rights obligations under international law.

The role of human rights as a foreign policy objective of the European Union has to be distinguished from the role of human rights as norms binding the European Union when engaged in external action. It is a political choice to make human rights a foreign policy objective. In addition, however, states and international organisations are obliged to respect human rights when engaged in external action. This is an issue of increased importance in a globalizing world where national borders tend to loose their importance. Articles 6 EU and the EU Charter of Fundamental Rights lay down an obligation on the European Union to respect human rights. This obligation extends to all EU action, including its external action. Thus the European Union has to ensure that its external activities are in conformity with the human rights norms binding upon the EU.

What changes would the entry into force of the Treaty establishing a Constitution for Europe bring? First of all, it constitutes an important, unprecedented, step forward for the European Union from a human rights perspective: it foresees the integration of the EU Charter of Fundamental Rights in the European Constitution. Thus the Union's commitment to respect the rights in the EU Charter—which as we saw in section II extends to the Union's external activities—is formally entrenched in the Treaty. The possibilities for the ECJ to supervise the Union's external policies will remain limited: it shall not have jurisdiction with respect to the provisions concerning the Common Foreign and Security Policy (Article III–376). An exception is made with respect to sanctions against natural and legal persons, which can be challenged before the Court in an action for annulment.

A positive development for the Union's external human rights policy is the abolition of the current pillar structure: the European Community will cease to exist and be absorbed in the European Union. External action of the European Union is dealt with in a single title of the new Treaty.[61] The only references to human rights are to be found in Article III–292:

> The Union's action on the international scene shall be guided by the principles which have inspired its own creation, development, and enlargement, and which it seeks to advance in the wider world: democracy, the rule of law, the universality and indivisibility of human rights and fundamental freedoms, respect for human dignity, equality

---

[60] PR Baehr and M Castermans, *The Role of Human Rights in Foreign Policy* (Basingstoke, Palgrave Macmillan, 2004) p 2.

[61] See for a general analysis of this new title: M Cremona, 'The Draft Constitutional Treaty—External Relations and External Action' (2003) 40 *CML Rev*, pp 1347–1366.

and solidarity, and respect for the principles of the United Nations Charter and international law.

The Union shall define and pursue common policies and actions, and shall work for a high degree of cooperation in all fields of international relations in order to: [. . .]

(b) consolidate and support democracy, the rule of law, human rights and international law.

In comparison to the current reference to human rights in Article 11 EU, Article III–292 is an improvement since Article III–292 applies to *all* EU policy areas, not merely to its CFSP. This means that in future (assuming that the Constitutional Treaty enters into force) the Union will be endowed with a general competence to make human rights a foreign policy objective, covering all policies areas.[62]

On the other hand, the new provisions on the Union's development relations (Articles III–316 to III–318), as well as its economic, financial and technical cooperation (Article III–319 to III–320) with third countries do not contain any specific reference to human rights. Does this mean that there would no longer be an obligation for the EU to subordinate (development) cooperation policies to respect for human rights, as is currently required by Articles 177 and 181 EC (see section III(a))? There does not seem to be much ground to fear that this is the case. In this respect it is important to note the reference to human rights as it can be found in the first paragraph of Article III–292. There it is made clear that all external EU action shall be guided by human rights and the other principles upon which the Union is based. This reference to human rights is largely similar to the reference to human rights as it currently can be found in the context of the Community's (development) relations. This would mean that the observations made by the ECJ in *Portugal v Council* on the relevance of human rights for the Community's cooperation policy would in future apply to all external policy areas.

Finally, it is important to note that the Constitutional Treaty introduces the Union Minister for Foreign Affairs (Article I–28), replacing the High Representative for the CFSP, who shall preside over the Foreign Affairs Council and shall be one of the Vice-Presidents of the Commission. He shall ensure the consistency of the Union's external action. The Union Minister for Foreign Affairs is to be assisted by a joint service (European External Action Service) composed of officials from relevant departments of the General Secretariat of the Council and of the Commission and staff seconded from national diplomatic services. Although there is cause not to be too optimistic,[63] these new

---

[62] See for a general analysis of EU external competence under the Constitutional Treaty: O De Schutter, 'L'adhesion de l'Union européene à la Charte sociale européenne révisée' EUI Working Paper Law, No 2004/11, pp 11–14.

[63] According to a Declaration to the Final Act to the Amsterdam Treaty, a Policy Planning and Early Warning Unit would be established in the General Secretariat of the Council. The tasks of the unit include monitoring and analysing developments in areas relevant to the CFSP. As the development and consolidation of democracy and the rule of law, and respect for human rights and fundamental freedoms is explicitly mentioned as one of the objectives of the CFSP, it may be expected that

actors may play an important role in ensuring consistency in the Union's human rights action. The fact that the Union Minister for Foreign Affairs is engaged with both Commission and Council external action provides an unprecedented opportunity for ensuring consistency between measures taken by both institutions.

V. THE FRA AND THE EXTERNAL POLICIES OF THE EUROPEAN UNION

In the decision of 13 December 2003 to reform the European Monitoring Centre on Racism (EUMC) and Xenophobia into a Fundamental Rights Agency, the European Council stressed 'the importance of human rights data collection and analysis with a view to defining Union policy in this field.' Apparently, the European Council sees data collection and analysis as the main tasks of the FRA. This is in line with the current mandate of the EUMC.[64] The Commission, in its public Consultation document suggests that the Agency should focus on two areas: data collection and analysis, and the drafting of opinions. In this section, we will examine to what these tasks would enable the FRA to pay attention to both aspects of human rights as an element of the Union's external policies that were distinguished in the preceding sections.

a) The Obligation to Respect Fundamental Rights and External EU Action

In some of the contributions to the discussion on the FRA, the suggestion that the FRA should play a role with respect to the Union's external policies seems to find little support. MEP Joke Swiebel, for example, observed:[65]

> Although it must be underlined that the EU's internal and external human rights policies must be co-ordinated and consistent, if they are to be effective and credible, this does not necessarily mean that data collection, analyses and advice in both areas should take place in the same institution.

In their observations on the FRA the French authorities submit:

> [L]a pertinence et la valeur ajoutée d'une agence communautaire chargée de la dimension extérieure des droits de l'homme ne paraissent pas démontrées ('[T]he relevance

the Policy Planning and Early Warning Unit will play a role in the EU's human rights policy. However, so far these ambitions have not been realised as the Policy Planning and Early Warning Unit has not yet been created.

[64] Art 2 Reg 1035/97, OJ 1997, L/151/1.

[65] Committee on Citizens' Freedoms and Rights, Justice and Home Affairs, Raporteur: J Swiebel, *Working Document on the proposal for a Council Regulation on the European Monitoring Centre on Racism and Xenophobia*, 25 March 2004.

and the added value of a Community Agency in charge of the external dimension of human rights do not appear to be demonstrated').[66]

These views, however, are difficult to reconcile with the paramount importance of respect for the fundamental rights laid down in the EU Charter for all EU policies, including its external policies. As we saw in section II, the EU institutions have to ensure that their external action is in conformity with the fundamental rights binding upon the European Union. As a consequence any task assigned to the FRA in order to ensure that the European Union takes fundamental rights fully into account when drafting and implementing its policies, comprises also the Union's external policies.

Consequently, if the FRA would be given the task to analyse the Union's (human rights) policies for their compatibility with the EU Charter, it should take up this task also with respect to the Union's external action. This would also be in conformity with the current practice of the NIE: it has taken up its mandate to monitor the situation of fundamental rights in the Member States and in the Union to comprise the Union's external action. Its second thematic comment focuses on fundamental rights in the external activities of the European Union in the fields of justice and asylum and migration in 2003. In view of the current mandate of the NIE, the question arises whether the task to monitor the situation of fundamental rights in the Member States and in the Union should be assigned to the FRA. That is an issue that needs to be discussed and that will be discussed elsewhere. Here, it is important to note that the mandate to monitor the situation of fundamental rights in the Member States and in the Union comprises monitoring whether their external activities are in conformity with the rights laid down in the EU Charter.

The FRA could also play a role in gathering information on the impact of the Union external policies on the human rights situation in third countries. As mentioned above, the Commission has undertaken to ensure that in the formulation of its (external) policies, 'any negative effect on human rights and democratisation is always avoided, and where possible, policies are adapted to have a positive impact.' However, no information is currently available whether Union practice is in conformity with this statement. As was noted in section II, the ECJ's control over the Union's external action, and thus its jurisdiction to ensure compliance with human rights norms, is restricted. Furthermore, judicial supervision may not be the best way to ensure that the rights in the EU Charter of Fundamental Rights are fully taken into account in external policies. The FRA—which does not have to adopt the strict legal approach of a court—may be in better position than the ECJ to clarify the practical relevance of the EU Charter of Fundamental Rights for the EU's external policies.

---

[66] Note des autorités françaises sur la transformation de l'observatoire européen des phénomènes racistes et xenophobes en agence européen des droits de l'homme, p 3.

b) Human Rights as a Foreign Policy Objective

In its Public consultation document, the Commission introduces an important restriction as to the geographical scope of the FRA's activities[67]:

> Confining the Agency's scope to the Union would clearly underline the will to empha-
> sise the importance of fundamental rights in the Union and would be an effective
> means of placing responsibility on its institutions in the field of fundamental rights. It
> would also help in determining the capacity and the expertise that the Agency will
> require.
>   This message might be diluted if the Agency's remit were to be extended to third
> countries; the Commission rejected this option in its Communication on the EU's role
> in promoting human rights and democratisation in third countries, and the Council
> shared its approach in its conclusions of 25 June 2001. In addition, respect for human
> rights in the Union's foreign policy is already taken into account in the context of
> cooperation with third countries.

Although the Commission does not make reference to the various aspects of human rights as an element of the Union's external policies, it thus seems to suggest that the role of the FRA should be confined to (making a contribution) to ensuring that the Union's external policies comply with the fundamental rights laid down in the EU Charter of Fundamental Rights. The arguments raised by the Commission, however, are not very convincing.

First of all, it is hard to see how an extension of the FRA's action to third countries would undermine the objective to emphasise the importance of fundamental rights in the European Union. That would only be the case if the FRA would pay attention to third countries at the expense of addressing fundamental rights in the European Union. Furthermore, information on the human rights situation in third countries is not merely a 'foreign affairs matter.' The human rights situation in third countries is of direct relevance for an important 'internal' policy area with obvious fundamental rights implications: the area of freedom, security and justice. It would seem that reliable information at EU level on the human rights situation in third countries (for example an EU list of safe countries) is a prerequisite for the establishment of a successful European asylum and immigration policy.

Also the argument that respect for human rights is already taken into account in the context of cooperation with third countries fails to convince. Are human rights not already taken into account in the context of other EU policies, which do fall within the FRA's intended scope of action? Are there not any deficiencies in the Union's external human rights policy that the FRA could help to overcome? In view of the importance of human rights as a foreign policy objective and the difficulties in establishing an external human rights policy that stands the test of

---

[67] See Communication from the Commission, *The Fundamental Rights Agency—Public Consultation Document*, SEC(2004)1281/COM(2004)693 Final, p 8 (footnotes omitted).

criticism (see section III), it should not be stated a priori—and on such unconvincing grounds—that the FRA's action should not extend to third countries.

For example, the FRA could be given the task to draw up reports on the human rights situation in third countries. In the Commission's Public Consultation Document, it is presented as a fact that 'the Agency will be required to monitor fundamental rights by area and not to prepare reports by country.'[68] In its 2001 Communication on the Union's external human rights policies, the Commission rejected the suggestion to draw up human rights reports on third countries without much ado:[69]

> [T]he Commission considers that the European Union does not lack sources of advice and information. It can draw on reports from the United Nations, the Council of Europe and a variety of international NGOs. Furthermore there is no monopoly of wisdom when it comes to analysing human rights and democratisation problems, or their implications for the European Union's external relations. The real challenge for any institution is to use the information in a productive manner, and to have the political will to take difficult decisions. An additional advisory body would not overcome this challenge. The Commission does not therefore intend to pursue this suggestion nor the related one which has been occasionally made that the Commission should produce, or subcontract an organisation to produce, a world-wide overview of the human rights situation by country, as is done by the US State department.

However, the fact that there is sufficient information available to the Union Institutions on the human rights situation in third countries, does not necessarily take away the need of an EU report on the human rights situation world-wide. It would enhance the transparency of the Union human rights policy if there would be an EU report on the human rights situation world-wide, that is, at the basis of all EU human rights action.

This does not mean that at the moment there is a complete lack of information on the human rights situation in third countries that is at the basis of the Union's external policies. Since 2000, the Commission has introduced so-called Country Strategy Papers. These papers set out the EU approach to the country concerned, on the basis of an assessment of its political and economic situation. In its 2001 Communication, the Commission suggested that these papers:

> encourage a more systematic approach by requiring an analysis of the situation in each country relating to human rights, democratisation and the rule of law.

While currently these Papers often contain only scarce information on the human rights situation in the third countries concerned, the Commission thus seems to be in a good position to collect information on the human rights situation in third countries and publish it in an EU report. Nevertheless, it would be better to assign the task of drawing up EU Reports to an independent agent,

---

[68] Communication from the Commission, *The Fundamental Rights Agency—Public Consultation Document*, SEC(2004)1281/COM(2004)693 Final, p 5.

[69] Commission Communication, *The European Union's Role in Promoting Human Rights and Democratisation in Third Countries*, COM(2001)252 Final.

such as the FRA. First of all, it is to be expected that for the FRA publishing information on the human rights situation in third countries is not as politicised as it is for the Commission. In the second place, since the information on the human rights situation in third countries is relevant for all EU institutions and bodies, it would be better if this information was not gathered and published by one of the actors concerned but by an agency with an independent status.

Another task that could be assigned to the FRA concerns the human rights policies of the EU Member States. On many occasions the need of consistency between the Union's and the Member States' external action in the field of human rights has been stressed.[70] Gathering information on the external human rights policies of the Member States may be a first step to ensure consistency between EU and Member State policies. It would also contribute to the coming into place of a true EU human rights policy. Notwithstanding the 'common' nature of the CFSP, different national views on the role of human rights in foreign policy still prevail. The following passage from Chris Patten's statement during the 56th Session of the Commission on Human Rights (20 March–28 April 2000), puts the role of the Commission in shaping to the Union's human rights policy into perspective[71]:

> And it is for the fifteen eu governments to decide whether or not the eu can agree a united view on the human rights record of an individual country, and to do so preferably in concert with other like-minded countries. The European Commission is not, of course, a government—however much of my compatriots may claim that it tries to behave like one! We can make our voice heard, but the member states are in the driving seat.

If the EU's human rights policy is to be more than technical and financial assistance and *ad hoc* responses to the human rights situation in third countries, then it is necessary that the Member States agree on the importance of human rights as an element of the Union's external relations.

Also, an advisory role of the FRA with respect to the Union's commitment to promote human rights by third countries would be most welcome. In general, the references to human rights in the various policy statements of the institutions are too vague to be of practical guidance in the day-to-days practice of the Union's external relations. The human rights clause, for example, states that respect for human rights is an essential element of the agreement. The Union's practice to include such a human rights clause in its external agreements is often referred to as an example of the Union's commitment to promote respect for human rights through its external action. However, in the absence of a clear practice of its implementation, it is not clear whether the Union's policy to include human rights clauses in external agreements really serves the promotion of human rights world-wide. There is thus an obvious need for further

---

[70] Commission, EP: Council Guidelines on Human Rights Dialogues, point 8.

[71] Speech at the 56th UN Human Rights Commission, available at: http://europa.eu.int/comm/commissioners/patten/speeches/index.htm.

implementation and concretisation of the principles and priorities of the Union's human rights policies. It is primarily the task of the institutions to take the necessary steps in this respect. The Commission Communication 'Reinvigorating EU actions on Human Rights and democratisation with Mediterranean Partners'[72] is a noteworthy example of a policy document containing concrete proposals on the use of the instruments available to the EU in order to strengthen the human rights dimension in the relations with the Union's partners.[73] While policy forming in the first place is a task for the institutions, the FRA could play an advisory role in that respect. Within the Netherlands the *Adviesraad Internationale Vraagstukken* (Advisory Council on International Affairs, or AIV)[74] provides impetus to the debate on various foreign policy related matters, including human rights issues. The AIV is composed of independent experts and reports on the request of the government or (exceptionally) on its own initiative. It regularly gives its views on issues with a clear EU dimension. In August 2004, for example, it presented its report 'Follow-up Report Turkey: towards membership of the European Union.' On the EU-level, the input of an independent expert body to this debate would also be of added value. For example, it would be very valuable if the FRA would be assigned the task of recommending on the application of the human rights clause to the Council. Obviously, the political decision to impose sanctions or to take any other measure in order to induce a third country to respect human rights must be taken by the Institutions. An advisory role of the FRA, however, would enable the Institutions to take such a decision on a more fully informed basis.

VI. CONCLUSION

There are obvious opportunities for the FRA to make a contribution to the European Union's external policies. First of all, it has to be acknowledged that the obligation to take fundamental rights fully into account applies to *all* EU policies. Consequently, any role of the FRA with respect to ensuring that fundamental rights are respected by the European Union by its nature will extend to its external policies.

In addition, however, it is evident the FRA could make a valuable contribution to the Union's external human rights policy, provided that the necessary tasks were assigned to it. One of the arguments of the Commission against such an extension of the mandate of the FRA, however, cannot easily be refuted: such an extension would have important repercussions for the capacity and expertise required by the FRA to function properly. For instance, if the FRA is endowed with the task of gathering information on the human rights situation in third

---

[72] COM(2003)294 Final.

[73] Algeria, Egypt, Israel, Jordan, Lebanon, Morocco, Syria, Tunisia and the Palestinian Authority.

[74] Information on the AIV and its reports, which are also published in English, are available at: www.aiv-advies.nl/.

countries, it cannot simply extend the data collection mechanisms used with respect to the EU and its Member States. The EU Charter of Fundamental Rights is of little relevance to third countries and the FRA would have to make use of other human rights documents that are of direct relevance to them. Also the methods to acquire information may need to be adapted, since third countries will probably not be as cooperative as the Union and the Member States in making sure that the FRA is provided with all relevant information.

In this respect, it is important to note the observation of the Commission that the Agency 'is intended to be a lightweight structure in terms of staff and budget.' It is obvious that extending the mandate of the FRA to the human rights situation in third countries will be a bit too much to ask from a 'light-weight structured' FRA. Preferably, and in line with the European Union's commitment to promote human rights world-wide, the necessary resources should be made available to the FRA to enable it to make a contribution to the Union's external human rights policy. If this should not happen, however, it will be necessary to make choices as to the tasks which should be assigned to the FRA as a matter of priority. For example, gathering information on the human rights situation in the candidate Member States would be a feasible and desirable option, if the FRA would be entrusted with the task to collect information on the human rights situation in the EU Member States. For this selected group of third countries the FRA could apply the same data collection mechanisms as with respect to the Member States. In view of their aspiration to be a Member of the European Union, the EU Charter of Fundamental Rights is of direct relevance for them, which is not the case for the world at large. Furthermore, in view of the number of countries concerned, it would not entail a substantial increase of the workload of the FRA. Another option would be to restrict the data collecting activities of the FRA with respect to other third countries to specific human rights or specific third countries. In this respect it could follow the thematic priorities and focus on countries as selected by the Commission and the Council.

Index